Humanism and Christian Letters in Early Modern Iberia (1480-1630)

Humanism and Christian Letters in Early Modern Iberia (1480-1630)

Edited by

Barry Taylor and Alejandro Coroleu

CAMBRIDGE SCHOLARS

P U B L I S H I N G

Humanism and Christian Letters in Early Modern Iberia (1480-1630),
Edited by Barry Taylor and Alejandro Coroleu

This book first published 2010

Cambridge Scholars Publishing

12 Back Chapman Street, Newcastle upon Tyne, NE6 2XX, UK

British Library Cataloguing in Publication Data
A catalogue record for this book is available from the British Library

ISBN (10): 1-4438-2227-2, ISBN (13): 978-1-4438-2227-5

CONTENTS

Part III: Visual Representation

INTRODUCTION

BARRY TAYLOR AND ALEJANDRO COROLEU

A movement based on the recovery, interpretation and imitation of classical texts, humanism has long been recognized as originating in Italy towards the middle of the fourteenth century. From there it spread to the farthest recesses of Europe within a period of a century and a half, influencing almost every facet of Renaissance intellectual life. Even though humanism derived its literary, moral and educational predilections from ancient Greek and Roman models, it was never an inherently secular movement and it soon turned to religious questions. Humanists were of course brought up with Christian beliefs, regarded the Bible as a fundamental text, and many of them were members of the clergy, either regular or secular. They also fully understood the historical and doctrinal significance of the Church Fathers, particularly Augustine, Lactantius and Jerome, translator of the Catholic Bible. While their importance as religious sources was undiminished, biblical and patristic texts came also to be read for their literary value. Renaissance authors who aspired to be *poetae christianissimi* naturally looked to the Latin Fathers who reconciled classical and Christian views of life, and presented them in an elegant manner.

It would, however, be foolish to think that the reception of classical literature and learning in Christian circles in the age of humanism was devoid of frictions and tensions. Nowhere is this truer than in the case of Petrarch (Francesco Petrarca, 1304-74), under whose guidance humanism took an irreversibly Christian direction. Charles G. Nauert has singled out Petrarch's historical importance, "not only for his efforts to rediscover lost works [from Antiquity], but also for his efforts to resolve some of the inner conflicts that Christian classicists had always faced".[1] Indeed, Petrarch was able to blend classical secular notions with traditional Christian concepts. In his *Bucolicum Carmen* he articulated a humanist ideal which brought together notions of constitutional government and

---

[1] Charles G. Nauert, Jr, *Humanism and the Culture of Renaissance Europe* (Cambridge: Cambridge University Press, 1995), 22.

civic liberty and the transcendent principles of Christianity. Indeed the *Bucolicum Carmen* is revealing of the author's longing for a moral regeneration of Christendom. This is true particularly of eclogues six and seven, those in which Petrarch voiced a call for reform of the church, by fusing the secular and ecclesiastical meaning of "pastoral". Similarly, in his *Secretum*, an imaginary dialogue between himself and Augustine, he expressed his anguish at not being able to turn his back on the ancient pagan writers he revered, for they had been the source of genuine eloquence and genuine moral wisdom.

The call for a return to (classical) sources voiced by Petrarch and early humanists was echoed by later generations of humanists, who turned their hand to biblical studies and began to apply philological methods to the scriptural text. One of the first to do so was Lorenzo Valla (1407-57), who, in his *In Latinam Novi Testamenti interpretationem annotationes* ("Annotations on the Latin translation of the New Testament"), produced a set of notes aiming at emending or clarifying erroneous or unclear passages which had crept into the Vulgate text. Valla's insistence on the need to consult the sources and to refer to the Greek original had far-reaching consequences. On the one hand, it resulted in new translations and interpretations of the scriptural text, which in turn led to conflict with Christian orthodoxy. But it also laid the groundwork for the transformation undergone by biblical studies in the sixteenth century, an evolution best represented by Erasmus of Rotterdam (1465/69-1536). Erasmus's direct link with Valla's philological activity is clear from his decision to publish Valla's annotations on the Gospels in 1505. This was the first step in a career which culminated in Erasmus's first edition of the New Testament of 1516, entitled *Novum Instrumentum*.

Erasmus's interest in the scriptural text went well beyond the task of establishing a correct Greek text of the Gospel. He also regarded the basic precepts of the Scriptures as the only moral values to be observed and as the only true form of knowledge. Erasmus first formulated these ideas (what is known as his *philosophia Christi*) in a book written in 1501, his *Enchiridion militis Christiani* ("The Handbook of a Christian knight"). A guide for the practice of Christian living by a layman, the *Enchiridion* highlights the importance of study of the Bible and the Church Fathers. Patristic literature would, in fact, prove a constant interest for Erasmus throughout his life, and he would edit many of the Church Fathers (Jerome, Cyprian, Chrysostom but, particularly, Origen) or commission editions of key patristic texts from other scholars. Determined to produce a revised text of the whole Augustinian corpus with commentaries but unable to undertake it alone, in 1520 Erasmus invited, for example, Juan

Luis Vives (1492-1540) to edit and annotate the *De civitate Dei*, a text which was included in Augustine's complete works published in Basle in 1529.

As with other parts of Europe, Erasmus's doctrine reached Iberia. With the arrival of the Flemish court of the first Habsburg king of Spain, the future Emperor Charles V, in 1516, Erasmianism was to have a transformative impact on Spanish society. In the early years of Charles's reign the most devoted disciples of Erasmus were men deeply involved with the imperial machine. Particularly receptive to Erasmian ideas was the influential lobby of humanists gathered around the emperor and led by Juan de Valdés and his brother Alfonso, secretary for Latin correspondence at the imperial court and *erasmicior Erasmo*. In addition, in the 1520s many of Erasmus's works—issued chiefly under the imprint of Miguel de Eguía at Alcalá de Henares—were translated into the vernacular, thus contributing to the popularity of his ideas. In 1526 Alfonso Fernández de Madrid, the archdeacon of Alcor, who had undertaken the translation of the *Enchiridion militis Christiani* two years earlier, wrote triumphantly to Erasmus that, whereas formerly the text had been read by the few who were skilled in Latin, "there is now hardly anyone who does not have in hand the Spanish version in the imperial court, in cities, in churches, in monasteries, and even in inns".[2] A letter of September 1527 from the humanist Juan Maldonado to Erasmus, praising his impact upon Spaniards (Allen, ep. 1742), evinces the confident enthusiasm which Erasmus's supporters in Spain felt at the time. Ironically, however, even those who called themselves supporters of Erasmus were inadvertently contributing to his unpopularity with the friars. Alfonso Fernández's translation of the *Enchiridion* gave ample ammunition to Franciscans and Dominicans, who were growing increasingly hostile to Erasmus's ideas and words. And, despite his good intentions, at Salamanca the theologian and Benedictine monk Alonso Ruiz de Virués antagonized Erasmus's critics by publishing a sample of the *Colloquia* in translation, which he prefaced with a letter to the Franciscan warden at Alcalá urging him to stop his attacks against Erasmus. He spread further confusion as to the orthodoxy of Erasmus's thought when he sent a copy of his *Collationes septem* to Erasmus, asking for clarification concerning a series of passages in his works. In the end, enthusiasm for Erasmus and for his reformist kind of humanism began to wane in the later 1530s, even though in post-Tridentine Spain the biblical

---

[2] *Opus Epistolarum Des. Erasmi Roterodami*, ed. Percy S. Allen et al. (Oxford: Oxford University Press, 1906-58), ep. 1904.

scholarship of Erasmus was still being used, even after many of his other works had been prohibited.

In Portugal King John III, dedicatee of Erasmus's *Lucubrationes aliquot* (1527), encouraged Portuguese students to study abroad and in 1547 recruited foreign teachers to staff the Colégio das Artes at Coimbra. In Iberia Erasmus's message was not, however, only transmitted through court circles. Central to the dissemination of Erasmian ideas was also the University of Alcalá, where copies of Erasmus's *Novum Instrumentum* arrived in late 1516. Inaugurated in 1498 by Cardinal Archbishop Francisco Jiménez de Cisneros, the University applied the programme of humanism to its curriculum and to the study of Scripture, even if conservative positions within it ultimately prevailed. As early as 1508 Cisneros himself initiated a great project of biblical scholarship which resulted in the printing between 1514 and 1517 (even though they were not actually published until 1522) of the six volumes of the renowned Complutensian Polyglot Bible, thus called from Complutum, the Latin name of Alcalá de Henares. The foundation of the University had, moreover, its roots in Cisneros's desire for religious reform. The institution became a centre for ecclesiastical education and among its professors and students were the first enthusiastic supporters of Erasmus in Spain. Oddly enough, however, Jiménez de Cisneros did not succeed in fully involving Spain's most renowned biblical scholar, Antonio de Nebrija (1444-1522), in the project for the publication of the Complutensian Polyglot. As early as 1507, Nebrija had sought Cisneros's protection by addressing to him the *Apologia*, in which he defended his right as grammarian to submit the text of Scripture to philological scrutiny. Nebrija had by then already completed a *Quinquagena*, namely a series of annotations to, or short essays on, fifty disputed words in Holy Scripture. Despite these impressive credentials, Nebrija was unable to make the humanistic method palatable to his patron and resigned from the project.

Like his hero Lorenzo Valla, for Nebrija Latin should not only facilitate knowledge of classical Latin writers but of Christian classics written in that language. In this he echoed Petrarch's view—famously epitomized by his own eulogy of Juvencus in the tenth eclogue of the *Bucolicum Carmen*—whereby the ancient tradition of poetry also embraced Christian Latin authors. Accordingly, Nebrija produced editions of, and commentaries on, liturgical hymns, Juvencus, Prudentius and Sedulius. The pedagogical possibilities of Sedulius's adaptation of the Gospels were quickly recognized by local printers. In the preface to his own edition of Sedulius (Valladolid, 1497) the Castilian humanist Diego de Muros praised the Christian poet as "elegans, sublimis, pius, verus et sanctus" and acknowledged the didactic value of the *Carmen Paschale* for young boys "who should become very familiar with the text already in their childhood". For his part, the Barcelona lecturer and Erasmian Martín Ivarra wrote a series of annotations to Sedulius's poem, which, together with Nebrija's own commentary on the text, were printed by Joan Rosembach in Barcelona in 1515. Both Diego de Muros's edition and Ivarra's notes are proof of the use of early Christian writings in the school and university curriculum across Renaissance Europe. As regards Ivarra, his decision to incorporate Sedulius into the educational curriculum at Barcelona seems to go hand in hand with his interest in fifteenth-century practitioners of Christian Latin verse such as Michael Verinus (1469-86). Indeed, from the last two decades of the fifteenth century Verinus's *Distichorum liber* was widely printed and read in Spain. Similarly, as many as eight editions of the poems of the Carmelite Baptista Mantuanus (1448-1516) were published in Spain between 1515 and 1536. This popularity reflected the fact that fifteenth-century Italian Neo-Latin poets were broadly incorporated into the Spanish educational curriculum in the early years of the sixteenth century.

   Alongside the poetic corpus of Christian classics, the homilies written by the Church Fathers and the Bible formed the substance of university studies in the arts faculties throughout Spain. More often than not, these texts were read with the aid of lengthy commentaries. The reading and teaching of biblical and patristic works in the classroom and erudite commentary soon encouraged native imitations, in Latin or in the vernacular. Central to this process was the translation of the biblical text and the corpus of Christian classics into Latin or into the various vernaculars of the Iberian Peninsula. As an example, Fray Luis de León (1527-91)—professor at Salamanca, theologian, and author of a small but exquisite collection of poetry in Spanish—produced eloquent translations of Job and the Psalms into Spanish. For his version of the Psalms Fray Luis chose metrical forms directly inspired by Horace, metres which would be subsequently employed in his own original poems. In doing so, he did not stand alone. Indeed, Benito Arias Montano (1527-98), contemporary of Fray Luis de León at the University of Alcalá, also recast the psalm texts in Horatian metres in his Latin translation of the Psalms published in 1574. He even went one step further and opted for Horatian metres for his own Neo-Latin poetry (the *Humanae salutis monumenta*, 1571, and the *Hymna et saecula*, 1593). Furthermore, Gregorio Hernández de Velasco's translation of Iacoppo Sannazaro's *De partu Virginis* in 1554 contributed not only to the dissemination of Sannazaro's poem among vernacular readers, but also to its sanction by literary critics as a model worthy of imitation.

The essays offered in this volume examine the influence of Christian Latin literature, whether biblical, patristic, scholastic or humanistic, upon the Latin and vernacular letters of the Iberian Peninsula in the period 1480 to 1630. The contributions have been organized into three thematically coherent groups, dealing with transmission, adaptation, and visual representation. The first section opens with two articles (González Vega and Coroleu) concerned, respectively, with Nebrija's biblical scholarship and with the circulation of devotional works and Christian Latin poets of Antiquity in the late fifteenth century. These are followed by three further essays (Ferrer, Allés and Harris) which attend to the process of translation from Latin into the vernacular. The six articles on adaptation deal with the manner in which fifteenth- and sixteenth-century Spanish and Portuguese writers looked to the Bible, the Church Fathers, and medieval and humanistic Christian authors for models and inspiration. Contributors show how, in accord with the practices of Renaissance imitation, writers in Latin or the vernaculars assimilated their sources thoroughly and created from them something personal and new. Essays in this section are concerned with epic poetry (Alves, Miralles-Valsalobre), biblical exegesis (O'Reilly), Neo-Latin and vernacular poetry (Fouto and Francalanci), and stylistic and scholarly issues (Taylor). The last two papers in the book (Andrews and Boyd) extend the study of Christian literature in Spain to the visual arts.

Contrary to most studies on the Iberian literature of the period in which practically no essays are devoted to texts other than in Spanish, this volume successfully accommodates authors writing in Portuguese and Catalan. Likewise, a significant part of the pieces presented here is concerned with literary texts written in Latin. This collection of essays therefore reflects the varieties of relationship between the Peninsular vernaculars and the continuing tradition of Latin letters. Moreover, it shows how the interests and preoccupations of the better-known authors of the Iberian Renaissance were also shared by contemporary figures whose choice of language may have resulted in their exclusion from the canon.

This book has its origin in a colloquium entitled "Latin and Vernacular in Renaissance Spain, IV: The influence of Christian Latin literature" held at University College Cork in April 2009, at which earlier versions of some of the chapters were read as papers. These have been adapted for this volume and supplemented with others in order to offer a wide-ranging, and yet coherent, picture of a complex and challenging topic. We would like to express our gratitude to Professor Terence O'Reilly and Mrs Kay Doyle for their moral and practical support.

PART I:

TRANSMISSION

EX GRAMMATICO RHETOR: THE BIBLICAL ADVENTURES AND RHETORICAL MATURITY OF ANTONIO DE NEBRIJA BETWEEN THE *APOLOGIA* AND THE *TERTIA QUINQUAGENA*

FELIPE GONZÁLEZ VEGA
(UNIVERSIDAD DEL PAÍS VASCO)

To the memory of José Perona, grammaticus

Nebrija's interest in biblical studies began as an earnest of his student years in Bologna and came to embrace almost his whole intellectual career. When in the eighteenth century Juan Bautista Muñoz published the first eulogy of our author he produced ample reason to consider him "the restorer of exegetical theology after the fatal shipwreck of the sciences in the dark ages". Erasmus included him among the "doctos et eloquentes viros" of Spain who would not figure in the catalogue of obsessive Ciceronians next to two eminent theologians, López de Zúñiga and Carranza.[1]

Nebrija's dedication to theological studies left a deep and lasting impression in the prefaces to his works. He dedicates the *Introductiones* of 1495 to Queen Isabella as his last efforts in grammar, determined as he

---

This study forms part of the programme of activities of the research group "Tradiciones Clásicas" of the Universidad del País Vasco (GIU07-26). I warmly thank Barry Taylor for translating my text into English.

[1] In a document of 1468 he appears as "domino de lebrixa theologo," as we know from the essential biography by Juan Gil Fernández, "Nebrija en el Colegio de los Españoles en Bolonia," *Emerita* 33 (1965): 347-49. *Elogio de Antonio de Lebrija leído en Junta Pública de la Real Academia de la Historia por su académico de número D. Juan Bautista Muñoz el día 11 de julio de 1796, con un prefacio de Alejandro Venegas y en facsímil* (Salamanca: Universidad, 1993), 28-37. Erasmus, *Dialogus Ciceronianus*, ed. P. Mesnard, in *Opera Omnia Desiderii Erasmi Roterodami*, I/2 (Amsterdam: North Holland Publishing, 1971), 690-91.

is to devote the remainder of his days to Holy Scripture ("extremum hunc artis grammaticae laborem meum: quia nobis in animo est ... omne reliquum vitae nostrae tempus in Sacris Litteris consumere"), the knowledge of which is the badge of the highest good.[2] But this knowledge is not to be separated from his other accumulated studies in medicine and civil law, ordered around his central humanistic idea of "knowledge of language",

> en que esta, no sola mente fundada nuestra religion & republica christiana, mas avn el derecho ciuil & canonico, por el qual los ombres biuen igual mente en esta gran compañia, que llamamos ciudad; la medicina, por la qual se contiene nuestra salud & vida; el conocimiento de todas las artes que dizen de humanidad por que son proprias del ombre en quanto ombre. Y como este sea el primer principio & entrada para todas ellas ...[3]

---

[2] I transcribe the first text from *Introductiones Latinae cum recognitione* (Salamanca, 1495), copy in the Biblioteca Histórica Marqués de Valdecilla, Madrid, I/335, fols [a]5r-v. The preface to the *Iuris Civilis Lexicon* (Salamanca, 1506), ed. José Perona (Salamanca: Ediciones Universidad de Salamanca, 2000), 70, gives this classification of the branches of knowledge: "Nam cum sint tria genera bonorum [...]: utilia, quorum fortuna dominatur; iucunda, quibus natura praesidet; honesta, quae sunt in animi nostri potestate, bonorum utilium quae infimum obtinent gradum leges arbitrae sunt, iucundorum quae sunt media medicina est conciliatrix, honestorum, quae sola simpliciter dicuntur bona, sacrae litterae sunt artifices. Itaque post iuris civilis vocabularium, dabimus id quod ad medicinam confert; deinde quod ad utriusque instrumenti multarum rerum earumdemque difficillimarum cognitionem maxime est conducibile et, ne artes homine libero dignas non desgustemus..." ['There are three classes of good, according to Peripatetic tradition: those which are useful, governed by fortune; those which are pleasing, governed by nature; and the honourable, governed by our souls. The useful goods which occupy the lowest rank are governed by laws; the pleasing which occupy the middle ground are counselled by medicine; the honourable, which alone can properly be called goods, are the concern of Holy Scripture. Therefore, after the dictionary of civil law we shall publish one concerning medicine; in order next to contribute with what may be most useful to the explanation of numerous inextricable subjects of both Instruments and, lest we fail to taste the arts worthy of a free man, I shall add five books on the Antiquities of Spain'].

[3] *Introduciones latinas contrapuesto el romance al latín (c. 1488)*, ed. M. Á. Esparza and V. Calvo (Münster: Nodus, 1996), p. 5, col. a. For this "saber humanista al servicio de un proyecto enciclopédico" see the late José Perona, "*Latina uocabula ex iure ciuili in uoces Hispanienses interpretata*. II,1 de Elio Antonio de Nebrija," *Cahiers de Linguistique Hispanique Médiévale* 16 (1991): 189-365. For medicine see *Dictionarium Medicum*, ed. Avelina Carrera de la Red (Salamanca: Ediciones Universidad de Salamanca, 2001).

At no point in his intellectual career does Nebrija abandon a philological perspective, the primordial starting point of grammar and rhetoric as the essential foundations of a wide-ranging culture. But this is a hierarchical culture, structured on three classes of good, which ascend from the lowest level of useful goods subject to fortune, to the middle level of pleasurable goods supplied by nature and mediated by medicine, to the highest level of the honourable, the only good which is good in itself and whose architect is Holy Scripture.

Such an orientation in Christian letters is the backbone of a development that is perceptible in Nebrija from the beginning of the sixteenth century onwards: he incorporated the Christian poet Prudentius in the *Suppositum de auctoribus* in the Seville edition of the *Introductiones* (1501) and *circa* 1502 published in Salamanca his *Enarrationes in Psychomachiam*, with the plain text of Prudentius edited separately. The *Enarrationes* are much influenced by the Aldine *Poetae Christiani Veteres* (Venice, 1501) and derive their edition from it. After these works come the commentary on the *Carmen Paschale* of Sedulius (Logroño, 1510) and an expansion of his Prudentius commentaries (Logroño, 1512). And at the end of his days he writes prologues to a work on preaching (*Compendium totius Sacre Scripture divinum Apiarium nuncupatum*, by the master of theology Enrique de Hamusco (Alcalá, 1520) and the *Thalichristia* or *Musa Christiana* of Alvar Gómez de Ciudad Real (Alcalá, 1522). I have not included in this list his scriptural writings, which I shall treat in their own right in this essay. I have also thought it most suitable to refer to his more creative and personal works, leaving aside his other tasks as a mere corrector of texts, as in the *Aurea expositio hymnorum* (1501 onwards).[4]

Nebrija's motivation lies in a strategic laicism which seeks to reconcile earthly knowledge with religious faith. Clearly confessing the

---

[4] For the history of the Prudentius, see *Aurelii Prudentii Clementis V.C. Libelli cum commento Antonii Nebrissensis,* ed. and tr. Felipe González Vega (Salamanca: Ediciones Universidad de Salamanca, 2002), 38-59 and 91-111; for the *Thalichristia* see Felipe González Vega, *"De poetica theologia*: presencias de alegorismo platónico en la exégesis humanista y una mediación de las *Siluae Morales* de Badio Ascensio (1492)," in *Humanismo y Pervivencia del Mundo Clásico III. Homenaje al profesor Antonio Fontán,* ed. José Mª Maestre, J. Pascual, L. Charlo (Alcañiz and Madrid: Instituto de Estudios Humanísticos, Laberinto and CSIC, 2002), III:2, 799-810. For Hamusco's *Apiarium* see Pedro M. Cátedra, "Nebrija y la predicación," in *Antonio de Nebrija: Edad Media y Renacimiento,* ed. C. Codoñer and J. A. González Iglesias (Salamanca: Ediciones Universidad de Salamanca, 1994), 481-90.

iudicium which governs and gives sense to his interpretation of Prudentius's Christian poetry he writes:

> Iudicium meum semper fuit synceri atque puri sermonis eos tantum fuisse autores, qui floruerunt intra ducentos annos qui sunt ab aetate Ciceronis ad Antoninum Pium, et ad phrasim eloquentiae faciendam hos tantum esse proponendos imitandosque; caeteros vero, quia plurimum conducunt ad multarum rerum cognitionem, non esse contemnendos atque in primis christianos, qui nos ad religionem erudiunt et magna ex parte facundiam augent.
>
> [It was always my judgment that genuine and perfect Latin was to be found only in authors who shone in the two hundred years from the time of Cicero to that of Antoninus Pius and that only these should be held up for imitation and learning of style; and that the others, however, because they contribute to our knowledge of many subjects, should not be despised, especially the Christians, who instruct us in religion and to a large extent increase our power of expression.][5]

This beneficial union of language and culture furthers the compatibility of knowledge and religion, between ancient eloquence and ancient and modern Christian values, a conciliation based on language as an historical social institution (the *iudicium meum* implied in *nos*). The philologist's role is directed at the arduous questions of the meaning of Holy Scripture, which are made all the more challenging by their difficulty and the more attractive and appropriate to the professional objectives which he has taken on, so close in many respects to those discussed by his counterpart Lorenzo Valla in the *Elegantiae* (*praef.* IV) when introducing his explications *de verborum significatione*. What else is this *Tertia Quinquagena* but a treatise on the meaning of words from the comparative perspective of the history of language(s) in the interests of an improved text of Holy Writ?[6] The same objective underlies the making of his *Rhetorica* (Alcalá, 1515), declared in the prologue dedicated to Cardinal Cisneros:

> ... sit adeuntibus rem tam arduam quasi opus introductorium. Ad quod faciendum tu me, Pater optime, identidem hortatus es, illa, opinor, ratione

---

[5] *Prudentii Libelli cum commento*, 202-03.

[6] F. Rico, *Nebrija frente a los bárbaros. El canon de gramáticos nefastos en las polémicas del humanismo* (Salamanca: Universidad, 1978), 63, rightly warns of the danger of "abultar la posible cargazón espiritual del biblismo de Nebrija, mejor inserto en una reforma de la cultura que en una reforma de la religión ... pero no se adentró en la *sacra pagina* por devoción—parece—sino por oficio (o *ars*)".

ductus, ut in hoc pulcherrimo totius orbis Hispani, ne dicam terrarum, gymnasio, eloquentiam cum sapientia iungens, hanc quoque partem inhonoratam non relinqueres, ad quam exequendam hic meus labor non nihil posset conducere.
[… a sort of introductory study for those who are approaching the subject for the first time. You, best Lordship, have encouraged me to do it, moved, I believe, by this purpose: so that in this University, the most distinguished of the entire Hispanic world, not to say the planet, unifying eloquence with wisdom, you will not leave this subject without honour: to attain it this effort of mine could help in some way.][7]

Here we see a tempered formulation of the obligatory confluence of rhetorical and theological interests; a substantial argument which Valla defended with vehement dialectic in the preface cited above, defending a history of patristic literature, headed by Jerome, which had set the precious stones of the divine word in the gold and silver mount of eloquence (the metaphor is Augustine's, *Doct.* 2, 40, 60) without sacrificing one type of knowledge to the other. This is the intellectual and literary context in which Nebrija carried out his philological activity. Using the evidence available I shall now attempt an internal and external history of the process that leads from the first *Apologia*, via the *Sacra Lemmata Quinque*, to the varying forms of the *Tertia Quinquagena*.[8]

---

[7] *Rhetorica,* ed. and tr. Juan Lorenzo (Salamanca: Ediciones Universidad de Salamanca, 2006), 48-49. For Valla, see *Prosatori Latini del Quattrocento*, ed. Eugenio Garin (Torino: Einaudi, 1977), 620: "Ac mea quidem sententia, si quis ad scribendum in theologia accedat, parvi refert an aliquam aliam facultatem afferat an non; nihil enim fere cetera conferunt. At qui ignarus eloquentiae est, hunc indignum prorsus qui de theologia loquatur existimo. Et certe soli eloquentes, quales ii quos enumeravi, columnae ecclesiae sunt … inter quos mihi Paulus nulla alia re eminere quam eloquentia videtur".

[8] In order: *Antonii Nebrissensis grammatici apologia cum quibusdam sacrae scripturae locis non vulgariter expositis* (Logroño: Brocar, *c.* 1507), copy in Biblioteca Nacional, Madrid, R/2212; *Sacra lemmata quinque* (Alcalá: Brocar, *c.* 1513), BNM R/2701[4]; *Tertia Quinquagena* [2nd edn without *apologia*] in full: *Aelii Antonii Nebrissensis ex grammatico rhetoris in complutensi gymnasio atque proinde historici regii in quinquaginta sacrae scripturae locos non vulgariter enarratos. TERTIA QUINQUAGENA* (Alcalá: Brocar, 13 April 1516), BNM R/1347; *Tertia Quinquagena* [3rd edn with *apologia*] in full: *Aelii Antonii Nebrissensis ex grammatico rhetoris in Complutensi Gymnasio atque proinde Historici Regii Apologia earum rerum quae illi obiiciuntur. Eiusdem Antonii Nebrissensis in Quinquaginta Sacrae Scripturae locos non vulgariter enarratos. Tertia Quinquagena. Eiusdem Antonii de digitorum computatione. Cum privilegio. Apud inclytam Garnatam Mense Februario D. XXXV.* (Granada: Sancho de Nebrija, 1535), BNM R/142.

The *Apologia cum quibusdam sacrae scripturae locis non vulgariter expositis* must have been printed by Brocar in Logroño around July 1507. We know its external history well, the trials suffered by Nebrija in order to see his explications of critical passages of Holy Scripture in print. It was his first attempt. In 1503, when Fray Diego de Deza was Inquisitor General, Nebrija was served a writ which for the moment did not go beyond the seizure of these annotations. He found the opportunity to print them in this first apologetic form almost certainly shortly after 17 May 1507, when Deza was replaced as Inquisitor by Cisneros. The *Apologia* is the programmatic introduction to the body of *lemmata* which would constitute the *Prima Quinquagena*, or simply *Quinquagena* if it had been possible to print the first attempt.[9]

Around 1513 the workshop of the faithful Brocar produced an edition containing several of Nebrija's *relectiones*, followed by the individual discussions of biblical words. The whole presents the uniform appearance of a specialized miscellany of aspects needing critical comment: the title which functions as a title page for the collections is *Aelii Antonii Nebrissensis relectio de numeris in qua numerorum errores complures ostendit qui apud auctores leguntur.* The order is: *relectio* 7[a] *de ponderibus* (13 June 1511); 8[a] *de numeris* (11 June 1512); 9[a] *de accentu latino* (11 June 1513). The *sacra lemmata* (which the wise don Antonio Odriozola named *Cinco anotaciones a la Sagrada Escritura*) follow, placed in *Tertia Quinquagena* in alphabetical order: "Cynus pro schino"

---

[9] The following are specific to *Apologia* [= *prima quinquagena*], but do not appear in the later editions: "Abimelech pro Achimelech" [*Biblica* I, 65-66; I, 105-106-107-108]; "Bersabee urie uxor pro Bethsabe" [I, 587; II, 442]; "Bersabee puteus pro Beersabe" [II, 440; I, 551; II, 441]; "Cyprus quae planta est" [I ,826]; "D. littera pro r. et contra r. pro d.", "F. litteram non debere poni prope h.", "H. nota aspirationis ubi non debere poni", "M. littera otiose adiecta", "Magi an tres et an reges" [independent manuscript edited by C. Gilly, "Otra vez Nebrija, Erasmo, Reuchlin y Cisneros," *Boletín de la Sociedad Castellonense de Cultura* 74 (1998): 257-340 (303-307)], "Praetorium et praetoliolum" [I, 2272]. Note that as his was work in progress, Nebrija recognized that he made supressions and additions, which are merely listed at the end of this *Apologia*, and are either not included in later editions or are terms which although briefly are defined in other lexica (the numeration is that of the *Nebrissensis Biblica*), or deal generally with aspects of historical phonetics which are incompatible with word-structure and are discussed individually under their respective lemmata. Its title places the (*Tertia*) *Quinquagena* in the train of the most brilliant and stimulating exegeses produced by humanism, such as the *Miscellaneorum centuria prima* of Poliziano or the *Annotationes centum* of Filippo Beroaldo: see Rico, *Nebrija,* 66.

X; "Sedere ad dextram" XXXIX; "Lustrum" XXIV; "Tibiicines" XLVI; "Digitorum supputatio" [= TQ "Dextera" XV].

In 1516 the work is printed under the title *Tertia Quinquagena*, although it contains only forty-eight lemmata, which will become forty-nine in the edition of 1535 printed by Nebrija's son Sancho in Granada. Both editions (TQ$_{16}$ and TQ$_{35}$) lack chapters XXXVI and XLI. In order not to disrupt the numeration the 1535 edition inserts a new chapter XLIII "Sin pro sed si", after chapter XLII "Simila et Similago", but leaves the following "Striatus" as XLIII, the same number it had in 1516. Thus the following chapters have the same lemma and number: "Stibium" XLIIII; "Talitha et tabitha" XLV; "Tibiicines" XLVI; "Traducere quid sit in Matthaeo" XLVII; "V. litterae varius usus" XLVIII; "Zelotes pro cananeus" XLIX; "Zona" L.

When Nebrija dies in Alcalá on 2 July 1522 the University makes a notarial record of the inventory of works kept "en vn arca del deposito del maest° antonio de lebrixa", given to his son Sebastián on 16 June 1523, to be taken to Granada. Carlos Gilly suspects on good grounds that MS. 19019 of the Biblioteca Nacional, Madrid, is a copy made in this city in the 1520s by a hand close to the family. Gilly had previously drawn attention to these works in the eighteenth-century MS. Ny kgl. Samling 18 2° of Det Kongelige Bibliotek, Copenhagen: *Apologia, Epistola del Maestro del Lebrixa al Cardenal, In Reuclinum Phorcensem et Erasmum Roterdanum quod de "talita" in Evangelio Marci et de "tabita" in Luca non bene senserunt, de magis observatio*, and the letter *Ad Cardinalem Hispanum* and *Lemmata ex utroque testamento*. The Madrid manuscript copies all these except the *Apologia*. The most interesting work, on account of its openly polemic tone against eminent humanists of the age, is the refutation of readings by Johann Reuchlin and Erasmus, although for our purposes it is important to know that he basically expounds the arguments of chapter XLV, "Talitha et tabitha". With it is "De magis observatio", which very likely reproduced the contents of the former chapter of the *Apologia* called "Magis an tres et an reges", which did not go on to be printed in subsequent editions.[10]

---

[10] The catalogue is published by P. Lemus y Rubio, "El Maestro Elio Antonio de Lebrixa 1441?-1522," *Revue Hispanique* 22 (1910): 459-508 (482). For Nebrija's apographs which although unpublished complement this *quinquagena* and contribute to the conceptual universe of the *Nebrissensis Biblica*, see the essential studies of C. Gilly, "Una obra desconocida de Nebrija contra Erasmo y Reuchlin," in *El erasmismo en España*, ed. M. Revuelta Sañudo and C. Morón Arroyo (Santander: Sociedad Menéndez Pelayo, 1986), 195-218; "Otra vez Nebrija, Erasmo, Reuchlin y Cisneros". BNM, MS. 19019 was pointed out by P. O.

Although dull and rapid, this summary panorama of external circumstances and textual materiality may suffice as a way into the detail of the ideas and methods used by Nebrija in what is beyond doubt his most mature philological work. Of course, all his prefaces shine in their careful prose and their high and innovative ideas. But in this case the particular rhetoric of the *Apologia* stands head and shoulders above the rest, perhaps because it evinces a greater conceptual rigour and a level of abstraction and method not achieved before.

In no other of his statements of intention—in dedicatory epistles—has Nebrija shown a greater consciousness of the novelty of his method than he does in this *Antonii Nebrissensis grammatici apologia cum quibusdam sacrae scripturae non vulgariter expositis*. Nebrija had absolutely no occasion for another *apologia* or "escusación del objecto" (*Lexicon* 1492), that is to say, a reasoned response on behalf of his exegesis of certain passages of Holy Scripture not according to customary method and manners (to be understood as meaning scholastic theology).[11] Nebrija explains the sense of "non vulgariter exponere" in his tract against Reuchlin and Erasmus:

> Inter caetera, quae Barachias somniat aut vigilans delirat, duo sunt cuius utriusque mentionem feci in Apologia in qua criminatores meos recriminatus sum et in Tertia quinquagena, in qua locos quinquaginta in sacris litteris no ex vulgi opinione, sed nova quadam ratione et a me primum excogitata, declaravi. Unus est ex evangelio Marci ...
> [Among the words about which Barachias either drowses or raves awake, there are precisely two, studied by me in the *Apologia,* where I recriminated with those who condemned me, as in the *Tertia quinquagena*, where I explicated fifty passages on Holy Scripture independently from the established interpretation, but according to a new and original method of my own devising. One is taken from Mark's Gospel ...][12]

Kristeller, *Iter IV (Alia itinera II)*, 577. See also C. del Valle Rodríguez, *"Corpus Hebraicum Nebrissense"*. *La obra hebraica de Antonio de Nebrija* (Madrid: Aben Ezra Ediciones, 2000).

[11] On Nebrija's biblical philology in Spain, see *Nebrissensis Biblica*, ed. P. Galindo and L. Ortiz (Madrid: CSIC, 1950). Outstanding studies of the last thirty years are Rico, *Nebrija*, and those of Gilly. See also D. Coles, "Humanism and the Bible in Renaissance Spain and Italy: Antonio de Nebrija (1441-1522)," 2 vols (unpublished dissertation: Yale University, 1983) and J. H. Bentley, *Humanists and Holy Writ. New Testament Scholarship in the Renaissance* (Princeton: Princeton University Press, 1983), 70-91 for Nebrija.

[12] Gilly, "Otra vez Nebrija," 286-87, with a few changes (semivocalic "u" to "v", a few commas, the order of initial predicatives and the translation of "non ex vulgi opinione sed nova...").

This "vulgaris opinio" refers to the meanings established for the Bible by the professional theologian and the "vulgariter exponere" of the title of the apologia is well explained by the "nova quaedam ratio"—with which he had highlighted the innovation of the *Introductiones* of 1481—, that is, not according to the logico-scholastic method of the time—however arranging a *dispositio iuxta obiecta*—, but in accordance with grammatical criteria and in stylish prose. His famous personality as "ex grammatico rhetor" will appear, as so often, when his protector Cisneros, at the time *protomystes* (cardinal primate), recruits him to teach rhetoric at the new University of Alcalá. Thus in the edition of 1513 he announces himself, without casting off his literary status, as the grammarian turned rhetorician, with the additional title of royal historian (since 1509): "Aelii Antonii Nebrissensis ex grammatico rhetoris in complutensi gymnasio atque proinde historici regii in quinquaginta sacrae scripturae locos non vulgariter enarratos". That is to say, he justifies his scriptural work with the methods of the *studia humanitatis* and protects himself against the attacks of the professional theologians with the immunity given by his membership of the circle of royal trust.

What is surprising about this *Apologia* is its latinity, its convincing and grammatical style, totally alien to the language of contemporary scholastic theology. Structurally it is a speech on classical lines, with *exordium, narratio* and *conclusio*, rounded off with a *protestatio* (public confession) before the conclusion. Having organized his battery of arguments out of patristic sources or *auctoritates* (basically Augustine on the sign and the textual criticism of *De doctrina christiana* II-III), Nebrija decides to oppose accusations of heresy regarding the exclusivity of Jerome's interpretation and restore "suo autori" what negligent scribes had corrupted, all this wrapped up in the periphrastic methods of humanistic grammatical commentary: literalist aims and a subjective sieving of sources giving primacy to linguistic precedent and the oldest witnesses.[13]

---

[13] "Idque partim fecimus partim facturi sumus conferendo recentiores codices cum vetustatis adorandae codicibus latinis, qui facile ostendunt quid Hieronymus nobis scriptum reliquerit, si modo consentit aut non discordat ab eo quod in Hebraeis Graecisque voluminibus habetur atque in eo laborare velim ab istis edoceri quod aereseos genus sit. Nam neque aereticum quid continet neque aeresin sapit neque ex verborum inordinatione potest aeresis sed neque aereseos ulla suspicio inferri." ["This task we have partly already done and partly we have still to do, collating the more recent Latin manuscripts with the venerable ancient ones, which enable us to know what Jerome wrote, and if at least it corresponds or not to the Hebrew and Greek books, and working on this I would like to teach what sort of heresy it is. For their content is not heretical, nor does it inspire

This formal exercise in classical deliberative oratory against scholastic theology might also be a substitute for an indirect but equally challenging censure "del medio de penetración y difusión más común del escolasticismo, el de la predicación, una censura del sermón escolástico en tanto que elaborado según las *artes praedicandi* medievales".[14]

Let us now read the exordium, divided here into two paragraphs. The intertexts are italicized in the text and recorded in the footnotes.

Aelii Antonii Nebrissensis Grammatici Apologia earum rerum quae illi obiiciuntur, quod in quosdam Sacrae Scripturae locos commentationes grammaticas edidit.

Ad perquam Reverendum in Christo Iesu Patrem ac Claementissimum Dominum Do. Fratrem Franciscum Ximenez S.R.E. Cardinalem Hispanum Archiepiscopum Toletanum atque Hispaniarum Mystarchen foeliciter.

[*Exordium*] Nondum satis constitutum habeo, claementissime Pater, utrum bene an potius male sit meritus de me genius meus qui eiusmodi luto praecordia mea finxit, ut nihil cogitarem nisi quod difficile, nihil aggrederer nisi quod arduum esset, nihil denique in vulgus ederem nisi quod mihi negotium facesseret. Quod si omne tempus meum amicorum temporibus accomodarem, si vigilias meas in fabulis ac poetarum figmentis consumerem, *si* in legendis aut scribendis historiis *bonas horas male collocarem* et, quod poeta inquit, "essent per me omnia protinus alba", me omnes amarent, laudarent nugisque meis congratularentur. Nunc vero quia *operor cibum qui non perit* atque, ut inquit Hieronymus, "investigo in terris quorum scientia nobis perseveret in coelo" temerarium, sacrilegum falsariumque appellant parumque abest quin impietatis reum peragentes *ex vinculis causam dicere cogant*. Neque enim deerit accusator, ut ait satyricus poeta, qui verum dixerit "hic est", ut de me iure possit illud ex Ecclesiaste dici "qui addit scientiam addit laborem", vel illud potius ex Plauto "ipsa avis sibi parit malum". Novimus namque ex turdorum stercore viscum gigni et *fronde virere nova quod non sua seminat arbos*, cuius glutino ipsae aves postea inviscatae capiantur. Quod si propositum legislatoris esse debet bonos ac sapientes viros praemiis afficere, malos vero atque a veritatis via aberrantes poenis coercere, quid agas in ea republica ubi Sacras Litteras corrumpentibus praemia proponuntur atque e diverso depravata restituentibus resarcientibus convulsa, mendosa emaculantibus infamiae nota inuritur an anathematis censura subitur? aut si positionem defendere coneris, mortem indignam oppetere cogaris?

[Defence of the grammarian Elio Antonio de Nebrija before the objections made to him when publishing his grammatical commentaries on

---

heresy nor it is possible to determine from their arrangement of words any heresy or suspicion of heresy"].

[14] P. M. Cátedra, "Nebrija y la predicación," in *Antonio de Nebrija: Edad Media y Renacimiento*, 129-50 (130).

certain passages of Holy Scripture. To the very Reverend Father in Christ Jesus and very Magnificent Don Fray Francisco Jiménez of the Sacred Roman Church, Cardinal of Spain, Primate Archbishop of Toledo and the Spanish Kingdoms greetings.

I still do not understand clearly, most magnificent Lordship, if I have well or ill deserved this guardian angel of mine who so formed my character that I think only of difficult things, that I take on only the arduous, that I certainly do not present to the public anything that does not cause me trouble. For if I spent all my time on my friends, if I devoted all my waking hours to the myths and inventions of the poets, if "I made ill use of my good hours", in reading or writing histories, and, as the poet said, "as far as I was concerned, everything would look rosy", everybody would love me, would praise me and would be delighted with my frivolities. But now, since "I seek the food that does not perish", and, as Jerome says, "I search on earth for the knowledge which will persevere in heaven", I am called reckless, sacrilegious and a falsifier, and it would take very little for them to accuse me of impiety and make me defend myself in chains. Nor shall I want for an accuser, as the satirist says, who in fact would have said "he is here", so that it could fairly be said of me "he who increases knowledge increases grief" in Ecclesiastes, or rather the Plautine "bird which seeks its own ruin". For we know that from the dung of the blackbird comes mistletoe and that "new leaves grow alien from the tree that grows them", in whose lime the selfsame birds are caught. And if the intention of the legislator must be to reward good and wise men, but punish the evil and those who turn aside from the path of truth, what can you do in that republic where they offer prizes to those who corrupt Holy Scripture while those who restore the corrupt, those who repair the uprooted, those who purge falsehood are branded with the sign of infamy? Are they besmirched with anathemas? Or if you attempt to defend your position, will you be forced to accept an unworthy death?][15]

In the exordium the accumulation of phrases and expressions from classical authors, and to a lesser degree of explicit biblical turns, is so

---

[15] Cf. nondum satis constitui [Cic. Fam. 11, 27, 1] / omne meum tempus amicorum temporibus transmittendum putavi [Cic. Pomp. 1] / poetarum figmenta [cf. Hier. In Is. 10, 34, 8]; figmenta poetarum [Aug. Civ. 2, 8; 4, 17; 6, 7] / male collocare si bonas voles horas [Mart. 1, 113, 3] / per me equidem sint omnia protinus alba [Pers. 1, 110] / operor cibum qui non perit [Io. 6, 27] / discamus in terris, quorum nobis scientia perseveret in caelo [Hier. Ep. 53, 10] / ex vinculis causam dicere cogant [Caes. Gall. 1, 4, 1] / accusator erit qui verbum dixerit "hic est" [Iuv. 1, 161] / qui addit scientiam addit laborem [Ecl. 1, 18] / ipsa sibi avis mortem creat [Plaut. frag. 47] / fronde virere nova quod non sua seminat [Verg. Aen. 6, 206] / propositum legislatoris esse debet bonos ac sapientes viros praemiis afficere, malos vero atque a veritatis via aberrantes poenis coercere [Arist. Eth. Nic. 1180a].

great as to place beyond doubt that Nebrija is appropriating classical antiquity and using it as a conceptual category in his discourse. It would be foolish to suppose that Nebrija uses his hard-won latinity merely to subordinate his own thought to a linguistic exercise or to stitch it together with other people's scraps. At the origin of this obsessive emulation of classical Latin (provided we understand "classical" to include the eclecticism with which the humanists modulated their language) lies his strategy, evident in this apologia, of demolishing medieval Latin and the scholasticism inherent in it. The change effected by the humanists in the Latin language is the essential driver for a change in mentality.

To this aim contribute the high number of idioms and turns of phrase. I register most of these in my notes and will discuss the most significant in the body of the text.[16] In the first paragraph Nebrija highlights the lack of understanding and even social danger which impels his activity as a grammarian; to exorcise these he does not hesitate to literally arrogate to himself Jerome's intention, claiming to investigate on earth things which will bring him benefits in heaven. These three Ciceronian expressions (the first with a positive meaning and the other two negative) are remade by Nebrija in a new context of depreciation of unproductive leisure wasted among friends and the reading and writing of fiction, ending with a line from Martial to refer poetically to the ill use of good time.[17] Even the commentator par excellence, Servius, can be raised as a model of

---

[16] *nondum satis constitutum habeo* [Cic. Fam. 11, 27, 1: "nondum satis constitui molestiae ne plus an voluptatis attulerit mihi Trebatius noster..."]; *genius meus*: in poetry and postclassical prose [Plaut. Aul. 725: "animumque meum geniumque meum"]; *luto praecordia finxit* [Iuv. 14, 33-34: "forsitan haec spernant iuvenes, quibus arte benigna / et meliore luto finxit praecordia Titan..."]; *cogitarem difficile* [Quint. Inst. 10, 7, 17: "namque et difficiliorem cogitationem exprimit et expellit dicendi neccesitas"] + *nihil nisi quod arduum* [Cic. Or. 33: "omnino et arduum, Brute, conamur, sed nihil difficile amanti puto"]; *temerarium-sacrilegum-falsarium* [Apul. Met. 11, 21: "qui non sibi quoque seorsum iubente domina, temerarium atque sacrilegum audeat ministerium subire noxamque letalem contrahere"; the term *falsarius* is recorded on only two occasions, in Cat. Or. frg. 11 and Suet. Tit. 3, 2]; *bonos viros praemiis afficere* [Cic. De or. 1, 247: "quod vero viros bonos iure civili fieri putas, quia legibus et praemia proposita sint virtutibus et supplicia vitiis..."].

[17] *tempus amicorum temporibus* [Cic. Div. Caec. 41: "ego... qui omne tempus quod mihi ab amicorum negotiis datur in his studiis laboribusque consumam"] + *fabulis ac poetarum figmentis* [Cic. Tusc. 4, 33, 70: "sed poetas ludere sinamus, quorum fabulis in hoc flagitio versari ipsum Iovem: ad magistros virtutis philosophos veniamus"] + *vigilias consumerem* [Cic. II Verr. 4, 144: "... cuius omnes vigilias in stupris constat adulteriisque esse consumptas".

writing. Thus "mortem indignam oppetere" seems to result from incorporating both concepts as defined by Servius to explain Virgil's poetic expressions; Nebrija makes them his own by applying them to the contradictions provoked in society by his profession as a grammarian.[18]

Let us now read the second paragraph with the beginning of the *narratio*:

An mihi non sit satis in iis que mihi relligio credenda proponit *captivare intellectum in obsequium Christi* <2 Cor. 10, 5>, nisi etiam in iis quae mihi sunt explorata, comperta, nota, manifesta ipsaque luce clariora, ipsa veritate veriora, compellar nescire quod scio? Non halucinans, non opinans, non coniectans sed adamantinis rationibus, irrefragabilibus argumentis, apodicticis demonstrationibus colligens. Quae malum haec servitus est aut quae tam iniqua velut ex arce dominatio, quae te non sinat pietate salva libere quae sentias dicere? Quid dicere? Immo nec intra parietes latitans scribere aut scrobibus immurmurans infodere aut saltem tecum volutans cogitare.

[*Narratio*] At quibus de rebus cogitare? Nempe quibus relligio christiana continetur quodque inter iusti et boni viri munera vel praecipuum Psalmographus <1, 2> commemorat: "In lege, inquit, Domini voluntas eius et in lege eius meditabitur die ac nocte".

[*Confirmatio*] Primum illud meditationis genus in lege Domini esse debere Augustinus praecipit, ut codices habeamus castigatos.

[It is not sufficient for me to "submit my understanding to the obedience of Christ" in the matter of my religious beliefs, unless I find myself obliged to ignore what I know in subjects I have investigated, discovered, known, made known and clearer than the light of day, truer than truth itself? Well, I do not hold forth, I do not hold an opinion, I do not conjecture unless it is with adamantine reasons, irrefutable arguments, demonstrative proofs. What damned slavery is this, or what injust and tyrannical domination, that does not allow one to say freely and without a lack of religious respect what one thinks? What do I mean "say"? Rather, I am not able either to write hiding myself behind walls or dig mumbling over the grave or at least think and ponder in your company.

So, on what subjects can one think? In truth, what the Christian religion is and what the Psalmist celebrates among the principal duties of the just and good man: "In the law of Yahweh, he says, he puts his will and will meditate on his law day and night".

Augustine prescribes that the first exercise of thought on the law of the Lord must be that we possess corrected books.]

---

[18] *mortem indignam oppetere* [Serv. Aen. 6, 163: "indigna morte: miserabili, non congrua eius meritis; vel propter animae etiam extinctionem elementi contrarietate"; Serv. Aen. 1, 96: "ergo dicimus et 'oppetit' et 'mortem oppetit', sicut et 'exspirat' et 'animam exspirat'"].

The second paragraph begins with the habitual turn in classical prose of questioning the certainty or basis of what follows (*an mihi*, derived from Prop. 1, 6, 13: "an mihi sit tanti doctas cognoscere Athenas"), by which the narrator relativizes and justifies—as the poet submits himself to his beloved—his dedication to theological studies. Thus Nebrija to target his religious beliefs is content to submit his intelligence to Christ. He clearly accepts that faith and religious beliefs are subordinated to theology, except for questions of culture, which unlike matters of faith require demonstration. We are close, albeit with some nuances, to the distinction between *probatio* and *religio* which Valla dissects in the *Elegantiae* (V, 30), when he defines Christian faith as equivalent to a *persuasio* which does not need confirmation:

> Fides [*sc.* quod Christiani dicunt fidem] enim proprie Latine dicitur probatio, ut "facio fidem" per instrumenta, per argumenta, per testes. Religio autem christiana non probatione nititur, sed persuasione, quae praestantior est quam probatio ... quod confutare non potest, non tamen acquiescit. Qui persuasus est, plane acquiescit nec ulteriorem probationem desiderat.
> [As "fides" in Latin is properly "proof", as in "I establish through documents, arguments, and witnesses". The Christian religion, then, does not rely on proofs but on persuasion which it finds more conclusive than proof [...] one does not trust what cannot be refuted. He who is persuaded trusts openly and does not deed further ratification.]

Nebrija extends and emphasizes all this field of "confirmation" with a display of rare or technical terms, poetical phrases and expressions which reveal his unease and intellectual anxiety in the face of the free investigative exhaustiveness to which he lays claim and the tyranny which enslaves him; a truly conscientious study of the Latin language and display of its rhetorical possibilities, for example the homeoptoton or tripartite rhymed alliteration (*non halucinans, non opinans, non coniectans*), which aid him in his aim to define and distinguish his concept of religion as a cultural rather than a faith object. The beginning of the *narratio* insists on this idea of religion as culture: religion as an activity of thought and reflection (*cogitare*). This too is the sense of his confirmation of the primacy given to the quotation from Augustine prescribing "textual correction" (*codices castigati*).[19]

---

[19] **halucinans— scrobis— infodere* [technical terms, which even seem to function as poetic words: Col. Rust. 7, 3: "ne fur aut bestia halucinantem pastorem decipiat", who also uses "scrobis"]; **adamantinis rationibus* [poetic adjective, Lucr. 2, 447: "adamantina saxa"; Hor. Carm. 1, 6, 13: "tunica adamantina"; and in

A rapid survey of the major features of medieval scholasticism will show the importance of what has been said so far. Medieval culture was a public affair governed by the institutional stability of Church and University, and the methodological unity of scholasticism, whose

---

postclassical prose: Apuleius, Pliny] + *irrefragabilibus argumentis* [specific adjective in Christian Latin, here suited to the tenor of his arguments] + *apodicticis demonstrationibus* [exclusive to Gell. 17, 5, 3, from Greek *apodeiktikós*]; **pietate salva* [poetic word, Sen. Phoen. 380-381: "... nil possum pie / pietate salva facere, quodcumque alteri"; also in Liv. 45, 19, 4: "quae vix salva pietate ei contingere poterant", but always in the order "s. p.", as also in Ov. Met. 15, 109, Sen. Ep. 81, 16, Aus. Ecl. 21, 14, which is different from Seneca tragicus and Nebrija]; **intra parietes latitans scribere* [the participial adjective shows poetic uses, Luc. Phar. 6, 712-713: "non in Tartareo latitantem poscimus antro / adsuetamque diu tenebris", but the image which Nebrija recreates is indebted to Quint. Inst. 1, 2, 1: "hoc igitur potissimum loco tractanda quaestio est, utiliusne sit domi atque intra privatos parietes studentem continere, an frequentiae scholarum et velut publicis praeceptoribus tradere"]; **scrobibus immurmurans infodere* [In the background of the censure which Nebrija suffers is the proverbial anecdote of King Midas punished by Apollo with ass's ears for having judged Pan's music better than his. I understand that "aut scrobibus immurmurans infodere" rewrites two sources: first, the participial adjective and the substantive are from Ovid's hexameters describing Midas's barber whispering his secret into the open grave, Ov. Met. 11, 187-189: "voce refert parva terraeque *immurmurat* haustae / indiciumque suae vocis tellure regesta / obruit et *scrobibus* tacitus discedit opertis". Second, he draws the substantive and infinitive from Persius 1, 119-120: "ne muttire nefas? nec clam? nec cum *scrobe*? nusquam? / Hic tamen *infodiam...*"; this satire, v. 110: "essent per me omnia protinus alba", had been used explicitly by Nebrija in the previous paragraph. Thus the intertext is not only linguistic or verbal, but also assumes the same satirical density of its source, positioning itself in the ancient succession of those who, conscious of the dangers they assume, demand the freedom of their writings. The independence of thought which Nebrija proclaims by claiming for himself the cultural truth of religious fact finds its radical expression in literary language and rewriting; **tecum volutans cogitare* [the participial adjective and verb are synonymous; their emphatic union is not documented either in Liv. 40, 8, 5: "multa se cum animo volutans inambulavit", nor Sil. Pun. 17, 185: "secum ipse volutans", nor Fronto Ep. 3, 17, 1: "haec mecum anxie volutans...", however, it does occur in Servius's prose paraphrase of Aen. 1, 50: "nam dixerat superius 'haec secum' <37> et modo ait 'volutans', id est cogitans"]. For our humanist the prose of the commentator and commentary takes on as much stylistic value as that of a literary author. In this respect "the commentary can itself become a kind of primary text". See A. Laird, "Juan Luis de la Cerda and the Predicament of the Commentary," in *The Classical Commentary. Histories, Practices, Theory*, ed. Roy K. Gibson and Christina Shuttleworth Kraus (Leiden-Bonn-Köln: Brill, 2002), 171-203 (183).

auctoritates are sacred and profane texts which act as guarantors of a tradition ratified as the patrimony of truth. This strong internal homogeneity ranked the branches of knowledge, with theology as the one undisputable and undisputed discipline which gathered and harmonized its disparate sources according to the criterion of "probability", but rejected anything subjective or innovative. This affected both history (Vincent de Beauvais) and theology (the *Sententiae* of St Bonaventure), where each with a tradition of cross-referenced texts had priority over personal judgement.[20]

However, in a deliberative essay like Nebrija's on critical passages in scripture the authorities are not mere texts but "persons", where argumentation proceeds from dialogue and the equality of ancient author and humanist, mediated by rational criteria of linguistic and historical comparison. Our humanist's battle against the medieval system of values can be read in one of the replies to the *obiectum* which riles him:

> [*Aliud obiectum*]   Sunt tamen complures qui hanc litterarum disquisitionem non multifaciant eamque disputationem de caprina lana esse contendant, novos vero atque ipsis inauditos vocabulorum significatus omnino excludant in illis praecipue locis ubi doctores alios sensus accomodarunt. Sed quaero ab istis an magis credendum sit in hac parte septuaginta, qui eo tempore ex Hebraeo in Graecum sermonem interpretati sunt quo utraque lingua vigebat cuiusque, ut omnes fatentur, erant doctissimi, magis Aquilae, Symmacho, Theodocioni, Luciano martyri, magis Hieronymo trium linguarum viro eruditissimo quam Nicolao, Hugoni, Papiae, Mamotrecto reliquisque omnibus neotericis autoribus qui in ea tempora inciderunt in quibus res litteraria Graeca pariter ac Latina dormiebat?
> [Nevertheless, many people give no importance to this literary disquisition and claim that this is a Byzantine discussion, rejecting all meanings of words new and unknown to them, principally where experts have given different meanings. But I ask them if more credit should be given in this matter to the translators of the Septuagint, who translated from Hebrew into Greek at a time when both languages were spoken and, as is recognized, were most cultivated in both, more to Aquila, to Symmachus, Theodotion [the biblical translator], to the martyr Lucian, more credit to Jerome, fluent in the three languages than to Nicholas, Uguccio, Papias, the Mamotrect and all the other modern authors who lived in the time when Greek literature slept like the Latin?][21]

---

[20] See R. Fubini, "Umanesimo e Scolastica. Saggio per una definizione," *Medioevo e Rinascimento* 18 (2004): 168-171.

[21] I advanced some of these ideas in "Retórica del comentario literario: un ejemplo desde la *Apologia* de Antonio de Nebrija (Logroño: Brocar, 1507)," in

If it is necessary to have recourse to the "rhetoric of enumeration" in order to range ancients against moderns, there will always be several *doctissimi* and more than one *eruditissimus* to bear the usual name of "baneful grammarians": Nicholas of Lyra (who is not always erroneous, as we shall see) and his *Glossa ordinaria*, Uguccio da Pisa and his *Magnae derivationes*, Papias and his *Elementarium*, Marchesini's *Mamotrect, nomina duriora.*[22]

In more than one question *iudicium* is strongly personal and directly oriented to reality, to the exclusion of any probabilism which is limited to authorized sources: the *auctoritas* which derived from a greater or lesser accord between witnesses can never impose itself on the emancipated judgment of the humanist.[23] To this universe of values Nebrija replies by defending his right to discuss and explicate scripture from the point of view of language, in accordance with his role as a grammarian. Protected by the reasons set out in his *Apologia* Nebrija launches into the debate in the alien territory of scholastic biblical study, like a curious explorer of the subject:

Retórica y educación: la enseñanza del arte retórica a lo largo de la historia, ed. G. Lopetegui Semperena (Amsterdam: Adolf M. Hakkert, 2008), 295-314.

[22] Cf. Rico, *Nebrija,* 11ff for the origins of the "baneful canon". Likewise, in another *obiectum* Nebrija questions the contradiction of prohibiting what Augustine encourages and states that he has based his decisions on the best authors, rejecting the baneful list of medieval authorities: "Quomodo igitur, o invide, tu me prohibes facere ad quod faciendum Augustinus hortatur? Sed dicunt rursus ex significatu illo sive vero sive falso iam doctores expresserunt alios sensus partim mysticos partim morales. Quid alii fecerunt, ipsi viderint, non meo periculo sed suo id fecerunt. Nos, quod autor Sacrae Scripturae atque proinde utriusque Instrumenti Spiritus Sanctus per os Prophetarum atque Apostolorum locutus est, ex ipsorum verbis interpretamur optimis autoribus freti, quos isti nunquam legerunt sed nescio quos Ebrardos, Mamotrectos, Papias, Hugutiones atque alia, ut inquit poeta <Mart. 4, 55, 9>, 'nostris nomina duriora terris'". [Why then, envious man, do you prohibit me from doing what Augustine encourages? But, they say, for such a meaning, true or false, the Doctors have already made clear other senses, in part mystic and in part moral. What others did, they will see, was not to my peril but their own. As for us, what the author of Holy Scripture and therefore of both Instruments, the Holy Spirit, said through the mouths of the Prophets and Apostles, we interpret on the basis of their own words, with the help of the best authors, who never read those I know not what Ebrards, Mamotrects, Papias, Uguccios and others, names "even harder for our land", as the poet says].

[23] Cf. Fubini, "Umanesimo e Scolastica," 167.

[*Aliud obiectum*]   Nam quod ad Pontificis autoritatem attinet, cotidie in cathedraliciis ecclesiis creat vel inde mortuorum locum substituit magistros scholarum, quibus impartitur munus ecclesiasticos libros castigandi. Ego quoque ipse Apostolicae sedis autoritate sum factus ingenuarum artium magister atque proinde grammaticae artis in Salmanticensi gymnasio cathedrarius concessa facultate de rebus ad professionem meam pertinentibus disputandi, disserendi, discernendi ac diiudicandi. Neque potest quis iurisdicionis meae terminos ita coercere, ut non possum discurrere per reliquas omnes artes et scientias, "non ut transfuga sed tanquam explorator" rerum quae illic gerantur <Sen. Ep. 1, 2, 5>, et si quid fuerit quod in censuram meam cadat, castigem illud corrigam et emendem. Neque enim fieri potest ut non in sua cuiusque disciplina aliquid deprehendam? Quod ipse turpiter ignoret ego pulcherrime intelligam.
[Regarding pontificial authority it creates the post or even relieves schoolmasters of the requirement to care for the dead so that they can correct ecclesiastical books. I myself have been appointed by apostolic authority master in liberal arts and professor of grammar in the university of Salamanca with the option to debate, expound, discern and judge subjects that concern my profession. And nobody can confine me within the limits of my jurisdiction without allowing me to expatiate on the other arts and sciences, not "as a desertor but an explorer" of the subjects treated there, if they were within my competence, in order to sanction, correct and emend what is said. Might I not discover something in others' disciplines? What one person in his dullness does not know, I will understand wonderfully.][24]

That Nebrija should call himself "not a desertor but an explorer" in the other disciplines must look like a prefiguration of a new Seneca guiding his Lucilius and interlocutors in the selection of readings and their exploitation. The authority of the *exemplum* will validate before the institution his right as a professor of grammar to "debate, expound, discern and judge" the subjects of his profession. But his recognition in the hostile field of theology does not come only from the fine-sounding exemplarity of the intertext. His best arms are without doubt the care which he takes so that language transmits this renewed erudition and persuades us to read it. And it is in this renewal of the Latin language or in its deliberate "linguistic change" that we find the authentic defining and substantial reality of humanism, its "Renaissance truth". Thus the *iuncturae* of the best classical authors, and of the Christian authorities, far

---

[24] As Marcel Bataillon says, with Nebrija's interpretative and editing decisions "queda netamente inaugurado el debate entre la rutina de las cuestiones escolásticas y la nueva disciplina del humanismo," *Erasmo y España*, 3rd edn (México, FCE., 1986), 32.

from being a lifeless certification or routine enumeration, validate a contestatory and interactive function which the humanists assign to the ancient in contemporary thought and literature, the literary vitality which transforms the ancient into something accessible and reproducible, congruent with the demands of true humanistic experimentation arranged to incorporate into life both rhetoric and classical scholarship.[25]

So far the intertexts identified are chiefly of classical origin. But we should not deceive ourselves. The norm was a complementary co-existence between pagans and Christians: because of their definite condition becoming ancients and classics. Towards the end, accused of having caused "scandal" Nebrija offers a blazing defence built on an intense paraphrase of New Testament morality of *scandalum* or "trompeçadero", as he renders it:

[*Aliud obiectum*]   Reliquum est ut brevi ad id quod de scandalo isti obiiciunt respondeamus. Nam eo confugiunt cum se vident undique circumventos. Sed quaero primum ab illis qui nam sunt ii quos nostra offendunt studia, doctive an indocti? An potius qui cum non sint se doctos putant? Non quidem docti, quoniam iisdem illi rationibus moverentur quibus et nos movemur. Non indocti, quia illi et cupiunt scire et non dedignantur a peritioribus erudiri. Atqui restat genus illud tertium de quibus Plato scripsit <Rep. 361a>: "ultimus iniustitiae cumulus est cum sis malus et ignarus velle bonus et sapiens videri"; ii sunt "qui Curios simulant et Bacchanalia vivunt" <Iuv. 2, 3>, "qui ambulant in stolis et amant primas cathedras in synagogis et primos accubitus in conviviis" <Lc. 20, 46>, "qui excolant culicem camelum vero deglutiunt" <Mt. 23, 24>. Quibus ego nihil recuso fieri scandalum, quandoquidem et Salvator noster Phariseis scandalum fuit. "Nos, inquit Paulus, praedicamus Christum crucifixum, Iudaeis scandalum gentibus autem stultitiam" <1 Cor. 1, 23>, et quod de illo Simeon iustus erat vaticinatus: "ecce hic positus est in ruinam et in resurrectionem multorum in Israel" <Lc. 2, 34>. Quod si "necesse est, ut scandala veniant" <Mt. 18, 7> et scandalizantibus Salvator noster grande malum interminatur, non id quidem ad Phariseorum scandalum pertinet quibus ipse scandalum fuit. Neque vereor ut pusilli et minimi in me scandalizentur sed illi tantum qui livore torquentur, qui invidia rumpuntur, qui quod se consequi posse desperant, carpunt, rodunt, detestantur.

---

[25] This truth assigned to linguistic change belongs to A. Moss, *Renaissance Truth and the Latin Language Turn* (Oxford: Oxford University Press, 2003). For the functionality of quotations and intertexts I follow V. Fera, "L'*imitatio* umanistica*,*" in *Il latino nell'età dell'Umanesimo. Atti del Convegno Mantova, 26-27 ottobre 2001*, ed. G. Bernardi Perini (Firenze: Leo S. Olschki, 2004), 17-33.

[It remains to us to briefly respond to the accusations of scandal they make against me. Indeed, they run away from them when they see they are surrounded on all sides. First, I ask who are they who meddle in our studies: the learned or the unlearned? Or rather, who think themselves learned without being so? Certainly they are not learned, as they would moved by the same reasons as we are. Nor are they unlearned, because they too feel the desire for knowledge and do not despise to be instructed by those who know. But there remains the third type to which Plato refers: "the acme of injustice is to wish to appear good and wise when one is evil and ignorant", they are those who "pass themselves off as Curiii and live Bacchanalia", "which desire to walk in long robes, and love greetings in the markets, and the highest seats in the synagogues, and the chief rooms at feasts"; "which strain at a gnat, and swallow a camel". I refute that I am a scandal to these, since Our Saviour too was an object of scandal to the Pharisees. "We," says Paul, "preach Christ crucified, unto the Jews a stumbling block, and unto the Greeks foolishness", and what Simeon had prophesied "behold, this child is set for the fall and rising again of many in Israel". And if "it must needs be that offences come", and those who are scandalized Our Lord threatens with a great misfortune: he does not mean precisely the scandal of the Pharisees, for whom he himself was a source of scandal. And I do not fear that these little squirts are scandalized by me. Only those who are tormented by jealousy, eaten by envy, who in the face of their desperation for gain steal, destroy and damn.]

When Nebrija, listing his objections, recognizes the rich polysemy of biblical language even in its literal sense (the Augustinian theory of the twofold *allegoria in verbis et ipsis in factis*) he does so presenting himself as a new Palaemon ("Non *est tamen* nostrum inter *tantos autores* tantas componere lites"), who is called in the Third Bucolic to arbitrate in a tense and bitter pastoral singing match between Menalchas and Dametas but refuses to give a verdict (Verg. Ecl. 3, 108: "non nostrum inter uos tantas componere lites"). The literalism of the quotation might mislead us regarding Nebrija's final plans in biblical interpretation, as if at the end he were allowing himself to be equidistant and seemed to throw in the towel in his personal fight for a profound revision of the Vulgate. However, with the echo of the recently discovered Virgilian hexameter shared with his reader he is swearing to his distance from the varied and mistaken interpretation of the Septuagint in order to limit himself to Jerome's interpretation alone, in what claims to be a new corrected version:

Non est tamen *nostrum inter* tantos autores *tantas componere lites*. Fieri namque potest, ut utrique se optimis rationibus defendant, cum praesertim Litterae Sacrae sub eisdem verbis atque sub eodem orationis contextu plures sensus non modo figuratos verum etiam litterales recipiant. Nam quod ab aliis scriptoribus amphibologicós dicitur, nisi ex industria id fiat, vitiosum est et quod quisque minus proprie dicit, magis obnoxium variis sensibus relinquit. At vero Sacrae Litterae quod spiritu divino foecundae sunt, hoc singulare habent, quod sub eisdem verbis res plures et rursus res ipsae res alias significant. Ex quo fieri potuit, ut alius interpres aliud sit secutus et quae nobis discordare videntur, minime sint discordia sed idem aut sibi non repugnantia designent. Sed de interpretum diversitate alias pluribus, nunc autem de unius tantum interpretis, hoc est Hieronymi, simplici interpretatione laboramus, ut quod librariorum negligentia depravatum erat, suo autori acceptum referatur.

[It is not our business to do battle so among such important authors. For it may happen that both defend themselves with the best reasons, especially because Holy Scripture under the same words and in the same phrase contains a plurality of meanings both figurative and even literal. Thus what other writers term "amphibological", unless the amphibology is done deliberately, is a defect and the less correctly it is expressed, the more harmful are the various meanings it produces. But Holy Scripture, having been fertilized by the Holy Spirit, possesses the peculiarity that the same word means several things and these things in turn have several meanings. Hence it could happen that a translator has interpreted something different, and what for us is in disagreement is only minimally discordant or the same thing or designate things that do not conflict with each other. But on the diversity of translators I have expressed myself enough on other occasions, now we work with the one interpretation of a single translator, namely Jerome, in order to transmit what his author has thought but is corrupted by the negligence of scribes.][26]

But the path of objection need not pass through exclusive classicism, however classical the context in which it is enunciated. It is quite possible that the unconvincing and unthinking scholastic arguments and concerns can be concisely ridiculed in the letter of their expression, in the close itself: "an non hoc melius quam disputare ridiculam illam quaestionem, utrum quiditates Scoti transeuntes per latera puncti possint implere ventrem Chimerae?". The humanistic preference for reasoned critical debate, summarized in the triad *disserere-discernere-disiudicandi*, goes against a simple ridiculous scholastic *quaestio*, expressed in a vulgar, far from classical, word-order (S-V-O: q. S. t. p. l. p. + p + i. v. Ch.; determinate-determinant: *quiditates Scoti, latera puncti, ventrem Chimerae*), capable of doing violence to the logic of the Latin language by creating this *quiditas*, a hard essentialist semasiologic neologism made

---

[26] Cf. non nostrum inter uos tantas componere lites [Verg. Ecl. 3, 108] / *amphibolos* interpretatur dubius sive ambiguus.a.um – *amphibolia sive amphibologia* interpretatur ambiguitas [Nebr. Dict$_{512}$].

by substantivizing the adjective *quid*, to designate the ideas of their intellectual leader Scotus, as fabulous and destructive by metaphorical association with the fire vomited by the chimera with its lion's head, goat's body and dragon's tail.

We will not be surprised to find that the body of the *Quinquagena* is coherent with the methodology and attitudes observed in its paratexts. In the *lemmata* the chance of resolving the problems between sign and reality is debated. The new method of incorporating into contemporary reality the knowledge contained in the ancient sources, expounded simply so that their arrangement leads the reader to the relevant clarification, is done. The argument always proceeds by sieving the ancient sources and if possible proposing solutions with the aid of direct observation of the thing itself. Thus the imprecise *camelopardalis* ("giraffe", VII), described by ancient authors and contemporaries like Poliziano:

> cornua vero hanc beluam habere quod Plinius, Solinus, Varro, Heliodorus, Dion atque alii siluerunt animadvertit Angelus Politianus <Misc. cent. pr. 3> in "girafa", sic enim vulgus camelopardalim appellat, quam Sultanus, idest Aegypti rex, misit dono Laurentio Medicae Florentinorum principi. Quod si cornua gestat bifidaque, ut Plinius scribit, merito ex genere mundarum quadrupedum Moses Hebraeis mandendam esse permittit.
> [And that this animal has horns, something on which Pliny, Solinus, Varro, Heliodorus, Dion and others were silent, is picked up by Angelo Poliziano under "giraffe", for this is the name commonly given to the cameleopard which the Sultan, that is, king of Egypt, sent as a gift to Lorenzo de' Medici leader of the Florentines. And if it has horns and there are two of them, as Pliny writes, it belongs to the class of quadrupeds which Moses rightly permits the Hebrews to eat.]

Or the *onocrotalus* ("pelican", XXXII), the "caath" which God forbids the Hebrews to eat (Lev. XI), described by Pliny (*Nat. Hist.* X) and which Nebrija claims to have seen twice in Bologna, seeing it once from a distance, the size of a year-old calf and once up close, exhibited dead to the public in the square; nobody could name it and he himself spoke up to identify it:

> ... et ne quasi de re incognita pluribus disputem, duos onocrotalos contigit mihi videre, alterum cominus in foro Bononiensi ad vulgi spectaculum publice expositum, alterum eminus ad Anae fluminis ripam ad cuius volantis monstrosam magnitudinem visendam multi mortales concurrerunt. Aequiperabat sane mole sua agnum anniculum. Sed cum nemo sciret avis nomen, quamquam alii dicerent se alias consimiles vidisse, ego illis dixi "croton" in Italia vocari et re vera ita appellabant Bononienses. Sed cum onocrotalus interpretetur "asinus crepitans", quoniam "onos" est asinus et

"crotao" crepito, videtur nomen impositum a voce quam avis illa edat, quam mihi audire non licuit, propterea quod quemadmodum dixi alterum cominus extinctum alterum eminus volantem conspicatus sum.

[And in order not to continue debating the unknown, I happened to see two *onocrotali*, one up close in the square in Bologna exposed to the common contemplation of the public, and the other from a distance on the banks of the Arno, a bird whose monstrous size a multitude of people had gathered to see. Without doubt it equalled in size a year-old calf. But as nobody knew the name of the bird, even though there were people who claimed to have seem similar, I myself said that in Italy they are called "croton" and so indeed the Bolognese called them. As "onocrotalus" means "crackling ass", as "onos" is ass and "crotao" crackle, the name is derived from the noise it makes, which I have never heard, as, as I have just said I saw the one up close and the other flying at a distance.]

This hightened sense of reality which presides over the grammatical and textual analysis does not arise from one or two lemmata, but makes the digression inspired by a critical reading into a real narration. See the rubric of chapter X "Cynus pro schino". In addition, it clarifies a textual trivialization commited by the seventeenth-century editors to compensate for the mismatch between the title and the number of chapters.[27] I hope it makes its structure clear, by doling out brief texts and paraphrasing the bulk, to lighten the weight of reading.

In Daniele propheta caput XIIII <Dn. 14>, ubi historia Susanae ex translatione Theodoctionis inserta scribitur, omnes codices vulgo habent "si vidisti eam, dic sub qua arbore videris". Qui ait "sub cyno" pro eo quod esse debuit "sub schino". Iacobus Constantius contra Nicolaum Lyram corruptam lectionem defendit asseveratque non "schinum", sed "cynum" eo in loco debere legi. Ego, cum ex mea consuetudine bibliopolia, quae Salmanticae complura sunt, excuterem, forte fortuna incidi in Observationes quasdam Iacobi Constantii …

[In Daniel XIIII, where the history of Susanna is told according to the translation of Theodotion, all the manuscripts read "if you saw her, say under which tree you saw her". He replied, "under the poplar", instead of the correct "under the acacia". Jacopo Costanzi, against Nicholas of Lyra, defends the incorrect reading, stating that here one should read "poplar" and not "acacia". Visiting, as is my custom, the many bookshops that there

---

[27] See compilations such as *De locis S. Scripturae Hebraicis Angeli Caninii Commentarius et A. Nebrissensis Quinquagena* (Antwerp, 1600), which according to Gilly, "Otra vez Nebrija," 264-65, worsened the text of lemma XLV "Talitha et tabitha" by putting the names in Hebrew, or *Tractatum Biblicorum, hoc est variarum in diversas materias biblicas commentationum volumen primus sive Criticorum Sacrorum tomus VI* (Frankfurt, 1696).

are in Salamanca, fortune wished that I came across certain *Observations*
of Jacopo Costanzi …]

The initial procedure is normal, specifying the Vulgate reading and the
Glossa ordinaria of Nicholas of Lyra next to the contrary alternative
reading of Constantius. The difference is in the *narratio* of the problem,
with the addition of the clear "ego" leading on to a customary digression
and erudition *ad vitam*.[28] Nebrija tells us in the first person of his habit of

---

[28] I prefer to relegate this long digression to a note: "Ego cum ex mea
consuetudine bibliopolia, quae Salmanticae complura sunt, excuterem, forte
fortuna incidi in observationes quasdam Iacobi Constantii viri plane litteratissimi,
sed quem antea nomine tantum noveram. Fuerunt autem observationes illae
numero centum, quas idcirco voluit graece 'Hecatostyn' potius quam 'Centuriam'
latine cognominare. Harum duae priores ac totidem posteriores pertinent ad
quosdam locos Divinae Scripturae. Sed cum reliquae omnes multum eruditionis
rerum saecularium contineant atque—ut ingenue fatear—omnes illas mihi facile
persuaserit, in quattuor tantum quas dixi hominis prudentiam desideravi, qui in
ipso statim initio ac deinde in operis clausula, ubi ex artis rhetoricae praecepto
consuetum est optima quaeque disponi frigidiora et pene puerilia collocarit, ut
quod in prima observatione quasi in re magna ac per difficili commoratur
ostendens eos aberrare, qui in Matthaei evangelio <2, 16> legunt quod Herodes
occidit 'omnes pueros a bimatu et infra', putantes non 'bimatu' sed 'imatu' esse
legendum ita ut 'b' littera non ad praepositionem praecedentem sed ad dictionem
sequentem pertineat, quod 'nec pueri quidem ignorant etiam qui nondum aere
lavantur' <Iuv. 2, 152>. Aut ostendat mihi Constantius oportet quis hoc unquam
dixerit, aut si harum rerum tam curiosus est illud potius est Laurentio Valla <Eleg.
II, 53> debuit adnotare in verbis illis non 'infra' sed 'intra' debere legi, propterea
quod 'infra' conditionem et locum designat, ut *infra omnes homines, infra tectum*,
'intra' vero numerum et spacium, ut *intra octo dies, intra urbis muros*'."
["Visiting, as is my custom, the many bookshops that there are in Salamanca,
fortune wished that I came across certain *Observations* of Jacopo Costanzi, a most
erudite man whom however I knew only by name. It was a hundred observations
which he preferred to call 'Hecatostys' in Greek rather than 'Centuria' in Latin.
Of course, the first two and a like number later on concern passages of Holy
Scripture. Although all the other observations present much erudition on profane
topics to which, in sincerity, I would feel easily inclined, in only four of those
mentioned I noted a lack of prudence on the part of one who, in the very opening
and then the close of the work—where rhetorical precept commands one should
place the best ideas—he raises insignificant and almost puerile questions. Quite
the opposite of the difficult, burning topic which he treats in the first observation,
laying out his differences with those who in Mark's gospel read that Herod killed
'all the children of two years and under', in the belief that one should read
'bimatu' not 'imatu', because the letter 'b' does not belong to the preceding
preposition but goes with the word that follows, something which 'even the

visiting the bookshops of Salamanca, where by chance he came by certain unknown most erudite *Observationes* by Jacopo Costanzi which he prefers to call by the Greek name of "Hecatostys" rather than the Latin "Centuria". Of these hundred annotations, the first two and nearly all the others treat passages from Holy Scripture. Nebrija admits he is easily attracted by civic and secular studies, in which these observations abound, but he would have wished for the prudence of one who, knowing that rhetoric requires the best material to be placed at the beginning and end, decides to put there insubstantial and quite childish thoughts. Our Costanzi is quite the opposite, as he launches from the first into a weighty subject. So against those who read in Matthew that Herod killed all the children "a bimatu et infra" ("two years old and under"), he believes that the reading should be not "bimatu" but "imatu", when it is correct to read that the "b" does not belong to the preposition but to the following word, something that even children who do not pay at the baths know. Or Costanzi tells me—says Nebrija—that anyone interested in the subject, basing themselves on Lorenzo Valla, should have noted that in the quotation one should not read "infra", but "intra", as "infra" designates social and physical position, as "infra omnes homines", "infra tectum"; while "intra" is used for number and space, as "intra octo dies", "intra urbis muros". There is more to be said ("sed de his alias, nunc ad rem") he tells us, but ending his digression he returns to what concerns us:

Constantius in observatione a finali proxima invehitur acerrime in Nicolaum quod eo in loco legat "schino", quam interpretatur "lentiscum" contenditque debere legi "cino", quam ipse somniat esse ex lauri generibus unum. Excutiamus igitur diiudicemusque uter illorum stet a causa potiori, constituatur inter eos causa, citentur partis utriusque testes. [Costanzi when concluding his observation bitterly attacks Nicholas of Lyra, because in this passage he reads "schino", in the sense of "acacia", and defends the reading "cino", dreaming that it is a type of laurel. So let us examine and explain which of the two has the more powerful reasons, and let a judicial reason be established between the two and let the witnesses to both sides be summoned.]

---

children who do not pay at the public baths know', or Costanzi shows me the correctness of this textual decison, or if he is so interested in these ideas, it is better to rely on Lorenzo Valla and realize that in this expression should be read not 'infra' but 'intra', because *infra* indicates social condition and position, as 'beneath all men', 'under cover'; *intra*, in contrast, refers to number and space, as 'in eight days' time' or 'within the city walls'"].

This dialogue with the authorities on "schinum" (which is not relevant to be pursued in full) is integrated in daily life, recreated by anecdote, and has much to tell of the life of Nebrija and the realities of humanism in general.[29] Some arise from habitual subjects of conversation with persons directly affected (*sacrificuli*, the friars) or simply curious to know the meanings of ritual words which play a strong social role, as "Drama. atis", in chapter XVI:

> Quaerunt me cotidie multi non solum ex sacrificulorum turba, sed ex illorum numero qui se sciolos putant, quid sibi vult drama illud, quod in celebritate Virginis Deiparae ac proinde in festis aliarum virginum ecclesia Romana canit: "Ante torum huius virginis, frequentate nobis dulcia cantica dramatis". Scribendum nanque est non per "ch", non per "g", non per duplex "m", ut in quibusdam depravatis codicibus legitur, sed simpliciter "dramatis". Atque ut semel me ab hac quaestione absolvam, volui hoc in loco scribere aliquid quo deinceps percontaturos remittam. Est itaque "drachma" per "ch"...
>
> [Many people ask me every day, no only from among the multitude of friars, but also of those who consider themselves somewhat wise, what this "drama" is that the Church sings in celebration of the Virgin Mother, and hence in the feasts of other virgins: "Before the altar of this virgin, come to use sweet songs of the drama". Well, it is not spelled with "ch", or with "g", or with double "m", as we read in certain corrupt manuscripts, but simply "dramatis". But in order to unburden myself once and for all of this question, I wished to write something to which to refer in the future when asked. Thus "drachma" with "ch" ...]

After giving the meanings of other words with which it is often confused, he offers a definition, descriptive and funcional, of its classical usage, taken from that encyclopedia of ancient learning, Servius on Virgil:

---

[29] This also explains in passing the query raised by Antonio Odriozola, "La caracola del bibliófilo nebrisense o La casa a cuestas indispensable al amigo de Nebrija para navegar por el proceloso de sus obras," *Revista de Bibliografía Nacional* 7 (1946): 1-112, who did not know the origin of the annotation "A bimatu et infra" which Angelo Caninio inserted between chapters VI "Bethdagon" and VIII, where he transferred the *lemma* "Camelopardalis". The passage is cited again by Nebrija in the commentaries on Prudentius, *Cathemerinon* 12, 105, where he glosses *Per Bethleem*: "Unde Christus erat oriturus, quasi dicat: etsi in Bethleem natus est quem ego timeo mihi successurum, tutius tamen est ut omnes pueri a bimatu et infra pereant" ["Where Christ was to be born, as if to say: although he who I fear will succeed me has been born in Bethlehem, it is still quite certain that all the boys of two years and less should perish"]. See *Prudentii Libelli cum commento*, 142 (textual criticism) and 422-23 (text).

Sed "drama.atis" simpliciter scriptum est representatio fabularum in quibus introducuntur variae personae, ut in comoediis et tragediis et poematis diversorum generum. Unde et Servius in Bucolicis <3, 1> illud dicit dramaticum dicendi genus in quo variae inducuntur personae, dictum a "drao", quod est "ago", in ea significatione qua Iuvenalis <3, 94> ait: "uxorem comoedus agit vel Dorida".
[But "drama.atis" spelled thus is the representation of fables in which various characters act, as in comedies, tragedies, and poems in various genres. Hence Servius too on the *Bucolics* refers to the dramatic style when various characters act. Constructed out of "drao" which is equivalent to "ago" in Juvenal's meaning when he says "the actor who plays a wife or Doris".]

Church Latin usages are linked seamlessly with classical ones, with a detailed indication of their forms of performance:

In quo sensu accipitur "drama" in versu quem ecclesia canit "dulcia cantica dramatis". Representat namque ecclesia Christi nuptias cum Matre virgine, aut cum aliqua ex virginibus quas evangelista vocat sapientes, aut cum defaecatissima aliqua fidelium anima, aut cum ipsa denique ecclesia, in quibus quidem nuptiis cavendum esse epithalamium, hoc est carmen nuptiale, admonemur, quale est illud Salomonis in Canticis Canticorum, in quo introducuntur personae representantes tum sponsam, tum sponsum, tum utriusque matrem, tum utriusque comites.
[This is the meaning of "drama" in the line "dulcia cantica dramatis" sung by the Church. There it means the marriage of Christ with the Virgin Mother, or another of the virgins that the evangelist calls wise, or any most purified soul of the faithful, or the Church itself, weddings in which we perceive without doubt the presence of the epithalamium, that is, a wedding poem, like that of Solomon in the Song of Songs, in which various characters are shown, representing the bride, the spouse, the mother of both and the companions of both.]

The history of the genre is likewise traced by listing authors from the Greeks and Romans to the Christians, co-existing in a single cultural universe. The whole ends with Origen on the epithalamium:

Quem deinceps imitati sunt poetae Latini et Graeci, qui epithalamia quoque scripserunt in nuptiis deorum atque hominum. Primus qui epithalamium cecinit apud Graecos autores fuisse dicitur Apollo in nuptiis Thetidis et Pelei et deinceps alii quos et Latini sunt subsecuti: Catullus, Ovidius, Claudianus, Ausonius. Talia igitur carmina in spiritualibus nuptiis esse canenda nobis monemur, qualia sunt illa ex Canticis Salomonis: "Dum esset rex in acubitu suo" <1, 11> et "leva eius sub capite meo" <2, 6> et "nigra sum sed formosa" <1, 4> et "iam hyems transiit et recessit" <2, 11>, quae sunt verba sponsi et sponsae, quae personae introducuntur ab autore. Et hoc est quod Origenes in Expositione <prol.> illius operis dicit: "Epithalamium—inquit—Salomonis, quod in morem dramatis compositum est", idest actionis vel representationis diversarum personarum.

[Epithalamium, imitated later by the Latin and Greek poets, who also wrote epithalamia on the weddings of gods and men. The first to sing an epithalamium among the Greeks was Apollo at the wedding of Thetis and Peleus, and then others who were followed by the Latins Catullus, Ovid, Claudian, Ausonius. We note that such poems, like the Song of Solomon, are to be sung at the exchange of vows: "while the king is on his couch", "his left hand under my head", "I am black but comely", "the winter has now passed", which are respectively words of the spouse and the bride as characters introduced by the author. And this is what Origen in his commentary says: the epithalamium of Solomon is composed in the manner of the drama, that is, of the action or representation of different characters.]

These are to be the directives that govern the pragmatic parameters of the study of language and intertexts, their contextualization in literary history. On the more general level of the opposition between the Renaissance mentality and scholasticism it means conceiving philology and the metaphorical word as a basic assumption of ontology, and not vice versa. Language and the observation of reality are the humanists' sensible way of confronting the meaning of being, the concrete reality which surrounds and preoccupies them, either via some modest grammatical commentaries or through these more refined miscellanies.

CHRISTIAN CLASSICS AND HUMANISM IN RENAISSANCE BARCELONA: THE CASE OF PERE MIQUEL CARBONELL (1434-1517)

ALEJANDRO COROLEU
(ICREA-UNIVERSITAT AUTÒNOMA DE BARCELONA)

In Renaissance Barcelona religious and moral texts amounted to an important part of the bibliographical output published and owned in the city.[1] Unsurprisingly much of this corpus is made up by liturgical material for offices and masses as well as prayers, hymns and sermons. In addition, the Barcelona presses issued editions of devotional and hagiographical works, and Christian Latin poets of late Antiquity also merited high regard among local printers and readers. An example of the attention paid to sacred and moral works in early modern Barcelona is provided by the printer, antiquary and bibliophile Pere Miquel Carbonell. Born in Barcelona in 1434, Carbonell was appointed public notary by king Alfons of Aragon (*el Magnànim*) in 1458. Eighteen years later, in December 1476, he was granted the positions of Royal archivist and Royal scribe, which he held until his death in 1517. As a result of his public duties, Carbonell was able to undertake extensive research in the local archives which led to his most accomplished works, the *Cròniques d'Espanya*, a narrative account of the Spanish past written with the full blaze of humanist rhetoric, and the *De viris illustribus Catalanis*, a collection of fifteen biographies aimed at

I am grateful to the audience for their remarks on the version read in Cork, and to Veronika Coroleu Oberparleiter and Lola Badia for their comments on a first draft of this essay. Abbreviations: BC [Biblioteca de Catalunya, Barcelona], BUB [Biblioteca Universitària, Barcelona], Girona, AC [Girona, Arxiu Capitular]. This article forms part of a Ministerio de Ciencia e Innovación team project *Poetae Latini Minores II* (FFI2008-01759).
[1] Jordi Rubió i Balaguer, "Notes sobre els llibres de lectura espiritual a Barcelona des de 1500 a 1530," in his *La cultura catalana del Renaixement a la Decadència* (Barcelona: Edicions 62, 1964), 113-29.

mapping out the state of Latin literature in the Catalan-speaking lands at the time. As with most humanists, Carbonell employed the epistolary form to communicate scholarly information and to express friendship. He corresponded in Latin with, among others, Jeroni Pau and the Italians Lorenzo Lippio and Alessandro Geraldini.[2]

Equally important as the texts written by Carbonell are the books which he acquired, assembled and annotated. Books were Carbonell's passion, at least his second passion, if we are to believe him when he confesses that he collected so many of them "not to continue being a womanizer" ("ne mulierosus persisterem").[3] Information on Carbonell's bibliographical interests can in any case easily be gleaned from several private documents. Apart from the volumes listed in his will, recently edited by Maria Toldrà, some twenty incunabula owned by Carbonell are now held in Barcelona University Library.[4] We also have at our disposal two miscellaneous manuscripts which include a number of texts from the Italian cultural world, copied by Carbonell and to which I shall return later in this essay.[5] In fact Carbonell's own library catalogue prior to 1484 survives in one of these two manuscripts (Girona, AC, MS. 69).[6] Last but not least, Carbonell's instructions to his booksellers attending, respectively, the

---

[2] For a biographical and bibliographical survey of Carbonell see Mariàngela Vilallonga, *La literatura llatina a Catalunya al segle XV* (Barcelona: Curial, 1993), 63-72. I have discussed the printing and readership of religious books in Renaissance Barcelona in "Printing Sacred Texts in Early Modern Barcelona (1480-1530)," *Ars Eloquentiae: Essays for Terence O'Reilly*, ed. Isabel Torres and Barry Taylor, *Bulletin of Hispanic Studies*, Special Number, 86: 6 (2009): 743-50.

[3] Quoted in Vilallonga, *La literatura llatina*, 63.

[4] Maria Toldrà, "El testament de Pere Miquel Carbonell," in *El (re)descobriment de l'edat moderna: Estudis en homenatge a Eulàlia Duran*, ed. Eulàlia Miralles and Josep Solervicens (Barcelona: Publicacions de l'Abadia de Montserrat, 2007), 9-31.

[5] These—BUB, MS. 123, and Girona, AC, MS. 69—have been discussed in Mariàngela Vilallonga, "Humanistas italianos en los manuscritos de Pere Miquel Carbonell," in *Humanismo y pervivencia del mundo clásico: Actas del II Simposio sobre humanismo y pervivencia del mundo clásico,* ed. José María Maestre Maestre, Joaquín Pascual Barea and Luis Charlo Brea, 3 vols (Cádiz: Universidad, 1997), III, 1217-24.

[6] The inventory of Carbonell's library prior to 1484 was transcribed and discussed by Jordi Rubió i Balaguer in his "Els autors clàssics a la biblioteca de Pere Miquel Carbonell, fins a l'any 1484," in his *Sobre biblioteques i biblioteconomia* (Barcelona: Publicacions de l'Abadia de Montserrat, 1995), 37-57.

Venice and Lyon Book fairs in 1488 and 1501 are available too.[7] All these documentation gives us a close insight into Carbonell's literary taste and intellectual preoccupations.

These sources have, however, often been presented as proof of Carbonell's intellectual turn. Thus, according to most scholars his inclination for humanistic texts and for the classics, as borne out by the large number of Italian, Greek (in Latin translation) and Roman writings included in the inventory prior to 1484, would have been superseded by an interest in the late 1480s and in the 1490s in theological texts, spiritual treatises, devotional works and Christian Latin poetry (most Christian books were indeed purchased in the late 1480s and above all in the 1490s).[8] Whilst the former would reflect Carbonell's humanistic credentials, the latter would confirm him, in Francisco Rico's words, as a "medieval throwback".[9] Yet, I believe that a more nuanced analysis of Carbonell's printing activity, largely spanning the 1490s, and of his library holdings may reveal how Carbonell's attention to religious texts was not motivated by one specific factor, but by different preoccupations and by an amalgamation of cultural traditions. In what follows I shall also attempt to draw parallels between Carbonell and his fellow printers in order to show how attention to spiritual texts in early Renaissance Barcelona is not unique to our man. Although my survey concentrates on Carbonell's activities at Barcelona, throughout this essay I will also make occasional references to other European cities.

From the last two decades of the fifteenth century onwards, Catalan humanists paid considerable attention to spiritual treatises and devotional works. One of the earliest volumes acquired by Carbonell (in 1481) was, in fact, a copy of a selection of devotional writings by Ioannes Carthusiensis under the title *De immensa caritate Dei* (Venice, 1480; BUB, Inc. 228). As Albert Hauf has shown, interest in this kind of text is closely related to movements for spiritual renewal such as the *Devotio Moderna*, a movement based on personal connection to God and the active showing of

---

[7] Whereas Girona, AC, MS. 69, includes instructions to booksellers in 1488, Barcelona, Arxiu de la Corona d'Aragó, *Memoriale* 55, includes instructions to booksellers in 1501.

[8] Rubió i Balaguer, "Els autors clàssics...," 48, n. 37. For a survey of scholarship on Carbonell, see Pere Miquel Carbonell, *Cròniques d'Espanya*, ed. Agustí Alcoberro, 2 vols (Barcelona: Barcino, 1997), I, 156-68.

[9] Jeroni Pau, *Obres*, ed. Mariàngela Vilallonga, pròleg de Francisco Rico, 2 vols (Barcelona: Curial, 1986), I, 7.

love towards Him.[10] The printed circulation of the devotional corpus in early modern Catalonia embraces both Latin and the vernacular. Inner spirituality is, for example, highlighted in the title of an edition of Bernard of Clairvaux's *Meditationes de interiori homine* which appeared in Barcelona in 1499. One of the first books published at Montserrat was also a Latin edition of Pseudo-Bonaventura's *Meditationes vitae Christi*, which came off the press of Joan Luschner in April of 1499. Just over a month later Luschner himself issued an edition of another work attributed to Pseudo-Bonaventura, the *De triplici via sive incendium amoris*. As attested by the colophon, the volume is directly relevant to the religious life at the Benedictine monastery: "ad permaximam utilitatem in vita spirituali proficere cupientium in Monasterio Beatae Mariae virginis de Monte serrato" (copy examined: BC, 9-III-48).

Local attention to Pseudo-Bonaventura predated, however, Luschner's printing activity at Montserrat and went beyond ecclesiastical and monastic circles. This is clearly the case with a bilingual Latin-Spanish edition of the *Meditationes vitae Christi* published by Carbonell in 1493. This edition presents the text in parallel columns. It has been noted that here "the line-lengths have been carefully coordinated to ensure that translation and original are perfectly aligned".[11] It therefore seems safe to assume that the volume was aimed at a reader whose level of proficiency in Latin must not have been very high. For Latinless readers or for those who did not need the assistance of a translation, that same year Carbonell prepared two separate Spanish and Latin editions from the same type-settings. Carbonell's decision to issue a Spanish (and not Catalan) edition of the text may have been determined by García Jiménez de Cisneros, Abbot of Montserrat after 1493 and a champion of the *Devotio Moderna*. We know that Carbonell's volume featured in Montserrat around 1500 as recorded among the books which would have made up the catalogue of the monastic library.[12] With the turn of the sixteenth century interest in the *Meditationes vitae Christi* did not decrease and lay readers soon had at their disposal a Catalan rendering of the text—"per un devot religiós del

---

[10] Albert Hauf, *D'Eiximenis a Sor Isabel de Villena: Aportació a l'estudi de la nostra cultura medieval* (València: Institut de Filologia Valenciana, 1990), 19-55.

[11] Barry Taylor, "Iberian-Latin Bilingual Editions, Fifteenth-Eighteenth Centuries," in *Latin and Vernacular in Renaissance Iberia, II: Translations and Adaptations*, ed. Barry Taylor and Alejandro Coroleu (Manchester: Manchester Spanish and Portuguese Studies, 2006), 149-69 (150).

[12] Anselmo Albareda, "Intorno alla scuola di orazione metodica stabilita a Monserrato dall'abate Garsías Jiménez de Cisneros (1493-1510)," *Archivum Historicum Societatis Iesu* 25 (1956): 254-316 (306).

monestir de Montserrat"—in, at least, two editions published by Joan Rosembach in 1518 and 1522.

The detailed evocations of moments from the Gospels included in the *Meditationes vitae Christi* occur in writings of similar subject-matter also published at the time by Carbonell and other Barcelona-based printers. The sufferings of Our Lord are described in several Latin texts (an edition of the *Passio Domini nostri* was issued by Pere Posa in 1498) but, above all, in works written in Catalan, as with the widely popular *Gamaliel* (1493, 1502 and *c*. 1510) or Francesc Alegre's *Passió de Jesucrist* (published by Carbonell around 1494). The life of Christ is the theme of a further local product, Isabel de Villena's vernacular *Vita Christi*, which first appeared in Valencia in 1497. Moreover, a Catalan version of the *Imitatio Christi*—a treatise commonly attributed to Thomas a Kempis outlining the concepts of Modern Devotion—was published by Posa in Barcelona in 1482. The popularity of Latin devotional texts in the Catalan-speaking lands in the early modern period is most apparent from the attention paid by local humanists and printers to Ludolph of Saxony's *Vita Christi*. Rigorously conforming to Scripture and to works by accredited authorities, the text first circulated in Latin as attested by a copy of the 1478 edition purchased by Carbonell in 1482 (BUB, Inc. 296), even though its phenomenal after-life was due to multiple vernacular renderings. Ludolph of Saxony's *Vita Christi* was very rapidly made available to vernacular readers in Joan Roís de Corella's Catalan translation. The popularity of Corella's version is obvious from its numerous reprints, in Valencia and Barcelona, between 1495 and 1518.[13]

Local printers and scholars drew inspiration from other cultural traditions, namely Christian Latin poets of late Antiquity. Of these Prudentius (348-405) was one of the first to receive Carbonell's attention. A letter sent to him by his cousin and fellow humanist Jeroni Pau in

---

[13] Details of the editions discussed on this and the previous paragraph are: Bernard of Clairvaux, *Meditationes de interiori homine* (Barcelona: Posa, 1499); *Meditationes vitae Christi* (Montserrat: Joan Luschner, 1499); *De triplici via sive incendium amoris* (Montserrat: Luschner, 1499); *Meditationes vitae Christi* (in Catalan) (Barcelona: Rosembach, 1518 and 1522); *Imitació de Jesu-christ* (Barcelona: Pere Posa, 1482); *Aquest libre ha nom Gamaliel en lo qual se compta tot lo proces de la passio de Iesu Crist* (Barcelona: Rosembach, 1493); Francesc Alegre, *Passió de Jesucrist* (*c*. 1494); *Lo quart del Cartoxà* [trans. Joan Roís de Corella] (Valencia: Lope de la Roca, 1495); *Lo terç del Cartoxà* (Valencia: Lope de la Roca, *c*. 1495); *Lo primer del Cartoxà* (Valencia: Hagenbach & Hutz, 1496); *Lo segon del Cartoxà* (Valencia: Cofman, 1500); Isabel de Villena, *Vita Christi* (Valencia: Lope de la Roca, 1497); *Passio Domini nostri* (Barcelona: Posa, 1498).

January 1486 bears witness to Carbonell's interest in poems from Prudentius's *Peristephanon* ("Crowns of the martyrs"), which Carbonell himself copied. In his letter Pau acknowledges having consulted a very old codex of Prudentius, which, he says, he was "rather pleased to read".[14] Pau's interest in Prudentius's hymns went well beyond the confines of textual criticism, and his own Latin poetry is heavily influenced by Prudentius's technique of composition. Although attention to Prudentius is, of course, not unique to Barcelona, and examples of the same trend can be found in Castile and the Low Countries, Carbonell and Pau's epistolary exchange regarding Prudentius's poetry is another proof of the circulation of early Christian writers in late fifteenth-century Catalonia.[15]

Carbonell's interest in Prudentius seems to go hand in hand with his attention to later practitioners of Christian Latin verse such as Pseudo-Albertus Magnus, a copy of whose *De laudibus Beatae Mariae Virginis libri XII, vel Mariale* (Strasbourg, 1493) was purchased by him that same year (BUB, Inc. 906). Carbonell was also well acquainted with Petrarch's *Carmen in laudem divae Mariae Magdalenae*, copied in the above-mentioned Girona manuscript sometime after 1473 (Girona, AC, MS. 69, fol. 210v). This composition in turn must have acted as a stimulus for Carbonell's own *Mariae Magdalenae oratio*. There is nothing strange in Carbonell's interest in Petrarch's poem on Mary Magdalene, a popular saint among early humanists.[16] Alongside poems by Prudentius or hymns in honour of Saint Ann, the text was, for example, published at least three times in the German- and Dutch-speaking world between 1508 and 1512 by printers undoubtedly committed to the *studia humanitatis*.[17]

---

[14] "Perlegi nuper vetustissimum codicem Prudentii poetae christiani, cuius lectione non mediocriter sum oblectatus", Jeroni Pau, *Obres*, II, 78.

[15] Information on the Renaissance reception of Prudentius can be gleaned from Felipe González Vega, "Poesía de la nueva espiritualidad en el primer Renacimiento español (con un excurso sobre la recepción de Prudencio y su primera traducción castellana)," in *Latin and Vernacular in Renaissance Iberia, II*, 23-47.

[16] Ann Moss, *Renaissance Truth and the Latin Language Turn* (Oxford: Oxford University Press, 2003), 95 and 101.

[17] See *Prudentii carmen de martirio divi Cassiani. Francisci Petrarche de diva Magdalena. Rodolphi Agricolae carmen de divo Iudoco* (Cologne: Quentell, 1508); *Carmina ornatissima trigintasex per modum orationis Francisci Petrarche ob laudem et reverentiam seraphice peccatricis Marie Magdalene. Hymnus in laudem dive et sanctissime matrona Anne* ... (Leipzig: Thanner, 1508); *Francisci Petrarche Aretini poete laureati Bucolicum carmen ... Sequitur carmen Francisci Petrarche ad divam Magdalenam compositum ...* (Deventer: Albert Paffraet, 1512).

Carbonell's familiarity with Petrarch's religious verse was not an isolated case. Rather, humanist Latin poetry on overtly Christian topics was very much in vogue at the time in Barcelona. This can be illustrated by an extremely rare edition of Giovanni Pontano's *De divinis laudibus* produced by Luschner in 1498. This is the only non-Italian incunable of Pontano, whose Latin poems must have undoubtedly appealed to readers in religious circles in Barcelona.[18] Yet, explicit references to Catalan and Aragonese poets and members of the nobility (Alfons of Aragon, *el Magnànim*; Pere Torroella; the Duke of Calabria), and the fact that Pontano's edition was dedicated to (Prince) John of Aragon, Joan II's (1397-1479) stepson and later Archbishop of Saragossa, must have also attracted the interest of the local public. Even though it is difficult to establish whether Carbonell was directly involved in Luschner's edition of the *De divinis laudibus*, he may have well persuaded the printer to bring out an edition of Pontano's collection of hymns. Carbonell's close links with the Luschner family and, above all, his prominent role at the court of Joan II some thirty years earlier may have been a determinant when deciding to publish a text which could serve a political function at the time when Catalonia was already weakened.[19]

Of all modern Christian authorities it was, however, the Carmelite Mantuan (Baptista Mantuanus or Battista Spagnuoli, 1448-1516) who merited the highest regard among Renaissance printers and readers. Mantuan's poetry included the *Contra poetas impudice loquentes*, ten eclogues on religious topics (the *Adulescentia*) and a poem on the Virgin Mary (the *Parthenice prima*). "A safe model"—to quote Ann Moss—"of assimilated classical language and culture", Mantuan's texts were frequently printed with commentaries aimed at grammar-class pupils and were employed in school and university courses throughout Europe.[20] Mantuan also enjoyed a certain degree of exposure in early modern Barcelona. We know, for example, that the *Contra poetas impudice loquentes* was read and annotated by Carbonell, as confirmed by a copy of

---

[18] A copy of Pontano's edition was listed among those held at Montserrat in 1500 (Albareda, "Intorno …," 313).

[19] Giovanni Pontano, *De divinis laudibus* (Barcelona: Luschner, 1498) (copy examined: Parma, Biblioteca Palatina, Inc. Parm. 238/II). On the links between Carbonell and Luschner (as well as other German printers active in Barcelona at the end of the fifteenth century), see Maria Antonia Adroher Ben, "Estudios sobre el manuscrito *Petri Michaelis Carbonelli adversaria 1492*, del Archivo Capitular de Gerona," *Anuario del Instituto de Estudios de Gerona* 2 (1956-1957): 109-62 (119-22).

[20] Moss, *Renaissance Truth*, 212.

Josse Bade's *Silvae morales* (in which Mantuan's poem was included) held at Barcelona University Library (Inc. 685). This volume bears a Latin manuscript note next to the colophon in which Carbonell proudly acknowledges having acquired the book in 1494 at his own expense.[21]

Apart from editions of devotional works and of Christian Latin poets, the Barcelona presses issued lives of saints. Carbonell followed this trend too. As an example, in 1493 he published an anonymous *Vita et transitus sancti Hieronymi* (in fact three long letters in Catalan attributed to Eusebius, Cyril and Augustine). The text was preceded by a life of Jerome (*Vida e transit del glorios sanct Iheronim*) extracted from Jacobus de Voragine's most popular *Legenda aurea sanctorum*. Significantly, the *Legenda aurea* appeared in Catalan in an edition prepared by Joan Rosembach in 1494—and by Lope de la Roca in Valencia two years later—and was published again—albeit "novament fet"—by Carles Amorós in 1519. Voragine's compilation must have provided the impetus for local products, like a life of St Severus bishop of Barcelona penned by Carbonell in 1512 which only survives in manuscript form.[22] Carbonell's interest in hagiography and in the lives of the Church Fathers is also apparent from his own library holdings. He owned a German edition of the Pseudo-Jerome's *Vitae sanctorum patrum* (Nuremberg, 1478; BUB, Inc. 52), which was purchased in 1482 and which must have had a relatively wide circulation. That the lives of the Fathers were at least regarded as material worthy of study at Montserrat is confirmed by Abbot García Jiménez de Cisneros's regulations: "Podrán tener los monjes para leer en sus celdas otros libros [...] como *Vitae Patrum*".[23] The collection seems to have been read by young boys in the vernacular if we are to believe Jiménez de Cisneros's own *Regula puerorum* ("Sunt autem legendi isti libri vulgariter").

Alongside spiritual treatises, lives of saints and religious verse, other Christian writings claimed the attention of Carbonell. He assembled texts by the so-called apologists as well as ecclesiastical chronicles. The term

---

[21] Felipe González Vega, "*Marginalia* de Pere Miquel Carbonell en el Incunable 685 de la Biblioteca Universitaria de Barcelona," in *La memoria de los libros: estudios sobre la historia del escrito y de la lectura en Europa y América*, ed. Pedro Cátedra, 2 vols (Salamanca: Instituto de Historia del Libro y de la Lectura, 2004), I, 273-292.

[22] The texts described above are: *Vita et transitus S. Hieronymi, sive epistolae de eodem in unum collectae* (Barcelona: Carbonell, 1493) and Iacopo da Varazze, *Legenda aurea = Flos sanctorum romançat* (Barcelona: Rosembach, 1494; Valencia: Lope de la Roca, 1496; Barcelona: Amorós, 1519). On Carbonell's life of St Severus see Vilallonga, *La literatura llatina*, 64.

[23] Albareda, "Intorno," 316.

"Apologists" designates a number of Christian Greek and Latin authors who defended the Christian faith against attacks from their pagan contemporaries. Carbonell showed interest in the work of one these writers, Lactantius Firmianus (240-320), whose *Divinae institutiones* were intended to refute all opponents, past, present and future. In the Renaissance Lactantius, the most classical of Christian writers, came to be known as the Christian Cicero. It should therefore not appear strange then that the text of Lactantius copied by Carbonell in a Barcelona manuscript (BC, MS. 1011) features together with fragments from Cicero's letters also copied by him. A further apologist who was well known to Carbonell was the fifth-century writer Paulus Orosius. In his *Histories against the Pagans* he compiled an apologetic response to the pagan argument that the coming of Christianity had brought disaster to the world. Orosius's *Histories* feature in Carbonell's inventory prior to 1484, and were quoted at length in the *Cròniques d'Espanya*. A similar example of a historical text owned by Carbonell and used in his own historical account is provided by the universal chronicle of Antoninus, archbishop of Florence, the *Chronicon*.[24] A copy of the Nuremberg edition of 1491 was bought by Carbonell three years later (BUB, Inc. 167). The text of the *Chronicon* is another source to the *Cròniques d'Espanya*, in which it is partially included in Carbonell's own Catalan translation.[25]

A further kind of text which commanded Carbonell's attention was works touching upon issues of moral philosophy. As is well known, in the second half of the fifteenth century a great number of texts, mostly of a compilatory character, appeared with the aim of consoling and instructing their readers against the precariousness and hardship of earthly existence. No work of Petrarch was more popular among early humanists than his *De remediis utriusque fortunae*, a Christian manual for meditation. Significantly (and seemingly unnoticed by scholars of Catalan humanism), a selection of *sententiae* from Petrarch's *De remediis* copied by Carbonell survives in the Girona manuscript (fols 246r-252v). Here selected passages from Petrarch's text are arranged thematically and reproduced alongside maxims from, among other, Augustine, Ambrose, Jerome and Aristotle.

We may dismiss Carbonell's approach to the *De remediis* as profoundly non-humanistic. After all what he did with Petrarch's manual was simply to abbreviate it and employ it (one would say) privately. Had he been serious, he would have published the whole text. Yet, the manner in which Carbonell used and read the *De remediis* is also typical of the last

---

[24] On Orosius and Antoninus as sources for Carbonell, see Carbonell, *Cròniques d'Espanya*, 90 and 91-92 respectively.
[25] See Vilallonga, "Humanistas italianos," 1218.

quarter of the fifteenth century, transitional years in which humanism was finding its feet in many parts of Europe. Petrarch's rather strange mixture of Christian and Stoic reflections on the troubles of the human mind very much appealed to humanists. They copied, read and, above all, abbreviated the *De remediis* over and over again, as with, for example, Jakob Wimpheling's *De adolescentia* of 1496, which includes a collection of maxims from the *De remediis*.[26]

Moreover, very often—in France and Holland—interest in Petrarch's text seems to go hand in hand with Stoic philosophy as illustrated by the large number of editions of the *De remediis*, of Boethius's *De consolatione philosophiae* and of Seneca and Pseudo-Seneca published in the same towns by different printers in a very short span of time.[27] Attention to this corpus in Catalonia at the time can also be documented. Antoni Ginebreda's old translation of Boethius's *Consolatio* was published in Lleida in 1489. Carbonell himself owned a copy of Seneca's *Opera philosophica* (Naples, 1475; BUB, Inc. 4), one of his dearest volumes, and copied the Roman humanist Paolo Pompilio's *De vita Senecae* (BUB, MS. 123, fols 47r-68r). Whether all this qualifies as humanism is, of course, open to debate. This essay has, however, tried to suggest that Pere Miquel Carbonell's humanistic credentials may also be enhanced in spite of (or more precisely in the light of) his interest in religious and moral writings.

---

[26] See Agostino Sotili, "Il Petrarca e l'umanesimo tedesco," *Quaderni Petrarcheschi* 9-10 (1992-1993): 239-91 (247, n. 30).

[27] Mariken Goris-Lodi Nauta, "The Study of Boethius's *Consolatio* in the Low Countries around 1500: The Ghent Boethius (1485) and the Commentary by Agricola/Murmellius (1514)," in *Northern Humanism in European Context, 1469-1625: From the "Adwert Academy" to Ubbo Emmius*, ed. F. Akkerman, A. J. Vanderjagt and A. H. van der Laan (Leiden: Brill, 1999), 109-30 (118-27); and Romana Brovia, "Du nouveau sur la fortune du *De remediis* en France (XIVe-XVIe siècles)," in *La Postérité répond à Pétrarque: Sept siècles de fortune pétrarquienne en France*, ed. Ève Duperray (Paris: Beauchesne, 2006), 87-110.

NOTES ON THE CATALAN TRANSLATIONS OF DEVOTIONAL LITERATURE WITH SPECIAL REFERENCE TO THE *EPISTLE OF LENTULUS TO THE SENATE OF ROME*

MONTSERRAT FERRER
(UNIVERSITAT DE BARCELONA)

Devotional literature in Catalan has not received the attention it deserves in the last half century. Albert Hauf is the only scholar who has endeavoured to provide an overview of the field. His studies on religious literature produced in the Crown of Aragon include the detailed analysis of specific works and a broad historical contextualization covering the period from the fourteenth to the sixteenth centuries.[1] Hauf has focused mainly on the Franciscans Francesc Eiximenis and Joan Eiximeno, and the Dominican Antoni Canals, all of whom were writing in the late fourteenth and early fifteenth centuries and were influenced by the devotional practices that emerged across Europe from the thirteenth century onwards, prior to the *devotio moderna*, a movement of religious spirituality from the late fourteenth to the sixteenth century, founded by Geert Groote, which emphasized meditation, individual prayer and inner life. Hauf has also

---

I am most grateful to Lluís Cabré for his suggestions and recommendations, and to David Barnett for his help with the English version of this article. This article is part of a Ministerio de Ciencia e Innovación team-project (Corpus Digital de Textos Medievales Catalanes II, FFI2008-05556-C03).
[1] In particular, see Albert G. Hauf, *D'Eiximenis a sor Isabel de Villena. Aportació a l'estudi de la nostra cultura medieval* (València: Institut de Filologia Valenciana; Barcelona: Publicacions de l'Abadia de Montserrat, 1990); "Corrientes espirituales valencianas en la baja edad media (siglos XIV-XV)," *Anales Valentinos* 48 (1998): 261-302; and "Profetisme, cultura literària i espiritualitat en la València del segle XV: d'Eiximenis i sant Vicent Ferrer a Savonarola, passant pel Tirant lo Blanc," in *Xàtiva i els Borja, una projecció europea* (Xàtiva: Museu de l'Almodí, 1995), 101-38.

studied those authors who wrote and translated religious works in Valencia in the late fifteenth century, in particular Isabel de Villena. The output of these authors and the sources they drew on provide an idea of the range of devotional texts that were being read at the time. A considerable part of the literature in this genre from the Crown of Aragon circulated in translation. Hauf has studied some of these—especially those by Antoni Canals—in relation to works originally written in Catalan, and has identified some relatively obscure sources. For example, he has established that the *Escala de contemplació* written by Canals between 1398 and 1410 is a version of a brief treatise entitled *De XV gradibus contemplationis et viridiarium Ecclesie*, based on the image of the ladder of virtues that the soul has to climb to reach paradise, an image commonly used by authors of devotional material.[2] (In contrast we know hardly anything of a Catalan *Scala celi* which corresponds neither to John Climacus's work nor that of Jean Gobi *junior*.)[3]

The corpus of devotional works translated into Catalan between the fourteenth and early sixteenth centuries is noteworthy not only for its scope, but also its quality. There is, however, no overall study of the translations in this genre and very few are available in modern editions. Some idea of the range and size of this corpus can be gleaned from the catalogue of devotional works in Catalan compiled by Pere Bohigas. This includes simple works aimed at a popular audience, which were largely unknown when the catalogue was published, and remain so today.[4] New works and manuscript witnesses have been added to Bohigas's original list

---

[2] Albert Hauf, "La *Scala de Contemplació*, de fra Antoni Canals, i el *De XV gradibus contemplationis* o *Viridiarium Ecclesiae*," *Anuari de l'Agrupació Borrianenca de Cultura* 8 (1997): 97-120.

[3] The Catalan version is found in Biblioteca de Catalunya, MSS 77 (fols 108-165) and 710 (fols 1-45) (as well as a lost manuscript, photographs of which have survived, from the Palau de Barcelona Archive). The same text in Castilian is found in manuscripts and early printed editions (Seville: [Meinhardus Ungut and Stanislaus Polonus], 1496). It is possible that the Catalan and the Castilian texts were from a common source, or that one is the source of the other. D. E. Rhodes, who is not aware of the Catalan, did not identify the source of this text and believes that it may be original ("The Spanish *Scala Celi*," *The British Library Journal* 7.2 (1981): 204-05). I am grateful to Stefano Maria Cingolani for some of this information.

[4] Pere Bohigas, "Petita contribució a l'inventari d'obres catalanes de pietat popular anteriors al segle XIX," *Analecta Sacra Tarraconensia* 28 (1955): 355-68. The date range of the catalogue is from the fourteenth to the eighteenth centuries.

by Lourdes Soriano and Glòria Sabaté.[5] Most of the works listed in these catalogues have still not been identified, and the source texts for those that are translations are unknown. It is also worth bearing in mind the devotional works that Jordi Rubió mentions in the chapters dedicated to religious literature in his *Història de la literatura catalana*, some of which are translations.[6]

Some of the classic works of the genre feature among the Catalan translations carried out in this period. For example, there are two versions of the *Stimulus amoris* attributed to St Bonaventure, one of the *Stimulus amoris minor*, now thought to be the work of James of Milan, and the other of the extended version known as the *Stimulus amoris maior*.[7] The translation of the *Stimulus amoris minor* is extant in only one manuscript from the second half of the fifteenth century (Paris, Bibliothèque Nationale de France, MS. Esp. 547). The Catalan *Stimulus amoris maior* is found in the Biblioteca Universitària in Valencia, MS. 980, from the fifteenth century. Neither version has been studied. Other works attributed (rightly or wrongly) to St Bonaventure circulated in Catalan: there is also a translation of the *Meditationes vitae Christi*, as well as one of the *Lignum vitae*.[8] The *Excitatorium mentis ad Deum* by the Augustinian friar Bernat Oliver was translated into Catalan before 1417, the date of one of the surviving manuscript witnesses.[9] A translation of Cassian's *Collationes*,

---

[5] Lourdes Soriano and Glòria Sabaté, "Literatura pietosa i edificant a la Corona d'Aragó. Aportació de textos inèdits i nous manuscrits per al seu estudi (segles XIV i XV) (1)," *Boletín bibliográfico de la Asociación Hispánica de Literatura Medieval* 16 (2002): 307-39. See the section entitled "Contemplacions, meditacions i tractats ascètics" on pp. 327-31. This list is based on information from the Biteca database of Catalan manuscripts (http://sunsite.berkeley.edu/Philobiblon/phbusc.html).

[6] Jordi Rubió i Balaguer, *Història de la literatura catalana*, 3 vols (Barcelona: Publicacions de l'Abadia de Montserrat, 1984 [1948-59]), I, 375-89 and 239-69.

[7] See Falk Eisermann, *Stimulus amoris: Inhalt, lateinische Überlieferung, deutsche Übersetzungen, Rezeption* (Tübingen: Niemeyer, 2001).

[8] Martí de Barcelona, "De codicografia franciscano-catalana," *Estudis franciscans* 42 (1930): 69-79 (69-76). For the *Meditacions*, see also Hauf's introduction to *Contemplació de la Passió de Nostre Senyor Jesucrist. Text religiós del segle XVI*, ed. Albert Hauf (Barcelona: Edicions del Mall, 1982), 5-12.

[9] The manuscript, Biblioteca dell'Archiginnasio di Bologna, MS. A-275, also contains the Catalan translation of the *Soliloquia* and the *Speculum peccatoris* attributed to Augustine. See Bernat Oliver, *Excitatori de la pensa a Déu*, ed. Pere Bohigas, ENC (Barcelona: Barcino, 1929), and Giovanni M. Bertini, "I *Soliloquia* e lo *Speculum peccatoris* dello Pseudo Agostino in catalano," in *Homenatge a*

no longer extant, features in the inventory of books belonging to Queen Maria of Castile (1458). The *Meditationes piissimae de cognitione humanae conditionis* ascribed to St Bernard were also translated into Catalan in the fourteenth century. This translation is extant in at least three manuscripts.[10] In recent times, some scholars have focused on identifying the source and witnesses for translations which might otherwise have gone unnoticed: namely, Sebastià Janeras's work on translations of Isaac of Nineveh in the Iberian Peninsula, one of which is in Catalan; and the study by Joan Requesens of the translation of the *De triplici via ad sapientiam et divinorum contemplationem* by Hugh of Balma, copied in a fifteenth-century manuscript (El Escorial, N.I.16) together with the translation of Isaac.[11] Later on, more classics of devotional literature appear in early printed editions, such as the translation of Thomas a Kempis's *Imitatio Christi* by Miquel Peres, published around 1482.

There are, therefore, a few broad studies as well as some monographs on particular authors or aspects of devotional literature, but currently it is an uphill task trying to trace a continuous history of the full scope of the transmission of this genre in Catalan during this period. Nevertheless, within this timeline, there are certain points worthy of note. Key devotional texts are found in Catalan from the late fourteenth century. The translation of Isaac of Nineveh's *De accessu animae ad Deum* is recorded in an inventory of books from 1373, although the only surviving manuscript witnesses are from the fifteenth century.[12] The translations of Antoni Canals all date from the late fourteenth and early fifteenth centuries. Most of them were carried out during the reign of Martí I (1387-1396), during whose reign we can also locate Joan Eiximeno's

---

Antoni Rubió i Lluch. Miscel·lània d'estudis literaris, històrics i lingüístics, 3 vols (Barcelona, 1936), II, 233-63.

[10] Paris, BNF, MS. Esp. 547; Roma, San Isidoro, MS. 1/18; and El Escorial, MS. N.I.16. The text is listed in an inventory of books from 1362 (Josep Hernando, *Llibres i lectors a la Barcelona del segle XIV*, 2 vols (Barcelona: Fundació Noguera, 1995), II, 364).

[11] Sebastià Janeras, "La Diffusion d'Isaac de Ninive dans la Péninsule Ibérique," in *Eastern Crossroads. Essays on Medieval Christian Legacy*, ed. Juan Pedro Monferrer-Sala (Piscataway, NJ: Gorgias Press, 2007), 247-74. And Joan Requesens, "Hug de Balma (s. XIII) en català (s. XV): la seva *Theologia mystica* en el *Tractat de contemplació* de Francesc Eiximenis i edició del pròleg traduït," *Arxiu de textos catalans antics* 26 (2007): 569-615.

[12] The Latin version of Isaac of Nineveh's work was written in the thirteenth century and had several titles in the Middle Ages (e.g. *De perfectione religiosa, De contemptu mundi, De vita solitaria*). It was the source of the Catalan translation. See Sebastià Janeras, "La Diffusion d'Isaac de Ninive".

Quarantena de contemplació.[13] As is well known, King Martí (and his wife Maria de Luna) were enthusiastic supporters of devotional literature and promoted the reading of these books at court.[14]

Another key period in this timeline is the life of Maria of Castile, the wife of King Alfons (1416-1458).[15] The role she played in the diffusion of devotional works in the first half of the fifteenth century was first pointed out by Anselm Albareda in an article from 1956 in which he highlights the influence of the Benedictines of Montserrat on the queen's literary tastes.[16] The monastery provided her with religious books—and especially devotional ones—and moral treatises, some of which were imported from Italy following the monks' regular visits there: copies of devotional works were also produced in the Montserrat *scriptorium* specially for her, and she received others either on loan or as gifts. The surviving correspondence shows Queen Maria requesting books that she knew of, and chasing up others that had been promised her.[17] The inventory of her books (1458) contains many Catalan translations of devotional texts, among which we can find the most important works in the genre that were circulating at that time in the Crown of Aragon.[18] We know that she also had Domenico

---

[13] Joan Eiximeno, *Quarantena de contemplació*, ed. Albert Hauf (Barcelona: Publicacions de l'Abadia de Montserrat, 1986).

[14] See Jordi Rubió, *Història de la literatura catalana*, 239-242. Joan Eiximeno dedicated to Martí I the *Quarentena de contemplació*, a work inspired by Ubertino da Casale's *Arbor vitae crucifixae Jesu*.

[15] From the time when Alfons the Magnanimous left (never to return) to embark on the conquest of Naples in 1432, Queen Maria acted as regent of Catalonia (until 1453) and of Valencia (until 1436) with the support of a council of nobles, one of whom was the abbot of Montserrat. Ferran Soldevila, "La reyna Maria muller del Magnànim," *Memorias de la Real Academia de Buenas Letras de Barcelona* 10 (1928): 213-345 (215).

[16] Dom Anselmo M. Albareda, "Intorno alla scuola di orazione metodica stabilita a Monserrato dall'abate Garsias Jiménez de Cisneros (1493-1510)," *Archivum historicum Societatis Iesu* 25 (1956): 254-316. The article focuses on Cisneros who introduced the "scuola di orazione metodica", commonly known as "devotio moderna", to the monastery. Albareda also provides a broader historical contextualization, emphasizing the cultural ties between the queen and the monastic house.

[17] See the letters published in Ferran Soldevila, "La reyna Maria," 333-45 (documents VI-X).

[18] It includes, among many others, Pseudo-Bonaventure's *Meditacions*, the *Stimulus amoris maior*, the work of Isaac of Nineveh, the *Book of Visions of Angela of Foligno*, Canals's *Escala de contemplació* and Oliver's *Excitatori*, all in Catalan. The inventory allows us to establish the *terminus ante quem* (1458) for some of these translations (the *Stimulus amoris* and the *Meditacions*, for example).

Cavalca's *Specchio di croce* translated by the Benedictine Pere Busquets, who completed the commission after 1445.[19] These data indicate the crucial role played by Queen Maria and her court in the production and dissemination of devotional works in Catalan.

A third key period takes us to the time of emergence of the printing press and the commercialization of books. In the final quarter of the fifteenth and the first of the sixteenth century, there was a marked increase in the number of translations of devotional works: new ones were commissioned specially for printed editions and earlier ones that were already circulating in manuscript form were also used. Devotional works, like the lives of saints, books of hours and other religious material, were the most commercially viable titles. And printers had to publish those works most in demand to sustain their businesses. So for example, the *Meditationes vitae Christi* attributed to St Bonaventure was printed in 1522 (Barcelona: Johann Rosembach).[20] The influence of the reading public's tastes for printed books can clearly be seen in the work of Joan Roís de Corella. As Francisco Rico explains: Corella had previously dedicated himself to secular prose and poetry, but the works of his that were printed—and with considerable success—are all on religious themes.[21] One of these is his translation of Ludolph of Saxony's *Vita Christi*, printed in parts between 1495 and 1497, and which became a bestseller.[22] Another prolific translator of this genre was Miquel Peres. His version of Kempis's *Imitatio Christi* was printed around 1482 (Barcelona:

Soldevila, "La reyna Maria," 320-32, who identifies most of the 71 volumes in the inventory.

[19] Domenico Cavalca, *Mirall de la Creu*, ed. Annamaria Gallina, 2 vols (Barcelona: Barcino, 1967).

[20] The *Meditacions* had been translated beforehand; it is conserved in fifteenth-century manuscripts (see n. 8). Whether the 1522 printed edition is the same as the manuscript translation or a separate translation has not been established. The rubric in the 1522 edition tells us that the work had been translated by a monk from Montserrat. Albareda suggests that a good candidate could be the monk Mateu de la Penya (Dom Anselm Mª Albareda, *Bibliografia dels monjos de Montserrat (segle XVI)* (Montserrat: Monestir, 1928), 198).

[21] Joan Roís de Corella, *Tragèdia de Caldesa i altres proses*, ed. Marina Gustà, introduction by Francisco Rico (Barcelona: Edicions 62, 1980), 18-19.

[22] For the printed editions of Corella's translation, see Diego Romero Lucas, "La traducción valenciana de las *Meditationes Vitae Christi* del cartujano Ludolfo de Sajonia. Las primeras ediciones valencianas impresas," *Quaderns de Filologia. Estudis literaris* 8 (2003): 299-314.

Pere Posa).[23] The frequency with which some of these translations were reprinted is a clear indication of their success and broad popularity. Peres's *Imitació de Crist*, for example, was reprinted in 1491 or 1493 (Valencia: perhaps by Nicholas Spindeler), again shortly after 1500 (Barcelona: Johann Luschner) and a third time in 1518 (Barcelona: Carles Amorós). In the rest of this article, I shall focus on an example from this later stage, that of early printing, with the specific aim of highlighting the new literary dimension that early printed versions—in other words updated versions—could acquire.

One of the works translated into Catalan and printed in this period was the *Epistle of Lentulus to the Senate of Rome*, which contains a physical description of Jesus Christ. This brief text is a by-product of the interest in Christ's life, on which authors of devotional texts placed particular emphasis: the meditation on the life of Christ, especially the Passion, was seen as a very fruitful spiritual practice. Pseudo-Bonaventure's *Meditationes Vitae Christi* and Ludolph of Saxony's *Vita Christi* are emblematic of this attitude—both works were rendered into Catalan, as we have seen. Such interest in Christ's life led to a curiosity about his physical description.

The *Epistle of Lentulus* is an apocryphal letter providing a description of Jesus Christ, especially his facial features, whose unknown author masquerades as a certain Publius Lentulus, Pontius Pilate's predecessor in the province of Judea. The *Epistle* circulated in Christian Europe from the end of the thirteenth century onwards and was translated into different languages, but reached its widest dissemination by the time Ludolph of Saxony included it in the prologue of his *Vita Christi* (1348-60).[24]

Two Catalan translations of the *Epistle of Lentulus* were produced between the late fifteenth century and the first quarter of the sixteenth century. One of them is the version included in Ludolph of Saxony's *Vita Christi*, which was translated into Catalan by Joan Roís de Corella. The first part of Corella's translation (*Lo primer del Cartoixà*), including the description of Christ taken from the *Epistle of Lentulus*, was printed in 1496 (Valencia: [Lope de la Roca]). Corella extensively expanded the

---

[23] Thomas a Kempis, *La imitació de Jesucrist, traducció catalana de Miquel Pérez*, ed. R. Miquel y Planas (Barcelona, 1911).

[24] The *Vita Christi* was first printed about 1472 ([Cologne: Arnold Ther Hoernen]) and then in 1474 (Strassburg: Heinrich Eggestein).

original text and added new passages to supplement the description of Christ.[25]

The other Catalan translation of the *Epistle of Lentulus* is anonymous and was printed in 1524 (Barcelona: Carles Amorós), together with three more works translated into Catalan: the last part of the *Monotessaron* (chapters 136-49) by Jean Gerson concerning the Passion of Christ, the *Epistle of Pontius Pilate to Tiberius* and the *Legenda aurea* by Jacobus de Voragine with the addition of new lives.[26] The *Monotessaron* extract, the *Epistle of Lentulus* and the *Epistle of Pilate* had been printed together in Castilian *c.* 1493 (Burgos: Friedrich Biel), and the extant copy of this edition[27] is bound with a Castilian translation of the *Legenda aurea* (Burgos: Juan de Burgos?, *c.* 1499).[28] Maria Mercè López established the relationship between the anonymous Catalan translation printed in 1524 and the Castilian translation of the *Epistle of Lentulus* printed *c.* 1493: both Catalan and Castilian translations are closely related.[29] Although the

---

[25] Corella's translation of the *Vita Christi* is not available in modern editions, but the passage concerning the description of Christ is: Hugo O. Bizzarri and Carlos F. Sainz de la Maza, "La *Carta de Léntulo al senado de Roma*: Fortuna de un retrato de Cristo en la baja edad media castellana," *RILCE* 10.1 (1994): 43-58 (56-57). For Corella's life and work, see Martí de Riquer, *Història de la literatura catalana*, 3 vols (Esplugues de Llobregat: Ariel, 1964), III, 254-320.

[26] The book was printed with the title *Flor dels sancts*. The *Legenda aurea* had already been translated into Catalan; the first manuscripts had been copied either in the late thirteenth century or at the beginning of the fourteenth century, and the first printed edition was published in 1494 (Barcelona: Johann Rosenbach). See *Vides de sants rosselloneses*, ed. Charlotte S. Maneikis Kniazzeh and Edward J. Neugaard, 3 vols (Barcelona: Fundació Salvador Vives Casajuana, 1977). The manuscript copies were the basis for the printed editions, which introduced various changes into the text. The 1524 edition, for instance, omits most of the introductions to each saint's life, in which the meaning of their names is explained.

[27] British Library, IB.53235. The Castilian incunable also contains an *Oración muy devota al crucifixo*.

[28] British Library, IB.53312. See the Incunabula Short Title Catalogue of the British Library (http://www.bl.uk/catalogues/istc/). A copy of an edition extant in Boston (Public Library, Q.403.88), which contains the *Monotessaron* extract and the two epistles in Castilian, seems to be a different edition (see Biteca, Manid 3719). The same works were translated from Castilian into Portuguese and printed twice in 1513 (Lisboa: Hermann von Kempen & Roberto Rabelo, and Lisboa: Joannes Petri de Bonominis de Cremona).

[29] Maria Mercè López Casas, "Una altra traducció al català de la *Carta de Lèntul al senat de Roma*," in *Edición y anotación de textos. Actas del I Congreso de Jóvenes Filólogos (A Coruña, 25-28 de septiembre de 1996)*, ed. Carmen Parrilla et al., 2 vols (A Coruña: Universidade da Coruña, 1998), I, 361-70.

Castilian translation was printed earlier, there is no textual evidence to determine which one was the source of the other. López suggests that an earlier version—now lost—of the Catalan *Epistle of Lentulus* was the source of the Castilian one.[30]

A comparison of the two Catalan translations of the *Epistle of Lentulus*—Corella's and the 1524 printed edition—allows us to see how a translator uses an earlier translation of the same work for stylistic reasons.

While the Castilian *Epistle* follows the Latin text closely, the Catalan translator expands the text by adding many extra adjectives and phrases not found in either the Castilian translation or the Latin text.[31] The description of Christ's face is far more detailed, and several features have been added. The result is a more polished and elaborate translation. This stylistic complexity is characteristic of the anonymous Catalan *Epistle of Lentulus* and Corella's translation. If one compares the insertions in these two translations, a connection between them becomes clear. The anonymous translator clearly consulted Corella's text to supplement his translation of the *Epistle*: some specific expressions and words in the extended passages were taken from the translation made by Corella; other passages echo Corella's translation too, and may also be modelled on it. The way in which Corella's translation is used in the anonymous *Epistle* can be seen in the following examples:

[1] CATALAN *EPISTLE OF LENTULUS*, ED. 1524: "És elegant home e d'una gentil i *mesurada granesa*, ço és a saber, més gran que petit, ab una formada i egual mijania. Mostra en lo gest de la sua cara molta graciositat, excel·lència i magestat, la qual és complidament bella *sens ninguna màcula.* ... Té la front plana, serena e condecentment *espaciosa*, ab la faç com he dit sens ruga o alguna taca. Lo nas té dret e *perfetament col·locat*, lo qual per una gentil egualtat e mesura li parteix

---

[30] López Casas's justification for the precedence of the Catalan text is based on the occurrence of the word *clencha* in the Castilian text, which she believes is a Catalanism. However, the word is already documented in Castilian at around the same time, and so its presence is not conclusive evidence. There are, nevertheless, one or two places where the Catalan text is closer to the Latin than the Castilian is: Lat. "discitur a gentibus", Cat. "és dit per les gents", Cast. "llaman las gentes"; Lat. "visus est ridere", Cat. "s'és vist riure", Cast. "vieron reír". Again, these readings are not conclusive evidence, but they do suggest that López Casas's hypothesis regarding an earlier Catalan text, now lost, is possible.

[31] The Castilian *Epistle of Lentulus* is very close to the Latin text found in Biblioteca Nacional de Madrid, MS. 4303, which has minor differences from Ludolph of Saxony's version. See Bizzarri and Sainz de la Maza, "La *Carta de Léntulo al senado de Roma*," 49, 53-54.

> les galtes, les quals són tant formoses que no crech sie cosa més amable e delectable a la vista, a la qual formosura és ajunt un mijancer e onestíssim color."
>
> CASTILIAN *EPISTLE OF LENTULUS*, ED. C. 1493: "Hombre de luenga estatura con medianía, y muy gentil. Tiene el rostro de grand acatamiento ... Tiene la fruente llana y muy serena, con la faz sin ruga o tacha alguna, a la qual fermosea un mediano color. En la nariz nin la boca no ay que decir."[32]
>
> CORELLA'S TRANSLATION OF *VITA CHRISTI*: "Jesu Crist ... fos de statura acostant-se a *granea proporcionada*. ... La sua faç *speciosa* sens algú defalt *ni màcula* ab una serenitat clara, reverend ensemps y affable ... Lo front pla sens alguna ruha. ... Lo nas aguileny que la sua cara enbellia, en lo mig ab una poca eminència que li donava *perfeta forma*."[33]

Some expressions match those from Corella's translation exactly, although often their location in the text is different. For example, the expression "sens ninguna màcula" qualifies the face in Corella's text, but in the anonymous translation it qualifies "lo gest de la cara". The same for "speciosa": it describes the face in Corella's translation, whereas in the anonymous text it occurs earlier and qualifies the forehead. Other expressions are not lifted verbatim, but appear to be closely related to his wording: for instance, in the description of Christ's nose, "perfetament col·locat" (cf. "li donava perfeta forma"), and "mesurada granesa" (cf. "granea proporcionada"), in the example quoted above. On other occasions, an idea rather than an expression or description seems to have been adopted from Corella's text:

> [2] CATALAN *EPISTLE OF LENTULUS*, ED. 1524: "En lo rependre se mostra terrible, mes en lo exortar, consellar i amonestar és molt benigne, alegre, *mansuet* e amigable, retenint emperò tostemps una increïble e maravellosa gravitat. En los braços e les mans té tanta *bellesa* corresponent a la *proporció* de tot lo cors, que és delit de mirar-los. Finalment té tots los altres membres *formats* e ornats de tant loable e

---

[32] All the quotations from the *Epistle of Lentulus* are taken from Maria Mercè López Casas, "Una altra traducció al català de la *Carta de Lèntul al senat de Roma*," 364-65. Italics are always mine. Cf. the Latin text: "Homo quidem stature procere mediocris et spectabilis. Vultum habens venerabilem ... Frontem planam et serenissimam cum facie sine ruga et macula aliqua quam rubor moderatus venustat. Nasi et oris nulla est prorsum reprehensio."

[33] All the quotations from Corella's translation are taken from Bizzarri and Sainz de la Maza, "*La Carta de Léntulo al senado de Roma*," 56-57.

inefable pulcritut que no crech sia mai nat tan excel·lent i *alegant home* entre los fills dels hòmens."

CASTILIAN *EPISTLE OF LENTULUS*, ED. C. 1493: "En el reprehender, terrible; en el amonestar, benigno y amigable, alegre, guarda empero su gravidad. ... En la estatura del cuerpo proporcionado y derecho. Tiene las manos y los braços que es deleite de verlos. En el fablar ralo, grave y discreto, de gran beldad entre los fijos de los hombres."

CORELLA'S TRANSLATION OF *VITA CHRISTI*: "... als penidents mostras la sua cara affable, *mansueta* y benigne. ... Larchs los braços y les mans proporcionades; drets larchs los dits y stesos, ab les ungles de color viva. Y así tot lo seu cors pujant dels peus fins a la part del cap més alta, era de tan *elegant bellea* que los ulls qui sens enveja miraven proporció de tan *elegant figura* donaven lahors a la Magestat Divina. ... Descriu en poques paraules lo Psalmista la sua bellea dient: 'Més bell, més gentil en la sua *forma* de tots los fills dels hòmens'."

The beauty and elegance are emphasized in the anonymous translation. The same intention can be found in Corella's description.

Finally, the Catalan translator added a description of Christ's eyebrows, mouth, lips and teeth. The same features are described in Corella's translation, whereas the Castilian translation and the Latin text make no mention of them. Even so, in this case Corella's description of these features does not match the anonymous translation exactly:

[3] CATALAN *EPISTLE OF LENTULUS*, ED. 1524: "Té les selles sobre los ulls en manera d'arch, esteses e per intervall degut separades. Té la boca *no molt gran*, mas compartida molt aptament. Los labis són *retirants a color de coral*. Les dents són cristal·lines, posades per gran orde, per les quals discorrent aquella sua discreta lengua no paraules humanes mas una divinal i suavíssima armonia resona."

CORELLA'S TRANSLATION OF *VITA CHRISTI*: "Les celles de color de castanya, distinctes, largues y molt fornides. ... La boca *de magnitud mijana*, ab los labis que sobre blanch *a color vermella se acostaven*. Les dents, de una blancor de orientals perles, molt poch les descobria, perquè no legim del Senyor algunes rialles."

There is no real coincidence in the descriptions of the eyebrows and teeth, but there are certain points in common in the way the two texts describe the mouth and lips. The Catalan translator could have adopted the idea from Corella's text and supplemented the description himself, or from another source. The phrase "los labis són retirants a color de coral" is quite similar to "los labis ... a color vermella se acostaven"; the expression "boca no molt gran" is semantically if not linguistically close to "boca de magnitud mijana". As can be seen in the example above, the Catalan translator composed the description of the features of the face following the order in Corella's text, which is not the same in the Castilian *Epistle*.[34]

We may therefore conclude that the anonymous Catalan translation of the *Epistle of Lentulus*, as printed in 1524, was made after Corella's translation (1496), which was widely disseminated soon after publication; the Castilian translation was already printed. The anonymous translator of the *Epistle* used Corella's translation, not to help him out with his comprehension of the original text, or to lift material directly from the earlier work, but rather to furnish his text with a more lofty style and to expand the content to a considerable degree.

The edition of the *Epistle of Pilate* printed with the *Epistle of Lentulus* in 1524 shows the same concern for style and for increasing the length of the text. Like the Catalan *Epistle of Lentulus*, the *Epistle of Pilate* is also extended, while the Castilian version follows the Latin text closely.[35] At the beginning of these epistles, there is a surprising textual correspondence between the Catalan *Epistle of Lentulus* and the Catalan *Epistle of Pilate*:

[4] CATALAN *EPISTLE OF PILATE*, ED. 1524: "aquests dies prop passats s'és esdevengut ... com los juheus e lurs adherents han mort cruelment sens ninguna rahó ... un digníssim home y propheta de gran virtut ... aprés d'haver-lo vist los jueus matexos fer innumerables miracles, ço és a saber, *il·luminar los cecs, mundar los lebrosos, sanar los contrets*, lançar los dimonis dels cossos humans, *fer parlar los muts e oyr los sorts*, ressucitar los morts, anar sobre les ondes de la mar sens mullar-se los peus, tenir imperi sobre tots los elements e fer moltes altres maravellas".

CASTILIAN *EPISTLE OF PILATE*, ED. *C.* 1493: "Poco ha que ha esto acahecido ... como los judíos e sus sequaces han cruelmente perescido por su

---

[34] These additions do not correspond to other Castilian versions of the *Epistle of Lentulus* either. However, there are some isolated coincidences between the anonymous Catalan translation and the Castilian translation of the *Vita Christi* made by Ambrosio Montesino in 1502: "És elegant home e d'una gentil i mesurada granesa, ço és a saber, *més gran que petit*" (see example [1] above), and the Castilian *Vita Christi* has: "fue de medida o estatura derecha et era *más alto que pequenno*" (Bizzarri and Sainz de la Maza, "*La Carta de Léntulo al senado de Roma*," 57-58). It could be a genuine coincidence, or maybe a proof of a common source.

[35] See the texts in Maria Mercè López Casas, "Versions hispàniques de la *Carta de Pilat a Tiberi*," in *Actes del VII Congrés de l'Associació Hispànica de Literatura Medieval (Castelló de la Plana, 22-26 de setembre de 1997)*, ed. Santiago Fortuño Llorens and Tomàs Martínez Romero (Castelló de la Plana: Universitat Jaume I, 1999), II, 303-13. This does not happen with the Catalan *Monotessaron*, which closely follows the original.

invidia ... después de haverle visto los judíos mismos *alumbrar ciegos, e alimpiar leprosos, e sanar contrechos*, e sacar demonios de los cuerpos, e resuscitar muertos, e andar sobre las ondas de la mar sin mojarse los pies, e tener imperio sobre los vientos, e fazer otros muchos miraglos." [36]

CATALAN *EPISTLE OF LENTULUS*, ED. 1524: "En aquest temps és apparegut i és viu encara un home i propheta de gran virtut nomenat Jesús ... Lo qual ab sola paraula sana tota manera de malalties: *il·lumina los cecs, guareix los lebrosos, dreça los contrets, fa hoir los sorts e parlar los muts*, e ressucita los morts."

CASTILIAN *EPISTLE OF LENTULUS*, ED. *C.* 1493: "En estos tiempos ha parescido y aun vive un hombre de grand virtud llamada Jesuchristo ... El qual sana dolientes y resucita muertos."

The Castilian *Epistle of Pilate* corresponds to the Latin text exactly. [37] The Catalan translation adds two miracles to the list: "fer parlar los muts e oyr los sorts". The passage that is added at the beginning of the *Epistle of Lentulus* (highlighted in italics) corresponds to the list in the Catalan *Epistle of Pilate*, with the extra miracles included. So this passage from the *Epistle of Pilate* has been added to the *Epistle of Lentulus*. The similarities between the beginnings of the two epistles transmitted together (the presentation of Christ as a virtuous man who performs miracles) makes this repetition easier. [38]

The 1524 Catalan printed edition is a clear example of consumer literature: lives of saints, and the Passion and physical description of Christ. It was reprinted twice: once in 1547 (Barcelona: Carles Amorós) and again in 1576 (Barcelona: Jaume Cendrat). It was common practice

---

[36] The quotations from the *Epistle of Pilate* are taken from López Casas, "Versions hispàniques de la *Carta de Pilat*," 305 (Castilian) and 306-07 (Catalan). The italics highlight textual matches.

[37] Cf. "... quem cum vidissent cecos illuminasse, leprosos mundasse, paraliticos curasse, demones ab hominibus fugasse, mortuos suscitasse, ventis imperasse, pedibus siccis super undas maris ambulasse, et alia multa miracula fecisse..." (López Casas, "Versions hispàniques de la *Carta de Pilat*," 309, revised).

[38] We also know of a manuscript that contains another Catalan *Epistle of Pilate* (Barcelona, Biblioteca de Catalunya, MS. 325, fols 48v-49). The manuscript is an eighteenth-century copy, made from an "ancient book", as the colophon says. López Casas ("Versions hispàniques de la *Carta de Pilat*") did not establish the relation between both Catalan witnesses of the *Epistle of Pilate*, but the text in MS. 325 corresponds exactly to the Castilian *Epistle* in the *c.* 1493 edition, with no added passages. Regardless of the authenticity of the information in the colophon, it was probably translated from the Castilian independently of the expanded version.

for printed editions to make use of earlier translations (like the *Legenda aurea*). And there are many cases of Castilian translations that are based on earlier Catalan translations (and one or two the other way round).[39] The anonymous *Epistle of Lentulus* is one such example. By using Corella's translation, the translator of the *Epistle of Lentulus* adapts the style of his text to the prose style characteristic of the second half of the fifteenth and early sixteenth centuries, of which Corella was a prime exponent. It is a rhetorical and elaborate prose that tends to include lexical and syntactical borrowings from Latin. Other contemporary translators follow the same model. For example, Bernardí Vallmanya does so in his translation of Gerard de Vliederhoven's *Cordiale de quattuor novissimis*: as in the case of the *Epistle*, he is not translating the original Latin, but rather an intermediate text, the Castilian translation of Gonzalo García de Santa María (1491), with its rather grandiloquent style (Valencia, 1495); or Francesc Prats, whose *Contemplació de la passió* is based on excerpts from Ludolph of Saxony's *Vita Christi*, translated with numerous rhetorical embellishments.[40] The additions to the 1524 Catalan *Epistle of Lentulus* that can be traced back to Corella highlight a literary practice still in use today: good translators write for a contemporary readership. Moreover, they date this practice to the early modern period when there was still sufficient demand for Catalan for it to be used for printed editions.

---

[39] For a list of Castilian translations from Catalan texts, see Jaume Riera, "Catàleg d'obres en català traduïdes en castellà durant els segles XIV i XV," in *Segon congrés internacional de la llengua catalana (1986). Àrea 7. Història de la llengua*, ed. Antoni Ferrando (València: Institut de Filologia Valenciana, 1989), 699-709. Some Catalan translations of devotional works precede the Castilian translations (often printed) of the same work, but in most cases the relationship has not been established. This and other translations are listed in the Catalogue of Medieval Translations into Catalan up to 1500 in the Translat project (available online: http://www.narpan.net/recerca/translat-db.html).

[40] For the Catalan *Cordiale* and the other translations by Vallmanya, see Curt Wittlin, "La valenciana prosa del traductor Bernardí Vallmanya," in *Miscel·lània Joan Fuster* 1, ed. A. Ferrando and A. Hauf (Barcelona: Publicacions de l'Abadia de Montserrat, 1989), 125-51. Vallmanya handled the second edition of García de Santa María's translation (Zaragoza, 1494). For the *Llibre de contemplació*, see Curt J. Wittlin, "De les *Meditationes vitae Christi* de Ludolf el Cartoixà a la *Contemplació de la Passió* de Francesc Prats," in *De la traducció literal a la creació literària* (Barcelona: Publicacions de l'Abadia de Montserrat, 1995), 119-36.

THE *VITA CAROLI MAGNI* OF DONATO ACCIAIUOLI, TRANSLATED BY ALFONSO DE PALENCIA (1491)

SUSANNA ALLÉS TORRENT
(UNIVERSITAT DE BARCELONA)

1. Text in Latin: the *Vita Caroli* of Donato Acciaiuoli (Florence 1429-Milan 1478)

Donato Acciaiuoli was without doubt one of the most distinguished figures of Florentine civic humanism. He was a philosopher actively involved in city life and more concerned with ethics, economics and politics than with metaphysics and theology. In fact, in *Medioevo e Rinascimento,* Eugenio Garin recalls the words of Angiolo Segni: "Donato Acciaiuoli, cittadino fiorentino, governando la Reppublica attese alla filosofia e filosofando governò la Reppublica",[1] meaning that politics did not hinder his ability to philosophize, and that his philosophical interests did not undermine his political pragmatism. Some of his works reflect his unconditional service to his city. This is the case of the *Life of Charlemagne* written, as we will see, representing the Republic and his family as a gift offered at the coronation of the new French king, Louis XI (1423-1483), for which he was given the title of councillor and "maistre d'hostel".[2]

---

[1] Eugenio Garin, *Medioevo e Rinascimento,* 5th edn (Roma-Bari: Laterza, 2005), 199, takes the notice from *Vita di Donato Acciaiuoli descritta da Angiolo Segni, e per la prima volta data in luce dal cav. avv. Tommaso Tonelli* (Firenze: nella stamperia di L. Marchini, 1841), 35; and the manuscript is conserved in Florence, Biblioteca Nazionale Centrale, MS. Naz. II, II, 325, fols 91r-111v and also in Florence, Biblioteca Nazionale Centrale, MS. Palatino 493.

[2] "Acciaiuoli, Donato," in *Dizionario Biografico degli Italiani,* dir. by Alberto M. Ghisalberti, 72 vols (Roma: Istituto della Enciclopedia Italiana, 1960-), I (1960), 81.

The *Life of Charlemagne*[3] belongs within the general framework of humanistic interest in historiography and the recovery of biographical classics with Plutarch's *Parallel Lives* as its archetype. During the Middle Ages, Plutarch was best known for his moral writings, but after 1400, when the *Parallel Lives* started to circulate in Italy, his biographical works began to be translated and circulated. At the same time, Italian humanists wrote new original biographies in Plutarchan style. Acciaiuoli translated from Greek into Latin the lives of Alcibiades (1454-1459) and Demetrius (1454-1459), and also wrote the lives of Charlemagne (1460), Hannibal (1467-68) and Scipio (1467-68).[4]

Coinciding with the coronation of Louis XI of the Valois dynasty, which took place in Reims on 30 August 1461, Florence sent an embassy as a sign of loyalty to the new monarch.[5] Donato Acciaiuoli formed part of it and for the occasion, he wrote a biography of Charlemagne "in segno di fede e dono". In the preface, preserved in several manuscript copies and in some subsequent editions, are words supposedly addressing the new French king. There were three reasons for choosing

---

[3] The specific works about this Life are: D. Gatti, "La *Vita Caroli* di Donato Acciaiuoli," *Bullettino dell'Istituto Storico Italiano per il Medio Evo e Archivio Muratoriano* 84 (1972-1973): 223-74; id., *La Vita Caroli di Donato Acciaiuoli. La leggenda di Carlo Magno in funzione di una Historia di gesta* (Bologna: Pàtron, 1981); M. Davie, "Biography and Romance: The *Vita Caroli Magni* of Donato Acciaiuoli and Luigi Pulci's *Morgante*," in *The Spirit of the Court: Selected Proceedings of the Fourth Congress of the International Courtly Literature Society (Toronto, 1983)*, ed. G. S. Burgess and R. A. Taylor (Woodbridge: Boydell and Brewer, 1985), 137-52; C. Pérez González, "La figura de Carlomagno en la *Vita Caroli* de Donato Acciaiuoli," in *Humanismo y pervivencia del mundo clásico: homenaje al profesor Antonio Fontán*, ed. J. M. Maestre Maestre, L. Charlo Brea, J. Pascual Barea, 5 vols (Madrid: Ed. el Laberinto, 2002), 1485-1504.

[4] Cf. M. Affortunati and B. Scardigli, "La Vita Plutarchea di Annibale: un'imitazione di Donato Acciaiuoli," *Atene e Roma* 37 (1992): 88-105; B. Scardigli, "C'è qualcosa di plutarcheo nella Vita di Scipione dell'Acciaiuoli?," in *L'eredità culturale di Plutarco dall'antichità al Rinascimento: Atti del VII Convegno Plutarcheo, Milano-Gargnano, 28-30 maggio 1997*, ed. I. Gallo (Napoli: M. D'Auria, 1998), 289-97.

[5] There are several sources which describe how the Florentines sent an embassy (which included Filippo de' Medici, the bishop of Pisa, Piero de' Pazzi and Buonaccorsi Pitti), to the coronation of the new king. One of the sources is Vespasiano da Bisticci who, in the life of Acciaiuoli, remembers how, at Piero's request, Donato formed part of the embassy and offered to write a biography of Charlemagne: see Vespasiano da Bisticci, *Vite di uomini illustri del sec. XV scritte da Vespasiano da Bisticci*, ed. A. Greco, 2 vols (Firenze: Istituto Nazionale di studi sul Rinascimento, 1970-1976), II, 187-88.

such a gift: firstly, the help that the French monarchs had given to the Florentine Republic, and in particular to the Acciaiuoli family; secondly, the chance to display to the world the image of a king who was "el lume e la gloria di tutto el mondo" and to portray him as an "esemplo e specchio di virtù" for future leaders; and lastly, the need to replace the biographies written up until then, all of which were incomplete, partly inaccurate and, above all, written in poor Latin. The three key points may be summarized as follows: 1) the political aim of the work was to gain the favour of the new French king by comparing him to the great Charlemagne; 2) the moral aim was to demonstrate the human and military qualities of Charlemagne as a role model to follow; 3) the humanistic aim was to triumph over the old texts written about Charlemagne, and to produce a biography capable of reconstructing the truth from the facts known and to write it in Ciceronian Latin.

It is from this angle that I intend to summarize the method followed by the Florentine biographer. The structure of the Life is divided into two sections, military feats and customs, as follows:

—Genealogy: Pepin the Short and his children.
—Charlemagne's military activity and conquests: the war of Aquitaine; the war against the Lombards and the dismissal of Desiderius; excursus on the history of the Lombards; the war against the Saxons; the expedition to Hispania; the ambush of the Basques in Roncesvalles and the death of Roland; the war against the Bretons and Beneventans; the Bavarian war and the betrayal of Taxilo; the war against the Velatabi; the war against the Huns, conflicts with Adalgis, son of Desiderius, against the Bohemians and the Linonians, the war against the Normans; assistance to the pope against conspiracy; named emperor.
—Excursus on imperial dignity.
—Charlemagne's expedition through Tuscany, reconstruction of Florence and return to Gaul.
—Charlemagne's journey to the East.
—Demarcation of the Frankish empire.
—Foreign affairs.
—Portrayal, private life and habits of Charlemagne: physical portrait (attire for festivities); habits (hunting and baths) and friends; family (his mother, Bertrada, his brother Carloman and his sister; conspiracy of his bastard son, Pepin the Hunchback); charitable works, benevolence and justice; religious feeling; public and cultural works.

—Eloquence, educated by Alcuin of York; foundation of the University of Paris; children educated in the *artes liberales.*

—The end of Charlemagne: coronation of Lewis the Pious and the death of Charlemagne; funeral and epitaph; premonitions surrounding his death; the royal will; distribution of his wealth.

The structure of the biography is based on conscious *imitatio* of Plutarch and this is evident on numerous occasions. Firstly, Charlemagne is depicted as a classic Plutarchan hero whose outstanding qualities, magnanimity and exceptional nature are accentuated. Furthermore, his characterization is defined through his actions. In other words, the ethical virtues of the hero are made up of the qualities he reveals through his constant moral choice. These qualities are manifested regularly through his actions, and this produces dramatic intensity. Therefore, for example, when Charlemagne is faced with a polemical situation, he is always motivated by an objectively just cause. Thirdly, as in the Plutarchan biographies, and as already seen in the preface, the character pursues an ethical purpose (the dialogue with classical authors encourages the assimilation of their values and conduct) and also a political aim (in Plutarch's case, his work is a bridge between Greeks and Latins and in Acciaiuoli's case, between Italians and Franks).

There is, however, another important biographical model to take into account: Suetonius and his *Lives of the Twelve Caesars,* discovered by Acciaiuoli through Einhard's *Vita Karoli.* The erudite method, structured *per species* is, in effect, that which is used in the Einhardian biography and, in fact, the selection and organization of the topics seem at first to coincide with the sequence of episodes that Acciaiuoli recounts.[6] A closer

---

[6] A simple comparison between Acciaiuoli's and Einhard's chapters illustrate the analogy (cf. Eginhardo, *Vida de Carlomagno,* ed. and trans. A. de Riquer (Madrid: Gredos, 1999) 27-28, from which I have taken the titles) can be found in: I. Preface; II. Fall of the Merovingians and rise of the Carolingians: the *Rois fainéants*; Charles Martel and his children; Pepin the Short and his children; III. Plan of the work; IV. Military activity and conquests of Charlemagne: the war of Aquitaine, the war against the Lombards; the war against the Saxons; expedition in Hispania and ambush in Roncesvalles; war against the Bretons and the Beneventans; the war in Bavaria; the war against the Welatabi, the war against the Avars; war against the Danes; V. Demarcation of the Frankish empire; VI. Foreign affairs; VII. Public works and naval defence; VIII. Character, private life and habits of Charlemagne: family and friends; conspiracies; relationships with foreigners; physical portrait; clothes; customs; cultural interests, religious views; charitable works and donations; IX. Coronation; X. Legislative and cultural reforms; XI. The end of Charlemagne; his funeral and epitaph; omens surrounding

analysis, however, shows that after this surface analogy, two very different human models emerge (for instance, Suetonian interest in human vices and descriptive details in particular disappear)[7]. In Acciaiuoli's case, for example, most of the biography is dedicated to the description of the subject's *res gestae,* focusing in particular on the history of the Lombards and their relationship with the Roman Church. By contrast, in Einhard's work, military feats are limited to a brief informative catalogue and the account focuses much more on details of Charlemagne's habits and his portrait as a human being. Furthermore, the portrayals by both writers are different: in Einhard's case that of a secular *Rex Francorum,* and in Acciaiuoli's case that of a king who established the Christian *renouatio imperii.* The method also varied, in that Einhard leans towards hyperbolic exaltation (as in the description of the borders of the empire), and Acciaiuoli remains true to historical truth thus highlighting the veracity of the information.[8]

Nevertheless, besides the *Vita Karoli,* different chronological sources can be detected in Acciaiuoli's text. On one hand, there are influences from classical authors such as Caesar[9] and Livy and on the other, from medieval tradition. One of the medieval influences is the myth of Florence's reconstruction by Charlemagne,[10] the founding of the University of Paris, the Basque defeat of the French in Spain, and lastly, Charlemagne's journey to the East.[11] Furthermore, Acciaiuoli made use

---

his death; distribution of his wealth.

[7] D. Gatti (1981: 29-52).

[8] Acciaiuoli's voice appears constantly in verbs such as *comperio, adducor, inuenio,* etc.

[9] When describing the regions of France, Acciaiuoli writes: "Aquitania pars Galliae est, quae antiquorum descriptione, a Garunna flumine ad Piraeneos montes et ad eam partem Oceani, quae ad Hispaniam pertinet, spectat inter occasum solis et septentrionem". And Caesar in his *Gallic War*: "Aquitania a Garumna flumine ad Pyrenaeos montes et eam partem Oceani quae est ad Hispaniam pertinet; spectat inter occasum solis et septentriones" (I, 1).

[10] According to D. Gatti (1981: 59), the unknown origins of Florence brought about the elaboration of a legend; ignorance of how it was created gave rise to all kinds of speculation and, eventually, ended up becoming a popular legend even though it had been produced in an aristocratic atmosphere. In this way, if the image was of a Christian French king as the creator of Florence, the legend was well received and the city acquired a founder of high lineage. This was a motive to connect Charlemagne's benevolence with that of the present French monarch and, in this way, gain his favour.

[11] This is another Carolingian topos which circulated in many places from the Middle Ages onwards, but the truth of the matter is that Charlemagne did not make

of more modern sources such as the *Liber pontificalis* (in particular the part which makes references to the biography of Pope Hadrian), Ricordano Malispini, and Giovanni Villani's *Chronicle*.[12] Two chapters in particular of Leonardo Bruni's *Historia Florentini populi* (translated by Acciaiuoli into Italian in the 1470s), must also be acknowledged: one chapter, at the time of writing the catalogue about the Barbarian nations, in particular the Lombards' settlement and fortune in the Italian peninsula. The other, the excursus on imperial dignity, documents a history of institutions in Ancient Rome from the period of the monarchy until the dissolution of the empire.[13]

I believe that the sources used by Acciaiuoli are a reflection of the portrait of Charlemagne that he creates: on one hand, the Plutarchan model, that of a classical hero, a *speculum uirtutis,* and a magnanimous and fair king, a true humanistic prince (who even knows Greek and Latin). On the other hand, a medieval character, a king rescued from the Dark Ages, author of the *renouatio imperii,* a *rex sacerdos*, a vassal of the Roman Church and one who posseses *uirtus christiana*. A model, therefore, of a ruler in a world governed by the ideals of the Catholic church and so not at all in conformity with the new model of humanistic ruler. However, despite the contrast between these two images, Acciaiuoli manages to merge them to create a new classically heroic Christian character who fights for "la commune libertà di tutti e' Christiani", relentless against barbarity and the growth of Christianity.

The *Life* was a success, as the preserved manuscript copies show.

---

any trips to the East, either to Constantinople or a pilgrimage to Jerusalem: see F. Monteleone, *Il viaggio di Carlo Magno in Terra Santa. Un'esperienza di pellegrinaggio nella tradizione europea occidentale* (Fasano: Schena, 2003), 311-20. In fact, the passage is very interesting as we can see the historical method Acciaiuoli uses: in the face of information of which he is unsure, he chooses only to provide it without categorically identifying if it is true or false.

[12] These are sources proposed by D. Gatti (1981: 32), but a complete analysis of the sources used by Acciaiuoli in this biography has yet to be carried out.

[13] In Bruni's case, the narration adopts a distinct philorepublican tone. On the other hand Acciaiuoli expresses a philoimperial tone (as could only be in a biography dedicated to an emperor) and an eminently positive vision of the *renouatio imperii.* Despite these copies, Acciaiuoli sometimes distances himself from Bruni's theories even though the latter gives historically sufficient reasons which are much more convincing than those of popular tradition; this is seen for example in the discussion of the reconstruction of the city of Florence and Bruni's opinion, different from that of Acciaiuoli: *Istoria fiorentina di Leonardo Bruni, tradotta in volgare da Donato Acciajuoli*; premessovi un Discorso su Leonardo Bruni aretino per C. Monzani (Firenze: Le Monnier, 1861), 44-45.

But, above all, it was made known thanks to being included in the first edition of the Latin translations of Plutarch's *Parallel Lives* first printed in Rome in 1470.

An interesting aspect of this biography of Charlemagne is the existence of a rough first draft in Italian by Donato Acciaiuoli used as a starting point for the Latin version.[14] This first draft is incomplete: we have only the first half which ends just after the war against the Velatabi who were helping the Abodriti. Comparison with the Spanish translation by Alfonso de Palencia of 1491 seems appropriate for seeing how two vernacular languages approach the same text, as well as for better understanding the connotations attached by Acciaiuoli himself to the Latin terms used. However, as we are dealing with something that is not exactly a translation, categorical affirmations and possible conclusions are risky.

2. Alfonso de Palencia's Translation

A second edition of Plutarch's *Lives,* in which its first editor Giovanantonio Campano had included Acciaiuoli's translation, was published in Venice in 1478 and Palencia used it to do a complete translation of the two volumes.[15] In order to carry out an initial analysis

---

[14] The only manuscript preserved was edited together with the Latin text by Gatti (1981).

[15] The identification of the edition used by Palencia has already been sufficiently clarified. See J. S. Lasso de la Vega, "Traducciones españolas de las *Vidas* de Plutarco," *Estudios Clásicos* 6 (1961-1962): 451-514 (471-83); A. Pérez Jiménez, "Plutarco y el humanismo español del renacimiento," in *Estudios sobre Plutarco, obra y tradición: Actas del I symposion español sobre Plutarco, Fuengirola 1988*, ed. A. Pérez Jiménez and G. del Cerro Calderón (Málaga: Vicerrectorado de Extensión Universitaria y Area de Filología Griega de la Universidad: Delegación Provincial de Cultura de la Junta de Andalucía, 1990), 229-47 (233); J. A. López Férez, "La traducción castellana de las *Vidas* realizada por Alfonso de Palencia," in *Estudios sobre Plutarco: ideas religiosas. Actas del III Simposio Internacional sobre Plutarco. Oviedo 30 de abril a 2 de mayo 1992* (Madrid: Ediciones Clásicas, 1994), 359-69; J. Bergua Cavero, *Estudios sobre la tradición de Plutarco en España (ss. XIII-XVII)* (Zaragoza: Universidad de Zaragoza, 1995), 15-16; S. Allés Torrent, "Alfonso de Palencia y la traducción de las *Vidas* de Plutarco (nuevos datos en torno al texto de partida)," *Cuadernos de Filología Clásica. Estudios Latinos* 28:2 (2008): 99-124. In the case of the *Vita Caroli*, the affiliation of Palencia's text to the Venetian edition of 1478 is shown by the following variation: 'Frisie' (Rome: Ulrich Han, 1470); 'Erisiae' (Venice: Nicolaus Jenson, 1478); Palencia translates 'Erisia' (Seville: Quatro compañeros alemanes, 1491) persisting

of the translation method used by the Spanish humanist, I took into account cultural and philological factors implicit in some of his lexical, morphological and syntactic choices.[16]

As in all the other lives, the translation of the *Vita Caroli* is preceded by a brief introduction acknowledging the author and translator. In Charlemagne's case, however, we read the following:

> Donato Acciolo, çibdadano florentino, escrivió en latín la vida del ylustre varón Carlo Magno, recolegida de las historias, y el cronista Alfonso de Palencia la traduxo en romançe castellano. Aquesta vida es más moderna y de príncipe católico y bien mereciente de la religión cristiana.

This brief introduction demonstrates that Palencia viewed Acciaiuoli's *Vita* as an interweaving of different sources ("recolegida de las historias"), even if the generic aspect of the reference prevents us from knowing exactly what his assertion is based on. In any case it helped him to highlight the historically reliable nature of the biography in which the author accurately identifies Acciaiuoli as a Florentine citizen, and chooses an interesting subject: the modern life of a "príncipe católico y bien mereciente de la religión cristiana" in contrast to the lives of so many pagans.

I would now like to shed light on the final words of the introduction: the presence of a Christian element in the compilation of the *Lives* made the volume more attractive and compensated for the predominance of pagan figures. The final biography of the volume is that of Charlemagne, an epilogue which is a culmination of a process and the best representative of modern times. Charlemagne was a promoter of the *renouatio imperii,* the bridge between Romans and Christians and the thread of western Catholic Christianity from its establishment until the present.

This Life was Palencia's last translation which he finished as an elderly man and would have undoubtedly interested him profoundly. The copy I have used as a point of reference (Madrid, Biblioteca Nacional,

---

in the error of the Venetian edition.

[16] A first attempt at philological analysis focusing on matters of nominal and verbal syntax such as unnecessary additions was made by J. A. López Férez, "Notas filológicas a la traducción en español de las Vidas Paralelas de Plutarco realizada por Alfonso de Palencia (1491)," in *Synodia: Studia humanitatis Antonio Garzya septuagenario ab amicis atque discipulis dicata*, ed. U. Criscuolo and R. Maisano (Napoli: M. D'Auria, 1997), 601-15. But a complete and systematic analysis of Palencia's translation method still needs to be carried out, a task which I hope to develop in my doctoral thesis.

I/573) was perhaps used by Palencia himself,[17] as some hand-written notes (*rubricae)* can be found to indicate the general topic, but on three occasions the marginalia are much more extensive. Two in particular, found precisely in the chapter about the defeat of Roncesvalles, deserve mention. In the first, when Charlemagne's expedition to Hispania is described ("De expeditione Caroli Magni / in Hispaniam de q*ua* plurima al*iter*...") he warns us that the facts do not resemble the truth. The second refers to the Basque ambush at Roncesvalles which resulted in the death of Roland and also refutes the version of facts put forward by Acciaiuoli: "Non est uerum res ...". If Palencia is the author of these notes, it would reveal the critical approach of an erudite Hispanophile. In addition and with the purpose of making the text more intelligible, Palencia adds detailed explanations in the body of his translation:

> *hunc* potissimum deligendum putarent, cui communi sententia regnum decernerent. > pensaron que devían muy principalmente *e con mayor razón a este Pipino*, al qual por común sentencia encomendassen el reyno [he specifies the demonstrative pronoun *hunc* with the intention of clarifying who is being referred to]; Carolo Magno, *ca el otro su hermano se nombró Carlo Mano* [added so that the reader does not confuse the characters]; quinto Kalendas Februarias. > quinto kalendas de febrero, que son a .XXVIII. días de enero [provides the exact date].

In order to clarify this point, I will refer to other important information extracted from the translation.

An effective indicator of Palencia's translation methodology is his vocabulary. The cases examined demonstrate some constant features of his techniques. Firstly, he highlights the use of binary constructions (copulative or disjunctive), which shows an awareness of semantics. Therefore, for example, when faced with the difficulty of translating certain Latinisms which require clarification, Palencia reproduces the original term accompanying it with an equivalent Spanish word:

> magno > Grande o Magno [he consequently translates *magnitudine > grandeza*]; militiae > miliçia o exerçiçio de guerra; eunuco > eunuco o castrado; fortitudine > en fortaleza y en robustidad de cuerpo; satellite > satélite o ombre de la guarda; figuram > la figura o effigie; basilicam > la basílica o esglesia cathedral.

At other times, the doublet corresponds to a semantic distinction:

---

[17] The script clearly seems humanistic and given the small circulation of the text in Spain, it is likely that we will find autograph notes by Palencia here.

opes > riquezas o favores; exinanitas [urbes] > affligidas y despobladas;
colentes > honrrando y adorando; nullum [...] praesidium > ningund
amparo nin ayuda; diuina ope > favor y ayuda divinal; in fines hostium > a
las fronteras y términos de los enemigos; tueri > amparar y defender;
insignem cladem > una grande y señalada pérdida; fortia facta > fazañas
fuertes y notables; per intestina arma > a causa de la guerra y armas
intestinas o entreñables; opes > poderío y riquezas; multis gemmis > con
muchas perlas y piedras preciosas; uenationibus > las monterías y caças;
sobolem > fijos y fijas.

Although the procedure is often that of the synonymous pairs of
medieval style:

clarisimum > notable y mentado; in locupletissimo regno > en un reyno tan
rico y tan bastado.

It is possible that a Latin concept can lack an exact opposite number
in contemporary reality, and so an equivalent must be offered to the
reader:

magistratum > magistrado o dignidad de mayordomía; ante armorum
castrorumque > ante capitanía de gente de armas y de governaçión de
aposentamientos en el campo; controuersiis hominum > en las diferençias
y pleytos entre los ombres litigantes.

There are also many instances of toponyms which are accompanied by
their corresponding modern name:

agrum Ticinum > campo de Ticino o de Pavía; Bisantium > Bysancio o
Constantinopoli; Pannonias > Panonias o tierras de Ungría

or are substituted directly:

Hetruria > Toscana; Galliae Citeriori > la Galia de aquende de los Alpes.

There are other translations which transpose the concept into modern
Castilian reality. This means that concepts used by Acciaiuoli, which
come from classical vocabulary, are translated along by Palencia with
others from his own time, always offering where possible a native word:

praefectos > mayordomos [ad praefectos regiae domus, sic enim eos
uocitabant > a los mayordomos de la casa del rey, a los quales ellos
llamavan prefectos]; oppidani > los de dentro; peditum equitumque copiis
> compañas de peones y cavalleros; dominationis > señorío; honore >

honrra; dominatione > señorío; egregie > señaladamente; Lupus > el duque
Lupo; controuersiis > differençias que eran entre los del reyno; praefectis >
comissarios; duces > cabdillos; Ecclesiae romanae patrocinio > abogaçía
de la Eglesia romana; suppellectilem > jaezes.

In this way the ancient world underwent an abrupt move towards
Castilian modernity; a purist tendency which sometimes encourages him
to use periphrasis even though the concept is not difficult to understand:

superiores > que antes dél fueron [subsequently translated thus: superiorum
regum > de los buenos reyes antepassados]; superstites filii > dos fijos que
le quedavan; primi > los que avían passado primero; posteriores > los que a
la postre venían; a posterioribus regibus > los reyes que suçedieron.

The same procedure can be found in some Latin expressions which
Palencia tries to express with the corresponding Spanish:

rerum gestarum > fazañas [although elsewhere: res egregie gestas > cosas
notablemente por él fechas]; liberam dominandi potestas > libre poderío de
señorear; contra ius fasque ultro > contra todo derecho y razón; contra ius
fasque > sin derecho y sin causa razonable; maximis itineribus > a todo
caminar; quam maximis potest itineribus > quanto más presto pudo
caminar; iure iurando > con firme y estrecho juramento; necessitudine aut
propinquitate > por parentesco o por affinidad çercana; auspicio
praefectorum > por buena dicha de sus governadores; certamine factionum
> contienda de las vanderías; ductu auspicioque > acabdillamiento e buena
dicha; sedes regni eiusque regia > silla del reyno y su morada real; unius
cuiusque ratione habita > guardada la condiçión de cada uno por razón.

The variety of Palencia's solutions of Latinisms is, in any case,
noteworthy and always depends on the context. In some cases, he adopts
the Latin term and in others he prefers the patrimonial word:

Latin term: referamus > refiramos, coniunctus > conjunto, monumento >
monumento [in the meaning of tomb]; resumere uires > resumir fuerças;
regem creauere > criar otro rey; a ceruicibus > de sobre las çervizes;
perfidia > porfidia; sinus > seno, impetrato > impetraron, etc. Patrimonial
word: indignabatur > pensava; multitudine > muchedumbre; suae perfidiae
> quebrantamiento de la fe, etc.

Of lesser importance is Palencia's method of translating verbal
morphology, although he always proves himself to be a skilled and
varied translator in his choice of technique. When translating verbal
constructions he always keeps the same person and almost always the

same tense (although, for example, the historic present is systematically translated into the past tense) but not the moods: there are translations which introduce a volitive modality (where misit > quiso enviar):

> caepit > quiso tomar; parat > quiso aparejar; parabat > quería mover; confirmat > quiso confirmar; ignouisse > quiso perdonar

or an element of possibility (dimouit > pudo quitar; comparauit > pudo conseguir), others which become a verbal periphrasis:

> reprimuntur > fizo que [...] se reprimiessen; persequitur > fue tras él persiguiéndolo; exercitum parat > dio obra a aparejar el exército; factum est > se ovo de fazer; misit > ovo de embiar.

Some verbal structures are not translated with total precision: for example, the ablative absolute is often translated by the personal form:

> regno inter se *parito > partieron* entre sí el reyno; *defuncto* Carolomanno > murió Carlomano; *superato* Vaifario duce > después que *venció* al duque Vaifario; Benigne hospitaliterque *suscepti*, auxilio *impetrato > Fueron reçebidos* y hospedados benignamente y *impetraron* lo que demandavan.

Furthermore, Latin nouns are expanded into sentences:

> antiquorum descriptione > según descriven los antiguos; post Pipini obitum > luego que su padre falleció; post longum bellum > acabada la luenga guerra que entre sí fizieran; in expectationem belli > que atendían la guerra, filios quoque [...] in disciplinam dedit > dio tanbién sus fijos para que los enseñassen y disçiplinassen

and vice versa relative sentences are reduced to nominal forms:

> populos qui ei aduersabantur > los pueblos contrarios a ella.

In any case, fidelity to the Latin text is not subordinate to clarity.

As for syntax, Palencia's translation proves very true to the Latin without losing the structure of the Spanish. In difficult cases, before constructing an unnatural expression, he resorts to explanatory paraphrases. At times he puts in two verbs corresponding to one Latin verb; at others, a simplification of two verbs in order to facilitate the construction. He is not, however, always systematic in his choices. In the following example we can see how two absolute participles are resolved in a different way:

quod *posthabitis* ferocissimis hostibus *relictoque* domestico bello, rem suam *neglexerit,* > pues que, *pospuestos* los enemigos muy feroçes, *quiso dexar* la guerra domésticá y *menospreciar* sus negocios.

In fact, if there is a conclusion to be drawn from this analysis, it is that his method is extremely varied: literal translations coexist with the free translations, explanatory paraphrases with translations which are a little uncertain and not wholly accurate:

> *Gothi* primi barbarorum, diuersis deinde temporibus Hunni, Vandali, Heruli, postremi omnium Langobardi > primeros entre todos los otros bárbaros y, desdende en diversos tiempos, los hugnos y los vándalos y los herulos [omitting the first in the list]; templum condidit ipsumque marmoreis columnis tum *argento auroque* caelato uehementer ornauit > edificó un templo y le adornó con colunas de marmol maravillosamente y le guarneçió de *esculpturas doradas y plateadas.*

However, it is equally evident that this is not a medieval translation *ad verbum,* but rather one much more conscious of the difficulties, more flexible and close to the method proposed by the Italian humanists, the *conversio ad sententiam,* where the most important factors are the content and the translator's ability to express himself effectively. In a nutshell, Palencia's commitment to the Latin language is considerable but not to the point of producing a hybrid of the two linguistic codes, Latin and vernacular. It is a translation which is true to the Latin text but does not stretch to lexical or syntactical transposition of the content and semantic equivalences. This is evident from the abundance of native terms and meanings which in the end demonstrates Palencia's deep commitment to the Spanish language.

All things considered, Palencia is a consciously manipulative translator who communicates the necessary information in the introduction to engage and influence the reader. He is an interactive translator who analyses the text to be translated and disputes its content where necessary; a translator with the sensitivity to relay the original message, making a substantial effort in his search for equivalent and varied solutions. He generally tends to transform the Latin into a concept which is familiar to Spanish readers. He shows determination in communicating all the nuances of Latin words and finds ways of translating syntactical structures from the source text to the target language.

In conclusion, I must say that the fortune of the *Life of Charlemagne* has always been associated with the volume of Plutarch's *Lives,* and it is undoubtedly owing to this that both the Latin and Spanish versions have been overlooked. Some authors refer to a 1508 edition which has however been lost.[18] Another edition of some of the *Lives* was published in 1792[19] but Charlemagne's was not included. Therefore, in the absence of a modern edition, I hope that this essay may inspire the circulation and deserved recognition of the first humanist biography of Charlemagne.

---

[18] Lasso de la Vega, 475; López Férez, 360; I. Muñoz Gallarte, "La presencia de Plutarco en España en el siglo XVI: La biblioteca del Seminario de Cuenca," in *Ecos de Plutarco en Europa. De Fortuna Plutarchi Studia Selecta*, ed. R. M. Aguilar and I. Alfageme (Madrid: Universidad Complutense de Madrid, Departamento de Filología Griega; Sociedad Española de Plutarquistas, 2006), 193-206 (204).

[19] Plutarco, *Vidas de los varones ilustres griegos y romanos escritas por Plutarco y traducidas por Alfonso de Palencia*, 2 vols (Madrid: Imprenta Real, 1792). In this edition only the first six couples which are in the Latin edition and in Palencia's (vol. I: lives of Theseus—Romulus, Lycurgus—Numa, Solon—Poplicola; vol. II: lives of Alcibiades—Corollius, Themistocles—Camillus, Pericles—Fabius Maximus) appear, suggesting that the intention was to continue with the reissue of all the remaining lives. This work is preceded by a life of Plutarch and a very interesting preface.

PLANTIN'S SPANISH ATLAS
AND THE POLITICS OF THE VERNACULAR

JASON HARRIS
(UNIVERSITY COLLEGE CORK)

The appearence in 1588 of a Spanish translation of the famous atlas of Abraham Ortelius, the *Theatrum Orbis Terrarum* (translated as the *Theatro de la Tierra Universal*)[1] is significant both as an unusual episode in the publication history of a highly influential work and as a case in which the prohibition upon importing Spanish-language books into Spain was obviated through careful manipulation of clientage networks. The Spanish translation naturally reflects these circumstances, which ought therefore to shape interpretation of the volume as a whole. Although it is common to think of a text gaining an international audience through its translation into Latin rather than into the vernacular, Ortelius's atlas went through the reverse process on several occasions and for varying reasons. In order to understand the particular circumstances of the translation into Spanish I will begin by examining the character of the atlas as it is manifested throughout the multiple editions in which it appeared; then I will comment on Plantin's motivation for publishing a Spanish version; and finally I will examine the Spanish text by way of further explicating its relationship to these wider contexts.

The contents of the first Latin edition of the *Theatrum* in 1570 are well known, having had considerable influence in determining the structure of atlases down to the present day; however, there were over thirty editions of the atlas published during the author's life-time and each new edition was up-dated and augmented to some degree.[2] While individual elements

---

[1] Abraham Ortelius, *Theatrum orbis terrarum* (Antwerp: Coppens van Diest, 1570); idem, *Theatro de la tierra universal* (Antwerp: Plantin, 1588). In 1602, after Ortelius's death, an expanded edition of the same Spanish translation was published in Antwerp by Jan Baptist Vrients under the title *Theatro d'el orbe de la tierra*.

[2] The various editions are described by Peter van der Krogt, "Appendix I," in *Abraham Ortelius and the First Atlas*, ed. Marcel van den Broecke, Peter van der

vary from edition to edition, the basic format of the atlas remains the same. An elegant title page executed in copper plate, a preface, and a collection of laudatory poems lead on to the contents page and a catalogue of geographical authors cited or used during production of the atlas. The first map is a depiction of the entire globe, followed by maps of each of the four continents. The remainder of the maps follow the Ptolemaic sequence from east to west, presenting a series of regions in greater or lesser detail depending on the information available to Ortelius. Each map takes up a full folio opening, while the reverse sides contain text relating to the map itself or the area depicted. The collection draws to a close with an extended version of one of these texts—a lengthy letter to Ortelius by Humphrey Lhuyd concerning the island of Anglesey and a Roman fort on the north coast of Belgium.[3] A catalogue of the historical variants in place names concludes the atlas.

The most striking feature of the series of editions of the atlas is the manner in which the material within it is continuously re-edited and updated. Ortelius clearly conceived of his book as a work in progress. The preface contains an appeal to the reader to submit more accurate maps or information to the author, and the publication history suggests that this was more than mere rhetoric. As subsequent editions appeared the atlas grew to almost double its original size, augmented not just in detail but by more and more new maps, to the extent that Ortelius had to issue five major *Additamenta* as supplements for those who had purchased earlier editions. The catalogues also grew; indeed, the list of historical place names was expanded into a large folio volume published separately as a historical dictionary of geography and chorography, the *Thesaurus Geographicus*.[4] Likewise, the selection of historical maps was expanded to form a publication in its own right, the *Theatri Orbis Terrarum Parergon*.[5] Finally, a number of reduced format editions of the atlas were produced

---

Krogt and Peter Meurer ('t Goy-Houten: HES Publishers, 1998), 379-82; but see Marcel van den Broecke, "Unstable Editions of Ortelius' Atlas," *The Map Collector* 70 (1995): 2-8.

[3] Iolo Roberts and Menai Roberts, "*De Mona Druidum Insula*," in *Abraham Ortelius and the First Atlas*, 347-362.

[4] Abraham Ortelius, *Thesaurus geographicus* (Antwerp: Plantin, 1587).

[5] Abraham Ortelius, *Theatri orbis terrarum parergon*, ed. Balthasar Moretus (Antwerp: Moretus, 1624). The *Parergon* was initially appended to the *Theatrum*, but was sometimes bound separately, prior to the posthumous publication of it as a separate work in 1624.

through the initiative of close friends of Ortelius, meeting market demand for a still smaller, less expensive, and more portable version.[6] The first few editions of the atlas were in Latin; subsequently, editions were produced in Dutch, German, French, Spanish, Italian, and English. This provided the opportunity to shape each publication specifically towards the intended readership in each country. Some marked changes in structure found their way into these editions, such as the provision of lists of trade goods instead of learned indices, and alteration of the texts accompanying each map to reflect the interests of each language community (most particularly in the Dutch and French versions, which were written by Ortelius himself).[7] The vernacular editions often lack the scholarly appendices and contain fewer classical and historical references in the texts accompanying each map. The text of the vernacular editions can also be stylistically different—for example, the French text is less scientific and more lyrical in tone, suggestive of the imaginative journey the reader is taking in viewing the atlas.[8] The Spanish edition of 1588 and the French edition of 1598 contain different short appendices supplying information on trade routes and products. On the other hand, the English edition of 1606 follows the most recent Latin text and scholarly apparatus very closely, but augmented it with new material that was particularly attuned to English ears. These variations underline the fact that, although the vernacular editions of the atlas might in a general sense be targeted at a wider mercantile readership with less of a scholarly interest, the balance between these elements altered from edition to edition. Nevertheless, before proceeding to an analysis of the Spanish version, it is important to draw attention to some general features of the market for atlases in the late sixteenth century.

Atlases then, as now, were primarily repositories of cultural information in geographical format. Their value for travel or navigation

---

[6] Peeter Heyns, *Spieghel der Werelt* (Antwerp: Plantin/Galle, 1577); Peeter Heyns, *Le miroir du monde* (Antwerp: Plantin/Galle, 1579); Hugo Favolius and Filips Galle, *Theatri orbis terrarum enchiridion* (Antwerp: Plantin/Galle, 1585); Giovanni Paulet, *Theatro d'Abrahamo Ortelio, ridotto in forma piccola* (Antwerp: Moretus/Galle, 1593. Numerous editions of these texts, often corrected or augmented, appeared subsequently.

[7] The most detailed discussion of the variant texts in editions of the *Theatrum* is Marcel van den Broecke, *Ortelius' Theatrum Orbis Terrarum (1570-1641): Characteristics and Development of a Sample of* on verso *Map Texts* (Utrecht: Koninklijk Nederlands Aardrijkskundig Genootschap, 2009).

[8] Descriptions of the various editions and translations can be found in Dirk Imhof, ed., *De Wereld in Kaart: Abraham Ortelius, 1527-1598, en de Eerste Atlas* (Antwerp: Museum Plantin-Moretus, 1998).

was limited, in part because of the scale of the maps, though kings and merchant tradesmen might use them to help visualize their overseas endeavours.[9] Atlases were also extremely expensive, becoming still more so if hand-coloured, printed on high-quality paper, or elaborately bound. Two inferences may be drawn from this: first, that the appeal of an atlas may often have been its display-value as a specimen of conspicuous consumption, and, second, that those who were more interested in its content than its display-value were unlikely to be seeking mere entertainment. The most common practical use to which the atlas was put is reflected in Ortelius's own marketing of it in his preface to the reader as "the eye of history" ("merito a quibusdam Historiae oculus appellata est")—an onomastic and geographical tool to aid comprehension of historical texts, but also an interpretative grid which allowed the humanist reader to understand his present-day world in terms of local histories.[10] In other words, the lists of sources, the catalogue of historical place names, and the schematic historical commentary accompanying each map are targeted at a humanist reader accustomed to conceptualizing the continuity of past and present. For this reason, although the book capitalized upon the thriving market for maps that developed in the wake of the voyages of discovery, in fact the great majority of the maps within the atlas depicted the regions of continental Europe.[11]

Reader reception can also be gauged by the many laudatory poems that were written to celebrate Ortelius's achievement in producing the *Theatrum*.[12] Most of these poems comment on his restitution of geography from ignorance, or on his glorious and useful reduction of the entire world into one book. The poem by Adolphus Mekerchus, which prefaced the *Theatrum*, is typical of the corpus:

Immensam Terrae molem, vastique meatu

---

[9] Prominent examples can be found in Geoffrey Parker, "Philip II, Maps and Power," in his *Empire, War and Faith in Early Modern Europe* (London: Allen Lane, 2002) and David Buisseret, ed., *Monarchs, Ministers and Maps. The Emergence of Cartography as a Tool of Government in Early Modern Europe* (Chicago: Chicago University Press, 1993).

[10] *Theatrum orbis terrarum*, fol. aiiij^r.

[11] For further discussion, see Jason Harris, "Reading the First Atlases: Ortelius, De Jode, and TCD volume M.aa.9," *The Long Room* 49 (2004): 28-53.

[12] There are three main sources for these poems: the prefatory matter in the various editions of Ortelius's *Theatrum orbis terrarum*; Franciscus Sweertius, *Insignium huius aevi poetarum lacrymae in obitum cl. v. Abrahami Ortelii* (Antwerp: Swingen, 1601); *Album Amicorum Abraham Ortelius, reproduit en facsimile*, ed. Jean Puraye and others (Amsterdam: van Gendt, 1969).

Oceani, toto sparsas et in aequore terras,
Scriptorum multi veterum, multique recentum,
Ingenio praestanti et rerum divite censu
Hactenus aggressi, triplices tantummodo partes
Invenere Orbis, quas nec describere plene
Posse datum est. Nostro id longe felicius aevo
Praestitit Ortelius multo majoribus ausis:
Ortelius, quem quadrijugo super aera curru
Phoebus Apollo vehi secum dedit, unde jacentes
Lustraret terras, circumfusumque profundum.[13]

Throughout this body of verse, four themes in particular stand out. First, Ortelius has created a self-contained world for the scholar's imagination, overcoming the dangers of physical travel by allowing the reader to indulge in what we might call armchair tourism. Second, Ortelius is a new Phoebus Apollo, the sun bringing light to the world. Third, his scholarship exceeds that of Ptolemy and all other previous cartographers. And fourth, a small number of writers ascribe to the atlas positive spiritual or religious effects through its symbolic depiction of the unity of God's creation. What is most striking is the repeated emphasis upon Ortelius's scholarly achievement, underlining the continuity between the maps themselves, the textual commentaries that accompany them, the learned indices of place names, and the subsequent onomastic dictionaries and historical atlases that developed out of the original map collection.

These poems provide eloquent testimony to the interest that the *Theatrum* held for the scholarly community; by contrast, the expensive bindings and blank margins of many surviving copies testify to the display-value that attracted many owners. As we will see, language could play a part in both regards—just as Latin could add either communicability or prestige, so could the vernacular. The goal of the publisher was, of course, to reach the largest audience possible. Records from the print shop of Christopher Plantin show that by the end of the decade the book was being issued in variant forms according to the design of the buyer, as was common for such books at the time—coloured or not, bound or not, and so forth.[14] These variations affected the price of the atlas and reflect the use to which the buyer intended to put it—practical, ornamental, and so forth.

---

[13] *Theatrum orbis terrarum*, fol. aii[v].

[14] Records can best be consulted in Leon Voet, *The Plantin Press, 1555-1589: A Bibliography of the Works Printed and Published by Christopher Plantin at Antwerp and Leiden*, 6 vols (Amsterdam: Van Hoeve, 1980-1983). See also Dirk Imhof, "The Production of Ortelius Atlases by Christopher Plantin," in *Abraham Ortelius and the First Atlas*, ed. Marcel van den Broecke, Peter van der Krogt, and

While most copies of the book were sold through the standard mechanisms of the publishing industry, an unusually large number of gratuitous presentation copies were distributed, as can be gauged from the correspondence of both author and publisher.[15] Each used the clientage networks to which they belonged to market and distribute the book. The importance of gratuitous copies should not be underestimated, both as a tool of clientage and as astute business practice. The *Theatrum* was one of the most expensive books of the sixteenth century, making it a prestigious gift, but also a necessary one if the leading scholars of Europe—rarely wealthy—were to own copies. Despite the fragmentary nature of the extant evidence, it is clear that Ortelius used the giving of gifts to ensure, by gaining endorsement from key scholars, that his book scored top of the citation index of early modern scholarship, as well as to play the patronage game so essential to all early modern society. On the other hand, the publisher Plantin had slightly different goals and accordingly different networks, largely grounded in his commercial interests. It is in this context that I wish to turn now to examine the production of the first Spanish edition of the atlas, published in 1588, which provides a particularly useful insight into the marketing of the work.

In fact, the initiative for this edition did not come from Ortelius himself, but from the publisher, Christopher Plantin. By contrast, of the three vernacular editions that had appeared prior to this, the Dutch and French were certainly initiated (and translated) by Ortelius, and, although the specific circumstances surrounding the production of the German edition are not known, it is likely that Ortelius was behind it, too. All three had appeared by 1573, were systematically updated with each new *Additamentum* to the Latin text, and exhibit a popularizing tendency which is in marked contrast to the other vernacular translations, which follow the Latin original more closely. It would not be unreasonable to see them as a co-ordinated part of the initial publishing venture undertaken by Ortelius.

Peter Meurer ('t Goy-Houten: HES Publishers, 1998), 79-92; idem, "Abraham Ortelius en Jan Moretus I: de produktie en verkoop van Ortelius' werken door de Plantijnse uitgeverij van 1589 tot 1610," in *Abraham Ortelius (1527-1598), cartograaf en humanist*, ed. P. Cockshaw and Francine de Nave (Turnhout: Brepols), 193-206.

[15] The standard editions are *Abrahami Ortelii (geographi Antverpiensis) et virorum eruditorum ad eundem et ad Jacobum Ortelianum (Abrahami Ortelii sororis filium) epistulae*, ed. Johannes Henricus Hessels (London, 1887, repr. Osnabrueck: O Zeller, 1969); *Correspondance de Christophe Plantin*, ed. Max Rooses and Jan Denucé, 9 vols (Antwerp-Ghent-The Hague: Society of Antwerp Bibliophiles, 1883-1918).

By contrast, it was not until sixteen years after the appearance of the original Latin text that production of a Spanish version was first mooted by Plantin.

Throughout the second half of 1586 Plantin was engaged in printing and distributing the *Breviarium Romanum* of Possevinus, which he eagerly advertised among court circles in Spain through the agency of Jean Moflin, Gabriel de Zayas, and Benito Arias Montano—three men who had been closely involved in the production of Plantin's polyglot bible as early as 1567.[16] Plantin had good reason to be eager to please the Spanish court, having spent from 1582 to 1585 in Leiden, the university established by the rebel Dutch Protestants in defiance of the authority of Philip II in the Low Countries. Throughout his stay in Leiden Plantin had protested his continued orthodoxy in a series of letters to his benefactors in Spain; he insisted that his motives for moving to Leiden were purely commercial and that he had avoided printing heretical works while there and, when asked to do so, had left.[17] On his return from Leiden to Antwerp in 1585 after its reconquest by Parma, he was understandably wary of the need to ensure the positive reception of these arguments at the Spanish court, where he knew he had enemies.[18]

Yet Plantin also had another goal. Although he had maintained throughout the previous decade the title "Prototypographer to the King" of Spain, a position which had gained him lucrative commissions for the publication of religious books in particular, the revolt of the Netherlands had caused him considerable financial difficulty. For much of the past decade Plantin had been complaining through his contacts at the Spanish court that he was seriously in debt, had been forced to sell parts of his business at less than half their value, and had even had to consider closure due to the incessant demands of his creditors.[19] In particular, his financial affairs had never fully recovered from the disastrous publication of his masterpiece, the elaborate and expensive polyglot bible which he had

---

[16] Leon Voet, "De Antwerpse Polyglot Bijbel," *Noordgouw* 13 (1973): 33-57; on Arias Montano in particular see Jeanine de Landtsheer, "Benito Arias Montano and the Friends from his Antwerp Sojourn," *De Gulden Passer* 80 (2002): 39-62.

[17] *Correspondance de Christophe Plantin*, VII, nos 1041, 1052, and 1056.

[18] On Plantin's career see Leon Voet, *The Golden Compasses. The History of the House of Plantin-Moretus*, 2 vols (Amsterdam/London/New York, 1969-1972); on his relations with Spain in particular see Francine de Nave and Dirk Imhof, eds, *Christoffel Plantijn en de Iberische Wereld* (Antwerp: Museum Plantin-Moretus, 1992).

[19] See, for example, *Correspondance de Christophe Plantin*, VII, nos 1072, 1074, 1079, 1080, and 1087.

published for Philip II in 1572/3.[20] This was an international scholarly collaboration of immeasurable prestige, but it nearly ruined Plantin, especially when completion and distribution of the work was delayed and ultimately undermined by accusations of unorthodoxy in the treatment of the biblical text. Further, the work had been commissioned by the king's own advisors, most notably Gabriel de Zayas and his chaplain Benito Arias Montano, who allowed costs to escalate on the understanding that Philip II would recompense Plantin for the financial outlay required to produce the book.[21] However, the impecunious king, beset by his own financial difficulties, failed to pay. Plantin tried every means possible within appropriate protocol to urge the king to loosen his purse strings and fulfil his financial obligations.[22] His recent sojourn in Protestant Leiden had not helped his case, but now that he had dramatically relocated to Catholic Antwerp he sought the opportunity to demonstrate his loyalty and provide a timely reminder of his value to the king; otherwise, he intimated, he would have to sell his entire business.[23]

In a lengthy letter written on 4 November 1586, Jean Moflin reveals that he and Plantin are already engaged in cultivating the patronage of García de Loaisa through exchange of goods and gifts. Moflin explains:

> Je luy ay recommandé voz affaires. J'ay espoir qu'il vous assisterat avec son credit aultant qu'il luy sera possible, comm' il m'at aussi escript, enquoy vous vous pourrez bien fier, car il est ung tresvertueux Seig^r qui ne promect riens sans l'effectuer, et pour aultant vous ne perdrez rien si vous luy envoyez choses d'architecture si vous en avez comm' il demande, aussi quelques abbreviaires qu'avez nouvellement imprimé.[24]

In the same letter, Moflin indicated that he had already presented Loaisa with a copy of a previous edition of the *Theatrum*. Within a few months, on 26 January 1587, he mentions in a letter to Petrus Pantinus his plan to present a new Spanish translation to young Prince Philip, smoothing the way by dedicating Ortelius's *Thesaurus Geographicus* to Loaisa, the prince's tutor:

---

[20] *Biblia regia* (Antwerp: Plantin, 1572/1573).

[21] For a discussion of the entire project see Leon Voet, *De Polyglot-Bijbel: de geschiedenis van een reuzenonderneming* (Antwerp: Museum Plantin-Moretus, 1972).

[22] Plantin provides a summary of his case in a letter that he wrote to Philip II on 31 December 1583: *Correspondance de Christophe Plantin*, VIII, no. 1014.

[23] See, in particular, his letter to Arias Montano on 6 February 1586: *Correspondance de Christophe Plantin*, VII, no. 1074.

[24] *Correspondance de Christophe Plantin*, VIII/IX, no. 1170.

Non ignoras amicum nostrum intimum Abrahamum Ortelium Geographum Regium olim edidisse Theatrum orbis terrarum latina lingua quod paullo post in Gallica et aliis linguis versum impressimus, in Hispanica vero hactenus cum non viderimus curavi meis sumptibus in eam verti et quoniam latina editio dedicata est nostro Regi catholico mihi venit in mentem hanc editionem Hispanicam Principi nostro tamquam hujus universitatis rectori futuro dedicare impetrara jam venia ab auctore qui et me donavit alio libro magno maximis laboribus et vigiliis aggregato [...] Hunc autem libenter dedicarem R.D. Praeceptori Principis si tu probaveris et hoc illi gratum esse intellexero.[25]

The next day he wrote to Loaisa himself, referring to both the projected works, and alluding to his letter to Pantinus for the provision of greater detail, promising that the work would appear within a few months, though in fact both publications took longer than he expected.[26]

If the creation of a Spanish edition of Ortelius's famous atlas seemed a fitting testimony of Plantin's loyalty both to the king and the Catholic faith, it was no less convenient for Ortelius, who had been investigated for his ties to heretics in the wake of the Spanish reconquest of Antwerp. Both men were vulnerable economically as well as politically and religiously. The collapse of the Antwerp economy caused by the flight of large numbers of its citizens before the approaching Spanish armies left an unstable situation which contained the potential for those who remained to make rapid and dramatic gains, but at the risk of looting, economic isolation, and recriminations from the Spanish authorities or their disaffected troops. In this context, Plantin's plan to secure patronage, protection, and the recuperation of old debts from the distant king was good business as well as good politics, especially since dedicating two new prestigious works to Spanish patrons was a reminder of previous debts as well as an attempt to pay for the proposed volumes.[27]

Although Plantin's idea was astutely conceived, it immediately ran into problems. His friend and patron in Spain, Jean Moflin, who had been in the process of translating the *Theatrum* into Spanish, died on 9 February 1587. Around the same time Plantin discovered that books printed in Spanish outside the Iberian peninsula were technically not allowed to enter

---

[25] *Correspondance de Christophe Plantin*, VIII/IX, no. 1200.

[26] *Correspondance de Christophe Plantin*, VIII/IX, no. 1201.

[27] Plantin's predicament is made clear in *Correspondance de Christophe Plantin*, VI, no. 840, and VII, no. 1078, as well as in many other letters to and from Arias Montanus and Zayas. The best account of his difficulties is Leon Voet, *The Golden Compasses*; but see also C. Clair, *Christopher Plantin* (London: Cassell, 1960), 161-78.

Spain. He had previously relied upon royal commissions and influential buyers within Spain to secure distribution of his books there, but his connections with Dutch Protestantism and the enemies of the king of Spain made him especially vulnerable to suspicion and so he expended considerable effort merely in trying to secure the right to print and sell a Spanish text. Although he proposed to dedicate the book to the young Spanish prince Philip (the future Philip III), it was a delicate matter to ensure that this dedication would be well received, and so he carefully tried to use his old contacts to identify the appropriate patron for both books.[28] This seems to have been the first time that he realized that his old protectors at court, Benito Arias Montano and Gabriel de Zayas, were no longer the best people to forward his cause, or could not do so successfully without backing from others. Both men had been affected by factional struggles at court and had lost the influence that they earlier possessed, a development of considerable concern to Plantin since they were also the two men who defended him most ardently from accusations of heresy at the Spanish court. Zayas, in particular, had been the original instigator of the Polyglot Bible scheme and so it was to him, initially, that Plantin turned to procure support for this project to recuperate funds. However, it became evident that the key person to be appeased was García de Loaisa, to whom he eventually dedicated the *Thesaurus*, and who was close to both the king and the young prince. Thus an astutely conceived deal was formulated—the more prestigious work, the atlas, was targeted at the prince; the more scholarly work at his broker, García de Loaisa. Thus, the *Thesaurus* appeared in 1587 with a dedication to Loaisa; the atlas the following year, dedicated to the prince.[29]

Yet the process of distribution of the atlas, which was central to gaining patronage, had only begun. Over the course of the months subsequent to publication Plantin sent multiple copies to Loaisa, Zayas and Arias, distributing his work to different members of the court, and making sure that the king received numerous ornamentally bound and illustrated versions. He seems to have identified figures at court strategically, although some copies inevitably were sent to friends and established patrons, and he asked friends there to distribute copies to

---

[28] *Correspondance de Christophe Plantin*, VIII/IX, nos 1210, 1230, 1231 and 1236.
[29] Abraham Ortelius, *Thesaurus Geographicus*, 1587; ibid., *Theatro de la Tierra Universal*, 1588. The arrangements with Vincentius are discussed in *Correspondance de Christophe Plantin*, VIII/IX, no. 1275.

appropriate individuals as they saw fit.[30] Although Plantin received financial return for some of these, the majority of the named recipients seems to have received copies unsollicited.[31] Plantin's broader goal of securing his long-term financial interest by creating a favourable atmosphere at the Spanish court seems to have pushed him beyond what he could hope to receive in immediate financial return.

Given the importance of the presentation value of this edition of the atlas it is particularly important to gauge the character of the translation. The death of Jean Moflin delayed production of the book so that it did not appear simultaneously with Ortelius's *Thesaurus Geographicus*, but an alternative translator was soon found—the Franciscan scholar Balthasar Vincentius. It is not clear whether the style of the translation was established by Moflin and followed by Vincentius, or whether the final texts represents Vincentius's work alone. Either way, the style appears uniform throughout. Under considerable time pressure, there was little scope for literary elaboration within the translation. Vincentius drew upon the latest Latin edition of the *Theatrum*, ignoring the alternative vernacular style offered by the Dutch, German and French versions, which were written in a more popular, accessible fashion, and appealed more directly to mercantile rather than scholarly interests. In fact, the Spanish translation set the trend for the subsequent translations into Italian and English, which appeared subsequent to Ortelius's death. Part of the explanation for this may lie in the fact that Ortelius was not directly involved in the production of these translations in the way that he had been for the earlier vernacular versions and that, accordingly, the translators had less licence to deviate from their source text. The specific text upon which the Spanish translation is based is that of the 1584 Latin edition. Where one might expect deviation, such as in the description of the Iberian peninsula, the Low Countries, or the British Isles, almost no substantial changes are made. In like manner, the maps in the Spanish edition are identical to those printed in the Latin edition of 1584 and the French edition of 1587. This is explained by the printing process. Ortelius owned the copper-plate exemplars of the maps, which had been updated for the 1584 Latin edition. When Plantin commenced production of the Spanish atlas, he

---

[30] *Correspondance de Christophe Plantin*, VIII/IX, nos 1264, 1272, 1376, and 1393.

[31] For the financial return from the king, Plantin's main target, see ibid., nos 1424 and 1445. The 1588 edition of the atlas was also distributed through the usual networks, such as via Torrentius to influential patrons in Rome; see Marie Delcourt and Jean Hoyoux, *Laevinus Torrentius Correspondance* (Paris: Les Belles Lettres, 1950-54), II, letter 577.

commissioned 255 printings of each map from Ortelius, having provided him with sheets on the reverse of which the Spanish text was already printed. As a work of scholarship there was, therefore, almost nothing new in this edition.

A comparison between a sample section of the Spanish translation and its source text serves to illustrate this point:

> Hispania Straboni corio bubulo humi protenso comparatur. Ea pelago vndique cingitur, nisi qua parte Pyrenaei montis obiecta a Gallis diuiditur. Habet Hispania ab Ortu, montem Pyrenaeum: qui a Veneris Templo siue Promontorio exortus, prope Illiberos (Colibre hodie) in Oceanum procurrit Britannicum, atque hac parte maxime angusta est; adeo vt ego, dum per Cantabriam iter facerem (inquit Vaseus) in Monte Diui Adriani, nisi fefellit aspectus, vtrumque mare me vidisse meminerim, Oceanum videlicet, cui eramus proximi: atque eminus, quantum oculorum prospectus ferre poterat, Mediterranei maris albicantes fluctus. A Septentrione autem clauditur Oceano Cantrabrico; ab Occasu mari Occiduo; a Meridie Freto Herculeo, et mari Balearico.[32]

> España dize Strabon que es semejante a vn cuero de buey tendido por tierra. Esta por todas partes ceñida de Mar, saluo a la parte donde es apartada de Francia por los montes Pyreneos. Tiene España al Leuante el monte Pyreneo, que vuo su origen d'el templo o promontorio de Venus, y junto a Colibre entra en el mar Bretannico, y por aqui es España muy estrecha. Tanto que quando yo caminaba por Biscaya (dize Vaseo) estando en el monte de S. Adrian, me acuerdo (si no me engañaron los ojos) auer visto entrambos mares, a saber el Oceano al qual teniamos cerca: pero d'el otro veyamos, d'el todo lo que la vista podia alcançar, el mar Mediterraneo blanquear las olas. A la parte Septentrional esta cercada d'el mar Cantabrico o de Biscaya, al Poniente d'el mar Occidental, al Mediodia d'el Estrecho de Gibraltar y mar Balearico.[33]

Two general changes may be observed: transposition of word-order from the subject-object-verb pattern of Latin to the subject-verb-object pattern of Spanish; and the analysis of compact inflected structures in Latin into Spanish perilocutions, e.g. the ethical dative "Straboni" becomes "dize Strabon". Where the Latin word-order is altered for effect, the Spanish translation follows suit if possible, e.g. "Habet Hispania ab Ortu, montem Pyrenaeum" becomes "Tiene España al Leuante el monte Pyreneo". Cognate words reinforce the similarity of the two passages (e.g. "corio bubulo" / "cuero de buey"), but false friends are avoided (e.g. "humi

---

[32] *Theatrum Orbis Terrarum*, 7.
[33] *Theatro de la Tierra Universal*, 16.

protenso" / "tendido por tierra"). There are numerous changes in idiom, but these are evidently intended to be direct equivalents (e.g. "exortus" / "vuo su origen"; "nisi fefellit aspectus" / "si no me engañaron los ojos"). The only conceptually significant alterations are to place names. Thus the Livian name "Illiberis" is not given in the Spanish translation, presumably because it was thought to be no longer in use (though in fact it is used locally even today as an ethnonym). Similarly, "Fretus Herculeus" is converted to "Estrecho de Gibraltar", replacing the classical toponym with the modern vernacular equivalent. On the other hand, "Oceanum Cantabricum" is translated directly but also glossed: "mar Cantabrico o de Biscaya". In summary, the Latin text is translated word-for-word, apart from the substitution of idiomatic expressions and, occasionally, the attempt to replace classical place names with early modern equivalents.

The most substantial deviation from the Latin text of the *Theatrum* is, of course, the dedicatory epistle that was designed exclusively for the Spanish publication. This was written for Plantin at the last minute by Benito Arias Montano—the delay being the result of Plantin's uncertainty about whether the dedication would be welcomed at court. The letter purports to be written by Plantin himself and expresses in the usual terms his hope for the favourable reception of the work under the auspices of such an honourable patron. The letter explains that Spanish dominance by land and sea, and prowess in exploration, render Spain the ideal nation to receive such an atlas translated into its language, and that the work should naturally appeal to those who lack the ability to read it in Latin but have good cause, as many in Spain do, to be interested in the text:

> Y porque entre todas las gentes que agora biuen en el mundo, ninguna ay que mas aya nauegado los mares d'el, no costeado y calado la tierra, que los naturales de España; y muchos d'ellos pudiendo approuecharse d'este libro tanto a proposito de su inclinacion y occupacion, por carecer de lengua Latina, no sienten el gusto y prouecho que podrian sacar; determine yo (con voluntad y beneplacito d'el Autor) traduzir en Castellano lo que los Romancistas dessearian tener traduzido, y communicarlo con todas naciones de España, que communmente entienden Castellano.[34]

Skilfully manoeuvring around Plantin's recent sojourn in rebel Leiden, Arias has him ingratiating himself by saying that he has always been and remains particularly fond of the Spanish because of their political ties under the same lord and their unfailing loyalty to the Catholic faith:

---

[34] *Theatro de la Tierra Universal*, unfoliated leaf.

por la affeccion que siempre los he tenido y tengo en particular, allende las generales obligaciones de ser hijos de vna Yglesia Catholica Romana, y biuir todos nosotros debaxo de vn dominio y gouierno de vn mesmo Rey y Señor proprio natural.[35]

The letter proceeds to express the value of the work for the upbringing and entertainment of the prince and future king of Spain. To him, therefore, the work is justly dedicated, just as the Latin version had been dedicated to his father.

The style of the Spanish translation and the terms in which it was presented at the Spanish court are not insignificant. Whether or not the close adherence to the Latin source text reflects time pressure and the fact that Ortelius was less involved in the production of the edition, the result is that the text appears in the guise of a work of vernacular scholarship, with the further consequence that the writings of many ancient and medieval authors about the diverse regions of Europe and Asia are transplanted directly into the Spanish texts, whereas to varying degrees they are transformed in the earlier vernacular editions. But what is most important about the translation is conveyed by the dedicatory epistle's demonstration of the Spanishness of the book as a whole—that an atlas is most fitting for the empire of Spain. By gaining permission to print this work in Spanish and distribute it in Spain, Plantin proclaimed himself and Ortelius to be loyal subjects of the king of Spain. It is no coincidence that this occurred immediately after the recapture of Antwerp by the Spanish troops of the Duke of Parma, nor that in the same year that the text was published a new bishop of Antwerp was installed, Laevinus Torrentius, who immediately proclaimed the triumph of orthodoxy in the city.[36]

While this particular edition of the *Theatrum* had a unique political and financial context, and problems specific to the production of Spanish books, the techniques and mechanisms that Plantin used to secure patronage and the maximum possible impact from the publication were not unusual. Distribution of multiple copies at the discretion of trusted friends in influential centres was widespread practice both by publishers and authors. Although this edition of the atlas contained none of the scholarly apparatuses included in the Latin texts, substituting instead appendices listing trade routes and products, it is quite clear from the above analysis

---

[35] Ibid.

[36] On Torrentius see Marie Juliette Marinus, *Laevinus Torrentius als tweede bisschop van Antwerpen (1587-1595)* (Brussel: AWLSK, 1989) and Jeanine de Landtsheer, "Laevinus Torrentius: auctor et fautor litterarum," *Zuidnederlandse Maatschappij van Taalkunde* 125 (1997): 131-147

that the prime target of the edition was the Spanish court, not Spanish merchants. The appeal to mercantile interest with the inclusion of such features was an attempt to underline the financial import of the Low Countries to the king of Spain. The Spanish translation of Ortelius's atlas is therefore a very particular breed of hybrid, mixing scholarly and mercantile elements within the wider framework of the pursuit of elite patronage.

To an extent, this is true of all versions of Ortelius's atlas; but whereas earlier editions leaned either more towards scholarship or more towards mercantile interests, the Spanish edition does neither. Indeed, it appears that the book as object (specifically, as a gift) was more important than the book as content, at least so far as the author and publisher were concerned. It represents an example of language as gift—the act of translation as an act of tribute. Neither Plantin nor Ortelius shared the political values of Spanish imperialism that are alluded to in the rhetoric of the volume's dedicatory letter; on the contrary, both showed sympathy, though not full agreement, with the Dutch rebels against Spanish authority in the Low Countries. Their profession of loyalty to Spain was a pragmatic response to economic, political and military circumstances. Whatever intellectual core animated the commercial enterprise of the atlas's first production in Latin had been disengaged by the time Plantin initiated the publication of a Spanish version, especially since Ortelius had by then turned his attention more specifically to historical onomastics. Nevertheless, the significance and impact of the book must be distinguished from the motivations that lay behind its creation. Aside from aiding in the promotion of modern geographical studies of Europe within the Iberian peninsula, the publication also inspired there a range of interpretative engagements with symbolic cartography, historical topography, and literary geographies. Thus the reduction of the atlas to the status of a mere object of exchange within the impoverished clientage networks of the Spanish Netherlands would ultimately be reversed as a consequence of the gift of translation so that Ortelius's atlas could find a life of its own in the imaginative world of Spain itself.

PART II:

ADAPTATION

Humanism and Lullism in Fifteenth-Century Majorca: New Information on the Case of Arnau Descós

Leonardo Francalanci

(Universitat de Girona, Institut de Llengua i Cultura Catalanes)

This paper concerns the Majorcan humanist and Lullist Arnau Descós and in particular one of his Latin letters, as yet unpublished, preserved in his extremely rich correspondence (Archivo de la Catedral de Mallorca, MS. 15530)[1]. This letter, which occupies fols 51r-51v, accompanied the poem "Causa tan gran, produint tal effecte" which Descós sent in response to the second call (*cartell*) for the Marian poetic contest (*certamen*) held in Valencia in 1486 in honour of the *Sacratíssima Concepció*;[2] the letter is addressed to the "noble mossen Ferrando Dieç, prevere", organizer and inspirer of the contest.[3]

As we shall see, the analysis of this letter will aid in the understanding of Descós's cultural and literary world, in his double role as humanist and Lullist, as well as certain particular aspects of the very close cultural and especially literary relations between the kingdoms of Majorca and Valencia; indeed, the participation of various Majorcan authors in the Valencian poetic contests is well known.

---

[1] Most of the letters are edited by F. Fita, "Escritos de fray Bernal Boyl, ermitaño de Montserrate. Correspondencia latina con don Arnaldo Descós," *Boletín de la Real Academia de la Historia de Madrid* 19 (1891): 267-348, and "Cartas inéditas de don Arnaldo Descós en la colección Pascual," ibid., 377-446.

[2] *Obra de la Sacratíssima Concepció* (Valencia: Lambert Palmart, 1487), Llibell II, "Perquè moltes obres detinguen la plaça".

[3] Antoni Ferrando Francés, *Els certàmens poètics valencians del segle XIV al XIX* (València: Institució Alfons el Magnànim, Institut de Literatura i Estudis Filològics, 1983), 461-64.

Furthermore, as will be described in the latter part of this paper, this letter allows us to add another grain of sand to the study of the *Certàmens poètics* which loom so large on the cultural and literary scene in Valencia: the letter includes a reference to another poem by this author "De triumphis in laudem B. Virginis Mariae, latino versu et patria lingua", which provides sufficient evidence for the more precise dating of the previously barely known *Certamen en llaors dels vint triomfs de Nostra Dona*, and confirms the active participation of Descós in the contest, something which has often been conjectured but had no documentary proof.[4]

But first one should introduce the true protagonist of this paper.

Humanist, writer and poet in Latin and Catalan, defender of Lullian doctrine, philosopher and theologian, Arnau Descós stands alongside figures of the calibre of Ferran Valentí as one of the most important representatives of fifteenth-century humanism in the Balearic Islands. Although his biography is still not clear in certain details such as his dates of birth and death, his large and rich correspondence allows us to reconstruct, at least in broad terms, the basic events of his life.

The son of Bartolomé Descós y Olesa, he must have been born in Palma de Mallorca in the second quarter of the fifteenth century. As a scion of one of the most illustrious Majorcan families, he was sent to study humanities at Naples, where he certainly had the opportunity to frequent the city's intellectual circles such as the *Accademia Pontaniana*, the true cradle of Neapolitan humanism, and thus come into contact with the principal humanists of his time, among them Il Panormita or Pontanus. From this period we have two Latin epistles addressed to his cousin, the renowned poet Jaume d'Olesa y Sanglada, son of Rafael d'Olesa, ambassador of the Kingdom of Majorca at Naples. After his studies he returned to Palma, where he married (possibly in 1476) and had children, all of whom appear to have died before 1493.

Here he stayed for the rest of his life, concerned with the administration of his family estate (he speaks of "urbana negotia"), the cultivation of letters (we have already mentioned his participation in the Valencian *certamen* of 1486), and above all the study and promotion of Lullist philosophy and theology, under the mastership of the famous theologian Pere Daguí, with whom he enjoyed a close friendship throughout his long life, reflected in their long exchange of correspondence. Daguí, chaplain of the Catholic Monarchs since 1487, was called to Palma—then called Ciutat de Mallorca—in 1481 as *mestre vitalici* of the chair of Lullian

---

[4] Ibid., p. 394.

philosophy, founded in the same year by Agnès Pacs de Quint and authorized by the king in 1483, occupying the post, albeit with interruptions thanks to persecution by the Majorcan inquisition (especially in the person of inquisitor Guillem Caselles), until his death in 1500, in Seville in the train of the Catholic Monarchs.

In the *Biblioteca de escritores baleares*[5] J. M. Bover claims Descós to have been his master's successor in the Lullist chair, while Hillgarth, for example, in his magisterial *Readers and Books in Mallorca 1229-1550*,[6] seriously doubts this on the grounds that if the *jurats* of Majorca really proposed him for the post it is probable that he would not have accepted it on account of his age. Indeed, our author must have died shortly after December 1504 (in any case after 1500), as this is the last time he is documented as living (his last letter is of *c.* 1495). All we can add is that in 1510 the manuscript of his correspondence already had a new owner: Miquel Descós, evidently a family member, although we do do not know his precise relationship to Arnau.[7]

Although, as we have seen, the documented facts of our author's life are few, allowing only an outline sketch of his biography, in contrast his intellectual background, and his political and especially cultural and philosophical thought, are I believe perfectly defined, as expressed in his own voice in his correspondence. The range of personalities who appear in it extends from his friend and classmate the Majorcan humanist Esperandeu Espanyol (tutor to Cesare Borgia in Rome), to Jeroni Pau, according to M. Vilallonga "el més gran humanista català del segle XV",[8] via, among others, Mateu Malferit, vicechancellor of Aragon, Luis de Santángel, his fellow student in Naples and then secretary to the Catholic Monarchs, and Juan de Malleón, bishop of Salamanca. In his letters, the classical models of Ovid and Cicero live alongside moral precepts from the Bible and Christian authors, and theological reflections with exquisitely classical stylistic and rhetorical turns, and even questions of a more informal, nay personal, character take on a humanist patina: thus, for

---

[5] J. M. Bover, *Biblioteca de escritores baleares* (Ciutat de Mallorca, 1868; repr. Barcelona-Sueca: Curial, 1976), I, 243-45.

[6] J. N. Hillgarth, *Readers and Books in Majorca 1229-1550*, 2 vols (Paris: CNRS, 1991), 221-28.

[7] Different sources identify him with the son of Arnau's brother, Bernat, or with the son of an unknown Bartolomé Descós, "ciutadà", married to Elionor Valentí; he is surely the same "reverendo maestro Miguel Cos, presbítero teólogo", documented as a "beneficiado" of the Cathedral de Majorca in 1554 who died in 1570.

[8] Jeroni Pau, *Obres*, ed. Mariàngela Vilallonga, 2 vols (Barcelona: Curial, 1986).

example, when he sends some mushrooms to his brother Bernat, he accompanies them with some verses inspired by the epigrams of Martial.[9] Such erudite expression in such a personal context, even though very probably meant as a joke, an act of complicity between brothers, must be seen as an unquestionable display of a grade of assimiliation of classical reading, and an undoubted proof of the intellectual maturity achieved by some of the representatives of humanism in Aragon.

Many of the strands of Descós's cultural origins have already been demonstrated in this brief summary of his life and works. Fifteenth-century Majorca, like most parts of the Crown of Aragon, was characterized by the strong survival of medieval traits on the one hand and the progressive assimilation of the new horizons of *Umanesimo*, received via continuous contacts between Majorcan intellectuals and Italian humanists, especially in Naples, at the court of Alfons the Magnanimous, but also in Rome, during the pontificates of the Borgias, and certainly in different Italian cities and universities. The presence of medieval elements, which were to a degree responsible for inhibiting the entry of new humanistic developments, is one of the reasons why some scholars question the legitimacy of the concept of *humanisme català* and express scepticism at the general application of the term "humanist" to the Catalan intellectuals. However, as will have become apparent, I personally see no problem in the use of the term, even though it could yield mixed results, especially at the level of assimilation of the new currents. Without reference to a humanism which although possibly superficial is wide-ranging it is impossible to understand authors such as Arnau Descós o Jaume d'Olesa, who, as we shall see, open their devout compositions to the Virgin with invocations in classical distichs.

Let us return to fifteenth-century Majorca. The one element to which we might point as distinctive of the Majorcan context, which marks it out from the other territories of the Crown of Aragon, is Lullism, or rather, as Lullism was a genuinely European phenomenon, the magnitude with which this doctrine is expressed on the island in the last quarter of the fifteenth century; not for nothing does Professor Hillgarth, in his *Readers and Books in Majorca*, devote the whole of his chapter VIII to "Lullism in Majorca", with a whole paragraph on Descós. Although it must be

---

[9] The epigram, unpublished, is on fol. 25r: "Accipe, mi frater, boletos accipe nostros; / Non quales edit claudius imperatore Nero, / Sed Iovis et mensa dignos omnique deorum / Combibio, cum sis dignior has habebas" [Receive, my brother, receive our mushrooms; / not like those that the famous Claudius Nero eats, / but worthy of the table of Jupiter / and the banquest of all the gods; because you are the most worthy receive them.]

recognized that there was not an unbroken tradition of interest in Llull in Majorca, it is also true that the last quarter of the fifteenth century saw one of the moments of greatest development and expansion in the study of Lullism. Following the example a few years earlier of the Catalan noblewoman Beatriu de Pinós, on 30 August 1481 Agnès Pacs de Quint, widow of the noble citizen Nicolau de Quint, donated her goods to found a chair of Lullism on the island and endow it with sufficient income to maintain a master and two students. Interest in the teachings of Llull in Majorca at this period is such that we find not one but two different Lullist schools: one, led by Daguí, in Puig de Randa (called the *Puxredenses*), and the other, headed by Bartomeu Caldentey, in Miramar (the *Trinitentes*, named after the nearby Ermita de la Trinitat). Professor Hillgarth argues that rather than competition it was a case of two different approaches to the subject: "In general, Prats—and it is reasonable to suppose Caldentey also, though we have nothing written by him—represents a more pastoral and less scholastic approach than that of Daguí, whose books tended to approximate Lull's theology as much as possible to Scotism and his logic to that of current Aristotelianism". And concludes that "there was no need for them to clash or compete", as "both schools, in different ways, sought to present Lull in terms intelligible to their age".[10]

The fascination which Llull evidently exerted throughout island society, and particularly in the aristocracy and urban patriciate, was not, however, exclusively devout in its origins: Llull was not only a great theologian and philosopher but a descendant of the Majorca nobility. This sort of social mimickry is in fact one of the most characteristic aspects of Majorcan Lullism; Descós gives a very clear example of this when in one of his letters he mounts a defence of Llull's doctrine against the attacks of the Italian humanist Paolo Pompilio saying "Quoniam videtur non solum detrahere fame nostre divi Raymundi Lulli, sed etiam nostro proprio honori, tum quia fuit conterraneus meus Balearis, tum quia eius pre ceteris sequimur doctrinam" ["Because, it appears, it not only harms the reputation of our blessed Ramon Llull, but also our own honour, not only because he was my fellow countryman, but because we follow his teaching above all others"]. The situation becomes even clearer when one analyses the constitution of circles concerned with the promotion of Lullism in Majorca in the second half of the fifteenth century: they consist for the most part of members of the urban oligarchy, formed of a relatively small number of closely interrelated families: the Descós, Olesa, Pacs de Quint, Espanyol, etc.

---

[10] Hillgarth, *Readers and Books*, I, 220.

With regard to Valencia, the city to which Descós's letter and poem are directed, it is worth recalling that this was one of the great capitals of the Mediterranean in the mid-fifteenth century, one of the richest and most influential cities in the Crown of Aragon and possibly the whole Peninsula. Culturally speaking it is one of the most fascinating, lively and cosmopolitan centres in the kingdom, open to a multiplicity of trends and productive of a brilliant literature: one need only recall outstanding poets such as Ausiàs March or Roíç de Corella, or works such as *Tirant lo Blanch*. However, what most interests us here, and what represents one of the most distinctive features of Valencian culture, is the poetic contests:[11] these are one of the most important literary expressions in the public sphere in the whole fifteenth century. Although closely linked to local culture, their fame in the second half of the century spread their prestige, both social and literary, all over the Crown of Aragon and the Peninsula. Their range is indicative of their nature: among the entrants we find, alongside the Valencians, Catalan, Castilian and (as we shall see) Majorcan poets. Here we will focus on two contests to which our letter refers, beginning with the *Certamen poètic en honor de la Sacratíssima Concepció* (1486), in which Desclós participated with his poem "Causa tan gran", to accompany which he wrote the Latin text which we shall analyse.

Beyond being written in good Latin, the letter has no literary pretensions; however, it provides a small example of Desclós's working methods, his sources, his concerns, and his adherence to Lullism. In it the author seeks to defend the orthodoxy of the Immaculist content of his poem, as we shall see inspired by Lullism, against those "qui libentius alios convitiis et fame detrimentis persequuntur et invident, quam eos ipsos in bonis artibus inutentur" ["who more insist on envying and harming with insults the names of others, than themselves practising the good arts"]; according to the author, these are the same "quos tuo tum sancto tanque devoto studio ac magno exellentique exposito premio ad bonas tu incitas et incendis artes; ipsi invidi rabule ac bilingues dehortentur omninoque perterreant" ["whom you [i.e. Ferrando Díeç] with such holy and devout study, and with great and excellent benefit, incite and inflame in the good arts; those same envious and false charlatans who in all cases discourage and terrify"]. The authors whom Desclós cites in his defence are, in accordance with his training, both classical and patristic. Thus, to show that his detractors put more effort into criticizing him than cultivating the "bonas artes", he does not hesitate to use both a

---

[11] See Ferrando, *Els certàmens poètics.*

passage from St Jerome, "Non enim me latet illud Hieronimi 'atque in eo se doctos arbitrantur, si aliis detrahant'" ["in fact it reminds me of that saying of Jerome: 'they think they are learned because they criticize others'"],[12] one from Cicero *De oratore*, "adest enim fere nemo, qui non vitia acutius atque acrius indicet, quam ea laudet que recta videt; ita quicquid est, in quo offenditur, id etiam ea, que laudanda sunt, obruit" ["there is scarcely anyone in fact who does not criticize errors more than he praises what he thinks rightful; in the same way, unpleasant things end up hiding those other things which are praiseworthy"][13] and a satire of Persius, "ut nemo in sese temptat descendere, nemo, sed precedenti spectatur mantica tergo" ["because no-one tries to dig into himself, no-one, but looks at the bag on the back of the person in front"].[14] Indeed, the entire letter seems to be inspired by the passage in Jerome's *Prologus in Libro Regum* which Desclós quotes: let us compare, for example, for example the way in which Desclós speaks of his detractors "caninidentes, os mordicus lacerare non desinent" with Jerome's "sed et vos famulas Christi rogo [...] ut contra latrantes canes, qui adversum me rabido ore desaeviunt et circumeunt civitatem atque in eo se doctos arbitrantur, si aliis detrahant, orationum vestrarum clypeos opponatis". But who are his detractors, those "invidi rabule ac bilingues", and what is their accusation? To judge from his defence, these must be the followers of nominalism, who were then the promotors of a heated polemic on the philosophical and theological lexicon in the works of Llull: his critics considered it unsuited, even obscure, while his defenders advocated the need to find new words to express new ideas. Desclós's argument, built on two quotations from Quintilian, *Institutio oratoria*[15] and one from St Augustine *De doctrina christiana*,[16] would seem to confirm this hypothesis, as the author uses them precisely to legitimate his position regarding the vocabulary used in poetry: "Et ideo merito his omnibus me verbis ussum existimo, dum modo ipsas theologicas sentencias integras vulgaribus exprimere rhythmis" ["And therefore I consider it legitimate to use all those terms so that I can

---

[12] Jerome, *Prologus in Libro Regum*.

[13] Cicero, *De oratore*, I, XXV.

[14] Persius, *Sat.*, IV, 23.

[15] Quintilian, *Institutio oratoria*, VIII, 1 and X, 4: "Ostendendo nil interesse, ut inquit Quintilianus 'quibus quicque nominibus appelletur, dum res ipsa manifesta sit', et alibi idem Quintilianus de verbis loquens: 'Quorum ea sunt'—inquit—'maxime probabilia, que sensum animi nostri optime promiunt'".

[16] St Augustine, *De doctrina christiana*, II, 15, 22: "'In ipsis autem'—inquit—'interpretationibus, Italia ceteris preferatur; Nam est verborum tenacior cum perspicuitate sentencie'".

express fully the same theological meanings in vernacular verses"].
According to Quintilian, supported by Descós, one should not pay
attention to the "nomina" by which one calls something, provided the "res
manifesta sit", and when choosing words, the most "probabilia" are those
which "sensum animi nostri optime promiunt".

Finally, regarding his poem "Causa tan gran", Descós, drawing again
on Quintilian, speaks of an "interpretationem quam greci *glossas*
vocant",[17] written with the intention of answering those backbiters whose
greatest strength is in "reprehendis vocabulis": "Quamobrem volebam, ut
ipsis maledicis, quorum maior vis in reprehendis vocabulis est, possem
respondere, facere aliquam interpretationem quam greci *glossas* vocant, ut
meum ipsum conceptum apertius exprimerem, tum in vocabulis ipsis
vulgaribus iure positis, tum in sententiis a veritate haud alienis"
["Therefore in order to reply to those ill-speakers whose principal strength
is in criticizing terms, I wished to make some kind of explanation—what
the Greeks call 'glosses'—to express my ideas openly, both in the
vernacular verses themselves and in phrases not far from truth"]. Later,
still following the *Institutio oratoria*, Desclós puts before Ferrando Díeç
an image, somewhat stereotyped, of the efforts devoted to poetic
composition: "Quamquam biduo perfecerim predictus opusculum,
verumtum non tanta festinationes editum est, quin deo favente pro meis
parvulis viribus elimaverim premendo tumentia, humilia extollendo,
luxuriantia stringendo, in ordinata digerendo, soluta componendo,
exultantia coercendo; hec enim emendatio, utilissima Quintiliano videtur,
non huic defuit sententia theologorum, quos et amore et studio persequor
non oratorum ornatus, non poetarum vivacitas, quibus apud italicos fontes
operam dedi" ["Although the aforementioned small work was finished in
two days, this does not mean that it has been composed hastily: with the
help of God and my humble capacities I have polished it, attenuating the
emphatic, raising the humble, trimming the superfluous, ordering what
was disordered, restoring hanging lines, and reining in the excessive
ornament of the phrase; for this correction which Quintilian considers
most useful does not contradict the meaning of the theologians, whom
with love and study I pursue, not the glory of the orators, nor the liveliness
of the poets, to which I devoted myself by the Italian springs"].[18] The
concerns expressed here are perhaps only to be expected in a humanist of
the time, but it is surprising to find such a lucid declaration of principle:

---

[17] Quintilian, *Institutio oratoria*, I, I, 35.

[18] Quintilian, *Institutio oratoria* X, 4: "premere vero tumentia, humilia extollere,
luxurantia adstringere, inordinata digerere, soluta componere, exultantia coercere".
Book X is entitled precisely *De emendatione*.

with "Causa tan gran", Descós aims to follow the dictates of the "oratorum ornatus" and "poetarum vivacitas" while respecting theological orthodoxy, giving both elements the same value and making clear their total compatibility.

The text of the poem is edited and analysed by Ferrando (see n. 3 above). However, some aspects merit further attention. First, Descós's fully humanistic approach makes him open the poem dedicated to the Virgin with an *invocatio* in elegiac distichs (he does however state that "Nil prossunt muse nil carminis auctor Apollo"). Second, his Immaculist beliefs are of clear Lullist descent, as is shown by a comparison of the opening lines of the poem "Causa tan gran, produint tal effecte / Compendre pot nenguna creatura, / Car excedex tan excellent objecte / L'enteniment nostre, que·s tant dejecte / Creat finit i baix de sa natura", with the last paragraph of chapter IX of Llull's *De ascensu et descensu intellectus*, where Llull admits that the Immaculate Conception is a true mystery for which his "enteniment" cannot find sufficient reason. These conclusions are merely partial, but I am certain that a more detailed analysis of the poem will bring out many more points of contact between the two authors.

Let us now look at the second poetic contest mentioned in the letter. This was in praise of the "vint triomfs de Nostra Dona", and is one of the contests of which least is known. According to A. Ferrando, it must have been held in Valencia between 1483 and 1492, and virtually nothing would have been known about it if not for the rubric of a poem composed for the occasion by the Majorcan poet Jaume d'Olesa: "Jhs. Triunphes de Nostra Dona en cobles capdenals biocades, per lo de mirable enginy Jaume d'Aulesa, ciutadà, compostes e trameses en València per la joya [que] era allí mesa al qui mils hi digués".[19] The rubric and its poem are copied in a Majorcan manuscript of the late fifteenth or early sixteenth century, once the property of the Jesuits of Palma and now in the Real Academia de la Historia in Madrid.[20] The only one of the contestants for whom we have certain information is Jaume d'Olesa himself; however Ferrando identifies other authors and works which although apparently not directly connected with the contest might well bear some relation to it. The first author is the Castilian Juan Tallante, probably of Murcian origin. His "Obra en loor de las XX excelencias de Nuestra Señora, hecha por mossén Tallante", presents the same structure as Desclós's poem and is printed in Hernando del Castillo's *Cancionero General* (Valencia, 1511) immediately

---

[19] See Ferrando, *Els certàmens poètics*, 361.
[20] Est. SS. gr. 1.ᵃ, número 15.

before the composition with which the author entered the Immaculist *certamen* of 1486 organized by Ferrando Díeç. If Tallante's participation is confirmed, the contest must have taken place at this date. Another candidate is Romeu Llull of Barcelona: his "Responsiva als vint triomfs de Nostra Dona" shares its form and theme with the other works, and may well have been presented at the same event, as Jaume Turró notes in his edition: "Composició en resposta d'algun certamen marià, el mateix al qual concorregué Juan Tallante [...] i, probablement, el mateix també en què Jaume d'Olesa presentà els seus *Triunphes de Nostra Dona*, tal com va proposar A. Ferrando".[21] The last of the possible participants is our Arnau Descós, although in this case his role is more hypothetical: "Ignorem", says Ferrando, "per haver-se perdut, si el segon dels esmentats opuscles immaculistes [*De triumphis in laudem B. Virginis Mariae*], expressat en *latino versu et patria lingua*, té res a veure amb el certamen valencià en honor del vint triomfs de Nostra Dona", and concludes that formal and stylistic comparisons with others of his poems (such as in the combination of Latin and Catalan) and his known links with the Valencian contests "no ho descarten precisament".[22] As we will see, some of the passages in Descós's letter supply answers to some of the questions raised by Ferrando, proving his connection with the *certamen* and contributing to a more certain dating for the event.

Such confirmation is given by Descós when he tells Ferrando Díeç with all the spontaneity of writing in the first person: "his proximis diebus opusculum meum de conceptione virginis una cum epistola ad te misi. Et cum incertum sim an ad tuas pervenerit manus, hac de causa iterum illud tibi mitto. Vereor enim ne mihi eveniat ut superioribus mensibus de triumphis quos in laudem beatissimae virginis et latino versu et nostra patria lingua cecini, qui id destinatum diem adesse non potuerunt, cum ob tempestatem maris navis qua differebantur ad tempus in eo destinatum non applicuerit. Cum presertim nullas a te huc usque habuerim litteras quibus profecto peroptabam certior a te fieri, an illud acceperis" ["Days ago I sent you, together with a letter, my little work on the Conception of the Virgin. And as I do not know if it reached your hands, I am sending it to you again. I am concerned especially that the same thing should not happen as happened months ago with the triumphs which I sent you, in Latin and our native language, in praise of the Most Blessed Virgin, which I was not able to present on the agreed day because the ship, blown off course by a sea storm, could not reach its destination on time. And the more so

---

[21] Romeu Llull, *Obra completa*, ed. Jaume Turró, ENC, A135 (Barcelona: Barcino, 1996), 83-84.
[22] See Ferrando, *Els certàmens poètics*, 394.

because I have still not received any letter from you, confirming as I had hoped that you had received it"]. It is curious that the lack of information about the contest is linked in Desclós's case to an event as fortuitous as a storm at sea. Be that as it may, what is clear is that this information opens new approaches for study, allowing us to show that our poet really did participate—or rather wished to participate—as Ferrando thought in the Valencian *certamen* in praise and honour of the Twenty triumphs, and that de did so with a poem "de triumphis [...] in laudem beatissimae virginis". Furthermore, this information demonstrates that the contest took place in 1484 or 1485, that is, some months before ("superioribus mensibus") the other *certamen* organized by mossén Díeç in honour of the *Sacratíssima Concepció* in 1486, to which the letter refers.

In this brief analysis of the figure of Arnau Descós and some of his works, we have sought to cast light on the multiplicity of influences which gave life to the cultural panorama of the Crown of Aragon, and bring new facts regarding literary relations between the different territories. It has also been shown that humanism and Lullism are two of the constituent elements which forged the particular nature of Majorcan cultural and literary life in the second half of the fifteenth century.

ST ISIDORE OF SEVILLE AND ST ILDEFONSUS OF TOLEDO AS MODELS OF STYLE IN THE RENAISSANCE

BARRY TAYLOR
(THE BRITISH LIBRARY)

While St Isidore preached classical decorum in his rhetorical treatises, he and his contemporaries were capable of turning away from such classical restraint in their more stylistically ambitious writing:

> En las *Etimologías* o en las *Diferencias* [Isidoro] utiliza esquemas simples, concisos y claros, como corresponde a géneros básicamente didácticos [...] El estilo necesariamente repetitivo y acumulativo propio de los *Sinónimos* acaba por aflorar en buena parte de la obra del sevillano, convirtiéndose en rasgo característico del *stilus Isidorianus* y también del *stilus scholasticus* visigótico.
>
> De todas formas, en la Hispania visigoda no siempre se respeta el ideal de equilibrio y de sencillez defendido teóricamente por Isidoro; más bien todo lo contrario, acaba predominando y consolidándose la tendencia en cualquier manifestación literaria a un estilo exuberante, a veces incluso alambicado, en el cual se deja ver con todos sus efectos el adiestramiento en retórica. Piénsese en el estilo cuidado, elevado y profuso de Julián de Toledo y, sobretodo, de Ildefonso de Toledo; el *De uirginitate perpetua sanctae Mariae* puede considerarse casi un *technopaegnion* sobre figuras retóricas, sobre procedimientos de estilo o sobre técnicas retóricas en general. Piénsese en el estilo grandilocuente, rebuscado y abigarrado de Valerio del Bierzo, a pesar de que lo encontramos trabajando en la región más aislada del Noroeste peninsular.[1]

Isidore had a variety of styles,[2] but stylistically, his most distinctive and influential work is the *Synonyma* alias *Soliloquia* or *De lamentatione*

---

[1] José Carracedo Fraga, "La retórica en la Hispania visigótica," *Euphrosyne* 30 (2002): 115-30 (123).

[2] Jacques Fontaine, "Théorie et pratique du style chez Isidore de Séville," *Vigiliae Christianae* 14 (1960): 65-101.

animae peccatricis. It has precedents in Augustine's *Soliloquia.*[3] It is written in clausulae in which the same idea is repeated, with a certain use of rhyme or near-rhyme. The synonymous style is reserved by Isidore for particular circumstances, especially penitence. In 1220 John of Garland, in his *Parisiana Poetria*, gives Isidore paternity of this style:

> *De stilo Ysydoriano.* In stilo Ysydoriano, quo utitur Augustinus in libro *Soliloquiorum*, distinguntur clausule similem habentes finem secundum leonitatem et consonanciam; et uidentur esse clausule pares in sillabis quamuis non sint. Item iste stilus ualde motiuus est ad pietatem uel ad leticiam:
>> Pre pudore genus humanum obstúpeat,
>> de communi dampno quilibet abhórreat,
>> admirentur sérui,
>> stupescant líberi,
>> conformantur magistris leues discípuli,
>> dum causa studii fauor est pópuli.
>> Prius legunt quam sillábicent;
>> prius uolant quam humi cúrcitent; […]
>> antequam sciant partes connéctere,
>> versus iactant miros compónere.
>
> [Let the human race be struck dumb at the shame, let every man shiver at the general blame, let slaves be shocked, free men appalled, when stuttering children are called to professorships, irresponsible schoolboys turned into masters, when the cause of scholarship is the plaything of the mob. They read lectures before they can sound out syllables, they fly before they can hop along the ground].[4]

The *Synonyma* were a medieval best-seller, "un des classiques de la spiritualité ascétique", as Jean Fontaine calls them.[5] Erasmus, however,

---

[3] Of which there were translations into Old Catalan, Portuguese and Spanish: Giovanni M.[a] Bertini, "I *Soliloquia* e lo *Speculum peccatoris* dello pseudo Agostino in catalano," *Homenatge a Antoni Rubio i Lluch*, 3 vols (Barcelona: Casa de Caritat, 1936), II, 233-63; Mário Martins, "Os *Solilóquios* e *Meditações* do pseudo-Agostinho, em medievo-português," *Brotéria* 55 (1952): 168-77. The Spanish translation is unpublished, but see *Philobiblon* (http://sunsite.berkeley.edu/Philobiblon), citing Biblioteca Nacional, Madrid MS. 463; Escorial MS. b.III.1; Escorial MS. a.II.7.

[4] John of Garland, *Parisiana Poetria,* ed. Taugott Lawler (Yale University Press, 1974), 107-9. I have laid out and accented the Latin to bring out the structure.

[5] Jacques Fontaine, "Isidore de Séville, auteur ascétique: Les énigmes des *Synonyma*," *Studi Medievali*, 3rd ser., 6 (1965): 163-95 (164). On the numerous medieval manuscripts of the *Synonyma*, see Jacques Elfassi and Dominique Poirel, "Isidorus Hispalensis Ep," in *La trasmissione dei testi latini del medioevo /*

was not impressed. Although he famously advocated copia (*De copia,* 1512)—that is, he thought an author should have a large number of synonyms at his disposal—he did not approve of using them all at once. He wrote to Colet about his *De copia*: "Nor am I disposed to mention authors like Isidore or Marius [Victorinus] or Philiscus [*floruit* 1453] who are at so many removes from *copia* that they are unable to express their thoughts in Latin even once".[6]

Leaving the sixteenth century, let us backtrack to Ildefonsus. He did not give his name to a style. He was the pupil of Isidore and in his *De virginitate* acknowledges Isidore as his stylistic master; and is generally held to have outdone his master in strangeness: "supera la praxis y la lexis retórica de [Isidoro]" ... "este arte de sinónimos, tratado con moderación hasta Isidoro, Ildefonso lo lleva al extremo".[7] This sample typifies his debt to Isidore:

> Auditu percipe tu, Iouiniane, corde sapito fátue, praecordiis cognosce stúlte, sensu disce cadúce. **Nolo** pudorem nostrae uirginis corruptum partu cáuseris, **nolo** integritatem generatione discérpas, **nolo** uirginitatem exitu nascentis scíndas, **nolo** uirginem genetricis officio príues, **nolo** genetrici uirginalis gloriae plenitudinem tóllas.
> [Perceive with your ears, Jovinianus; know with your heart, fool; know with your heartstrings, stupid; learn with your mind, dullard. I do not wish you to contend the pudor of our Virgin to have been corrupted by childbirth; I do not wish you to separate wholeness from motherhood; I do not wish you to separate virginity from the birth of the child; I do not wish you to deprive the Virgin of the office of mother; I do not wish you to take away the plenitude of virginal glory from the mother.][8]

Like Isidore, Ildefonsus also had a later medieval tradition.[9] Indeed, he was the subject of what may be the first ever piece of Spanish literary criticism, when in the thirteenth century Gonzalo de Berceo (*Milagros de*

Mediaeval Latin Texts and their Transmission, ed. Paolo Chiesa and Lucia Castaldi (Firenze: Sismel, Edizioni del Galluzzo, 2004), 186-226 (218-26).

[6] Erasmus, *De copia; De ratione studii,* ed. Craig R. Thompson, Collected Works of Erasmus, 24 (Toronto: University of Toronto Press, 1978), 227.

[7] Juana Balleros Mateos, *El tratado "de Virginitate sanctae Mariae" de san Ildefonso de Toledo* (Toledo: Estudio Teológico de San Ildefonso, Seminario Conciliar, 1985), 141-42.

[8] Balleros, 42.

[9] José María Canal, "Tradición manuscrita de la obra de san Ildefonso de Toledo de *Virginitate sanctae Mariae,*" *Revista Española de Teología* 28 (1968): 51-75; Matilde Cupiccia, "Ildephonsus Toletanus Archiep.," in *La trasmissione dei testi latini del medioevo* (as in n. 5), 177-86 (176-81).

Nuestra Señora, LI) praised his book as a "libro de dichos colorados", a reference to the colours of rhetoric.[10] In the fifteenth century, Alfonso Martínez de Toledo and the Beneficiado de Ubeda wrote lives of him (although Martínez's responsibility has been questioned),[11] and Martinez de Toledo translated the *De virginitate* into Spanish, keeping the style:

> Oye tú, Joveniano non sabio; entiende nescio e sin coraçón; conosce loco e sin entendimiento; aprehende, ciego e sin seso. Non quiero que en la nuestra virgen pongas mancilla nin corrupción del parimento, la entreguedat del engendramiento, la virginidad del nascimiento. Non quiero que prives la nuestra virgen de officio de madre; non quiero que prives la madre de conplimiento de gloria virginal.[12]

---

[10] Berceo's comment is of course positive. However, there is reason to believe that in the majority of Old Spanish authors *colorado* suggests "specious". *Partida* VII, tit XVI, ley 1: "*Dolus* en latin tanto quiere decir en romance commo engaño: et engaño es enartamiento que los omes facen unos á otros por palabras mintrosas ó encubiertas ó coloradas que se dicen con entençion de los engañar ó de los deçebir," ed. Real Academia Española (Madrid, 1807); Don Juan Manuel, "razones coloradas et apuestas," *El conde Lucanor*, ex. XXXVI; Juan Ruiz, "mentir colorado," *Libro de buen amor*, 635d; Bernat Metge, "evasions colorades," *Lo somni*, ed. Stefano Maria Cingolani, ENC (Barcelona: Barcino, 2006), bk II, p. 179; "Mas com aquell que amb manifestes delictes haveu del tot la vergonya perduda, sercau amb colorades e vils paraules desviar-vos del que falsament haveu amprés," Vicent Turol i Reig, "Unes lletres de batalla en temps del Tirant: Joan Francesc de Pròixita contra don Pero Maça de Liçana," *Caplletra* 34 (primavera 2003): 143-69 (167); Hernando del Pulgar: "¡Oh rey! Mal lo miras, si todo cuanto te dicen crees; porque muchos vienen a ti, dellos con mentiras coloradas, dellos con malicias que tienen imagen de bondad," *Letras*, ed. Jesús Rodríguez Bordona, Clásicos castellanos (Madrid: Espasa-Calpe, 1958), "Para su fija monja," 148; "penso el arçobispo de buscar causas coloradas como de la corte se fuesse," *Crónica de Enrique IV,* ed. María Pilar Sánchez Parra (Madrid: Ediciones de la Torre, 1991), 488. One example of the positive sense: Alonso de Palencia: "podrán meior ver quánto mueve en las deliberaciones, que en los comienços de las enpresas se fazen, el artificio de bien fablar i las razones coloradas con esperanças de grandes provechos," *Batalla campal de los perros contra los lobos*, Prologue, in *Dos tratados de Alfonso de Palencia*, ed. Antonio M. Fabié (Madrid: Librería de los Bibliófilos, 1876), 11.

[11] Ralph de Gorog and Lisa de Gorog, "La atribución de las *Vidas de San Ildefonso de Toledo y San Isidoro* al Arcipreste de Talavera," *Boletín de la Real Academia Española* 58 (1978): 169-93.

[12] *San Ildefonso de Toledo a través de la pluma del Arcipreste de Talavera*, ed. José Madoz (Madrid: CSIC, Patronato "Raimundo Lulio"—Instituto "Francisco Suárez," 1943), 109, rendering the passage from Ildefonsus quoted above. Cited by

Martínez's own style in the *Corbacho* is typified by synonymy.
Ildefonsus was edited by Miguel Alfonso Carranza in Valencia in 1556.[13]
Carranza's prefatory material makes little reference to Ildefonsus's style,
merely praising it in commonplace terms. A curiosity of Carranza's epistle
to Gregorio de Miranda, Inquisitor of Valencia, is that Carranza appears to
be imitating the Saint's style:

> **Tantum** enim in hoc opere sanctissimus ille praesul apparet in Virginem
> Mariam charitate *refertus*: **tanto** ipsius intactae virginitatis zelo *commotus*:
> **tanto** denique beatissimae illi dilectae amore *copulatus* (sig. *iii^v)

In an important article of 1965, María Rosa Lida drew attention to what
she saw as a continuous tradition of highly-wrought Spanish artistic prose
stretching from Ildefonsus to Antonio de Guevara (*c.* 1481-1545).[14] I am
broadly in agreement with her argument (as I am with everything Lida
wrote). One example which I would take out of her tradition of art prose is
a passage from Don Juan Manuel (fourteenth century), as it is closely
modelled on a passage in the *Bocados de oro*. Similarly, the lamentation
over the fall of Spain in the *General Estoria* owes its artistic prose to its
nature as a close translation of Jiménez de Rada's *Historia gothica* (381-
82).[15] One work in a highly wrought prose style which Lida does not
mention (because it was unpublished in her time) is the fourteenth-century
Soliloquios of Fr. Pedro Fernández Pecha, in the tradition of Augustine.[16]

María Rosa Lida de Malkiel, "Fray Antonio de Guevara: Edad Media y Siglo de
Oro español," *Revista de Filología Hispánica* 7 (1965): 346-88 (380).
[13] *Sanctissimi Patris Illefonsi Archiepiscopi Toletani ... aureus libellus de illibata
virginitate sanctae Mariae, genitricis Dei, ac dominae nostrae industria fratri
Michaelis Carrançae ... Carmelitarum familia, nunc primum in lucem editus, &
scholiis ... illustratus ; accessit operi epitome sententiarum quas sanctissimi patres
in laudem virginitatis Mariae decantarunt autore eodem fratre Michaele Carrança
...* (Valentiae: excudebat vidua Ioannis Mey, 1556). Biblioteca Nacional, Madrid,
R-29420.
[14] María Rosa Lida de Malkiel, "Fray Antonio de Guevara: Edad Media y Siglo de
Oro español," cited n. 12 above.
[15] Jiménez de Rada is indebted to Isidore: Stéphanie Jean-Marie Guirardel,
"L'*Historia gothica* de Rodrigue Jimenez de Rada (1243): écriture et discours"
(Ph. D. thesis, Université de Toulouse, 2007) (hal.archives-ouvertes.fr/docs
/00/.../THESE_corrigee_17dec2007.pdf).
[16] Fernando Lapesa, "Un ejemplo de prosa retórica a fines del s. XIV: los
Soliloquios de fray Pedro Fernández Pecha," in *Studies in Honor of Lloyd A.
Kasten* (Madison: HSMS, 1975), 117-28.

Lida addresses an obvious but little-studied aspect of *Celestina*: its synonymous style:

> Lee los ystoriales, estudia los filósofos, mira los poetas. Llenos están los libros de sus viles e malos exemplos, e de las caydas que levaron los que en algo como tú las reputaron (Act I)
> Ya me reposa el coraçón, ya descansa mi pensamiento, ya reciben las venas e recobran su perdida sangre, ya he perdido temor, ya tengo alegría (Act VI, both cited by Lida, 384)

To her comments on *Celestina*, I would add that *Celestina* scholars have hardly ever addressed the question of style. Samonà's monograph is largely descriptive.[17] Scholars allude occasionally to Diego de San Pedro as an inspiration for Rojas, in part because we know Rojas owned a copy of his works.[18]

According to Lida, in the sixteenth century the foremost exponent of the Isidorian style is Antonio de Guevara, author of several best-sellers such as the *Libro áureo de Marco Aurelio* (1528), a fictionalized life of Marcus Aurelius, revised a year later as the *Reloj de principes*. (Englished respectively by Lord Berners as *The Golden Book of Marcus Aurelius* in 1535 and by Thomas North as *Dial of Princes* in 1557):

> En cuanto en este mundo vivimos todo lo deseamos,
> todo lo tentamos,
> todo lo procuramos
> y aun todo lo probamos.
> Y al fin, después de todo visto y gustado con todo nos cansamos y con todo nos ahitamos.

> En la corte, como no hay justicia que tome las armas, no ay campana que taña a queda, no ay padre que castigue al hijo, no ay amigo que corrija al prójimo, no ay vecino que denuncie al amancebado, no hay fiscal que acuse al usurero, no ay provisor que compela a confesar, no hay cura que llame a comulgar; el que de su natural no es bueno, gran libertad tiene para ser malo.[19]

---

[17] Carmelo Samonà, *Aspetti del retoricismo nella "Celestina"* (Roma: Facoltà de Magisterio dell'Università di Roma, 1953). On synonymy in *Celestina*, see Samonà, 41-57, 134-62.

[18] See Samonà, passim.

[19] Antonio de Guevara, *Menosprecio de corte y alabanza de aldea; Arte de marear*, ed. Asunción Rallo (Madrid: Cátedra, 1984), 133, 182.

There was a time when Guevara was thought to have been an influence on the highly wrought style of John Lyly in his *Euphues* of 1578. This was the argument of Landmann in 1882;[20] an argument which has steadily been losing ground ever since. English studies nowadays hardly ever mention Guevara as the source of Euphuism; he is occasionally listed as one source among many.[21]

This to me is an indication of the closing of the minds of students of English to any literature other than their own. There is a very strong case to made for the influence of Guevara on any contemporary stylist. His works were widely translated, sometimes issued in bilingual editions for the student of Spanish.[22] And in any case knowledge of Spanish among educated Britons was greater then than it is now.

In a classic article of 1950 on "La lengua en tiempos de los Reyes Católicos" Menéndez Pidal memorably dubbed the development of Spanish prose style "Del retoricismo al humanismo".[23] His thesis contrasted the over rhetorical prose style of writers such as Juan de Mena in the fifteenth century with the more natural, simpler ("natural" and "simple" being his words), more moderate style of sixteenth-century authors unnamed; *Celestina* representing a half-way house (15). (We might note in passing his use of "rhetoric" in a pejorative sense; after all, all writing is rhetorical.) He makes no mention of Guevara, an author typified even by broad contemporaries as uncontrolled in his use of certain rhetorical figures. This was the opinion of George Puttenham:

> Isocrates the Greek Oratour was a litle too full of this figure [antithesis], & so was the Spaniard that wrote the life of Marcus Aurelius, & many of our moderne writers in vulgar, use it in excesse & incurre the vice of fond affectation: otherwise the figure is very commendable.[24]

---

[20] Friedrich Landmann, *Der Euphuismus, sein Wesen, seine Quelle, seine Geschichte* (Giessen, 1881).

[21] There is for example no mention of him in Janel Mueller, *The Native Tongue and the Word: Developments in English Prose Style 1380-1580* (Chicago: University of Chicago, 1984) or Sylvia Adamson, "Synonymia: or, in Other Words," in *Renaissance Figures of Speech*, ed. Sylvia Adamson, Gavin Alexander and Katrin Ettenhuber (Cambridge: Cambridge University Press, 2007), 16-35, 253-55.

[22] See Barry Taylor, "Éditions bilingues de textes espagnols," *Opera romanica* 11 (České Budějovice), in press.

[23] *Cuadernos Hispanoamericanos* 13 (1950): 9-24.

[24] George Puttenham, *The Art of English Poesie*, ed. Gladys Doidge Willcock and Alice Walker (Cambridge: University Press, 1936), 211, cited by Eduard Norden,

What were Guevara's stylistic sources? Like most authors, Guevara had more than one style. A great deal of work on Guevara is concerned with this question. Eduard Norden in 1898 gave him a fair amount of attention: indeed, his position at the end of *Die antike Kunstprosa* casts Guevara as the culmination of a tradition of artistic prose stretching back to early Antiquity. Norden has comparatively little to say of the Middle Ages, and it was not until 1965 that Lida argued that Guevara was to be seen as *retardataire*, modelling himself on Isidore and Ildefonsus.

More recently, López Grigera has challenged this view by arguing that Guevara in fact is following Hermogenes (only known in the Latin West from 1420 thanks to George of Trebizond), and should therefore be seen as a Renaissance man; indeed, this knowledge would place him at the cutting edge of the revival of learning.[25] Lázaro Carreter in 1988 identified Guevara's style as Ciceronian *concinnitas*, a source rather less *recherché*.[26] On *concinnitas* the locus classicus is Cicero, *Orator* 12.38:

> Datur etiam venia concinnitati sententiarum et arguti certique et circumscripti verborum ambitus conceduntur, de industriaque non ex insidiis sed aperte ac palam elaboratur, ut verba verbis quasi demensa et paria respondeant, ut crebro conferantur pugnantia comparenturque contraria et ut pariter extrema terminentur eundemque referant in cadendo sonum; quae in veritate causarum et rarius multo facimus et certe occultius. [The epideictic style likewise indulges in a neatness and symmetry of sentences, and is allowed to use well defined and rounded periods; the ornamentation is done of set purpose, with no attempt at concealment, but openly and avowedly, so that words correspond to words as if measured off in equal phrases, frequently things inconsistent are placed side by side, and things contrasted are paired; clauses are made to end in the same way and with similar sound. But in actual legal practice we do this less frequently and certainly less obviously.][27]

La prosa d'arte antica dal VI secolo a.C. all'età della Rinascita (Roma: Salerno, 1986), 798 [German original 1898].

[25] Luisa López Grigera, "Algunas precisiones sobre el estilo de Antonio de Guevara," *Studia Hispanica in honorem Rafael Lapesa*, 3 vols (Madrid: Gredos, 1960-63), III, 299-315; "Los estilos de Guevara en las corrientes retóricas de su época," in her *La retórica en la España del Siglo de Oro* (Salamanca: Universidad, 1994), 107-20.

[26] Fernando Lázaro Carreter, "La prosa de fray Antonio de Guevara," in *Literatura en la época del Emperador* (Salamanca: Universidad, 1988), 101-17.

[27] Cicero, *Brutus and Orator*, tr. G. L. Henderson ad H. M. Hubbell, Loeb Classical Library (London: Heinemann, 1939), 332-33; see J. König, "Concinnitas," in *Historisches Wörterbuch der Rhetorik* (Darmstadt: Wissenschaftliche Buchgesellschaft, 1982-), II, cols 317-35.

Cicero's definition does indeed sound like Guevara, but his practice is clearly different. I think it is clear from these examples that Guevara bears a much closer affinity to the Visigothic saints than to Cicero or to the Greek rhetoricians mediated by Trapezuntius. Quite simply, Guevara is too extreme to be Ciceronian. When Puttenham recommends *concinnitas* ("parison or the figure of even") he warns: "in prose there should not be used at once of such even clauses past three or foure at the most".[28]

There was no explicit prohibition in classical rhetoric of multiple members, but we may note the supremacy granted to the number three by the pseudo-Ciceronian *Rhetorica ad Herennium*:

> Membrum orationis appellatur res breviter absoluta sine totius sententiae demonstratione, quae denuo alio membro orationis excipitur, hoc pacto: "Et inimico proderas". Id est unum quod appellamus membrum; deinde hoc excipiatur oportet altero: "Et amicum laedebas". Ex duobus membris haec exornatio potest constare, sed commodissima et absolutissima est quae ex tribus constat, hoc pacto: "Et inimico proderas et amicum laedebas et tibi non consulebas". Item: "Nec rei publicae consuluisti nec amicis profuisti nec inimicis resististi".
> [Colon or Clause is the name given to a sentence member, brief and complete, which does not express the entire thought, but is in turn supplemented by another colon, as follows: "On the one hand you were helping your enemy". That is one so-called colon; it ought then to be supplemented by a second: "And on the other you were hurting your friend". This figure can consist of two cola, but it is neatest and most complete when composed of three, as follows: "You were helping your enemy, you were hurting your friend, and you were not consulting your own best interests". Again: "You have not consulted the welfare of the republic, nor have you helped your friends, nor have you resisted your enemies".][29]

We might distinguish the Isidorian style from the Ciceronian by saying that both strive for copia, but where Cicero aims for closure at the end of the period, Isidore's structures are infinitely extendible. Or put another way, Ciceronian periodicity is to be contrasted with Guevara's schematics. ("schematics" indicating sentences that combine parataxis with a lack of interest in conclusion.)[30]

---

[28] George Puttenham, *The Art of English Poesie*, 214.
[29] *Ad C. Herennium de ratione dicendi*, with an English translation by Harry Caplan, Loeb Classical Library (London: Heinemann, 1954), IV, xix, pp. 294-95.
[30] See for example John Lyly, *Euphues: The Anatomy of Wit & His England,* ed. Morris William Croll and Harry Clemons (London: Routledge, 1916), xxxiii-lxiv.

The sixteenth century in Spain saw a revival in interest in the Visigothic past, as witnessed by a number of publications from the 1540s onwards (admittedly after Guevara's death in 1545).[31] I believe that we can relate Guevara to sixteenth-century Spanish interest in the Gothic inheritance, and that this context therefore strengthens the case that his source was more likely Isidore than Hermogenes or Cicero. The publishing history of Isidore's *Synonyma* and Ildefonsus's *De virginitate* bears witness to an interest at European level in these authors: "L'histoire des éditions témoigne aussi des vicissitudes de la fortune des *Synonyma*, très lus dans la première moitié du XVIe s. et ensuite victimes d'un oubli presque total: ils furent édités 21 fois jusqu'à 1566 […] mais à partir de 1580, ils furent publiés seulement parmi les oeuvres complètes d'Isidore".[32] Post-medieval manuscripts of these works do of course exist, but scholars have understandably paid minimal attention to these *recentiores*.[33] In England in the 1560s, Thomas Tallis set to music the text of the *Synonyma*.[34]

The contrast between the Visigoths and Cicero seems to have played no part in the Spanish debate on Ciceronianism and Anti-Ciceronianism. Although there were anti-Ciceronians in Spain as elsewhere, the models they proposed as alternatives to Cicero were not medieval Christian authors but the laconic Silver Age Seneca and Tacitus.[35] Nor could anyone hold up the Visigoths as examples of Christian *sermo humilis*.

In conclusion, the influence of the synonymous style of Isidore and Ildefonsus on Martínez de Toledo, translator of Ildefonsus, needs little argument. I believe with Lida that the source of Guevara's mannered style

---

[31] Barry Taylor, "Gothic Revival: The 1599 *Opera* of St Isidore," in *Manuscripts, Texts and Transmission from Isidore to the Enlightenment: Papers from the Bristol Colloquium on Hispanic Texts and Manuscripts*, ed. David Hook (Bristol: HiPlam, 2006), 131-46.

[32] Jacques Elfassi and Dominique Poirel, "Isidorus Hispalensis Ep". See also Jacques Elfassi, "La Réception des *Synonyma* d'Isidore de Séville aux XIVe-XVIe siècles: les raisons d'un succès exceptionnel," *Cahiers de Recherches Médiévales* 16 (2008): 107-18.

[33] Jacques Elfassi, "Les *Synonyma* d'Isidore de Séville; un livre de sagesse? Aperçu de la réception médiévale, moderne et contemporaine de l'oeuvre," in *Le Livre de sagesse: supports, médiations, usages. Acte du colloque de Metz (13-15 septembre 2006)*, ed. Nicolas Brucker (Bonn, etc.: Peter Lang, 2008), 11-26, notes some manuscripts of the *Synonyma* from the seventeenth and eighteenth centuries.

[34] Kerry McCarthy, "Tallis, Isidore of Seville and *Suscipe quaeso*," *Early Music* 35 (2007): 447-50.

[35] Juan María Núñez González, *El ciceronianismo en España* (Valladolid: Universidad de Valladolid, 1993).

lies with the Visigoths. Although the Visigoths were never held up explicitly as models, I think they can be seen as contributing to the mannered Guevaran style which thanks to Guevara and Lyly in the original and in translation, held sway in Europe, for good or evil, for half a century.

San Juan de la Cruz and the Fathers of the Church: Song 1. 3 in the *Cántico espiritual*

Terence O'Reilly
(University College Cork)

Our understanding of San Juan's debt to the Fathers of the Church has been deepened in recent years by a number of studies of his exegesis of biblical texts, in particular the Song of Songs. These have shown that his prose commentary on the *Cántico espiritual*, which he composed in the early 1580s, was modelled in its format and methodology on Latin commentaries on the Song, a genre, established by the Fathers, that flourished throughout the Middle Ages, and continued into his own time.[1] The subject, however, requires more detailed study, as Cristóbal Cuevas has observed: "El día en que se estudie en detalle la influencia de la exégesis bíblica en la técnica glosatoria de nuestro místico, tal como la aplica en sus comentarios, se habrá dado [...] un paso muy importante en la comprensión de sus mismas peculiaridades literarias".[2] Two questions,

---

[1] Henri de Lubac, SJ, *Exégèse mediévale: Les quatre sens de l'Écriture*, 2 vols (Paris: Aubier, 1959-1964), II, 498-505; Manuel Diego Sánchez, "La herencia patrística de San Juan de la Cruz," in *Experiencia y pensamiento en San Juan de la Cruz*, ed. Federico Ruiz (Madrid: Editorial de Espiritualidad, 1990), 83-111; Denys Turner, *Eros and Allegory: Medieval Exegesis of the Song of Songs* (Kalamazoo, MI, and Spencer, MA: Cistercian Publications, 1995), 175-214; Colin Thompson, *St John of the Cross: Songs in the Night* (London: SPCK, 2002), 155-86; *San Juan de la Cruz: Cántico espiritual y poesía completa*, ed. Paola Elia and María Jesús Mancho (Barcelona: Crítica, 2002), xxxix-liv. On the origins and development of the *Cántico espiritual*, see Eulogio Pacho, *San Juan de la Cruz: Historia de sus escritos* (Burgos: Monte Carmelo, 1998).

[2] "The day one studies in detail the influence of biblical exegesis on the glossing technique of our mystic, as it is applied in his commentaries, one will have taken a most important step forward in the understanding of his specific characteristics as a writer", Cristóbal Cuevas, "Estudio literario," in *Introducción a la lectura de San Juan de la Cruz*, ed. Salvador Ros García and others (Salamanca: Junta de Castilla

in particular, remain to be asked. First: in what ways was San Juan influenced in his exegesis of the Song by the renewal of patristic studies in the sixteenth century? And second: to what extent was he aware of commentaries on the Song by sixteenth-century authors who developed the patristic tradition in new ways? The purpose of this essay is to seek an answer to these questions in San Juan's exegesis of a verse of the Song that he cites on two occasions in the *Cántico*: "trahe me post te curremus" (Song 1. 3).[3]

1. The Fathers in the Sixteenth Century

In its fourth session, in April 1546, the Council of Trent noted that the Latin translation of the Bible known as the Vulgate, which dated from patristic times, had been "tested in the Church by long use over many centuries", and it decreed that it should, accordingly, "be kept as the authentic text in public readings, debates, sermons and explanations".[4] No one, it added, should interpret Scripture "in opposition to the meaning which has been and is held by holy mother church", nor should any interpretation of it run counter to "the unanimous consent of the Fathers" ("contra unanimem consensum patrum"). The Council's decree explains the tendency among religious writers of San Juan's time to support their teachings by citing the Church Fathers, a tendency justified by the Dominican theologian Melchor Cano in his influential work, *De locis theologicis*, which shaped Catholic theological studies in the period after Trent:

> In expositione sacrarum literarum communis omnium sanctorum veterum intelligentia certissimum argumentum Theologo praestat ad Theologicas

---

y León, 1991), 160. The same point is made by Thompson, 167: "The centrality of the Bible to San Juan is beyond question. But little attention has been paid to his exegetical techniques, or to the literary qualities of his interpretations".

[3] References to the *Cántico* are to the first recension of the work (*Cántico A*): see *San Juan de la Cruz: Cántico espiritual. Primera redacción y texto retocado*, ed. Eulogio Pacho (Madrid: Fundación Universitaria Española, 1981). References to the Vulgate version of the Song of Songs are to *Biblia sacra iuxta latinam vulgatam versionem: libri Salomonis* (Rome: Vatican, 1957), 175-97.

[4] "ut nemo [...] contra eum sensum, quem tenuit et tenet sancta mater ecclesia [...] aut etiam contra unanimem consensum patrum ipsam scripturam sacram interpretari audeat". *Decrees of the Ecumenical Councils*, ed. Norman P. Tanner, SJ, 2 vols (London: Sheed and Ward; Washington: Georgetown University Press, 1990), II, 664.

assertiones corroborandas. Quippe cum sanctorum omnium sensus Spiritus sancti sensus ipse sit.[5]

Nicolás Doria, San Juan's Carmelite contemporary and eventual foe, promoted the practice, advising that half of every sermon should consist in *autoridades* (que "la mitad del sermón sea autorizada por Doctores y dichos de Santos"), but San Juan himself appears to have thought differently: in his writings, explicit references to the Fathers are rare.[6] In their substance, however, they reveal a profound understanding of patristic exegesis, as Henri de Lubac showed.[7] This is true, especially, of his approach to the Song of Songs.

In the early sixteenth century, one of the commentaries on the Song best known in Europe was by a Spanish author, Jaime Pérez de Valencia, a hermit of Saint Augustine who taught canon law and theology in Valencia. His *Expositio in cantica canticorum* was first published in 1486, and it went through twenty-two editions between then and 1541, the year before San Juan was born.[8] His reading of the biblical poem follows the line established a century earlier by Nicholas of Lyra. Within it he finds two levels of meaning, one historical, the other prophetic. In the literal sense of the text, as he sees it, King Solomon, the author, uses the imagery of human love to recount the history of Israel, from the time of Adam to the prosperity of his own reign. But this historical account is, in the spiritual

---

[5] "In the exposition of the Sacred Scriptures, the unanimous interpretation of all the holy Fathers offers to the theologian a most secure argument in confirmation of theological statements. And this is so because the unanimous judgement of the saints is the judgement of the Holy Spirit himself". Melchor Cano, *De locis theologicis libri duodecim* (Salamanca: Matías Gastio, 1563), book VII, chapter 3, translated into Spanish in Melchor Cano, *De locis theologicis*, ed. Juan Belda Plans (Madrid: Biblioteca de Autores Cristianos, 2006), 428. The Latin text of the first edition is available online at www.bac-editorial.com.

[6] Diego Sánchez, 83-84. On the reception of the Fathers before and after the Council, see Ralph Keen, "The Fathers in Counter-Reformation Theology in the Pre-Tridentine Period," in *The Reception of the Church Fathers in the West from the Carolingians to the Maurists*, ed. Irena Backus, 2 vols (Boston: Brill, 2001), II, 701-43 (735-37).

[7] De Lubac, II, 500-05.

[8] Jaime Pérez de Valencia, *Expositio in cantica canticorum* (Valencia: Lambertus Palmart, 1486). The printing history of the work is traced in Max Engammare, *Qu'il me baise des baisers de sa bouche. Le Cantique des Cantiques à la Renaissance. Étude et bibliographie* (Geneva: Droz, 1993), *164. See also Nigel Griffin, "Spanish Incunabula in the John Rylands University Library of Manchester," *Bulletin of the John Rylands University Library of Manchester* 70 (1988): 5-141 (48-54).

sense, prophetic: it traces allegorically the history of the Church, from its beginnings in the New Testament to its triumph after the conversion of Constantine.[9]

The exegesis of the Song popular in Spain a hundred years later could not be more different. During the 1570s and 1580s, the decades in which San Juan composed the poetry and prose of the *Cántico*, several new Latin commentaries by Spanish writers appeared in print (see Table 1):[10]

Table 1

Tomás de Villanueva, *Commentarii in Cantica Canticorum,* in *Conciones sacrae* (Alcalá de Henares: Ioannes a Lequerica excudebat, 1572).
Cosme Damián de Hortolá, *Paraphrasis in Canticum Canticorum* (Barcelona: Jacobus Cendras, 1579).
Luis de León, *In Cantica Canticorum Salomonis explanatio* (Salamanca: excudebat Lucas à Iunta, 1580).
Alonso de Orozco, *Commentaria quaedam in Cantica Canticorum* (Burgos: apud Philippum Iuntam, 1581).
Cipriano de la Huerga, *Commentaria in [...] Cantica Canticorum Salomonis* (Alcalá de Henares: ex officina Iñiguez à Lequerica, 1582).
Jerónimo de Almonacir, *Commentaria in Canticum Canticorum Salomonis* (Alcalá: Ioannes à Lequerica excudebat, 1588).
Luis de León, *In Canticum Canticorum triplex explanatio* (Salamanca: apud Guillelmum Foquel, 1589).

---

[9] De Lubac, II, 366-67 (n. 5); Engammare, 59-60.

[10] See Klaus Reinhardt, *Bibelkommentare spanischer Autoren (1500-1700)*, 2 vols (Madrid: CSIC, 1990-99).

In these the Song is interpreted, primarily, not as a coded guide to salvation history, but as a record of the intimate relations between Christ and the Church or the individual soul. The historical and prophetic senses give way to others that are moral and mystical. This is how San Juan interprets the Song himself in the *Cántico espiritual*. In the prologue, addressed to Ana de Jesús, he writes of the mystical images in his poem:

> Las quales semejanças, no leýdas con la sencillez del espíritu de amor e inteligencia que ellas lleuan, antes parecen dislates que dichos puestos en raçón, según es de uer en los diuinos Cantares de Salomón y en otros libros de la Escriptura diuina, donde, no pudiendo el Espíritu Sancto dar a entender la abundancia de su sentido por términos vulgares y usados, habla mysterios en estrañas figuras y semejanças. De donde se sigue que los sanctos doctores, aunque mucho dicen y más digan, nunca pueden acabar de declararlo por palabras, así como tampoco por palabras se pudo ello decir; y así, lo que de ello se declara, ordinariamente es lo menos que contiene en sí.[11]

The biblical poem, he indicates, is a sacred text, inspired by the Holy Spirit, who uses the language of human love ("términos vulgares y usados") to convey a meaning that is mystical. This meaning, however, is so abundant that the comparison with human love breaks down, producing images puzzling to reason ("estrañas figuras y semejanças") that can only be interpreted faithfully when read in a contemplative mode ("con la sencillez del espíritu de amor e inteligencia"). The principles of exegesis implicit here (as de Lubac, Diego Sánchez and Turner have remarked) recall the Alexandrian reading of the Song, initiated in the third century by Origen, which was preserved and transmitted in the West by a succession of influential writers, including Cassian, Gregory the Great, Bede, Bernard of Clairvaux, and the authors of the *Glossa ordinaria*. In the late Middle

---

[11] *Cántico espiritual*, p. 578: "These similitudes, if not read with the simplicity of the spirit of love and understanding that they convey, seem to be nonsense rather than expressions of a reasoned kind, as may be seen in the divine *Songs* of Solomon and in other books of Sacred Scripture, where the Holy Spirit, being unable to express the abundance of his meaning in everyday and long-used terms, utters mysteries in strange figures and similitudes. From which it follows that the holy doctors, however much they say or might say, can never fully expound it [his meaning] in words, any more than words sufficed to express it; and thus what is expounded of it is normally the least part of what it contains in itself".

Ages, when the interpretation of Nicholas of Lyra held sway, the tradition was maintained by Denis the Carthusian.[12]

Origen's homilies on the Song, in the Latin version of St Jerome, and his commentary, translated into Latin by Rufinus, were printed for the first time *c.* 1468, when three editions appeared in Italy (Rome) and France (Argenteuil), and they were republished a further eighteen times between then and 1512, when the first edition of Origen's *Opera*, edited by Jacques Merlin, was printed in Paris. A quarter of a century later they were included in the great edition of Origen's works prepared by Erasmus, which appeared shortly after his death, in 1536.[13] Erasmus revered Origen, and laboured to make his works better known, seeing in them a first flowering of the *philosophia Christi* by which the troubled Church of his time could be healed. In the *Ratio verae theologiae*, of 1518, he described Origen as, "in tractandis allegoriis felicissimus artifex", and he affirmed, "sic est primus ut nemo cum illo conferri possit".[14] Later in the *Ecclesiastes*, published in 1535, he judged him to be, "in Scripturarum expositione nulli secundus", and in the same work, following Origen, he evoked the mysterious depths of Scripture, in terms with which San Juan would have concurred:

> Tanta est, tamque inexhausta Scripturarum opulentia, in mysteriis recondita, ut nunquam defuerit neque defuturum sit, quod rimetur eruatque studiosorum pia sedulitas, semper inconcussis fidei catholicae dogmatibus.[15]

The recovery of the patristic tradition, which Erasmus and his fellow humanists pioneered, made available to sixteenth-century readers a wide

---

[12] De Lubac, II, 504; Diego Sánchez, 90-109; Turner, 184, 192-94. On the exegesis of Denis the Carthusian, see de Lubac, II, 365-67, and Denis the Carthusian, *Selected Writings*, ed. Íde M. Ní Riain, with an introduction by Terence O'Reilly (Dublin: Four Courts, 2005), x-xii.

[13] Engammare, pp. *163-64, 90-93.

[14] Cited in de Lubac, II, 446.

[15] "The riches of the Scriptures, concealed in mysteries, are so abundant and inexhaustible, that there never will be, nor may there ever be, any deficiency in what the devout application of scholars, working with unfailing respect for the teachings of the Catholic faith, may seek out and discover". Cited in de Lubac, II, 450.

range of commentaries on the *Song*, which Max Engammare has recorded (see Table 2):[16]

Table 2

Ambrose of Milan: 17 editions, 1492-1586. Gregory the Great: 25 editions, 1473-1588. Gregory of Nyssa: 1571, 1573. Origen: 71 editions, *c.* 1468-1586. Philo of Carpasia: 1537, 1570, 1579, 1589. Theodoret of Cyrrhus: 4 editions, 1563-1573. Alan of Lille: 1514. Anselm of Laon: 1573. Apponius: 1538, 1589. Bede: 1536, 1545, 1563. Bernard: 56 editions, 1481-1596. Denis the Carthusian: 12 editions, 1533-1555. Gilbert of Hoyland: 13 editions, 1485-1547. Haymo of Auxerre: 7 editions, 1508-1592. Henry Herp: 6 editions, 1538-1587. Honorius of Autun: 1490. Hugh of Saint-Cher: 4 editions, 1498-1600. Hugh of St Victor: 1526. Richard of St Victor: 5 editions, 1506-1592. Rupert of Deutz: 9 editions, 1526-1577. Giles of Rome: 7 editions, 1505-1587.

The interpretations of the *Song* proposed by the two Western Fathers, Ambrose and Gregory, were printed often, but the most popular patristic commentator was Origen, whose homilies and commentary went through seventy-one editions between 1468 and 1586. The Greek tradition was known also through the exegesis of Gregory of Nyssa, Theodoret of Cyrrhus, and Philo of Carpasia. Most of the texts printed, however, were not patristic but medieval, and of these the larger part were by monastic authors of the sixth to the ninth centuries. Later monastic works selected

---

[16] See the "Répertoire bibliographique des auteurs des éditions du texte et des commentateurs du Cantique des Cantiques au XVᵉ et XVIᵉ siècles," in Engammare, *1-*775, and in particular the "Index des auteurs," *159-*165.

for printing included those of Rupert of Deutz, Bernard of Clairvaux, and Bernard's continuator, Gilbert of Hoyland, while the mystical tradition of the late Middle Ages was represented by the exegesis of Denis the Carthusian and Henry Herp. Texts on the Song by scholastic writers were generally ignored, with one notable exception: the commentary by the thirteenth-century Augustinian, Giles of Rome. This was published under his own name on one occasion only, in 1554, but otherwise it appeared under that of Thomas Aquinas, a point to which I shall return.[17]

2. Song 1. 3 in *Cántico* 16

San Juan's approach to the Song belongs to the Alexandrian tradition, not only in its broad sweep, but also in its finer details. In the seventeenth century Richard Simon observed: "La plupart des Pères qui ont vécu après Origène n'ont fait presque autre chose que copier ses commentaires et ses autres traités sur l'Écriture".[18] This is apparent in the case of the Song, whose initial verses acquired, through Origen's works, a series of connotations and associations on which subsequent exegetes drew. Often one commentary is distinguished from another, not by its interpretation of an image or phrase, but by the theological acumen or literary elegance with which conventional elements are articulated. San Juan's reading of individual verses of the Song reflects this. Normally, though not always, he reworks traditional motifs in his exegesis.[19] An example is his interpretation of Song 1. 3, which he cites for the first time when commenting on stanza 16 of the *Cántico*:

> A çaga de tu huella
> las jóuenes discurren al camino,
> al toque de centella,
> al adobado vino,

---

[17] Engammare, 88: "Que la plupart des commentaires édités appartiennent à l'état monastique de la seconde moitié du premier millénaire signale que les critiques portées à l'encontre de la scolastique, tant chez les réformistes de l'Église que chez les premiers Réformateurs, ont été entendues".

[18] Richard Simon, *Histoire critique du Vieux Testament* (Amsterdam: pour la Compagnie des libraires, 1685), book 3, chapter 10 (p. 403). Cited in de Lubac, I, 212.

[19] See Terence O'Reilly, "The *Cántico espiritual* of Saint John of the Cross and the Mystical Interpretation of the Song of Songs," in Terence O'Reilly, *From Ignatius Loyola to John of the Cross: Spirituality and Literature in Sixteenth-Century Spain* (Aldershot: Variorum, 1995), and Terence O'Reilly, "La figura de Aminadab en los escritos de San Juan de la Cruz," *San Juan de la Cruz* 31-32 (2003): 187-96.

emisiones de bálsamo diuino.

San Juan composed this stanza during his months of solitary confinement in Toledo, when he was dependent on his memory for the text of the Song, and it is likely that Chapter 1. 3 was one of the verses that he had in mind when doing so.[20] In his prose commentary, written in the years that followed, he cites the Song verse explicitly, when reflecting on the second line, "las jóuenes discurren al camino":

> Es a saber: las almas deuotas, con fuerças de juuentud recebidas de la suauidad de tu huella, discurren, esto es, corren por muchas partes y de muchas maneras (que eso quiere decir discurrir) cada vna por la parte y suerte que Dios la da de espíritu y estado, con muchas diferencias de exercicios y obras espirituales, al camino de la vida eterna, que es la perfectión euangélica, por la cual encuentran con el Amado en vnión de amor después de la desnudez de espíritu y de todas las cosas. Esta suauidad y rastro que Dios deja de sí en el alma, grandemente la aligera y hace correr tras de Él; porque entonces el alma muy poco o nada es lo que trabaja de su parte para andar este camino; antes es mouida y atraída de esta diuina huella de Dios, no sólo a que salga, sino a que corra de muchas maneras, como auemos dicho, al camino. Que por eso la Esposa en los Cantares pidió al Esposo esta diuina atractión, diciendo: *Trahe me: post te curremus in odorem unguentorum tuorum*, esto es: Atráeme tras de ti, y correremos al olor de tus ungüentos.[21]

---

[20] See *Cántico espiritual. Primera redacción*, ed. Pacho, 594-95; José L. Morales, *El Cántico espiritual de San Juan de la Cruz: su relación con el Cantar de los Cantares y otras fuentes escriturísticas y literarias* (Madrid: Editorial de Espiritualidad, 1971), 164-65.

[21] *Cántico espiritual*, 784: "In other words, the souls that are devout, with the youthful energy received from the sweetness of your scent, *discurren*, that is, *they run* in many directions and in many ways, for such is the meaning of *discurrir*, each one in the direction, and in the manner, of the spirit and state of life given by God, with a great variety of spiritual exercises and works, *to the path* of eternal life, which is evangelical perfection, where they meet the Beloved in a union of love, after attaining nakedness of spirit and of all things. This fragrance and trace that God leaves behind him in the soul greatly lightens her step and makes her run after him; for then the soul, for its part, strives little or not at all to tread this path; instead it is moved and attracted by this divine fragrance of God not only to go forth but to run in many ways (as we have said) to the path. Hence the Bride in the *Song* asked the Bridegroom for this divine attraction, saying: *Trahe me: post te curremus in odorem unguentorum tuorum*, that is: Draw me after you, and we will run to the fragrance of your oils".

At no point here does San Juan allude to the Fathers, but in his remarks a number of traditional elements of exegesis are adapted and developed. First among them is the image of the attractive scent of God which enables the soul to run after Him with effortless ease: "Esta suauidad y rastro que Dios deja de sí en el alma, grandemente la aligera y hace correr tras de Él". The comparison, implicit here, between divine beauty and a "trace" or "fragrance" is found in Origen, who wrote: "odoratum sponsae et adulescentularum, quo odoratae sunt *odorem unguentorum* sponsi, non corporis sensus, sed divini odoris illius et interioris qui appellatur hominis dici".[22] Subsequent commentators developed the theme. Gregory the Great observed: "Habet hic sancta ecclesia aromata [...] sed longe excellentior est illa unctio contemplationis dei, ad quam quandoque ducendi sumus",[23] and St Bernard, in his sermons on the Song, affirmed: "Currimus cum internis consolationibus et inspirationibus visitasti, tamquam in suaveolentibus unguentis respiramus".[24]

Second, there is the image of the young women, "las jóuenes". These, San Juan remarks, are devout souls, whose youth has been renewed by the Bridegroom's fragrance: "las jóuenes [...] es a saber: las almas deuotas, con fuerças de juuentud recebidas de la suauidad de tu huella". The image goes back to Origen, who interpreted the maidens in Song 1. 2 (Vulgate: "adulescentulae") as, "adulescentulae in augmento scilicet aetatis et pulchritudinis positae animae, quae semper innovantur et de die in diem renovantur, novum se induentes hominem, qui secundum Deum creatus

---

[22] Origen, *Commentarium in cantica canticorum*, trans. Rufinus of Aquilea, ed. W. A. Baehrens, in *Origenes Werke*, vol. VIII (Leipzig, 1923), 105-06; *The Song of Songs: Commentary and Homilies*, trans. and annotated by R. P. Lawson (London: Longmans, Green and Co., 1957), 80: "the sense of smell by which the bride and the maidens perceived the fragrance of the Bridegroom's ointments, denotes not a bodily faculty, but that divine sense of scent which is called the sense of the interior man". On patristic readings of Song 1. 3, see the detailed study by Pietro Meloni, *Il profumo dell'immortalità: L'interpretazione patristica di Cantico 1, 3* (Rome: Studium, 1975).

[23] Gregory the Great, *Commentaire sur le Cantique des Cantiques*, ed. Rodrigue Bélanger (Paris: Cerf, 1984), 100-01: "Holy Church possesses perfumes here below [...]. But far more excellent is that perfumed oil of the contemplation of God, to which one day we shall be led".

[24] St Bernard, Sermon 21:11, in *Sermones sobre el Cantar de los Cantares*, trans. Iñaki Aranguren (Madrid: Biblioteca de Autores Cristianos, 1987), 302-03: "We run when you visit us with interior consolations and inspirations, thus inhaling, as it were, the delicious odour of (the Bridegroom's) ointments".

est".[25] His interpretation became part of the tradition. St Ambrose asked, in the fourth century: "Quae sunt istae adolescentulae nisi animae singulorum, quae deposuerunt istius corporis senectutem, renovatae per Spiritum sanctum?".[26] Later, St Gregory the Great applied it to the Christian churches: "adolescentulae uocantur, non iam uetustate per culpam, sed nouellae per gratiam; non senio steriles, sed aetate mentis ad spiritalem congruae fecunditatem".[27] His reading was cited by Bede, and disseminated in the later Middle Ages in the *Glossa ordinaria*.[28]

Third, there is the image of the "camino". San Juan explains that the path on which the maidens run is the way of evangelical perfection. It leads to eternal life, and culminates in union with the Beloved, once everything else has been left behind: "corren [...] al camino de la vida eterna, que es la perfectión euangélica, por la cual encuentran con el Amado en vnión de amor después de la desnudez de espíritu y de todas las cosas". Origen, similarly, pictures the maidens catching up with the spouse and becoming one with him in love: "Ego puto quod [...] iam non ambulent neque currant, sed vinculis quibusdam caritatis eius adstrictae adhaereant ei nec ultra mobilitatis alicuius ullus in iis resideat locus, sed sint cum eo unus spiritus".[29] Gregory the Great, in turn, sees the chase as a figure of the soul's longing for the divine vision: "In odorem unguentorum dei currimus, cum donis eius spiritalibus afflati, in amore visionis eius

---

[25] Origen, *Commentarium*, 101-02; *Commentary*, 75: "Young souls growing up in years and beauty, who are always being made new and renewed from day to day, as they put on the new man, created according to God".

[26] Ambrose of Milan, *De Sacramentis*, Book 5:2, cited in *Patrologia Latina*, CXV, col. 1856: "Who are these young women, if not individual souls who have put off the old age of this body, renewed by the Holy Spirit?".

[27] Gregory the Great, *Moralia in Iob*, Book 19:12, ed. M. Adriaen, Corpus Christianorum Series Latina, CXLIII, 2 vols (Turnhout: Brepols, 1979), II, 970: "They are called maidens, no longer old through sin, but new through grace; not sterile in extreme old age, but of the age of mind consonant with spiritual fruitfulness".

[28] Bede, *In cantica canticorum*, ed. D. Hurst, OSB, Corpus Christianorum Series Latina, CXIXb (Turnhout: Brepols, 1983), 374 (Book VI, lines 594-97); *Glossa ordinaria: In canticum canticorum*, ed. Mary Dove, Corpus Christianorum Continuatio Medievalis, CLXX (Turnhout: Brepols, 1997), 88-9.

[29] Origen, *Commentarium*, p. 103; *Commentary*, p. 77: " I think [...] they would no longer walk or run, but bound, as it were, by the bands of love, they would cleave to him, and would have no further power ever to move again, but would be one spirit with him".

inhiamus".[30] Bernard writes of the Bride as leaving all things in order to hasten after her beloved: "Sic itaque et dilecta tua, relictis omnibus propter te, concupiscit semper ire post te, semper tuis inhaerere vestigiis".[31] And for Denis the Carthusian, her words express the soul's passionate longing for union, in complete poverty of spirit: *"Trahe me post te*: id est, da mihi lucem et gratiam contemplationis tam altae, et tantum sanctae caritatis ardorem, ut cuncta creata trascendam, et tibi soli inhaeream".[32]

3. Giles of Rome

In ways such as these, San Juan draws on, and adapts, longstanding traditions of exegesis. But in two respects his interpretation of the biblical image is unusual. First, there is his description of how the young girls run in different directions, and in different ways: "discurren, esto es, corren por muchas partes y de muchas maneras (que eso quiere decir discurrir) cada vna por la parte y suerte que Dios la da de espíritu y estado, con muchas diferencias de exercicios y obras espirituales, al camino de la vida eterna". Here he exploits the Latin root and overtones of the verb *discurrir* to underline that the response to the divine attraction varies according to a person's calling and gifts.[33] His teaching may be found in embryo in the commentary of Origen, who returns to the image of the running maidens when considering the next line in the Song, "introduxit me rex in cubiculum suum". There he pictures them following the spouse at different speeds, depending on the strength of each one: "Currunt ergo adulescentulae post ipsum et in odorem eius, unaquaeque tamen pro viribus, alia quidem velocius, alia paulo tardius, alia etiam inferius ceteris

---

[30] Gregory the Great, *Commentaire*, 106-07: "We run after the scents of the fragrance of God when, inspired by his spiritual gifts, we are left filled with loving desire to behold him".

[31] Bernard, Sermon 21:3, in *Sermones sobre el Cantar de los Cantares*, 294-95: "In this way, then, your beloved, having left all things for you, desires to follow you always, to always walk in your footsteps".

[32] Denis the Carthusian, *Enarratio in canticum canticorum Salomonis*, in *Opera omnia*, vol. VII (Montreuil: Typis Cartusiae Sanctae Mariae de Pratis, 1898), 315: *"Draw me after you*: that is, grant me the light and the grace of a contemplation so exalted, and grant me so much fervour of holy love, that I may surmount all things, and cleave to you alone".

[33] Eulogio Pacho, "Glosas al léxico sanjuanista," in *Estudios sanjuanistas*, vol. I (Burgos: Monte Carmelo, 1997), 796-97; *Cántico espiritual. Primera redacción*, ed. Pacho, 594, n. 23.

et ultimo aliquo in loco".[34] Despite the authority of Origen, this aspect of his exegesis does not normally recur in subsequent commentaries on Song 1. 3. It is given prominence, however, by Giles of Rome, who asks why the Bride speaks of herself initially in the singular ("trahe me"), and then switches to the plural ("curremus"). His answer is that God draws all things to himself in the same way, but that his drawing is experienced differently according to the receiver:

> Deus quantum est de se, uno modo trahit [...] non tamen trahimur uno modo: quia licet Deus uno modo se habeat ad omnia, non tamen se habent omnia uniformiter ad ipsum, quia eadem influentia diversimode recipitur in creaturis.[35]

The second unusual feature in San Juan's remarks has to do with how he formulates the soul's dependence on God that the *Song* verse emphasizes:

> entonces el alma muy poco o nada es lo que trabaja de su parte para andar este camino; antes es mouida y atraída de esta diuina huella de Dios, no sólo a que salga, sino a que corra de muchas maneras, como auemos dicho, al camino.

The notion of divine power at work in human weakness was associated with Song 1. 3 from the Fathers onwards. Ambrose, for instance, writes: "Habemus [...] cupiditatem sequendi, quam unguentorum tuorum inspirat gratia, sed quia cursus tuos aequare non possumus, *attrahe nos*, ut auxilio tuo fultae vestigiis tuis possimus insistere".[36] The theme recurs

---

[34] Origen, *Commentarium*, 109-10; *Commentary*, 86: "The maidens, then, run after him and into his fragrance, each of them according to her powers, one faster, one somewhat more slowly, while another runs behind the rest, and brings up the rear".

[35] Giles of Rome, in *Salomonis cantica canticorum cum [...] commentariis divi Thomae Aquinatis* (Paris: apud Bartholomaeum Macaeum, 1587), fol. 199v: "God, considered as he is in himself, draws in one way [...], but we are not all drawn in one way, because although there is one way in which God relates to everything, there is not one way in which everything relates to God, for the same influence is received by creatures in different ways". On Giles, see Turner, *Eros and Allegory*, 357-80. His commentary has been edited in Thomas Aquinas, *Opera omnia*, ed. Roberto Busa, SJ, 7 vols (Stuttgart: Bad Cannstatt; Fromann: Holzboog, 1980), VII, 29-43.

[36] Ambrose of Milan, *De Isaac et anima*, chapter 3, cited in *Patrologia Latina*, CXV, col. 1859: "We have [...] the desire to follow, which the grace of your perfumes inspires, but because we cannot keep pace with you, *draw us*, so that, supported by your assistance, we may press closely upon your steps".

subsequently in Bede, Haymo of Auxerre, Denis the Carthusian, and Tomás de Villanueva.[37] However, the commentary closest to the interpretation San Juan advances is, once again, Giles of Rome, who draws the same distinction between "not only moving, but running" ("no sólo a que salga, sino a que corra"):

> Non ad insipientiam dico *trahe me post te*, quia tuus tractus est suavis et validus, quia si tu me traxeris, non solum movebor qualitercumque, sed etiam curram *in odorem unguentorum tuorum*, id est, velociter movebor.[38]

These parallels raise the possibility that when writing his commentary San Juan recalled or consulted Giles. It is, indeed, plausible, that he did so, for he revered the works of Saint Thomas, to whom Giles's commentary was normally ascribed, and we know that he was familiar with other apocryphal works of Aquinas (some of which have been published by Miguel Díez González).[39]

4. *Song* 1. 3 in *Cántico* 21

The second citation of the Song verse in the *Cántico* occurs in the commentary on stanza 21:

> De flores y esmeraldas,
> en las frescas mañanas escogidas,
> haremos las guirnaldas
> en tu amor florecidas,

---

[37] Bede, *In cantica canticorum*, Book 1:3, lines 152-53 (p. 194): "precamur nobis manum dare digneris nos tuo subsidio ad te currentes adiuues"; Haymo of Auxerre (Pseudo-Cassiodorus), *Commentarium in cantica canticorum*, *Patrologia Latina*, LXX, col. 1057: "meam infirmitatem cognosco, et video me nihil meis viribus boni posse agere, tua gratia *trahe me* ad tui imitationem"; Denis the Carthusian, *Enarratio in canticum canticorum Salomonis*, p. 300: "recolens sponsum suum dixisse, *Sine me nihil potestis facere*, invocat gratiosum ejus auxilium, dicens, *Trahe me post te*"; Tomás de Villanueva, *Commentarii in cantica canticorum*, in *Conciones sacrae* (Alcalá: Ferdinandus Ramirez excudebat, 1581), fol. 120r: "non ipsa venire per me possum, sed tu trahe, sequar te, si trahis me".

[38] Giles of Rome, fol. 199v, translated in Turner, 367: "I do not say idly, *Draw me after you*, because your drawing is gentle and strong. For if you will draw me I will not move in just any fashion; rather I will run *in the fragrance of your ointments*; I will, in other words, move swiftly".

[39] Miguel A. Díez González, *Lecturas medievales de San Juan de la Cruz* (Burgos: Monte Carmelo, 1999).

y en vn cabello mío entretegidas.

The garlands woven by the Bride and her spouse, San Juan explains, are the virtues and gifts of the soul, in which the soul and God take delight. This shared delight, he continues, is an expression of their intimate cooperation, conveyed by the plural verb in line three:

> Y no dice haré yo las guirnaldas solamente, ni haráslas tú tampoco a solas, sino haremos entrambos juntos; porque las virtudes no las puede obrar el alma, ni alcançarlas a solas sin ayuda de Dios, ni tanpoco las obra Dios a solas en el alma sin ella. Porque, aunque es uerdad que *todo dado bueno y todo don perfecto sea de arriba, descendido del Padre de las lumbres*, como dice Santiago, todauía eso mesmo no se recibe sin la habilidad y ayuda del alma que lo recibe. De donde, hablando la Esposa en los Cantares con el Esposo, dijo: *Trahe me, post te curremus in odorem, etc*; que quiere decir: Tráeme, después de ti correremos. De manera que el mouimiento para el bien, de Dios a de uenir—según aquí da a entender—solamente; mas el correr, no dice que Él solo, ni ella sola, sino correremos entrambos, que es el obrar Dios y el alma juntamente.[40]

This exegesis is extremely rare in the tradition, as Eulogio Pacho has pointed out (it is, he writes, "muy singular").[41] It does not occur in the patristic and medieval commentaries I have examined, nor in the Spanish commentaries published in the 1570s and 1580s. The question therefore arises: is it original to San Juan, or did he draw it, directly or indirectly, from a writer of his time? A possible answer is indicated by the fact that a similar reading of the Song is advanced in the work of his younger contemporary, St Francis de Sales, who wrote in his *Traité de l'Amour de Dieu*:

---

[40] *Cántico espiritual*, 846: "And she does not say, 'I will make the garlands by myself', nor 'you will make them alone' either, but 'we will make them with each other together', for the soul cannot practise the virtues, nor attain them, by herself, without God's help, nor does God effect them in the soul alone and without her. For though it is true that *every good thing given, and every perfect gift, is from above, coming down from the Father of lights*, as St James says, none the less, that [gift] itself is not received without the ability and help of the soul which receives it. Hence the Bride in the Song, speaking with the Bridegroom, says: *Trahe me, post te curremus in odorem, etc*, which means: *Draw me, we shall run after you to the fragrance etc*. So that the impulse to good has to come from God (as she indicates here) alone; but the running is not attributed by her to Him alone, nor to herself alone, but 'we shall run with each other', which is God and the soul working together".

[41] *Cántico espiritual. Primera redacción*, 784-85, n. 6.

Tirez-moi, dit l'Épouse sacrée, c'est à dire, commence le premier, car je ne saurais m'éveiller de moi-même, je ne saurais me mouvoir si vous ne m'émouvez; mais quand vous m'aurez émue, alors, ô le cher Époux de mon âme, *nous courrons* nous deux![42]

The *Traité* was published in 1616, more than two years before the *Cántico* appeared in print (1618-19), and although St Francis had Discalced Carmelite contacts and friends, there is no firm evidence that he knew the writings of San Juan in manuscript.[43] The parallel, for this reason, suggests the likelihood of a common source.

To trace it we need to examine a Reformation debate that became connected with the exegesis of Song 1. 3 long before San Juan composed the *Cántico*. Luther's disagreement with Erasmus about grace and free will, which came to a head in the mid-1520s, established the issue as a bone of contention between Catholics and the Reform, and his views left their mark on his lectures on the Song, which he delivered in 1530 and 1531.[44] In line with patristic and medieval tradition, he saw in the words "Trahe me" an admission of the soul's complete dependence on grace:

Scire et posse duo sunt. Quando igitur verbum habemus, non statim possumus illud sequi, sed retrahunt a verbo caro nostra, mundus et Satan. Subiicit igitur iam orationem: Dedisti verbum, pro quo tibi gracias ago. Nunc fac, ut etiam faciamus, quae verbum docet, et sequamur id in vita nostra.

And he stressed the same theme of moral weakness in his subsequent remarks on "curremus": "Si tu afflaveris spiritu tuo, libenter agam [...]. Si non afflaveris, nihil quisquam, quantumvis magno studio et cura,

---

[42] *Traité de l'Amour de Dieu*, Book II, Chapter 13, in *Saint François de Sales: Oeuvres*, ed. André Ravier and Roger Devos (Paris: Gallimard), 450.

[43] It has been argued that St Francis could have known the works of San Juan in manuscript through his contacts with French Carmels founded from Spain in the early 1600s, but the similarities noted in the writings of the two saints are not conclusive. See André Bord, "La influencia de San Juan de la Cruz sobre San Francisco de Sales y Santa Juana de Chantal," *San Juan de la Cruz* 14 (1994): 155-72; Pierre Serouet, *De la vie dévote à la vie mystique: Sainte Thérèse d'Avila et Saint François de Sales* (Paris: Desclée de Brouwer, 1958), 385-87, 395.

[44] Diarmuid MacCulloch, *Reformation: Europe's House Divided, 1490-1700* (London: Allen Lane, 2003), 150-52. On the impact of the debate in Spain, see Jorge de Montemayor, *Omelías sobre Miserere mei Deus*, ed. Terence O'Reilly (Durham: University of Durham, 2000), 9-11.

promovebit".[45] Here the moral freedom signalled by the adverb "libenter" is seen, not as a gift of nature, but as a fruit of justifying grace, and a similar notion of moral weakness informs the commentaries of two other Protestants of the time. First, Francis Lambert of Avignon, a Franciscan provincial who joined the Reform in Wittenburg in 1523, and published his lectures on the Song the following year. He writes of the Bride's plea: "Propter veteris Adami perniciosissimam senectutem, tanta est in omnibus debilitas, ut neque credere, neque Deo gratum aliquid efficere possint".[46] Second, Conrad Pellican, also once a Franciscan, who joined the Reform in Zurich in 1525, and published his Song commentary in 1534. For him the words of the Bride are a request by the Church to be liberated from the fear of eternal damnation, a grace granted to the elect.[47]

A very different approach is evident in the commentary of Frans Tittelmans, a Franciscan who remained a Catholic. In his lectures on the biblical book, he argued that Song 1. 3 runs counter to two heresies: "Unica hac et brevissima oratione duae haereses destruuntur: quarum prior, hominem ex solis naturalibus, sine peculiari Dei gratia, salvari posse; altera, sine hominis cooperatione, per solam Dei gratiam in homine operantem, ipsum salvari, stulte contendebat".[48] Commenting on the verb

---

[45] *Auslegung über das Hohelied (1530-1531)*, in *D. Martin Luthers Werke*, vol. XXXI.2 (Weimer: Hermann Böhlaus Nachfolger, 1914), 601-02, 604; translated by Ian Siggins in *Luther's Works*, vol. XV, ed. Jaroslav Pelikan and Hilton C. Oswald (Saint Louis: Concordia, 1972), 198: "To know, and to be able to do, are two different things. When we therefore possess the Word, we are not immediately able to follow it, but our flesh, the world, and Satan draw us away from the Word again. Now, therefore, he adds this prayer: 'You have given us your Word, and I thank you for it. Now grant that we may also perform what the Word teaches, and follow it in our lives'; [...] 'If you breathe your Spirit upon me, then I shall freely act [...]. If you do not, no one will accomplish anything, no matter how great his zeal and care'".

[46] François Lambert, *In cantica canticorum Salomonis libellum* (Nuremburg: apud Io. Petreium, 1524), fol. 22v: "Because of the most pernicious old age of the Old Adam, there is so much weakness in everyone, that they can neither believe nor do anything pleasing to God". See Engammare, 148.

[47] Conrad Pellican, *Commentaria bibliorum. Tomus quartus* (Zurich: Christophorus Froschouerus excudebat, 1540), (at Song 1. 3): "Clamat fidelium ecclesia: Per gratiam electionis tuae ô Deus, *trahe me* [...] ut non tam de iusto tuo iudicio terreamur". See Engammare, 148-49.

[48] Frans Tittelmans, *Commentarii doctissimi in cantica canticorum Salomonis* (Paris: apud Ioannem Roigny, 1547), fol. 9r: "By this one and most brief plea, two heresies are destroyed: the first [held] foolishly that man may be saved by his natural efforts alone, without a special grace of God; the second argued foolishly that he may be saved, without his cooperation, by the grace of God alone working

"curremus", he emphasizes the implication of active cooperation: "Qui enim currit, non solum patitur, sed agit et operatur, seipsum movendo, motivamque in seipso virtutem exercendo".[49] And he concludes, with Protestant exegesis in his sights:

> Nec enim sic trahi petit a sponso sponsa quomodo truncus ab equo trahitur nihil cooperans; sed quomodo puer qui per seipsum nequit currere, manibus trahitur maternis, ut possit hoc adiutorio infirmos pedes ad cursum movere celerius.[50]

Tittelmans's lectures were delivered in 1534, but they were not published until 1547, a significant date. In that year the Council of Trent issued its decree on justification, which affirmed the two doctrines that Tittelmans had wished to defend: first, the Christian's total dependence on grace; and second, the need for his (or her) willing cooperation.[51]

In his exegesis of Song 1. 3, San Juan alludes directly to both these aspects of the Council's teaching, and it seems that he took pains to get his wording right: the manuscript evidence, at this point, indicates extensive revision of the text.[52] The Council had given the two doctrines equal weight, but without explaining how they might be reconciled, a task that fell in following years to the theologians, who failed, acrimoniously, to agree. San Juan may have been aware of the disputes about grace and free will that arose in the University of Salamanca during the early 1580s, and, if so, he may have been keen to avoid contention.[53] But another reason for

---

in him". On Tittelmans see Jerry H. Bentley, *Humanists and Holy Writ: New Testament Scholarship in the Renaissance* (Princeton: Princeton University Press, 1983), 198-211; Paolo Sartori, "Frans Titelmans, the Congregation of Montagu and Biblical Scholarship," in *Biblical Humanism and Scholasticism in the Age of Erasmus*, ed. Erika Rummel (Leiden: Brill, 2008), 215-23.

[49] Tittelmans, fol. 9v: "For one who runs is not simply acted upon, but acts and works, moving himself, exercising within himself both motive and power".

[50] Tittelmans, fol. 9v: "The Bride certainly does not ask to be drawn by the Bridegroom as a tree trunk is drawn by a horse, without cooperating at all, but as a child who, unable to run by himself, is drawn along in his mother's hands so that he may, with this help, move his feeble feet forward more speedily".

[51] Engammare, 152, 270-73. See, in particular, Chapter 5 of the decree, in *Decrees of the Ecumenical Councils*, ed. Tanner, II, 672.

[52] *Cántico espiritual. Primera redacción*, ed. Pacho, 846-47.

[53] The controversy flared up in the University in January 1582, following three disputations on the merits of Christ and human predestination. See Colin P. Thompson, *The Strife of Tongues: Luis de León and the Golden Age of Spain* (Cambridge: Cambridge University Press, 1988), 80-83.

his care is possible too. The two points that the Council emphasized were central to his thought, and they underlie the teaching he advances in the *Cántico* as a whole. On the one hand he affirms that the journey of the soul to God (of the Bride to union with her spouse) is entirely the work of God's love, made visible in Christ, the Bridegroom. On the other, he holds that the Bride is utterly changed, becoming, by grace and with her active cooperation, what the Bridegroom is by nature: "[la amada] en el Amado transformada".[54]

It may be that when preparing his text, San Juan consulted commentaries on the Song, and the possibility that he did so is strengthened by the fact that the exegesis he sets out in stanza 21 is found earlier, in a work by Gilbert Génébrard, a Benedictine scholar who was lecturer in Hebrew in the Collège des Lecteurs Royaux in Paris. In his first commentary on the Song, published in 1570, we read:

> *Trahe me*: initium iustificationis nostrae a solo Deo est, qui nos ad sui cognitionem et amplexum [...] trahit. *Post te curremus*: iam iustificata curram non ego sed gratia Dei mecum.[55]

Fifteen years later, in a second edition, he added: "Observa ordinem salutis. Primus gradus est electio sive attractio. Secundus, ex parte nostri, apprehensio et concursus".[56] Génébrard is the source also of the exegesis

---

[54] The phrase occurs in San Juan's poem *En una noche oscura* (stanza 5, line 5). See Thompson, *John of the Cross: Songs in the Night*, who discusses the poem on pp. 84-95, and the theme of deification, or divinization, on pp. 181-82, 189.

[55] Gilbert Génébrard, *Canticum canticorum Salomonis regis* (Paris: apud Martinum Iuuenem, 1570), fol. 6v: "*Draw me*: the start of our justification comes from God alone, who [...] draws us to his knowledge and embrace. *We shall run after you*: once justified, I shall run, not alone, but with God's grace accompanying me". Génébrard's exegesis of Song 1. 3 was foreshadowed in the commentary of Michele Ghislieri, later Pope Pius V (1504-1572), which was not published, however, until the early seventeenth century. See his *Commentarii in canticum canticorum Salomonis* (Paris: apud Viduam Adriani Beys, 1613), 56, col. 2: "Bene vero statim, ac dixit *Trahe me*, subintulit, *post te curremus in odorem vnguentorum tuorum*, quia etsi hominum redemptio sit mere a Christo: etsi erectio, atque prima iustificatio a peccatis sit absque vllis operibus, ac meritis nostris, vsus tamen ipsius iustificationis, eiusque effectus, non solum est a Christo, sed etiam a nobis atque a nostro libero arbitrio, per quod Christi cooperamur redemptioni".

[56] Gilbert Génébrard, *Canticum canticorum Salomonis* (Paris: apud Aegidium Gorbinum, 1585), fol. 26v: "Note the order of salvation: the first step is election or attraction; the second, our contribution, is to seize what is offered, and run alongside". See B. Heurtebize, "Gilbert Génébrard," *Dictionnaire de Théologie Catholique*, VI:1, cols 1183-85; *Le Temps des Réformes et la Bible*, ed. Guy

of Francis de Sales, mentioned earlier. Towards the end of the *Traité*, Francis refers with praise to the lectures of Génébrard on the Song that he attended as a student in Paris in 1584: "Le savant Archevêque d'Aix, Gilbert Génébrard, que je nomme par honneur et avec consolation pour avoir été son disciple, quoique inutilement, lorsqu'il était lecteur royal à Paris et qu'il exposait le *Cantique des Cantiques*."[57]

In seventeenth-century Spain, other writers took up Génébrard's exegesis of the Bride's words, among them Juan de los Ángeles, who, in his *Consideraciones sobre el Cantar de los Cantares* of 1607, attributes it to the French writer explicitly, and Luis de la Puente, who resumes it in his commentary of 1622.[58] San Juan, however, writing in the 1580s, is the earliest witness we have to the impact of Génébrard's commentary in Spain, and the fact is not without importance for our understanding of the saint's writings. For Génébrard was famous throughout Europe for his studies of Origen. In the late fifteenth and sixteenth centuries, Origen's commentary and homilies on the *Song* were regularly attributed to Saint Jerome, and they were often included in editions of the Latin Father's works.[59] In 1512, Jacques Merlin argued for Origen's authorship, but doubts remained. When Erasmus's edition of Jerome was published by Froben, between 1516 and 1520, the humanist Bruno Amerbach, in his preface to volume VII, affirmed that neither Origen nor Jerome had written them, and two decades later, in his edition of Origen, Erasmus expressed the same view. For a generation the issue hung in the air, and it was not resolved until 1574, when Génébrard published his own edition of Origen's *Opera*, and showed that, *pace* Erasmus, the commentary was by

---

Bedouelle and Bernard Roussel (Paris: Beauchesne, 1989), 272, 361. Génébrard's defence of Benito Arias Montano in the controversy surrounding the Antwerp Polyglot Bible is noted in *La Biblia Políglota de Amberes en la correspondencia de Benito Arias Montano*, ed. Baldomero Macías Rosendo (Huelva: Universidad de Huelva, 1998).

[57] *Traité de l'Amour de Dieu*, Book XI, Chapter 11, in *Oeuvres*, 908. Génébrard held the post of *lecteur royal* in Hebrew from 1566 or 1569 until his death in 1591: see *Les Origines du Collège de France (1500-1560): Actes du colloque international (Paris, décembre 1995)*, ed. Antonio Alvar Ezquerra and others (Paris: Collège de France, 1998), 325; 358-59; 370-72.

[58] Juan de los Ángeles, *Consideraciones sobre el Cantar de los Cantares de Salomón* (Madrid, 1607), in *Obras místicas*, ed. Jaime Sala and Gregorio Fuentes, 2 vols (Madrid: Bailly Bailliere, 1912-17), II, 114, 124; Luis de la Puente, *Expositio moralis et mystica in canticum canticorum* (Cologne: apud Ioannem Kinckium, 1622), 318.

[59] See the references in Engammare,*163.

Origen himself.[60] San Juan's acquaintance with Génébrard's exegesis connects him firmly with the recovery of Origen, and with the revival, in the sixteenth-century Church, of the Alexandrian reading of the Song. But San Juan, though a learned man, was not an academic, and his knowledge of the Fathers did not give rise to works of scholarship. Instead it fed the meditative reading of Scripture that his Carmelite rule prescribed, and it found expression in the mystical works that he composed, without thought of publication, for other contemplatives. In the *Cántico espiritual*, the absence of patristic references gives to his reading of specific verses of the *Song*, such as Chapter 1, verse 3, a freshness often lacking in Latin commentaries of the time, and it reminds us that his approach to the Bible was much more than the prolongation of a hallowed tradition. It was, in de Lubac's memorable phrase, "un renouveau de scève": a new rising of the sap.[61]

---

[60] *Origenis Adamantii magni [...] opera*, ed. Gilbert Génébrard (Paris: ex officina Petri l'Huillier, 1574). See Engammare, pp. 90-94; *119.

[61] De Lubac, II, 505.

CHRISTIAN AUTHORS AS MODELS
OF *IMITATIO* IN THE AFTERMATH
OF THE COUNCIL OF TRENT:
DIOGO DE TEIVE'S *EPITHALAMIUM IN LAUDEM NUPTIARUM ALEXANDRI ET MARIAE PRINCIPUM PARMAE ET PLACENTIAE* (1565)

CATARINA BARCELÓ FOUTO
(ST PETER'S COLLEGE, UNIVERSITY OF OXFORD)

On 22 May 1565, the Portuguese Infanta D. Maria (granddaughter of King Emanuel and niece of the late King John III) married Prince Alessandro Farnese, the son of Octavio Farnese and Princess Margaret of Austria, the illegitimate daughter of the Emperor Charles V, and Philip II's half-sister.[1] This marriage was of great significance to the Portuguese royal family, who made the necessary diplomatic efforts to ensure that the marriage would be agreed upon by both the Dukes of Parma and Piacenza and Philip II. It was, in fact, Philip II who imposed the wedding, thus establishing yet another important matrimonial alliance between Portugal and Spain.[2]

I would like to thank Professor Thomas F. Earle for his kindness in reading, commenting on and correcting the English translation of the excerpts of the *Epithalamium*.

[1] A. Martínez Pereira, "Alejandro Farnese en las relaciones de sucesos españoles," in *D. Maria de Portugal princesa de Parma (1565-1577) e o seu tempo: as relações culturais entre Portugal e Itália na segunda metade de Quinhentos*, ed. José Adriano de Freitas Carvalho (Porto: Centro Universitário de História da Espiritualidade, 1999), 85-108.

[2] A. Buescu, *D. João III* (Lisboa: Círculo de Leitores, 2005), 260-70; A. Polónia, *D. Henrique* (Lisboa: Círculo de Leitores, 2005), 168 and 205-17; M. A. Cruz, *D. Sebastião* (Lisboa: Temas e Debates, 2009), 40-44 and 130-33.

As one would expect on such an important occasion, the celebrations lasted for several days,[3] reflecting that the Portuguese royal family were both committed to and rejoicing with the nuptials. Portuguese authors, on the other hand, also celebrated the royal wedding, and at least three writers composed extensive epithalamia[4] on this highly important political fact: Diogo de Teive,[5] António Ferreira[6] and Pêro de Andrade Caminha.[7]

All three poets knew each other: both as humanists and as court poets, they knew each other's work as the epithalamia themselves prove: intertextuality plays an important role in this corpus of poems, as Ferreira's text was the first to be written; Andrade Caminha's epithalamium is clearly an *amplificatio* of Ferreira's poem, and Teive's text alludes to a particular *passus* in Ferreira's epithalamium, which until now has not been noted. This is a clear sign that more research should be carried out on the interaction between Neo-Latin and vernacular literatures, which will only contribute to a deeper understanding of both forms of literary expression, as well as cultural interaction.

As the title of this essay indicates, there are particular aspects of the poem composed by Diogo de Teive which make this epithalamium so unique. First of all, it was written in Latin and in iambic metre, and not in Portuguese. And secondly, Teive used a Christian medieval author as the model of structural *imitatio* in his poem, combining both Christian and pagan elements, whereas Ferreira and Andrade Caminha set the wedding of the Infanta D. Maria and Alessandro Farnese against the background of a pagan mythological narrative. The differences in the general framework of the three poems should be explained: why did Teive decide to write such a *different* poem?

---

[3] G. Bertini, *Le nozze di Alessandro Farnese. Feste alle corti di Lisbona e Bruxelles* (Milano: Skira, 1997).

[4] V. Anastácio, *Uma introdução à poesia de Pêro de Andrade Caminha* (Lisboa: JNIT—Fundação Calouste Gulbenkian, 1998); eadem, "Poetas e Príncipes: algumas considerações acerca de dois epitalâmios dedicados ao casamento de D. Maria de Bragança com Alexandre Farnese," in *Discursos de Legitimação* (CD-rom) (Lisboa: Universidade Aberta, 2003); L. Fardilha, "A celebração poética em Portugal do casamento de D. Maria e Alexandre," in *D. Maria de Portugal princesa de Parma (1565-1577) e o seu tempo*, 29-48.

[5] Included in Diogo de Teive, *Epodon siue Iambicorum libri tres* (Lisbon: Franciscus Correa, 1565), III.

[6] A. Ferreira, *Poemas Lusitanos*, ed. Thomas F. Earle (Lisboa: Fundação Calouste Gulbenkian), 227-37.

[7] V. Anastácio, *Uma introdução à poesia de Pêro de Andrade Caminha*, 805-28.

I shall start by presenting a brief account of Diogo de Teive's life,[8] for it is representative of an entire generation of Portuguese sixteenth-century humanists. I will mention the most significant literary works Teive composed[9] whilst outlining his biography. Finally, I will present Teive's last printed work in a few words: the epithalamium subject to analysis in this article was published in the volume *Epodon siue Iambicorum libri tres* (Lisbon, 1565).

The main purpose of this study is to discuss the concept of *imitatio* underlying Teive's epithalamium. Therefore, after a concise presentation of the poem, the source of structural *imitatio* will be identified, thus allowing further discussion of the nature of the concept of *imitatio* adopted by Teive. The causes and implications of assuming this concept of *imitatio* will be brought to debate, whilst clarifying in what way it reflects a particular historical and cultural ambience in Portugal at the time, in the aftermath of the Council of Trent. It should not be forgotten that Teive was a humanist, a courtier and a priest who lived side by side with the main political and religious personalities of his day. Hence the need to answer the following questions: Did Teive use this particular model of *imitatio* given his acknowledged Christian profile? Was there an underlying ideological motive for the use of this author? If so, what particular historical circumstances led to this ideological usage of a literary model?

But, first, let us briefly recall Teive's life and work, for this too will provide some essential information to answer the questions raised above. According to the information Teive himself gave during his trial before the Inquisition, he was born in the northern town of Braga, around 1514. The date of his death, on the other hand, is uncertain: it is a fact that he was alive in 1569, and that he was already dead by 1579. Recently, in the Library of King Emanuel II in Vila Viçosa, I have discovered manuscript evidence that places Teive in Lisbon in 1565.

Unlike some of Portugal's most renowned sixteenth-century authors, Teive wrote exclusively in Latin (under the Latin form of Iacobus Tevius), and published all of his works during his lifetime. And like the majority of the Portuguese humanists of his day, Teive spent the decisive years of his

---

[8] M. Brandão, *O Processo na Inquisição de Mestre Diogo de Teive* (Coimbra: Universidade de Coimbra, 1943); A. C. Ramalho, "Sobre os últimos anos de Diogo de Teive," *Biblos* 55 (1979): 137-48.

[9] M. Díaz y Díaz, *HISLAMPA: Hispanorum index scriptorum Latinorum Medii Posteriorisque Aevii; autores latinos peninsulares da época dos Descobrimentos (1350-1560)* (Lisboa: Imprensa Nacional—Casa da Moeda, 1993); B. Taylor, "Recent Acquisitions: A Rare Work by Jacobus Tevius," *Electronic British Library Journal* (2003), article 5, 1-9.

intellectual and cultural formation abroad, thanks to the support of King John III. The ruler awarded scholarships for Portuguese alumni to study in France, at the Collège Sainte-Barbe; the young Teive left Portugal to study abroad in 1526, at the age of twelve. Later on, he briefly returned to Portugal, summoned by his father who wished his son to take a degree in law. Teive then headed to Salamanca, where he lived between 1532 and 1534. He returned to France to pursue the study of law at Toulouse, but met with economic difficulties which forced him to tutor the sons of a rich nobleman in Montalbon. Teive later moved to Bordeaux, and, there, at the Collège de Guyenne, he was one of the members of an international group of scholars invited by King John III to come to Portugal and staff the Colégio das Artes at Coimbra.[10]

Thus, foreign intellectuals as well as a generation of Portuguese humanists arrived in Portugal in 1547 to educate the cultural and administrative élite of the Portuguese Empire. Amongst the foreign scholars appointed at the Colégio das Artes one could find Nicolas de Grouchy, Guillaume de Guérente, Elias Vinet, Arnould Fabrice and George Buchanan. The group invited by King John III also featured renowned Portuguese academics such as André de Gouveia, João da Costa, António Mendes, and finally Diogo de Teive, who taught Greek and Latin. In 1547, in an atmosphere of clear optimism, Teive published his first work, the *Commentarius* on the second siege of Diu. This Commentary was dedicated to King John III, and included epigrams by João da Costa and George Buchanan. Little did the authors know that the state of affairs would change so dramatically.

The appointment of André de Gouveia as principal of the Colégio das Artes was a clear sign of the king's favour, and the rivalry between the Bordeaux group and the Parisian scholars who also taught at the Colégio das Artes led to a gradual tension within the institution. Personal antagonism undermined the daily life of the Colégio, and the conservative group of Parisian scholars grew stronger. Both João da Costa and Diogo de Teive had studied and taught at the Collège Sainte-Barbe where the principal, Diogo de Gouveia, was an active defender of Catholicism. Owing to their liberal religious views, Teive and João da Costa came into conflict with Diogo de Gouveia and, because of this dispute, the two Portuguese scholars left for the Collège de Guyenne where they met the Scotsman George Buchanan, also considered suspicious.

---

[10] M. Brandão, *A Inquisição e os Professores do Colégio das Artes*, 2 vols (Coimbra: Universidade de Coimbra, 1948-69).

After the sudden death of André de Gouveia in 1548, King John III succumbed to the pressure of the conservative Parisian group, and Teive, da Costa and Buchanan were removed from the Colégio das Artes, and brought before the Inquisition. They were accused of Protestantism, and in Teive's case he was also accused of possessing a copy of Calvin's *Institutio Christiani Religionis*, and of being a Lutheran: at this point in the trial, his relations with Etienne Dolet and André Zébédée at Bordeaux were recalled. The three humanists were condemned, deprived of their posts, and imprisoned: Teive was released after a year spent in prison, but his conviction did little harm to his relationship with the royal family—he would return to be rector of the Colégio in 1552, and he delivered orations when Prince John, the heir to the throne, married the daughter of Charles V, and died within a year. When Teive was appointed principal of the Colégio in 1554, the conservatives reacted so negatively that the king handed control over the institution to the Jesuits.

Teive left Coimbra, and embraced religious life in the village of Santa Cruz da Braciosa, in Miranda do Douro, thanks to the intervention of Queen Catherine of Austria: Santa Cruz was a remote parish, but quite wealthy, and while Teive was a priest in Santa Cruz, he managed to publish one of his books in Salamanca in 1558. This work, the *Opuscula aliquot* includes official speeches, epistles, a tragedy based on the death of Prince John, and the *Institutio Sebastiani primi*, a poem that draws closely from the Erasmian text of the *Institutio Principis Christiani*. While in Miranda do Douro, Teive met the Spanish bishop Don Julián de Alba,[11] who had been appointed by Queen Catherine—this man would prove to be extremely important in Teive's life, for it was most likely thanks to him that Teive returned to Lisbon in 1563, the year Don Julián de Alba himself returned to the capital. Teive published minor works between 1563 and 1564, dedicated to the members of the houses of Braganza and Aveiro, and in 1565, he published his last printed work, the *Epodon libri,* a clear sign that the poet had returned to the political scene in Lisbon.

The epithalamium Teive wrote on the occasion of the royal wedding of the Infanta D. Maria and Alessandro Farnese was published in the third book of the *Epodon libri*, which include a collection of texts addressed to members of the royal family. The structure of the work itself and the corresponding dedicatees of each of the books are highly significant from a political point of view. Book I is dedicated to Don Julián de Alba (close

---

[11] J. da Silva Terra, "Espagnols au Portugal au temps de la Reine D. Catarina. D. Julião de Alva (c. 1500-1570)," *Arquivos do Centro Cultural Português* 9 (1975): 417-506.

to Queen Catherine, the former Regent), book II is dedicated to the future King Sebastian, and the dedicatee of book III is Cardinal Henry, who was regent of the country at the time.

The *Epodon libri* include various poems, some of which had been previously published. Book I consists of two bilingual editions: the *Sententiae* (addressed to the heir to the throne) and a second edition of the *Institutio Sebastiani primi* (first published in the *Opuscula* of 1558). Book II, on the other hand, comprises a series of hymns addressed to the patron saints of Portugal, and, finally, book III includes the poem *De perfecto episcopo,* a "speculum prelati" dedicated to Cardinal Henry, certainly motivated by the fact that he was regent during Sebastian's minority. The "De perfecto episcopo" is followed by occasional poems, including the epithalamium on the marriage of Alessandro Duke of Parma and Piacenza and the Infanta D. Maria of Portugal. This last book of the *Epodon libri* is a sort of poetic journal of those days at the Portuguese court. The poems are organized in chronological order, and both the epithalamium and the last poem of the book, an ode celebrating the victory over the Turks during the siege of Malta, refer to events of 1565.

At this stage, it should be stressed that the dedicatee of the epithalamium was no other than Cardinal Henry himself, Regent and Inquisitor. And yet Teive dedicated to him this peculiar epithalamium which combines both Christian and pagan elements. It is, in fact, crucial for understanding the uniqueness of this poem to see how Christian and pagan elements are combined in different sections of the poem.

In the opening lines of the epithalamium, the narrator states it is his purpose to sing of the royal wedding. The author then introduces the topic of God's Creation of the World, drawing his inspiration from the biblical narrative of Genesis: the Creation of Man is described and the author dedicates several lines to the institution of the holy sacrament of matrimony, referred to as the first sacrament. Divine protection is then requested for the royal wedding, along with wishes for a happy life and many descendents. There follows a political section in the text, which clearly contributes to lessening or even neutralizing the erotic content of a poem of this particular genre. A particular remark is made to the future offspring of the couple: may they be worthy of their ancestors, and be known for fighting the Turkish menace, and for expanding Christianity. Then, the author proceeds, offering his advice to the future Dukes of Parma, particularly on the importance of not yielding to passion, and obedience to God's will and submission to virtue. Teive also gives his advice to the people under the couple's rule, and God's blessing is requested.

The following section of the poem is highly interesting for it presents the pagan elements of the epithalamium. This part of the text begins with the *recusatio* of the artificiality of the classical poets. But this, of course, is merely a *topos*, for the poetical explanation for the royal marriage is presented under the form of a mythological narrative. At this point, a new character emerges in the poem, the *uates* or *poeta*, who will sing of the council of the gods, summoned by Jupiter at Hymenaeus's request. Hymenaeus recognizes he has been unable to find a suitable match for the Portuguese Princess. Cupid, who had not been given a seat, intervenes, boasting that Maria and Alessandro were both in love with each other thanks to him, in a clear demonstration of his power before the gods. Jupiter then orders Maria and Alessandro to marry, and the *uates* sings of the celebrations and of the joys of marriage.

Nonetheless, this section of the poem ends rather peculiarly: the narrator refuses to reproduce the songs of the choirs of Tritons and Nereids, alluding to the epithalamium which António Ferreira had written on the same occasion, and which finished with an alternating sequence of choirs of Tritons and Nereids, following the model of Catullus's *carmen* 64, which had also been adopted by Sá de Miranda in his *Epitalâmio Pastoril*.

At the very end of the mythological narrative the narrator also comments on the previous section, referring to these pagan deities as "figmenta ueterum poetarum" ("fabrications of the ancient poets"). I will return to these lines later.

Finally, and unlike the poets of his day, Teive requests the protection of the Virgin Mary, for the royal couple, particularly for Infanta D. Maria who would travel by sea to Brussels where she would eventually meet her future husband. Both Ferreira and Andrade Caminha request the protection of Venus. In the closing lines of the poem, the narrator wishes a safe journey to the Portuguese princess, and predicts future glory for all the members of the Portuguese royal family, under God's protection.

Now that the reader is acquainted with both the author and the text, let us draw our attention to the complex question of *imitatio* in Teive's epithalamium.

First of all, it is impossible to identify direct quotations from both classical and medieval Latin authors in the epithalamium, as metrical restrictions usually complicate the matter.[12] Furthermore, according to the results of textual analysis, Teive read both classical and medieval Latin authors, and there is no distinction between the usage or presence of classical authors, on the one hand, and medieval, on the other, in the two different sections of the poem which I previously identified. From the classical authors such as Catullus, Lucretius, Virgil, Livy, Seneca and Lucan, to Paulinus of Nola and Prudentius, Teive seems to master an array of different genres: epic, didactic, epithalamium, tragedy, historiography, hymns, etc.. Moreover, the phraseology of the epithalamium testifies that the author uses both poetic and prose sources whilst writing his text.

As mentioned earlier, the epithalamium can be found in the third book of the *Epodon libri*. The choice of the title indicates a clear literary model: that of Horace's *Epodes*. The title, the use of iambics, and the metrical technique—these elements would allow the Renaissance reader to establish an immediate connexion between Teive and Horace. However, Horace is simply the formal model: both in theme and in tone Teive and the Latin poet could not be more different. The critical adoption of Horace's model is discussed by Teive himself in the prologue of book III: the author states he considers Horace's poetry as a model of formal perfection and of *Latinitas*. Teive praises Horace's "uerborum cultum et elegantia", as well as his "suauitas ornatissimi carminis", only to refuse to recognize the gravity of its "argumentum". It is true that during the Renaissance period this was a topic, but I should stress that in the prologue of book III of the *Epodon libri* Teive is very much concerned to show Cardinal Henry that the contents of his book are highly worthy of his priestly status. It must not be forgotten that Teive had been condemned by the Inquisition, and had only recently returned to the Portuguese court. In 1565 he was writing on the most important political events of his day, and dedicating such poems to the main political and religious authorities of the Portuguese élite.

Therefore, the concept of *imitatio* adopted by the Portuguese poet is both complex and dynamic. If Teive is not imitating Horace from the point of view of the "argumentum" of his poetry, whom then is he imitating? Unlike Ferreira who drew inspiration from Catullus and the Italian poet Angelo Poliziano (and his incomplete *Stanze per la giostra di Giuliano de'*

---

[12] I have used the corpus of the Database of Latin Dictionaries and the Corpus Lexicographicum Lusitanum.

Medici, 1475),[13] Diogo de Teive chose to use Paulinus of Nola's *carmen* 25 as a model of structural imitation.[14]

This composition by Paulinus of Nola, dedicated to the marriage of Julian of Eclanum and Titia, is central in the tradition of the Latin Christian epithalamium. This text is considered to be an "adaptation for Christian purposes of a classical genre":[15] when comparing Paulinus's epithalamium with two epithalamia written by the contemporary poet Claudian, one cannot help to notice the striking differences both in tone and in content. It is clear how Paulinus is attempting to build a Christian superstructure on the classical foundation in the epithalamium.[16]

In the exordium, the poet addresses Christ and banishes Venus, Juno and Cupid from his text, condemning them for their lust. Following this is the narrative of the institution of marriage by God, after man and woman had been made in His own image (lines 13-26). In the history of the epithalamic genre, Paulinus was the sole Latin Christian poet to take the Bible as his model when composing his text, and like Teive Paulinus presents the aetiology of the sacrament of holy matrimony. Teive could have had access to the epithalamium through an edition of Paulinus's *Epistolae et poemata* published in Paris in 1516,[17] and a second edition of Paulinus's poems came to out years later, in 1560, in Cologne, entitled *Quotquot extant opera omnia.*[18]

---

[13] A. Poliziano, *Poesie Volgari*, I, ed. Francesco Bausi (Roma: Vecchiarelli, 1997).

[14] A. Bouma, *Het Epithalamium van Paulinus van Nola. Carmen xxv met inleiding, vertaling en commentaar* (Assen: Van Gorcum, 1968), 22-36 (text).

[15] S. Costanza, "I generi letterari nell'opera poetica di Paolino di Nola," *Augustinianum* 14 (1974): 637-50; H. Crouzel, "L'epitalamio di S. Paolino: il suo contenuto dottrinale," in *Atti del convegno XXXI Cinquantenario della morte di S. Paolino di Nola (431-1981)* (Roma: Herder, 1983); R. Gelsomino, "L'epitalamio di Paolino di Nola per Giuliano e Titia," in *Atti del convegno XXXI Cinquantenario della morte di S. Paolino di Nola*, 213-30; R. P. H. Green, "Paulinus' Use of Poetic Forms," in his *The Poetry of Paulinus of Nola* (Bruxelles: Latomus, 1971), 21-40.

[16] M. Roberts, "The Use of Myth in Latin Epithalamia from Statius to Venantius Fortunatus," *Transactions of the American Philological Association* 119 (1989): 321-48; Andrea Ruggiero, *I carmi di Paolino di Nola* (Roma: Città Nuova, 1990); Anna Sbrancia, "L'epitalamio di S. Paolino di Nola," *Annali della Facoltà di Lettere e Filosofia della Università di Macerata* 11 (1978): 83-119; Virginia Tufte, *The Poetry of Marriage: The Epithalamium in Europe and its Development in England* (Los Angeles: Tinnon Brown, 1970).

[17] Paulinus, bishop of Nola, *Epistolae et poemata* (Paris: per Iodocum Badium Ascensium et Ioannem Paruum, 1516)

[18] Paulinus, bishop of Nola, *Quotquot extant opera omnia* (Cologne: per Maternum Cholinum, 1560).

The choice of Paulinus as a model of structural imitation must be explained. In fact, when comparing Teive's poem with the epithalamia written by the contemporary Portuguese poets Ferreira and Andrade Caminha, the differences are striking. The texts composed by the two poets are exclusively based on mythological narratives, while in Teive's poem the narrative of the council of the gods is preceded by an account of the creation of marriage.

What reasons, then, made Paulinus's poem so appealing to Teive? It offered an interesting precedent in the tradition of the epithalamic genre by presenting the aetiology of the sacrament of holy matrimony.

At a time when the Church had restated the sacramental nature of marriage at the Council of Trent; and at a time when Cardinal Henry decided Portugal would be the first country in Western Europe to put the Tridentine decrees into practice, there is reason to suspect that Teive's selection of Paulinus's epithalamium was ideologically motivated. But the Portuguese humanist did not limit himself to a servile imitation of his model, and introduced differences which amount to an ideological interpretation of his text, mirroring deep changes in the historical and cultural ambience of the poet's day.

Unlike Paulinus, Teive does not quote the text of the Bible: the account of Genesis is present on two occasions in the first section of Paulinus's epithalamium, when the poet states that God "ex una fecit carne manere duos" (l. 18) ("made two abide in one flesh", Gen. 2. 24), and when Adam himself recognizes Eve as his partner in life, Paulinus writes "seque alium exsese sociali in corpore cernens / ipse propheta sui mox fuit ore novo. / "haec", inquit, "caro mea est, os ab ossibus istud / nosco meis, haec est costa mei lateris" (ll. 23-26) ("Once he [Adam] beheld this other self sprung from himself in the flesh they shared, he then became the prophet of his own situation, speaking with tongue renewed. "This flesh," he said, "is the flesh of my flesh. I recognize the bone of my bones. She is the rib from my side.") (Gen. 2. 23). Teive, on the other hand, does not quote the Bible. For the narrative of the creation of the world by God, Teive drew inspiration from Ovid's *Metamorphoses* (XV, 239ff), and quotes from Genesis are absent from his narrative of the creation of Adam and Eve. I quote the relevant section of the epithalamium, side by side with the decree of the 24th session of the Council of Trent, which discussed the doctrine of marriage:

Teive, *Epithalamium*... (Lisbon, 1565)

Doctrine on the Sacrament of
Matrimony (24th session of the
council of Trent)

Mortale ac istud prole crescat ut genus
et excitetur, pulluletque latius
α mens una, pectus unum, et una sit caro,
una et uoluntas, denique unus sit thorus α
quod ergo summus coelitum iussit pater,
quod ipse lege statuit aerterna Deus,
quod alligauit **uinculo firmissimo**
β quod ille nodis strinxit arctioribus,
quos nulla uis mortalium distringeret. β
Illudque robur, tam uetus, tam nobile
**primumque sacramentum ab ipso
numine,**
auctore rerum constitutum maximo.
cur non sacerdos et senex, antistitis[19]
teretes ad aures concinam integerrimi,
si Christus ipse nostra spes, salus decus,
deique uerus natus, et uerus deus,
quae prima terris edidit miracula[20]
uoluit in ipsis edita esse nuptiis,
nec adesse celebri respuit conuiuio?
Haec fixa terris, clara cur uestigia
Non insequemur? Non quidem miracula
humana ut edere queat imbecillitas,
sed quae ille rector omnium, ac uerus parens
praesentia ornauit sua. Nos uersibus
nostris canamus, regias nos nuptias,
non infaceta concinamus tibia,
laetoque laetos explicemus carmine
lusus amorum, quos pudor sanctus probet.
(ll. 63-90)
[And may the offspring of the race of
mortals be multiplied, / and may it renew
itself, and be dispersed widely. / And may
there be but one mind, one spirit and one
flesh, / and may there be but one will, and
one marriage bed / for the supreme father
ordained it from heaven / for God Himself

Matrimonii **perpetuum
indissolubilemque nexum** primus
humani generis parens divini
Spiritus instinctu pronunciavit,
cum dixit: α *Hoc nunc os ex
ossibus meis, et caro de carne mea.
Quamobrem relinquet homo
patrem suum et matrem, et
adhaerebit uxori suae et erunt duo
in carne una.* α
Hoc autem **vinculo** duos
tantummodo copulari et conjugi,
Christus Dominus apertius docuit,
cum postrema illa verba tamquam
a Deo prolata referens dixit: *Itaque
jam non sunt duo, sed una caro,*
statimque ejusdem **nexus
firmitatem** ab Adamo tante ante
pronunciatam his verbis
confirmavit: β *Quod ergo Deus
conjunxit, homo non separet.* β
Gratiam vero, quae naturalem
illum amorem perficeret, et
indissolubilem unitatem
confirmaret conjugesque
sanctificaret, **ipse Christus
venerabilium sacramentorum
institutor atque perfector** sua
nobis passione promeruit, quod
Paulus Apostolus innuit dicens:
*Viri, diligite uxores vestras, sicut
Christus dilexit ecclesiam, et se
ipsum tradidit pro ea*, mox
subjungens: *Sacramentum hoc
magnum est, ego autem dico in
Christo, et in ecclesia.* [...][21]
[The perpetual and indissoluble

---

[19] i.e. Cardinal Henry.
[20] Teive is referring to the biblical episode of the Marriage at Cana.
[21] H. J. Schroeder, *Canons and Decrees of the Council of Trent: Original Text with English Translation* (London: B. Herder, 1960), 451.

instituted it as a perennial law / for He united [them] with a bond so strong / for He bound [them] with knots so tight / which no human power shall pull apart. / And that power so ancient, so noble, / and the first marriage instituted, by the supreme creator of all things / by his own divine will, why would I, a priest and an old man, not sing them / to the cultivated ears of the most upright minister, / if Christ, our hope and glory of Salvation, / God's true offspring, and true God / who performed these first miracles on earth wished that marriage to be proclaimed / and did not refuse to attend the celebrated festivity? / If this took place on earth, why should we not follow / those eminent steps? For I would be unable / to sing of human miracles, / but these events, He who presides over all things, / and true Father, has honoured them with His presence. We, who sing in verse, / shall not sing the royal wedding, / with the coarse sound of the flute, / but we shall present the joyful play of the cupids / with a joyful song which pious decency shall approve.]

bond of matrimony was expressed by the first parent of the human race, when under the influence of the divine Spirit, he said: *"This now is bone of my bones, and flesh of my flesh. Wherefore a man shall leave father and mother, and shall cleave to his wife, and they shall be two in one flesh"*. But, that by this bond two only are united and joined together, our Lord taught more plainly, when referring to those last words as having been spoken by God, He said: *"Therefore now they are not two, but one flesh"*, and immediately ratified the firmness of the bond so long ago proclaimed by Adam with these words: *"What therefore God hath joined together, let no man put asunder"*. But, the grace which was to perfect that natural love, and confirm that indissoluble union, and sanctify the persons married, Christ Himself, the institutor and perfecter of the venerable sacraments, merited for us by His passion, which Paul the Apostle intimates when he says: *"Husbands love your wives, as Christ also loved the Church, and delivered himself up for it"*; adding shortly after, *"This is a great sacrament, but I speak in Christ and in the Church"*.]

In italics and identified with letters α and β are the passages in which Teive paraphrases the quotations of the Holy Scriptures included in the decree of the 24th session of the Council.

Teive carefully avoids direct quotation of sacred texts. At Trent the edition, the use and the quotation of the Bible was naturally also one of the most significant topics of debate. The fourth session of the Council issued a decree regarding the edition and use of the Sacred Books. I quote the relevant paragraph:

Post haec temeritatem illam reprimere volens, qua ad profana quaeque convertuntur et torquentur verba et sententiae Sacrae Scripturae, ad scurrilia scilicet, fabulosa, vana, adulationes, detractiones, superstitiones, impias et diabolicas incantationes, divinationes, sortes, libellos etiam famosos, mandat et praecipit, ad tollendam huiusmodi irreverentiam et contemptum, et ne de cetero quisquam quomodolibet verba Scripturae Sacrae ad haec et similia audeat usurpare, ut omnes huius generis homines, temeratores et violatores verbi Dei, iuris et arbitrii poenis per Episcopos coerceantur.[22]

[Furthermore, wishing to repress that boldness, whereby the words and sentences of the Holy Scriptures are turned and twisted to all sorts of profane usages, namely, to things scurrilous, fabulous, vain, to flatteries, detractions, superstitions, godless and diabolical incantations, divinations, the casting of lots and defamatory libels, to put an end to such irreverence and contempt, and that no one may in the future dare use in any manner the words of Holy Scripture for these and similar purposes, it is commanded and enjoined that all people of this kind be restrained by the bishops as violators and profaners of the word of God, with the penalties of the law and others that they may deem fit to impose.]

It is clear this decree targeted specifically heterodox and heretical interpretations of the Bible, but a reference to the profane use of quotations from the Bible is included in the decree. Bearing in mind that the dedicatee of the poem was Cardinal Henry, one cannot help but notice how Teive is behaving carefully: he never quotes the Bible in this poem.

The second difference between Teive's epithalamium and that of Paulinus is that the latter does not state that marriage is a sacrament, whereas Teive repeatedly insists on this topic. When analysing the poem from a conceptual point of view, it becomes clear that Teive was aware of the main doctrinal conclusions of the Council of Trent, which ended in 1563, two years before the epithalamium was composed and published.

The text of the decrees of the 24th session of the Council established Counter-Reformation doctrine on the sacrament of matrimony. The Catholic Church reaffirmed that marriage was perpetual and indissoluble, and that it had been instituted by God at the Creation. Again, I will quote an excerpt of the decree, underlining coincidences in the phraseology of both texts:

Matrimonii **perpetuum indissolubilemque nexum** primus humani generis parens divini Spiritus instinctu pronunciavit [...]. Hoc autem **vinculo** duos

---

[22] Schroeder, *Canons and Decrees of the Council of Trent,* 298.

> tantummodo copulari et conjugi, Christus Dominus apertius docuit, [...]
> statimque ejusdem **nexus firmitatem** ab Adamo tante ante pronunciatam
> his verbis confirmavit [...] **indissolubilem unitatem** confirmaret
> conjugesque sanctificaret, *ipse Christus venerabilium sacramentorum
> institutor atque perfector* sua nobis passione promeruit

Teive insists upon the sacramental nature of marriage, and situates the
origin of matrimony in the creation of Adam and Eve, stating that it is
indissoluble and perpetual—marriage is the first sacrament instituted by
God.

There are echoes of the vocabulary used in the decree in the poem,
which contribute to the creation of meaning in the epithalamium clearly
akin to that of Catholic doctrine. Two years before Teive composed this
text, in November 1563, the Council of Trent had restated that matrimony
had been the first sacrament created by God, after the creation of man; and
that this sacrament was indissoluble, and ever-lasting. Latin words such as
"nexus", "uinculum", and "indissolubilis" occur in both the text of the
decrees and in Teive's epithalamium.

Finally, and perhaps more significantly, Teive partially addresses the
criticism of the Reformation when he includes a reference to the biblical
episode of the Marriage at Cana in his epithalamium. The Tridentine
decree also declared that the sacramental nature of matrimony was
confirmed by Jesus himself, while Luther claimed that marriage should not
be considered a sacrament for it had been instituted by God, and not
Jesus.[23] In the epithalamium, Teive incorporates a reference to the
Marriage at Cana and to the miracle Jesus performed, and this reference
can also be found in Paulinus.

In Paulinus's poem, the biblical episode expresses the divine nature of
matrimony confirmed by Jesus with a miracle; in Teive's epithalamium on
the other hand this reference justifies the very composition of the poem: if
Jesus himself attended the marriage and performed a miracle, why should
not a priest sing of the joys of marriage, and dedicate his work to another
priest, that is to Cardinal Henry (see l. 75 ff)? Again, Teive is eager to
demonstrate that his poetry is befitting his priestly status.

So, in conclusion, Teive's usage of Paulinus is ideologically motivated
within the context of the Counter-Reformation in Portugal. Two years
after the end of the Council of Trent, the poem testifies how the decrees

---

[23] E. Carlson, *Marriage and the English Reformation* (Oxford: Blackwell, 1994),
3-8.

were enthusiastically welcomed in Portugal. Teive constantly refers to the sacramental nature of marriage in the epithalamium, and he avoids quoting directly from the Bible, according to the decisions taken at Trent. The adoption of the medieval author as a model of structural imitation is dynamic: Teive's imitation is innovative and original, updating its source within a new ideological and historical context.

In the second part of this study, the concept of poetic *imitatio* adopted by the Portuguese humanist will be subject to further analysis. The study of the techniques of poetic composition of the epithalamium reveals that Teive favours eclectic and transformative *imitatio* in his work. He does not use direct quotations, and he transforms the texts. Teive is, in fact, highly original, and it is his own voice that the reader hears in the *Epodon libri*. His compositional technique resembles that of patchwork. This makes it all the more difficult to identify the sources of the poem, and the authors to which he had had access.

First of all, Teive uses archaic forms in his text: apart from the ablative plural form *queis* (which occurs in the poem for metrical reasons), the humanist prefers forms such as *foemina* or *coelitum* instead of *femina* and *caelitum*. The use of medieval vocabulary on the other hand is also a distinctive feature of Teive's poetry: examples of this are *neptem*, *pertimescit* and *fulcita*. Forms such as these ultimately contribute to a more solemn style, but it should also be taken into account that one of the reasons why Teive used archaic forms and vocabulary in his poem may well be connected to the fact that he establishes a contrast between himself and the younger generation of poets. Teive depicts himself in the epithalamium as an old poet, free of any artificiality—his pious and fearful attitude towards God offers a clear contrast with that of the *uates* who sings in the company of the gods; the younger poets, on the other hand, are presented as the representatives of learned poetry of classical inspiration.

The analysis of the poem also revealed the existence of some textual coincidences between Teive's epithalamium and Paulinus's poems: for instance, *modulamen* is frequently used by Paulinus, and the phrases "conscia mater" (*carm.* 6, 183), "mundi sator" (*carm.* 10, 47), "sinu pleno" (*carm.* 21, 84) and "edens miracula" (*carm.* 23, 38) occur in both authors.

The phrase "vocibus dei" can only be found in the work of Augustine, and the same sort of textual coincidences can be observed regarding the work of Prudentius, for example: "cedant nubila" ("cedunt nubila", *Hamartigenia,* 877-78), "tollit oculos in altum" (*Cathemerinon*, 12, 1-2: "Quicumque Christum quaeritis / oculos in altum tollite"); "Beate uiuere [...] audiat" (*Peristephanon*, 10, 209: "si beate uiuere audit Iuppiter").

Nonetheless, one should bear in mind that rather than deliberate imitation, the use of similar phraseology in Latin may well be the result of either coincidence or unconscious reminiscence.[24] This could be the case particularly in poetry for metre constrains the choice of words and their position in the line, and indeed many phrases would come naturally to the poet's mind because they fit the required metrical pattern. For example, Teive wrote his historiographical account of the siege of Diu, based on Livy and Tacitus, and used Seneca's tragedies in his *Tragedy of Prince John*. Similar textual coincidences of Livy and Seneca can be found in Teive's epithalamium, but that does not imply that Teive is trying to emulate his models.

Teive's technique of poetic composition shows similarities with the Erasmian concept of *imitatio*. Teive, who had spent the early years of his life in France, would have been easily aware of the controversy surrounding Erasmus's *Ciceronianus*. It is important to remember that some of Teive's acquaintances in France were involved in the polemic. Gouveia (who invited Teive to teach at Bordeaux) was an Erasmian, but Sussanneau, Julius Caesar Scaliger and Dolet were well-known Ciceronians.

In this sense, the close analysis of Teive's technique of poetic composition reveals an original author with a personal style and expression, as Erasmus himself had proposed in his *Ciceronianus*.

But Erasmus had criticized the use of pagan mythology in Sannazaro's *De partu Virginis*, where gods and goddesses are depicted as witnessing the birth of Jesus. It was demonstrated that Teive's choice of a Christian theme for his epithalamium is, in fact, ideologically motivated. But how then can one explain the presence of pagan deities in that poem which draws inspiration from a Christian epithalamium? And what is the role of the mythological narrative in the framework of an epithalamium with distinctive Counter-Reformation contents? Intertextuality will shed some light upon this complex problem.

The mythological narrative in Teive's epithalamium is preceded by a *recusatio* of the artificiality of the Italian poets:

---

[24] G. W. Pigman III, "Neo-Latin Imitation of the Latin Classics," in his *Latin Poetry and the Classical Tradition: Essays in Medieval and Renaissance Literature* (Oxford: Clarendon Press, 1990), 200-01.

Omnis ornatus procul, / comptique crines, nimiaque elegantia / pulchra calamistris. Eruditis uatibus / quos Itala terra nutrit, haec relinquimus.
[Be gone all artifice, / and false tresses, and fair and excessive beauty in writing. / I shall leave all this to the learned poets Italy nurtures.]

This reference to the "learned poets" of Italy may be interpreted as an allusion to the epithalamium written by António Ferreira, who adopted Poliziano's *Stanze per la giostra di Giuliano de' Medici* as his model, but further research is being carried out to clarify the meaning of these lines.

On the other hand, Teive also proclaims his unwillingness to accept mythological devices in his poem at the very end of the mythological narrative: "But we shall leave [these songs of Nereids and Tritons] to other poets, who are pleased with the fabrications of the ancient poets" ("Nos ista at aliis deseramus uatibus, / figmenta ueterum queis poetarum placent").

Therefore, Teive is cautious when he overtly rejects pagan mythology in his poem: the fable of the love of Maria and Alessandro offers a poetic explanation for the royal wedding leaving politics aside, and rests on a poetic plane. Also, while respecting one of the conventions of the Renaissance epithalamium, Teive's priestly status is not questioned. In fact, even though Teive criticizes "vain fables and fictions" in the prologue of the *Epodon libri*, he cannot simply erase classical mythology and the literary tradition surrounding it.

In that sense, these lines are the key to understanding the meaning of classical mythology in the poem. Camões himself will later tell the reader of the *Lusiads* something quite similar. Thetis, the nymph, reveals to the Portuguese captain Vasco da Gama that the gods

fingidos de mortal e cego engano / só pera fazer versos deleitosos / [servem] ; e, se mais o trato humano / [lhes] pode dar, é só que o nome [seu] / nestas estrelas pôs o engenho vosso. (X, 82)
[Are mere fables / dreamed by mankind in his blindness. / [They] serve only to fashion delightful / verses, and if human usage offers / [them] more, it is [their] imagination awards [them] / each in heaven a constellation.][25]

Camões explicitly refers to the gods as merely allegories, and by acknowledging they are false, they can be included in the epic poem, without seriously compromising the author's position. Both in Teive's epithalamium and in Camões's *Lusiads* the concept of poetic fiction bears

---

[25] L. de Camões, *The Lusiads*, translated by Landeg White (Oxford: Oxford University Press, 1997).

directly upon the role of the pagan gods in the poem, and it is crucial to the creation of meaning: the *narrator* of the poem distances himself from the feigned gods and the *poet* overtly recognizes the fictionality of the narrative.

Associated with the *recusatio* of classical mythology is the shift from a first person to a third-person narrator in Teive's epithalamium. Hence, Teive (re)presents himself as a humble and suppliant poet devoted to the one true God:

> clarum ac micantem lucidis stellis polum / oneremus ergo precibus, et cantu pio, / propicia ut istis numina adsint nuptiis / Christusque sancto faueat ut connubio./ Illi offeram pectore ab humili preces, / sancto offeramus sancta uota numini, / cantus suaues, dulcia modulamina. / Numquam recusat supplices Deus preces, / nec dulce carmen perbenignus respuit / cui uatum ab ore profluens cantus placet. / Pectus requirit humile, pectus candidum, / pectusque purum, pectus expers sordium.
> [And let us now fill the noble sky, gleaming with bright stars, / with prayers, with a pious song, / so that propitious divine spirit may attend these nuptials / and that Christ may favour this union. / To Him I shall offer my prayers with a humble heart, / We shall offer our holy vows to the sacred god, / smooth songs, sweet melodies. / Never does God refuse supplicant prayers / nor does He, who in His kindness is pleased with the song that flows from the lips of the poets, / reject the sweet song. / He requires a humble heart, an innocent heart, / and a pure heart, free of all vileness.]

On the other hand, in the mythological narrative Teive presents the reader a new persona, that of the glorious and elegant *uates* who plays Apollo's cythara side by side with the gods. However, God listens to the Christian poet's prayers, and his poetry pleases God, whereas nowhere in the poem is it clear that the pagan poet obtains any sort of reward from the gods for his poetry. Therefore, Teive is cautious when he overtly rejects pagan mythology in his poem: the fable of the love of Maria and Alessandro rests on a poetic plane, and while respecting one of the conventions of the epithalamic genre, Teive's priestly status is not questioned. This is a clear sign that, even though Teive condemns "vain fables and fictions" in the prologue of the *Epodon libri*, the poet cannot simply dismiss classical mythology from his poetry, as it was surely a significant part of his humanistic background.

In conclusion, the adoption of a medieval Christian author as a model of structural imitation reveals the enthusiasm surrounding the reception of the decrees of the Council of Trent. Teive was both quick and original in the way he responded to the Tridentine cultural atmosphere of his day. On the other hand, the poet was neither ready nor willing to discard his cultural background. Teive used Paulinus's text as his model, and updated the text to a new ideological scene. However, unlike his medieval predecessor, he does not banish the classical gods from his text, and he cautiously includes them in his poem.

In fact, one cannot help but notice that the author's life and work are representative of the changes that took place in the second half of the sixteenth century in Portugal. Under King John III, Portugal experienced cultural openness: the kingdom was the head of a vast empire from the east to the west, the members of the royal family and its entourage were literary patrons and supporters of the visual arts; its most promising scholars had lived and travelled abroad, and some of them were widely read in Europe. When Portugal went into crisis and the cosmopolitan team that King John III had brought from abroad was replaced at the Colégio das Artes, Teive's situation changed, and he lived with the suspicion of Protestantism hanging over his head. After the death of King John III, the struggle for power between Queen Catherine and Cardinal Henry would eventually lead to the rise of a new cultural scene in Portugal under the influential and powerful Inquisition and the Jesuit Order. In this sense, Teive's epithalamium mirrors the tensions (and often the contradictions) of deep historical and cultural changes in Portugal in the second half of the sixteenth century: the choice of Paulinus's epithalamium as a model of structural imitation is a sign of Teive's commitment to a new cultural scene, and yet the poet is unable and unwilling to reject his humanistic background.

FROM LLUÍS JOAN VILETA TO JOAN PUJOL: LATIN AND VERNACULAR POETRY ON THE BATTLE OF LEPANTO IN CATALONIA

EULÀLIA MIRALLES
(UNIVERSITAT AUTÒNOMA DE BARCELONA)
PEP VALSALOBRE
(UNIVERSITAT DE GIRONA, INSTITUT DE LLENGUA I CULTURA CATALANES)

Learned poetry of the sixteenth century in Catalan is characterized, as it is all over Europe, by the tension between native tradition and the assimilation of newer features, not in conflict, but rather in a process of progressive amalgamation. Catalan poetry is a reaction less to a simple dichotomy than to a notable plurality of stimuli. The most remarkable of these new features are found, as was to be expected, in the adoption of Italianate strophic forms and the dictates of Petrarchism. Other aspects which coincide with the poetry of Renaissance Europe are the cultivation of the imitation of popular poetry and learned glosses on oral poetry.

There are, however, some poetic tendencies which are suggestive of traditionalist belatedness. By which we mean the imitation and poetic celebration of Ausiàs March, a poet of the previous century, as well as several translations of his work into Castilian and numerous editions of the original in the Kingdoms of Aragon and of Castile; these editions became increasingly rigorous as the century wore on, reflecting the desire to edit a classic. Now, as March was crossed with Petrarch by the most Italianizing lyric poets writing in Castilian (starting with Boscán of Barcelona through Garcilaso de la Vega, Hurtado de Mendoza or Gutierre de Cetina, among others)[1] and this admixture was spread in Italianized metrical and stanzaic

---

This article has been written within the framework of the HUM2006-08326/FILO Project for the Spanish Ministry of Education and Science.
[1] See Kathleen McNerney, *The Influence of Ausiàs March on Early Golden Age Castilian Poetry* (Amsterdam: Rodopi, 1982).

forms, there can be no doubt that the presence of March among the Catalan poets inclined towards Petrarchism cannot be interpreted in terms of traditional inertia or medieval survival, as is usually considered, but of innovation.

Perhaps the most noteworthy poet of the century, displaying a simultaneous blend of practically all of these models in his work, is Pere Serafí, professional painter and literary aficionado, whose *Dos llibres de Pedro Serafín de poesia vulgar en llengua catalana* was printed in Barcelona in 1565.[2] The considerable interest of the poetry of Serafí should not lead us to forget other equally important names, such as Joan Pujol, on whom, along with his contemporary the Latin poet Lluís Joan Vileta, we shall focus in this paper.

So, despite the existence of some outstanding poets, we would be deceiving ourselves if we did not say that the learned poetic production of the sixteenth century in Catalan was quantitatively low, surprisingly low, if we compare it to the preceding and subsequent centuries. It seems as if Catalan poetry were immersed in a permanent search for its own voice after the break from medieval tradition (with the exception of March) and the appearance of new poetic forms from abroad. And in this uncertain period few authors dared launch a new poetic initiative. We prefer to see the sixteenth century in Catalan poetry as an age of crisis, in the sense of a complex period of active exploration, of divergent poetic initiatives, without any particular poetic tendency establishing itself.

This is a situation which, undoubtedly, must be seen in relation to the rapid decline in the traditional literary patronage of royal, vice-regal and noble courts, and of the higher ecclesiastical hierarchy, due to the large-scale aristocratic relocation to more ambitious courtly environments at the centre of the Iberian Peninsula, especially through the marriage policy of the upper nobility.

One should distinguish the diversity of poetic evolution in the different territories of the Catalan linguistic domain; while in Valencia the Castilianization of learned poetry is almost absolute by mid-century, in Majorca the production of Catalan poetry is outstanding in the first half, an era of intense cultural relations with Valencia, only to drop off considerably in the second.[3]

---

[2] Pere Serafí, *Poesies catalanes*, ed. Josep Romeu i Figueras (Barcelona: Barcino, 2001).

[3] On the poetry of the 1500s, see the recent syntheses by Pep Valsalobre, "La poesia catalana del Cinc-cents: a la recerca d'una veu pròpia," *Revista de Catalunya* 210 (October 2005): 79-111, and P. Valsalobre, "La poesia al

A few points must now be mentioned regarding new features of the cultural panorama in Catalonia in the second half of the century. On the one hand, there was a certain literary production which adopted the religious and cultural formulations of the so-called Counter Reformation. On the other, there arose a movement for cultural retrenchment which appears to be linked to groups connected to the University of Barcelona and certain minor nobility whose aim was to define a cultural tradition of their own. To this end, they opposed the cultural exchange that Catalonia maintained with Castile during the first half of the century.

Involved in the literary promotion of this dual aim—Counter Reformation and cultural retrenchment—we find the poet Joan Pujol, priest of Mataró, a coastal town near Barcelona. His work in verse is preserved in two witnesses: an edition printed in Barcelona in 1573 and a manuscript preserved in the Bibliothèque Nationale in Paris. The principal language in his verse is Catalan, though there are also poems in Castilian and Latin. His oeuvre can be classified into three broad categories: a poetic cycle on the victory at Lepanto, a group of texts related to the figure and work of Ausiàs March and a third more heterogeneous group of moral-didactic poems, spiritual works, etc.[4]

In the first two sections, referring to Lepanto and to March, there are patent signs of the dual aim mentioned above. Regarding March, Pujol offers a Counter-Reformation moralizing, even theological, reinterpretation, of his poetry, encouraged by his "master" Lluís Joan Vileta. This is shown in the poem *Visió en somni*, in which Pujol launches an effusive panegyric of Vileta, especially praising his activity in defence of Ramon Llull, considered the cultural glory of the Catalan tradition, and declaring Vileta the only valid interpreter of March; all of which is sanctioned in this poem by the fifteenth-century poet himself, when he appears to the author in the poetic dream. Furthermore, Pujol opposes the Renaissance diffusion of March and especially the translations into Castilian of his work, which he considers untranslatable, and therefore, inalienable from the Catalan tradition in which he writes.[5]

Cinccents," in *Panorama crític de la literatura catalana. Segles XVI-XVIII*, dir. by Albert Rossich (Barcelona: Vicens Vives, 2010, in press).

[4] A single edition of his Catalan work is available: Joan Pujol, *Obra poètica*, ed. Karl-Heinz Anton (Barcelona: Edicions 62, 1970). For the quotations from the work of Pujol and Vileta we have used the edition of E. Miralles and P. Valsalobre, currently in preparation.

[5] For the Marchian element in Pujol see Pep Valsalobre, "Joan Pujol: una lectura contrareformista d'Ausiàs Marc," *Estudi General* 14 (1994 [1995]): 105-35.

The most important text in Pujol's Lepanto cycle is an epic poem in three cantos describing the battle and its immediate antecedents: *La singular y admirable victòria que, per la gràcia de Nostre Senyor Déu, obtingué el Serveníssim Senyor don Juan d'Àustria de la potentíssima armada turquesca,* which gives its title to the epic and the collection of Pujol's poetry published in Barcelona in 1573.[6] The plot is developed as an epic of Catholicism against the Turkish enemy, based on the reworking of material taken from chronicles, verse chapbooks and newsbooks, using the schemes of learned epic as well as, according to the poet, oral accounts of the sea battle. Pujol's epic poem again allows a glimpse of his dual aim: to compose a homage to the Catholic victory seen as a sacred victory; and at the same time put on record the participation of Catalan soldiers in this mythic event of post-Tridentine Catholicism and, by extension, of the Catalan nation.

We said above that Pujol's work places him at the centre of the literary diffusion of the dual project of the Counter Reformation and the definition of a native cultural tradition. However, the man behind this project seems to be a figure with a well-known profile: Lluís Joan Vileta. Canon of Barcelona Cathedral, Professor of Philosophy and Theology at the University, Lullist and promoter of editions of Llull's philosophical work, Vileta published neo-Aristotelian works, attended the Council of Trent as a theologian in the company of the Bishop of Barcelona and there became involved in a dispute about the Eucharist which was printed in Venice. His successful defence of the exclusion of Llull's work from the Roman index of prohibited books won great renown in Catalan cultural circles and in general among Lullists across Europe. He was present also as a jury member in poetry competitions. Vileta was also a poet in Latin but above all he was the most important Catalan Lullist of the sixteenth century. And

---

[6] On Pujol's epic poem, see Antoni Comas, "Introducción" in Joan Pujol, *La singular y admirable victoria que per la gràcia de N. S. D. ...* (Barcelona: Diputación Provincial de Barcelona, 1971; repr. Barcelona: Pere Malo, 1573), IX-XL; Eulàlia Duran, "La historiografia catalana en el pas del Renaixement al barroc: el poema èpic sobre Lepant de Joan Pujol (1573)," in *La cultura catalana tra l'umanesimo e il barocco.* Atti del V Convegno dell'Associazione Italiana di Studi Catalani (Venezia, 24-27 marzo 1992), ed. Carlos Romero and Rossend Arqués (Padova: Programma, 1994), 271-80; and Eulàlia Miralles, "Muses i Fama: notes per a la lectura del *Lepant* de Joan Pujol," in *Formes modernes de l'èpica (del segle XVI al segle XX),* ed. Eulàlia Miralles and Jordi Malé (Santa Coloma de Queralt: Obrador Edèndum, 2008), 11-38.

for Vileta, the defence of Llull was also the defence "del nom català" ["of the Catalan name"], of Catalan identity itself.[7]

Vileta's neo-Latin poetry is printed twice in this period, in the preliminaries of two books: one published by Jeroni Costiol and another by Joan Pujol himself—and also copied in the Paris manuscript. Which books are they? Texts related to the Battle of Lepanto: historical narrative poetry, epic poetry and a prose historical chronicle. With the Council of Trent barely concluded, Lepanto was, without doubt, the fundamental myth of the Catholic Reformation. To sing and recount the victory of troops in the service of the Catholic God against the feared and hitherto invincible Turk was an act of service to Counter-Reformation propaganda. And this is the context in which the works cited here belong.

The acclaimed victory of the Holy League over the Ottoman fleet in the Gulf of Lepanto on 7 October 1571 was interpreted by the allies not only as a military victory, but also as a demonstration of Catholic pre-eminence. The narration of the battle and the Christian victory were thereby converted into a prime element of propaganda: Europe learned that the Ottoman armada was vulnerable and that the Christian faith had triumphed. In the Iberian Peninsula, it also served to exalt the figure of Philip II and the House of Austria, and to highlight the strength of the Hispanic Monarchy as a world power. The King had been one of the figures behind the alliance, and his illegitimate brother, John of Austria, was the commander of the Holy League fleet which had brought victory to the Christians.[8]

Such was its significance that Lepanto became the motive for an important number of outstanding cultural productions throughout Catholic Europe. Writers penned narratives of the victory, artists captured it in paintings, ceramics and woodcuts, musicians dedicated compositions and civic and religious festivals were held in celebration of it. In the Iberian Peninsula, literature in Latin and the vernacular took an interest in this historic episode which highlighted the House of Austria as the standard-bearer of the defence of Catholicism: the Habsburgs, Philip II and John of Austria, assuming the inheritance of the late Charles V, played a central, active and decisive role in the conquest of the infidel.

---

[7] On Vileta, see José M.ª Madurell y Marimón, "Luis Juan Vileta," *Analecta Sacra Tarraconensia* 37 (1964): 19-76.

[8] See Frank Pierce, *La poesía épica del Siglo de Oro*, 2nd ed. (Madrid: Gredos, 1968), and Lara Vilà, *Épica e imperio. Imitación virgiliana y propaganda política en la épica española del siglo XVI* (Bellaterra: Universitat Autònoma de Barcelona, 2003) < http://www.tdx.cat/TDX-1021103-175052 >.

Let us return to Vileta and his compositions in Latin on the victory of the Holy League, printed in the works of Costiol and Pujol. Costiol, about whom we have scarcely any information, published in Barcelona in 1572 the *Primera parte de la Chrónica del muy alto y poderoso príncipe Don Juan de Austria*, in prose, followed by the *Canto al modo de Orlando, de la memorable guerra entre el gran Turco Selimo y la Señoría de Venecia, con la felicíssima victoria del sereníssimo señor Don Juan de Austria* in octaves, which is mainly a translation from the Italian.

Besides his relationship with Costiol and Pujol, Vileta also appears linked to another poet who likewise praised the victory at Lepanto also in Castilian octaves: the Sardinian military officer Antonio de Lo Frasso, author of the pastoral novel *Los diez libros de Fortuna de Amor* (Barcelona, 1573), a work praised ironically by Cervantes the preliminaries of which feature a sonnet by the author in praise of Vileta. Now, two years before, Lo Frasso had published a long historical narrative poem on Lepanto, *El verdadero discurso de la gloriosa vitoria que Nuestro Señor Dios a dado al sereníssimo Señor Don Joan de Austria contra la armada del Turco en las mares de Lepanto* (Barcelona, 1571).

The series of major poetic texts printed in Catalonia relating to the maritime victory of the Holy League is as follows: 1571, Lo Frasso; 1572, Costiol; finally, in 1573 and in Catalan, Pujol. The most noticeable fact is that all of these, as we have seen, are linked to the figure of Vileta, who would appear to be the intellectual mentor of the group. However, the divergences between the texts of Lo Frasso, Costiol and Pujol are also very clear, to the extent that the few coincidences that can be found between the three are strictly the result of their use of the same historical sources, that is to say, the chronicles and chapbooks which were previously in circulation. So, despite belonging to the same intellectual group, with Vileta at the centre, we can conclude that the preceding texts did not constitute a model or a source for the Pujol poem. This was probably because they belonged to different literary genres.

Be this as it may, the historical importance of Pujol's epic poem in the Hispanic literary world, as yet unrecognized, must be stressed.[9] It is, without doubt, an epic poem: such was the intention of the author, confirmed by the models he used. It is, moreover, the first epic poem dealing with Lepanto in a vernacular language published in the Iberian Peninsula. The text regarded as the first to be the printed in the Peninsula about Lepanto is in Latin: *Ad Catholicum ... Philippum Dei gratia*

---

[9] For poetry on Lepanto, we must still turn to the classic work of José López de Toro, *Los poetas de Lepanto* (Madrid: Instituto Histórico de la Marina, 1950).

Hispaniarum regem De foelicissima ... Austrias carmen ..., by Juan Latino, published in Granada in 1573, the same year that Pujol's book appeared.[10] The other epics printed in the vernacular by Hispanic authors on Lepantine themes come much later. In fact, the third Hispanic epic dedicated entirely to Lepanto, the *Felicíssima victoria concedida del cielo al señor don Juan d'Austria, en el golfo de Lepanto de la poderosa armada Othomana*, by the Portuguese Jerónimo de Corte Real, composed in blank verse in fifteen cantos, did not appear in print in Lisbon until 1578. Other Hispanic poets recounted episodes from the battle in epic form, but these were mainly fragments inserted into texts dealing with unrelated or more general topics. Such was the case with Alonso de Ercilla who dedicated canto XXIV of the second part of *La Araucana*, published in 1578, to Lepanto.[11] Similarly, in *La Austriada* (Madrid, 1584) Juan Rufo described the battle in cantos XXII-XXIV, as did the Valencian soldier Cristóbal de Virués, who deals with it in canto IV of *El Monserrate* (Madrid, 1588).[12] Of a different cut is the lyric *Canción en alabança de la divina magestad, por la vitoria del señor don Juan,* by Fernando de Herrera, which begins "Cantemos al Señor, que en la llanura" (1571?), of only 212 lines, a passionate panegyric of the victory and an execration of the Turk in the form of an ode to God, without entering into any historical details.

As regards Vileta, he celebrated the Battle of Lepanto and the consequent victory of the Holy League with an enthusiastic *De mira et singulari uictoria quam nupter diuino fauore ab ingenti turcarum classe reportauit dominus Ioannes ab Austria, classis christianae inuictissimus imperator*, a set of three brief poems in Latin distichs. The general heading of these three poems, *De mira et singulari uictoria ...*, serves also as the title of the first and longest (22 verses); the others are two *oktastikha*, the first entitled *Ad fortunatam Barcinonem, unde dominus Ioannes ab Austria felice omine soluit, factis pie uotis diuae Eulaliae octasticon extemporaneum* and the second, *Ad Philipum regem catholicum extemporaneum octastichon inuitans ad fructum uictoriae.*

The theologian Vileta is neither the first nor last poet in the Peninsula to celebrate the famous victory in Latin: this would also be done by Juan

---

[10] The royal printing licence for Latino's text is October 1572 and for Pujol's 13 May 1573. The licence for Latino's text states that the book has not been written yet and that once completed, it must be reviewed before printing; for Pujol's text, the licence was granted once the text had been reviewed.

[11] On another occasion, it will be useful to explore the coincidences detected between the texts of Pujol and Ercilla.

[12] On the epic in Castilian, see most recently Lara Vilà, *Épica e imperio*; see also Pierce, *La poesía épica.*

Latino in his epic, the Aragonese Antonio Agustín in an epyllium, Fernando Ruiz de Villegas of Burgos in hexameters, or the Valencian Jaume Joan Falcó, to mention only the most eminent names. Therefore, Vileta is only one more writer who turns this episode into literature using Latin. Now, his compositions in Latin were a source of inspiration for Pujol, who would gloss them in Catalan shortly afterwards; Pujol, moreover, would write in the same language about the same theme, his epic poem *La singular y admirable* ..., also known as the *Lepant*.

The relationship between Vileta and Pujol might be defined as that of the intellectual master whose cultural concerns are furthered by the disciple by literary means, rooted in the double axis of Counter Reformation and Catalan cultural retrenchment: the reinterpretation of March, propaganda for the master's pro-Lullian and pro-Tridentine activity, and the literary apotheosis of Lepanto as the ultimate symbol of the Tridentine Catholicism of the time and Catalan participation in it. Although Vileta was only one year older than Pujol, it would appear that the latter considered him a model: this is clearly demonstrated in the highly-valued *Visió en somni* and in specific parallels in his work as a whole. Two poets will be glossed by Pujol: March and Vileta himself. This parallel is not of course fortuitous. At other points in his oeuvre, Pujol will also praise his master, as in the first octave of his gloss on Vileta's Latin Lepanto poem:

Les Muses fan   per si bell aposent
y gran ciutat   d'una gentil vileta,
perquè molt temps   cercant posada feta
may han trobat   alberch a son content;
demostren-ho   ab subtil argument
lo bell concert   dels versos qui·s seguexen,
qui tal renom   assí vivint li dexen
que aprés de mort   veuran sempre crexent.[13] (*Introductió*, lines 1-8)

The Muses change a charming "vileta" (a village or small town) into a great city: the play on Vileta's name is obvious. The pen of Vileta, a great poet, has been blessed by the daughters of Jupiter.

---

[13] Working translation: "The Muses make a fine room / And great city from a genteel village / For a long time searching firm repose / Never have they found lodgings to their pleasing; / They demonstrate it with subtle arguments / Beautiful agreement of the verses that follow / Who with such fame in life thus leave him / That after death shall be seen to grow eternal".

Several of Pujol's texts form what we have call the "Lepantine cycle" in his poetic work: preceded by some preliminaries—dedicated to the nobleman Jeroni de Pinós—the main body is composed of the *Lepant* and the Latin poems of Vileta with Pujol's glosses; the cycle is closed by some poems lauding the author and Pujol's responses. The main body is, at the same time, fragmented into two parts, as can be seen. The first of these (the *Lepant*) precedes the second (poems by Vileta and glosses by Pujol) in the arrangement of the witnesses. The fact that it precedes it does not mean that it was written first: Vileta's poem was written before April 1572 (the date of the printing licence of Costiol's work), the gloss by Pujol must have been composed at the same time or not much later, and the *Lepant* was possibly written before May 1572.[14] We have, then, a series of compositions written in a very short period, between the time that news of the victory reached the Peninsula and the first months of 1572.

Pujol's glossed translation appears headed by an *Introductió de l'auctor dels següents versos latins*, in two octaves. There follows the gloss of Vileta's three poems: the first under the rubric *Traductió de l'autor dels sobredits latins versos*, and the following two *A la fortunada Barcelona* and *Al rey Philip*—with some differences depending on the witnesses. Each of Pujol's octaves corresponds to a distich of Vileta's: thus the first gloss consists of eleven octaves, and the next two of four each.

Pujol's epic is a relatively brief text if we compare it to other works of the same genre; 1600 lines in three cantos. The first two cantos narrate the historical background of the battle, the Turkish conquest of Cyprus and the establishment of the Holy League, and the third tells of the encounter between the fleets in the Gulf of Lepanto and the victory of the Catholic armada.

The *Lepant* is important in the context of literature in the Peninsula in the sixteenth century although, perhaps because it was written in Catalan, it has gained little attention from specialists, a situation which strikes us as incomprehensible: it is one of the first epic poems about Lepanto to be written after the battle and the first in the vernacular. Thus it is of importance that Pujol had no epic predecessors for his theme, and certainly not in Catalan. Pujol's poem must be included in the context of Renaissance Hispanic epic and displays some clear characteristics which must be related to the twin aims—Counter Reformation and cultural retrenchment—of literary production which we have indicated; Catalan national assertiveness is to the fore in the second half of the sixteenth

---

[14] Miralles, "Muses i Fama," 13.

century and we find it in the *Lepant*: first, in the importance given to the
city of Barcelona, the port of departure for the fleet; second, in the lengthy
naming of Catalan lineages (the Requesens and Cardona families are
treated as the paradigm of the heroes of Lepanto); finally, and perhaps
most significantly, in the lack of reference to the earlier feats of arms of
the House of Austria (poets from the Peninsula usually took as precedents
the campaigns of Charles V against the Turks, or the celebrated revolt of
the Alpujarras which John of Austria helped to quell). Pujol recreates a
Hispanic framework but makes visible the Catalan participation in the
great deeds of the monarchy, which are normally attributed to figures from
the Kingdom of Castile.

Let us now look at how Vileta's Latin poetry on Lepanto, translated
and glossed by Pujol, is reflected in the latter's epic. The themes dealt with
by Vileta are announced in the rubrics of his Latin poems and Pujol's
glosses: the victory at Lepanto, the city of Barcelona, and lastly, Philip II.
The incorporation of these themes in the *Lepant* is predictable: the victory
at Lepanto is the occasion of the poem; the House of Austria is the right
arm of the Catholic Church, and by extension, of God, in the battle; the
city of Barcelona, its patron saint, St Eulalia, and natives of the city (here,
by extension, the combatants of Catalan lineage), play an active, decisive
part in the naval warfare. Vileta's exhortation to continue fighting against
the infidels is also present in the *Lepant* of Pujol.

The subjects and their treatment in Vileta's compositions, their
spiritual themes, their plastic and acoustic images of battle are also found
in Pujol's glosses and the *Lepant*. An episode from the celebrated battle
serves as an example: in Vileta, Jupiter and Neptune hold a dialogue
where they agree that control of the world, until then in their hands, is in
danger. There occurs an inversion of established roles because "occupat
oceanum glomerata potentia papae / et mare Ioannes temperat austriacus"
["John of Austria occupies the ocean with the allied strength of the Pope
and [with this strength] tempers the sea"] (*De mira et singulari uictoria*,
lines 9-10). The verbs used by Vileta to recreate the moment (*tremefacio,
clamo, increpo, intono*), and the substantive (*fulmen*), serve to reinforce
the idea of an inversion of established values: the desire of "Iupiter
Altitonans" to have his voice heard, to communicate with his gods, has
been broken by a superior presence, that of God, who accompanies the
combatants. The same dialogue appears in Pujol's gloss, though more
developed: here, he presents a fearful Jupiter ("ab gran terror", *Traductió*,
1); and Neptune fleeing the deafening battle, trembling and voiceless: "qui
fugitiu d'aquelles parts venia / tot tremolant, que parlar no podia" (26-27).
Since then, the power of Jupiter shall never again be absolute:

Aquell poder   qui puja·ls crestians
a l'etern goig   de la divin·altura
del Sanct Pastor,   qui ab divina cura
pot concedir   als seus tresors molt grans,
tot en un munt   plegat y ajustat,
té lo gran mar   constret ab sa puxança,
y el Austrià   la tempr·ab tal bonança
que va pertot   segur y molt guiat.[15] (*Traductió,* 33-40)

Absolute power is in the hands of almighty God, and his representative on Earth, the Pope, shall be charged with guiding the combatants of Lepanto. John of Austria ("el Austrià"), captain general of the Mediterranean and fleet commander for the Holy League against the Turkish armada, is to be the right arm of Catholicism.

In the third canto of the *Lepant*, John of Austria urges his combatants to fight to the death, raising the Cross in his hand as a standard (908, 953, 1261, 1570). It seems as though the end of the world is approaching ("Semblà que fos vingut lo darrer jorn, / que tornaran tots los mortals reviure" ["It seemed as if the final day had arrived / when all mortals shall live again"]; 1061-62), since the combat witnessed cannot be compared to any other ("Perquè fonch tal y de tanta furor, / qu·en nigun lloch s'és vista may tal cosa" ["For such fire and fury / nowhere have been seen before"]; 1073-74), and at this time, the description of the battlefield (especially lines 1053-84) refers to the thunderous uproar that Vileta describes in the words of Jupiter and Neptune, when these two see that their empire is threatened:

Si may haveu   oyit un boniment
d'espessos trons,   quant ab rellamps desparen,
la hu seguint   a l'altre, que may paren,
sens reposar   ni sols un xich moment,
tal fonch lo jorn   d'aquell cruel combat,
l'encontre dur   y fúria molt terrible,
ab un remor   tan gran y tan orrible
que no·s pot fer   fingir major esclat.[16] (*Lepant,* 1077-84)

---

[15] "That power which lifts the Christians / To the eternal joy of divine heights / Of the holy shepherd who with divine care / May concede his great treasures / All in a mound folded and trimmed / It holds the great sea constrained with its rise / And Austria tempers it with such goodness / That he goes forth sure and well guided".

[16] "If ever was heard a break / Of heavy thunder with lightning bursts / One after the other, neverending, / Without pause not even for a moment / Such fire that day

Lightning bolts and thunderclaps govern the world, although this time it is not Jupiter who throws them, but the Christian heroes.

This Christianization of the pagan themes is present throughout the *Lepant*. Pujol opens his epic by asking the Muses for their help and conversing with Fame, a Fame who writes in her book the names of the Christian warriors as the battle progresses, a battle in which God intervenes in a decisive manner: the list is populated solely by men of the Holy League. In the gloss of the poem dedicated to the city of Barcelona, it is also God who is responsible for establishing the list of names of the heroes of Lepanto.

It is Vileta who describes with precision, in the episode of the dialogue of the gods, the inversion of the established order: his God, the strength that God gives to men, dethrones the pagan gods. The world order has shifted, old governors lose strength, thunder and lightning, elements that characterize Jupiter, now frighten him and his brother, Neptune. The idea that the Christian victory is more divine than human in this episode appears in other contemporary sources and so is not strange, although without being aware of the inversion effected by Vileta, it would be more difficult to understand Pujol's war images in his *Lepant*.

There are other elements that invite discussion of the echoes of Vileta found in Pujol: the treatment of the figure of Charles V is one of these. Vileta's two references to the Emperor must be seen in relation to his sons: firstly, John of Austria is referred to as "hanc Caroli sobolem" ["this offspring of Charles"] (*De mira et singulari uictoria* 12), or, as Pujol puts it, of "un fill senyalat / de Carles quint" ["an appointed son / of Charles the Fifth"] (*Traductió* 41-42); the second is found in the *oktastikhon* dedicated to Philip II. Here we see a star which, from the world of the dead, guides King Philip, who will follow the same destiny as the star which shines and guides him now. The star is Charles V, and Philip II follows in his father's footsteps:

> stella micat, propera occiduo te ducet ab orbe.
> Te manet hocce decus, diue Philippe, tuum;
>   perpetuo uiues felix caeloque coruscum
> fulgebit sidus, diue Philippe, tuum.[17] (*Ad Philippum*, 5-8)

---

from that cruel combat / That hard encounter and most terrible fury, / With a noise so great and horrible / A greater din could not be imagined".

[17] "The star shines [which] will rapidly lead you from the western world. This honour, which is yours, divine Philip, will remain with you. You will always live happily and in heaven, divine Philip, the bright star which is yours will shine".

Pujol's gloss reinforces the idea that the star refers to the father, Charles V:

L'estela veig   que gran claredat llança
qui us guiarà   del ponent molt segura:
seguiu, cuytau,   seguiu vostra ventura,
no y ha perquè   dupteu de sa mudança;
a vós ha pres   lo Rey de l'etern sostre
per acabar   un fet de tal valia
y tal honor   a vós sol se devia
y al gran poder,   divino Philip, vostre.

Sempre viureu   ab benaventurança
ab los elets   en la divin-altura,
hon convertit   en clarejant figura,
fruint a Déu,   pendreu nova semblança.
Creheu de ferm   sens dupte lo que us mostre,
qu·entre los sancts   oyint sanct-armonia,
claror més gran   que·l sol enmitg del dia
darà l'estel,   divino Philip, vostre.[18] (*Al rey Philip*, 17-32)

In this way, the poet tells us that Philip is chosen by God to continue the work of the father on Earth (21-22); by doing do, he will be converted "en novella figura" ["a new figure"] according to one witness to his gloss or "en clarejant figura" ["the figure of a new dawn"] according to the other (27). Pujol underlines this idea in the following verse: "pendreu nova semblança" ["you assume a new appearance"] (28).

The motif of the conversion into a star after death, or *catasterism*, comes from ancient literature where it is frequently applied to kings, emperors and pagan gods; here it is emphasized that these new stars are placed "en las alturas" ["on high"], close to God. In the *Lepant*, the presence of a Charles figure who watches over and guides his offspring from Heaven is recurrent and significant: the poet informs us that John of Austria is the "fill valerós" ["valiant son"] or "l'animós fill" ["spirited

---

[18] "The star I see throws great clarity / That guides you on a sure, west wind / Follow, take care, follow its destiny. / There is no reason to doubt its movement / The King has taken to the eternal roof / To end a deed of such bravery / And honour it directs itself to you alone / And to great power divine Phillip, yours. // You shall live on with blessings / With the elect in the divine heights / Where, become a bright figure, enjoying God, you will assume a new appearance / Believe firmly without doubt what I show you / Who among the saints hearing sacred harmony, / A greater light than the sun at midday / Shall give, divine Phillip, yours".

son"] (509-10, 974, 1278) of the Emperor Charles and that it is Philip who passes on to his brother the power and honour which are due to him: "Jo vull que vós aneu en lo meu lloc / [...]; per vós serà de Carlos renovat / lo bell renom y les grans valenties, / qui gloriós entre les hierarchies, / alt en lo cel, viu benaventurat" ["I want you to go in my place / [...]; by you shall be Charles's beautiful renown and great bravery be renewed / who, glorious among hierarchies, / high in heaven, lives in good fortune"] (525, 529-532). And it is Charles who will close the *Lepant* from the "divina altura", reinforcing his decisive role in the composition.

There are other elements to be found in Vileta and Pujol which stem from their shared vision of the world, as we mentioned at the beginning of this paper: the assumption of certain cultural and religious aims of the Counter Reformation and the assertion of Catalan national culture and politics. They are elements which can be tied to what has been suggested here: the idea of the renewal of time through the figure of Charles's sons, the weight of Catalonia in the composite monarchy of the House of Austria, etc.

The poems of Vileta with Pujol's glosses, and the *Lepant*, feed back into each other. Differences aside (of metre, language and especially length), they are works which present remarkable coincidences and complement one another. Not only do they deal with a common theme, like so many others dedicated to the historic episode and its diffusion as propaganda, either in Latin or the vernacular, in prose or in verse, but they do so on the basis of shared references. Pujol reads and interprets Vileta very well in his gloss (though at first he tells us, in an inescapable *captatio beneuolentiae*, that his verses are for him "no ben conversos / o traduïts en lengua vulgarment" ["not well converted / or translated into vernacular language"]; *Introductió*, 7-8),[19] whilst in works on more than one occasion he exhibits his admiration for the Lullist Vileta and subjects his thoughts and actions to Vileta the theologian (*Visió en somni*).

It is clear that Vileta influences Pujol, that the former permeates the work of the latter directly (in person) and indirectly (through his ideas), and it is fair to assume that they shared moments of debate on how the subject of Lepanto should be addressed. It is also clear that the dates of composition of the poems are very close and that the influence could have come from personal contact between the two authors.

---

[19] This is from the reading of the printed book; for the later reading of the manuscript, see the octave quoted above (p. 166).

THE EUHEMERISM OF LACTANTIUS IN CAMÕES'S *LUSIADS*

HÉLIO J. S. ALVES
(UNIVERSIDADE DE ÉVORA)

In a highly thought-provoking essay published in 2007, João Ricardo Figueiredo of the University of Lisbon wrote that I, in my "brilliant analysis of Euhemerism in the *Lusiads*", demonstrated, through "acute philological work", that Camões's main source for that doctrine was Lactantius.[1] I naturally felt flattered. Unfortunately, however, I am not sure that he was right ...

To begin with, as far as I am aware, no reference to Lactantius has ever occurred with relation to Camões in the scholarship. Worse, the presence of Euhemerism as a whole in the poet's work was flatly denied by some reputed scholars, among them the foremost cultural historian of Portuguese sixteenth-century letters, J. S. da Silva Dias. After stating that "the dialectics and polemics of Italian and Christian humanism do not resonate, in the slightest, in the life or the work of the Poet" (p. 41), Silva Dias writes:

> With the news that reached [Camões] about the New World, and above all from what he personally observed in Africa and Asia, the obvious fact that Christianity was a minority religion in global terms—and, more than a minority, actually unknown even to the greater number of the Earth's inhabitants—could not have gone unnoticed. This fact, known to him, did not express itself in Euhemerism in his thinking. We shall look in vain for Euhemerism in his works. Even stanzas 80-82 of the Tenth Canto of the *Lusiads* [...] are far from Euhemerism. They are only a demystification of

---

[1] João R. Figueiredo, "Pais Tiranos: o Baco de *Os Lusíadas* e Camões," in *A Teoria do Programa. Uma homenagem a Maria de Lourdes Ferraz e a M. S. Lourenço,* ed. António M. Feijó and Miguel Tamen (Lisboa: Universidade de Lisboa, 2007), 32. Translations here and throughout this article are my own, unless stated otherwise.

pagan mythology, a late confirmation of this mythology's death over a millenium earlier.[2]

Silva Dias seems to identify Euhemerism with rationalist tendencies in sixteenth-century European philosophy; and because he rejects any sign of these tendencies in Camões's poetry, the historical interpretation of the pagan gods signified by Euhemerism falls short of real consideration in his work. This is, at least, my argument for the present purpose, as supported by Silva Dias's denial of any inkling of Renaissance "free-thinking" in Camões's poetry (67).

It cannot be denied, however, that Euhemerism played an important role in early Christian polemical writing against classical paganism. This, of course, is where Lactantius, but also other Christian thinkers from the early Middle Ages, come into play. By revealing the hidden human nature of gods like Jove, Juno, Venus, Mars and so on (to use their Roman names), Christian writers were ready and willing to debunk their divine nature and, therefore, their supernatural attributes and aptitudes.

At the same time, by showing the base nature of individual names and figures of the Greek and Latin pantheon, Christian polemical writing opened the way to the inclusion of such arguments in Christian literature in general. This is true of Camões as of everybody else. Expounding Euhemeristic theory and binding the pagan gods to it, a writer could perfectly well stay within the bounds of Christian dogma. In this case, rationalization of divinity was tantamount to proselytizing for the one and only true Christian God.

I would therefore argue that Silva Dias is right in identifying in Camões a Scholastic framework to his thought and a firmly Catholic grounding to the poetic expressions we know of him—no one, in any case, has covered the difficult groundwork as well as Silva Dias in the fields of Portuguese Renaissance philosophy and theology—but I would add that Euhemerism was included, within, again, a perfectly Catholic perspective, in the structural procedures and strategies which served Camões's rhetorical and poetic purposes.

This is not to say, of course, that Euhemerism was totally safe and innocent ground. Faria e Sousa, the most abundant and influential commentator on the *Lusiads,* seems to make no reference at all to Euhemerus, or this mysterious character's theory, at least in explicit terms. In any case, it does not seem that the tradition of Camonian studies made

---

[2] J. S. da Silva Dias, *Camões no Portugal de Quinhentos,* Col. "Biblioteca Breve" (Lisboa: ICALP—Ministério da Educação e Cultura, 1981), 71.

much use of the interpretation of the gods *historialiter* that characterizes Euhemerism. It is true that the fragment of Cicero's *Republic* which survived as *The Dream of Scipio* throughout the Middle Ages has been mentioned *à propos* the Portuguese epic ever since the first commentary proper in the language, Manoel Correia's text—probably interpolated by Pedro de Mariz—published in 1613. But the critics disagree, not only on the dream's meaning for Camões, but even more so on the passage of the *Lusiads* to which it could apply. The commentator of 1613 notes Scipio's dream as an aid to understanding stanza 73 of Canto X, while twentieth-century critics mention it with regard to other tracts: a piece of Canto IV (Rebelo Gonçalves) and another from Canto IX (Carvalhão Buescu).[3] The latter scholar recalls Scipio's dream in its eschatological significance, derived from mixed philosophical origins including Platonism and the Stoa.

However, Euhemerism is mentioned nowhere in these Camonian interpreters. We can imagine why. Manoel Correia wrote about "the turpitude of ancient idolaters, who made men out of gods" ("a torpeza dos antigos idólatras, que faziam seus deuses homens") (fol. 71r)[4] and it is unimaginable that Camões, for the mainstream of commentators, could have been, at any time, confused with an idolater. The *nobility* of Cicero's dream was not conducive to recalling such base thoughts. And therefore, the idea that Camões could have made structural use of a pagan doctrine that literally "transformed gods into men" was, or could be understood to be, at the very least disagreeable, at the most sinful and dangerous. Idolatry and paganism come together before Christian eyes, as both may suggest that divinity originates from humanity, an idea that can risk denying the very creation of humankind by a God.

Where I disagree with Silva Dias's rejection of the presence of Euhemerism in Camões is in that he focuses on the passage at the end of Canto IX where the gods are made human, without checking whether that schema could apply to the *poetic* use of the gods in the epic. In other words, it is true that the poet is making an anachronistic demystification of pagan mythology in a perfectly dogmatic, Counter-Reformation, way, but Camões is at the same time revealing that the narrative *fabula* of the Greek gods in the *Lusiads* pertains, in some fundamental way, to this

---

[3] Rebelo Gonçalves, *Dissertações Camonianas* (São Paulo-Rio de Janeiro-Recife: Companhia Editora Nacional, 1937), 79-80. Maria Leonor Carvalhão Buescu, *Ensaios de Literatura Portuguesa* (Lisbon: Presença, 1986), 33 and 60-61.

[4] Cited by Edward Glaser, "Manuel de Faria e Sousa and the Mythology of *Os Lusíadas*," reprinted in his *Portuguese Studies* (Paris: Fundação Calouste Gulbenkian, Centro Cultural Português, 1976), 135-57 (153).

understanding of their presence and role in the poem. This is why the end of what could be called, albeit inadequately, the "plot of the gods", which occurs on the Isle of Love with its connubial and apotheotic central attributes, comes together with the following "denunciation" of their meaning:

> Que as imortalidades que fingia
> A antiguidade, que os ilustres ama,
> Lá no estelante Olimpo
> [...]
> Não eram senão prémios que reparte,
> Por feitos imortais e soberanos,
> O mundo c'os varões que esforço e arte
> Divinos os fizeram, sendo humanos.
> Que Júpiter, Mercúrio, Febo e Marte,
> Eneias e Quirino e os dous Tebanos,
> Ceres, Palas e Juno com Diana,
> Todos foram de fraca carne humana.
> [Those immortals whom men of antiquity,
> In their love of great deeds, imagined
> Living there on starry Olympus [...]
> Were enjoying only those rewards
> The world bestows for the superb,
> Deathless achievements of heroes
> Who, though human, became divine;
> Jupiter, Mercury, Phoebus, and Mars,
> Aeneas, Romulus, and the two Thebans,
> Ceres, Pallas, Diana, Juno they
> Were all composed of feeble human clay.] (IX, 90-91)[5]

After this, there is no more involvement of the gods in the historical human endeavour, and I think one can conclude without much controversy that this passage provides one key for our hermeneutical efforts.

Alas, readers and critics have not enjoyed the idea! Sir Maurice Bowra actually thought that this "explanation is worse than an anticlimax; if we treat it seriously, it spoils much of the poem".[6] And there you have another reason why even modern criticism did not develop the Euhemeristic connection: it ruins the realistic presence of these gods full of "personal" traits, it ruins the illusion so essential to fiction; in a word, it ruins the entertainment. In the context, it is not surprising, therefore, that critics and

---

[5] Luís Vaz de Camões, *The Lusíads*, translated with and introduction and notes by Landeg White, The World's Classics (Oxford: Oxford University Press, 1997).
[6] *From Virgil to Milton* (London: Macmillan, 1945), 117.

literary historians bent on praising Camões's masterpiece were not enthusiastic, to say the least, about referring to Euhemerism.

However, the entire point of epic poems such as the *Lusiads,* in their sixteenth-century encyclopaedic purposes, is that they had high didactic intentions and, at the same time, were quite eager to convey depth of meaning throughout the text. To summarize my view, the readers' illusion resides precisely in taking the *Lusiads* as essentially realistic fiction rather than something else, i.e., rhetorical discourse committed to making an impact in virtually all fields of human activity and culture. Allegory was certainly one of the means to achieve this, and there is no need, I think, to explain why the pagan gods were such ideal vehicles for narrative allegory.[7] The possibility that the gods signified a "translation to the stars" of mere human beings, and therefore that they *also* could mean humanity in one or another of its features, is a possibility clearly open and encouraged by the excerpt from Camões just quoted.

Whether this poetic Euhemerism implies a strict focus on Lactantius is a different matter ... Lactantius seems to be the oldest known Christian source on Euhemerus, mentioned by name in the *Divine Institutions* (I, xi, 33). More than that, the book discusses Euhemerism in abundance and in some detail. The *Divinae Institutiones*, as is to be expected, were published in very many sixteenth-century editions all over Europe, not to mention abbreviated versions and citations. If it were not for the obvious reluctance felt by commentators in scrutinizing the *Lusiads'* Euhemerism or even accepting its existence in the poem, it would be surprising that they granted so little scholarly attention to Lactantius, given his importance to medieval and Renaissance culture.

Let us begin with one example of how attention to Lactantius can suppose a radical reevaluation of the *Lusiads* and of its signifying structures. The epic's preeminent commentator, Faria e Sousa, equates the god Jupiter, as represented in the poem, with Christ or the Godhead.[8] He found some support in the passage in the epic, X, 83, 1-2, which states flatly that "Holy Providence" ("a Santa Providência") is meant in the poem by Jupiter ("que em Júpiter aqui se representa"). Jupiter, in Faria e Sousa's view, should then consistently allegorize God or Christ, and the poet thus establishes, from the beginning, a hierarchy of the characters' existence and presence that is clear and coherent. More than that, the

---

[7] See Michael Murrin, *Allegorical Epic* (Chicago: University of Chicago Press, 1980), for an extensive discussion.

[8] *Lusiadas de Luis de Camoens, Principe de los Poetas de España [...] comentadas por Manuel de Faria i Sousa,* 2 vols (Madrid: Juan Sánchez, 1639; facsimile repr. Lisboa: Imprensa Nacional-Casa da Moeda, 1972).

Lusiads becomes, in such hermeneutics, a kind of theological master poem, expressing the deepest mysteries of the Christian Church in a ciphered manner second only to Holy Scripture itself. This at least was Faria e Sousa's project and conclusion. And although most critics did not follow him, to this day the *Lusiads* often raises in readers the temptation to explore issues of metaphor, to search for "secret" deeper meanings, which tend to find in the gods the ideal excuse for such exercises.

In Canto I, stanza 22, Camões describes Jupiter in his divine and human nature. Faria e Sousa explains the fact by reminding the reader that God became flesh and so Jupiter can be portrayed as assuming both natures. Now, the *Divine Institutions,* one of the greatest defences of figurative literature in Early Christianity, affirms quite straightforwardly that those who give to the supreme God the name of Jupiter are vain and empty, and cannot be confused with poets (I, xi). Lactantius says: "Poets spoke of men; what happened was that, to praise those whose memory they celebrate, they said they were gods" (I, xi, 17). This represents, of course, basic rhetorical and epideictic knowledge, both during the time of Lactantius, and in the time of Camões. Applying this to the *Lusiads* naturally overturns Faria e Sousa's allegorization of Jupiter in Canto I, stanza 22. In the light of Lactantius, the Portuguese epic's Jupiter is a human being who became a god. The consequence of this is far-reaching, because Lactantius teaches the reader—with many and very clear examples—to understand how the poets proceed in their myth-making and to clarify the limits of poetic licence and *elegantia*. If we are to accept that Camões knew and followed Lactantius, the "Christian Cicero", as one of the very major Christian authorities on the poetic representation of the gods, then Faria e Sousa's reading of Jupiter becomes impossible, while the god turns out to be, on the other hand, one of the supreme examples of Euhemeristic doctrine exposed explicitly in the poem.

Other Christian hermeneutical authorities have been identified by Camonian scholarship. Edward Glaser showed, in a still fundamental essay,[9] how important it was for Faria e Sousa that St Clement of Alexandria expounded a theory in which epic poets could reveal Christian truth through pagan fable. But in the passage cited, Faria e Sousa identifies Jupiter with the "Alto Poder, que só co'o pensamento / governa o céu, a terra e o mar irado" (I, 21), ("the High Power which rules heaven, earth and the angry sea with His thought only") i. e., an abstract all-powerful and single God, even though, both syntactically and cosmographically, the

---

[9] "Manuel de Faria e Sousa and the Mythology of *Os Lusíadas*". The passage on *Lusiads* I, 20-22 occurs on pp. 141-45.

preparation of the council of the gods in the *Lusiads* (I, 20-22) militates against this identification. Glaser's summary and source-finding of Faria e Sousa's interpretation of Jupiter becomes essential to understanding the seventeenth-century commentator, but misses the mark with respect to Camões's text.

In spite of the fact that Camões, like any other Renaissance poet, would only naturally superimpose on occasion the chief gods of both religions, it is nevertheless remarkable how few the instances are where it is unclear what particular divine being is involved, be it pagan Jupiter or a Christian (and Stoic, Platonic and perhaps other) single God. Camões's Jupiter, in fact, resists throughout identification with God or Christ, a fact that is not incompatible, within the epic tradition itself, with the Thunderer's metaphorical translation as divine providence. Virgil's *Aeneid* shows that Jupiter could mean both divine providence, and a certain field of perspectives which could not fit into any concept of divine providence.[10] As we saw, Camões explicitly identifies Jupiter with divine providence in Canto X, but in Canto I Jupiter means the king of the gods and the planet, a being in both cases subject to the Fates ("Fados") and who therefore cannot be compared to God. Furthermore, as we have also seen, in this same Canto, Jupiter is introduced as a human-become-god, a notion devoid of the slightest inklings of Christian thought.

In the passage where Camões identifies Jupiter with divine Providence, he also allegorizes the other gods as ministers of the Almighty God, by stating that Scripture itself sometimes employs the word "god" as a synonym for an angel, good or fallen:

> Quer logo aqui a pintura, que varia,
> Agora deleitando, ora insinando,
> Dar-lhe nomes que a antiga Poesia
> A seus deuses já dera, fabulando;
> Que os anjos da celeste companhia
> Deuses o sacro verso está chamando;
> Nem nega que esse nome preminente
> Também aos maus se dá, mas falsamente. (X, 84)
> [The painter with words, in his varied aims,
> At times to delight, at time instructs,
> Applies to them names the ancient poets
> Once gave their imagined gods;
> Even the Bible describes as "gods"
> The angels of the sacred company,

---

[10] See D. C. Feeney, *The Gods in Epic: Poets and Critics of the Classical Tradition* (Oxford: Clarendon Press, 1991), 154-55.

Though this pre-eminent name is misapplied
To fallen angels, wrongly deified.]

What Camões says of the Bible ("sacro verso") is true and was pointed out
specifically by a Church Father like St Augustine in *The City of God*, IX,
23, with reference to Psalms (49: 1; 135: 2) and First Corinthians (8: 5).
Lactantius, however, finds the mixture of names unacceptable. He writes:
"God elected ministers of his government; but these are neither gods, nor
do they wish to be called or adored as such" (*Divine Institutions*, I, vii, 5);
and, later on, he repeats: "angels do not permit or want to be called gods"
(*Divine Institutions*, II, xvi, 6). It is hard to imagine that Camões could
have named God's ministers "gods", and even less so evil angels ("maus"),
if he were well-read in Lactantius's work. Camões's justification of poetic
practice through theological means (notice the relative "que" joining the
first to the second half of the stanza) indicates that the poet is not merely
invoking poetic licence here; he is concerned with theological authority.
And the authority for naming Jupiter, Venus, Bacchus and the others as
"gods" runs definitely against the *Divine Institutions*.

Stanza 84 of Canto X, however, has very little to do with Euhemerism,
so it is still possible that Lactantius continued to be a main theological
source for Camões. A definitive view about the impact of Lactantius in the
Lusiads will be impossible until fundamental research on the Portuguese
poet's theology has been done. Thus far, I have found no consistent
evidence that the *Divine Institutions* are alluded to specifically by Camões.
Even with respect to Bacchus, perhaps the individual god in the *Lusiads*
who invites most citations from the *Divine Institutions*, Camões does not
portray him quite like Lactantius and significantly misses many of the
god's traits featured by the latter.[11] If one argues, as I do, that Euhemerism
is a structural device employed in the *Lusiads* to convey symbolic wealth
of meaning to the narrative of Gama's voyage, the fact remains that
intertextual evidence is missing for Lactantius's contact with Camões. The
early Christian author did act as the main intermediary between
Euhemerism and the European Middle Ages, but the Portuguese poet, who
lived many centuries later, could possibly have found sufficient
information about the doctrine from other sources.

This is not to say, of course, that the *Divinae Institutiones* were
unknown to Camões. It just means that the *Lusiads*, as far as I can see,
employs Euhemerism as an ethical and aesthetic device to suit the poem's

---

[11] For a direct comparison of Bacchus's traits in the *Lusiads* and in earlier
authorities on Euhemerism, see my *Camões, Corte-Real e o sistema da epopeia
quinhentista* (Coimbra: Por Ordem da Universidade, 2001), 629.

own strategies and symbolizations, to a degree in which Lactantius's important discussion of the pagan gods and of their role in rhetoric and poetics would have been profoundly useful to Camões in more ways than one.

PART III:

VISUAL REPRESENTATION

LUIS DE MORALES'S REPRESENTATIONS OF ST JEROME

JEAN ANDREWS
(UNIVERSITY OF NOTTINGHAM)

Luis de Morales (*c.* 1520, Badajoz – 1586, Badajoz) is a painter whose name and some of whose work are known to all serious students of Spanish sixteenth-century art. He is also a painter about whose life, artistic influences and painterly development comparatively little is known. There is no certain account of his having travelled beyond his native Extremadura, although there is much supposition that he may have studied in Seville or Portugal or both as a young man, perhaps even travelled to Italy though that is extremely doubtful, and visited Valencia much later, under the patronage of Juan de Ribera, formerly bishop of Badajoz and his erstwhile protector.[1] There is consensus that his work shows elements of Flemish style, notably in his figure drawing; he may even have worked under the Flemish painter Pieter de Kempeneer (known in Spain as Pedro de Campaña) who was based in Seville from 1537 to 1562. There is also very evident use of Leonardesque *sfumato*, perhaps gleaned from exposure to the techniques employed by followers and contemporaries of Leonardo such as Bernardino Luini and Giovanni Antonio Boltraffio, some of whose work had reached Spain, and coincidences of composition and palette with such as the Portuguese master, Fray Carlos. Isabel Mateo Gómez further

---

[1] See Isabel Mateo Gómez, "Flandes, Toledo y Portugal en la obra de Luis de Morales," *Archivo Español de Arte* 80: 317 (enero-marzo 2007): 7-24 (7-14). Mateo Gómez provides a succinct summary of the views on Morales's biography from the seminal Juan Antonio Gaya Nuño, *Luis de Morales* (Madrid: Instituto Diego Velázquez/CSIC, 1961) and Ingjald Bäcksbacka, *Luis de Morales* (Helsinki: University of Helsingfors/Societas Scientiarum Fennica, 1962) to the most recent collection of documents relating to Morales compiled by Carmelo Solís Rodríguez, *Luis de Morales* (Badajoz: Fundación Caja de Badajoz, 1999). I would like to express my deep gratitude to my colleague Jeremy Roe for invaluable advice on bibliography for this chapter.

argues that possible influence from the Toledan school and the work of Juan Correa de Vivar, for example, must not be overlooked.[2]

All in all, Morales presents a rather unique conundrum, summarized neatly in 1911 by Gaston Sortais:

> His favourite themes, frequently reproduced without any change, are "Ecce Homo", "Christ at the Column", and "The Blessed Virgin holding the Dead Christ". The drawing is clean and firm, the anatomy correct, the figures, which recall primitive German and Flemish work by their slenderness, are not wanting in grace, and at times are characterized by a certain air of melancholy. The colouring is delicate and as brilliant as enamel. Morales excels in the faculty of making his modelling stand out by the skilfully graduated employment of half-tones; like the early Northern painters, he exercises minute care in the reproduction of the beard and hair, and makes a point of rendering faithfully the drops of blood falling from the thorn-crowned brow of Christ, and the tears flowing from the eyes of the afflicted Mother.[3]

In the words of his most distinguished recent champion, Carmelo Solís Rodríguez, Morales was, in the landscape of sixteenth-century Hispanic art, "un árbol exótico, por cuyo tronco reptasen savias dispares, que hacen de él un ser solitario—por ecléctico—".[4] By choice or circumstance, then, Morales attempted a very restricted range of subject matter, even within the strictures imposed by Church patronage at the time: vignettes from the life of Christ and those of a small number of saints, to which he returned time and time again, either as panels for altarpieces or small pieces for private devotion. Because of this, and because of a certain austere spirituality to be discerned in his work, he became known as El Divino.

The origin of this appellation may be traced back to Antonio Palomino, who, writing in the early eighteenth century, asserted that:

> Fuè cognominado el Divino, assi porque todo lo que pinto, fueron cosas sagradas, como porque hizo cabezas de Christo, con tan gran primor y sutileza en los cabellos; que a èl mas curioso en el Arte, occasiona a querer

---

[2] Mateo Gómez, "Flandes, Toledo y Portugal," 8.

[3] Gaston Sortais, "Luis de Morales," in *The Catholic Encyclopedia* (New York: Robert Appleton Company, 1911), vol. X, accessed 9 Nov. 2009 <http://www.newadvent.org/cathen/10557a.htm>.

[4] Solís Rodríguez, 7. Solís's collection of documents was initially put together as part of the restoration of the Morales panels at Badajoz cathedral, in 1975.

soplarlos, para que se muevan, porque parece que tienen la misma sutileza, que los naturales.[5]

A century earlier, Francisco Pacheco had no such fine opinion of the high finish of Morales's work. Indeed his own mark of a great painter was a gradual move away from any high finish techniques mastered in the painter's youth, these latter being mere accomplishments:

> Y así da buenas esperanzas quien en sus principios acaba mucho las pinturas, de ser gran pintor, y de dar, si quisiere después, en pintar menos acabado. Y aunque digo que este segundo modo abraza la perfección del otro, entiéndese en los grandes maestros; que muchos hay y ha habido que han pintado dulcemente, y para muy cerca, a quien falta lo major de l'arte y el estudio del debuxo y aunque han tenido nombre, no ha sido entre los hombres que saben: exemplo es Morales, natural de Badajoz.[6]

Palomino apart, Pacheco seems to have established a consensus, evident to this day among many Spanish art historians and critics, that Morales was in some way sub-standard, a quasi autodidact unable to produce anatomical verisimilitude in the Italian manner, more complex figure composition or the use of a more vibrant palette, again in the Italian manner. This readiness to condemn can be seen, for example, as recently as in Jesús Manuel López Martín's excoriation of Morales's panels for the church of San Martín in Plasencia, which he undertook between 1565 and 1570, at the height of his popularity.

López Martín sees these panels as derivative, overly dependent on Morales's studio painters and ultimately dishonest:

> Nos volvemos a encontrar a un Morales, en la etapa culmen de su vida, que abrumado por la cantidad de encargos para la realización de retablos, no duda en utilizar la monotonía temática, el abandono en manos de sus ayudantes y el recurso seriado de las estampas flamencas, alemanas o italianas, reservándose únicamente la pintura de rostros y manos, el toque personal que remata la obra colectiva, donde el artista esconde, y no muestra, su personalidad.[7]

---

[5] Antonio Palomino de Castro y Velasco, *Las vidas de los pintores y estatuarios eminentes españoles* (London: impresso por Henrique Woodfall, a costa de Sam. Baker, & T. Payne, 1744), 13.

[6] Francisco Pacheco, *El arte de la pintura*, ed. Bonaventura Bassegoda i Hugas (Madrid: Cátedra, 2001), 418.

[7] Jesús Manuel López Martín, "Las tablas de Luis de Morales en el retablo de la Iglesia de San Martín de Plasencia (Cáceres)," *Espacio, Tiempo y Forma,* serie VII, *Historia del Arte*, vol. VII (1994): 57-71 (71).

Yet, Morales did not sin more in this respect than others of his era. Perhaps his assistants were less accomplished. Even so, in the view of Jonathan Brown, there is no doubt that Morales is "beyond question one of the great devotional painters of the period" and happily, the new millennium appears to have ushered in the contributions of scholars more willing to echo Brown unequivocally.[8] One such, for example, is Dionisio Ángel Martín Nieto who proclaims Morales to be "una de las figuras más refulgentes de la historia de la pintura española".[9]

St Jerome was one of the few saints of the Church included in Morales's oeuvre. Backsbäcka's 1962 catalogue raisonné attributes four images of Jerome to Morales: a panel in the altarpiece of the Church of Sta María de la Asunción in Arroyo de la Luz, near Cáceres (1563-68); one in the altarpiece of San Martín, Plasencia (1565-70), a painting in the National Gallery of Ireland (1570-80) and one in Badajoz cathedral (1580). These were all completed just before the great burgeoning of interest in St Jerome which came to fruition with the new century.

Interest in Jerome had grown in Western European Catholic pictorial art from the Renaissance onwards. The factors influencing this phenomenon are several. Firstly, the patronage of the Order of St Jerome, established in 1374 in Toledo (obliged by the Avignon Pope, Gregory XI, to obey the Rule of St Augustine while following faithfully the spiritual writings of St Jerome) and set to achieve great prominence in Spain and Portugal in the Renaissance, brought about many new commissions.[10] Secondly, the acceptance of the Latin Vulgate Bible as the Catholic standard by the Council of Trent, in April 1546, gave Jerome much greater prominence in Church life.[11] Thirdly, and perhaps less concretely, Jerome's erudition and mastery of rhetoric rendered him attractive to the eyes of humanists, this

---

[8] Jonathan Brown, *Painting in Spain, 1500-1700* (New Haven and London: Yale University Press, 1998), 44.

[9] Dionisio Ángel Martín Nieto, "Luis de Morales y Lucas Mitata en el Sacro Convento de la Orden de Alcántara: nuevas aportaciones documentales," *Revista de Estudios Extremeños* 58: 1 (2002): 31-92 (31).

[10] See *The Catholic Encyclopadia* entry at http://www.newadvent.org/cathen/07345a.htm; Peter and Linda Murray, *The Oxford Dictionary of Christian Art* (Oxford: Oxford University Press, 1998), 269-70 (see entries s.v. Jerome and Jeronymites); Gaston Duchet-Suchaux and Michel Pastoureaux, *La Bible et les saints: Guide iconographique* (Paris: Flammarion, 1994/2003), 198-99; Alain Saint-Saëns, *Art and Faith in Tridentine Spain (1545-1690)* (New York: Peter Lang, 1995), 31.

[11] See *Canons and Decrees of the Council of Trent: The Fourth Session, Celebrated on the eighth day of the month of April, in the year 1546*, at www.bible-researcher.com/trent1.html.

being a quality reflected in his modern designation by the Catholic Church as the patron saint of librarians.

Eusebius Sophronius Hieronymus, a cantankerous, difficult controversialist who often departed both post and abode under a cloud, was born in 345, in Strido(n), a town near Aquileia (in Italy, near the border with Slovenia), in the Roman province of Dalmatia (modern-day Slovenia and Croatia), which was sacked by the Goths in 379 and subsequently lost to history. His parents were well-off and Christian but they did not have their son baptized as a child. He grew up to become one of the four Doctors of the Western Christian Church, along with Gregory the Great (Pope Gregory I), Ambrose of Milan and Augustine of Hippo. He went to Rome in 363 to study Latin, Greek and rhetoric under the grammarian Aelius Donatus and, according to his own account, had plenty to repent of later on. In 366 he was baptized, it is believed, by Pope Liberius and thus began a long life of scholarship and prayer. As there were no monasteries as such in his time, but rather loose associations of like-minded ascetics who congregated together under some sort of self-selected authority, Jerome first gravitated towards a community of educated, pious people in Rome. From 374 to 379 he lived among a community of hermits in communities in the Middle East, seeking a more challenging form of devotional life in the Desert of Chalcis, near Antioch, in Syria. This is the period of his life represented in later Catholic iconography as Jerome undergoing various purgations of the flesh in order to atone for his sins and being tempted by visions of sirens and other carnal pleasures, undoubtedly remembered from very real observations and experiences during his student days in Rome. Of course, while he did live as a hermit in a cave or cavern, wore sackcloth, earned his meagre meals through labour and subjected himself to a regime of rigorous penance and prayer leading on occasion to spiritual trance or ecstasy, he also received letters and books, learned Hebrew from a Jew who had converted to Catholicism and copied and translated the Hebrew gospel.[12] He eventually returned to Rome, after a couple of years spent studying under Gregory Nazianzen, the great rhetorician of the day, in Constantinople, and papal service under Pope Damasus. While in Rome, which he finally left in 385 to live permanently in the Middle East, he became part of an informal spiritual network prominent in which were several patrician Roman widows and their equally pious-minded daughters. Eventually, he would establish a proto-monastic, ascetic and

---

[12]*Jerome, Letters and Select Works*, translated by W. H. Freemantle, G. Lewis and W. G. Martley (Edinburgh: T. & T. Clark, 1893), xvi,
at www.ccel.org/ccel/schaff/npnf206.iv.I.html

mixed gender community with some of these women, notably Paula and Eustochium, in Bethlehem. From this originates his association with the origins of Christian monasticism, an attribution more properly rendered to St Augustine. He is more enduringly cherished as the creator of the Latin Vulgate Bible, on which he worked while resident in Bethlehem from 391 to 404.

Jerome is usually depicted in three main ways: as a penitent, partially clothed in the desert (and, as mentioned above, sometimes, though much less frequently, flagellating himself in the desert while trying not to look upon sinful visions of voluptuous female flesh); as a scholar in his study translating the Bible (in this version he is sometimes accompanied by the apocryphal lion from whose paw he is reputed to have removed a thorn); as an elderly cardinal of the Catholic Church, a representation more current in the later seventeenth century. In most depictions, he is shown with the symbols ordained by that censor and lawmaker of Catholic iconography in Spain, Francisco Pacheco, in his *Arte de la pintura* (1649):

> Píntasele una calavera, Crucifixo, o Cruz o Calvario y una trompeta al oído, por la continua memoria de la muerte y juicio final, y muchos libros, porque en aquella soledad le ayudaban los estudios, junto con la modificación de su carne. Y también se han de guardar para otra ocasión donde se pinta escribiendo y estudiando lenguas, pues siempre lo exercitaba.[13]

Pacheco identifies two main representations of Jerome: his penitence in the desert, which he considers to be the most frequently seen, and Jerome in cardinal's attire.[14] He also mentions, in passing, the depiction of Jerome in his study translating the Bible. His comments on the saint are, as he acknowledges, almost entirely sourced in José de Sigüenza's *Historia de la Orden de San Jerónimo* (1595-1605). He cites Sigüenza's justification for the custom of depicting Jerome in cardinal's robes: that he carried out the office of a cardinal, even though there was no such rank in Jerome's time, and is content to add that he should be shown in this dress "con venerable barba blanca, color tostado, de setenta y ocho años de edad". He takes greater issue, however, with the depictions of Jerome in penitence, noting, more astutely than pedantically, that Jerome was a young man when he lived in the Syrian hermit community: "estando en el yermo, haciendo penitencia, siendo de treinta años y se llama mochacho [...] se

---

[13] Pacheco, *Arte de la pintura,* 691.
[14] Pacheco, *Arte de la pintura,* 691-94.

pinta viejo impropriamente".[15] This practice he views, however, as so ingrained as to be impossible to correct. The other objection he makes is typical of his concern with decorum: both the decorous representation of the saint and proper modesty on the part of the artist. He believes that the degree of nakedness shown in many of these images is excessive. When Jerome is shown unclothed and shoeless beating his breast with a stone in his penitence, Pachecho declares that:

> advierto que los santos amaron muncho la honestidad, y no es necesario para darse en el pecho, desnudarlo hasta los zapatos, porque basta descubrir aquella parte, dexando lo demás vestido de un saco, como él dice, que antes parece ostentar los pintores lo dificultoso de su arte, que conformarse con la razón y la verdad [...][16]

The most striking Spanish example of the naked Jerome executed in the early seventeenth century is, without question, El Greco's late, unfinished *St Jerome* (1610-1614), kept at the National Gallery of Art, Washington.[17] The painting was in the possession of the artist's son, Juan Manuel, after his death (mentioned in 1624) and was inventoried at the convent of San Hermenegildo in Madrid in 1786.[18] As Bassegoda i Hugas supposes that Pacheco almost certainly visited El Greco's studio in Toledo in 1611 during the artist's lifetime, it is likely that Pachecho may have seen this St Jerome; he may also have come across it later on in Madrid, in 1625.[19] This work, by a painter whose greatness Pacheco recognized but for whom his admiration and approbation was always qualified, offends the critic's principles under both headings.[20] Firstly, this Jerome is an old man. Secondly, the entirety of his nearly naked body, his modesty preserved by a flimsy piece of drapery, is depicted and such that even his discalced state (one which seems to bother Pacheco in particular) may be observed against the harsh landscape. Thirdly, the artist, while representing

---

[15] Pacheco, *Arte de la pintura*, 691.

[16] Pacheco, *Arte de la pintura,* 691.

[17] El Greco also painted a more formal St Jerome: as a cardinal, in three-quarter portrait. Several versions of this image exist, dated from about 1595 to his death, with greater and lesser collaboration from studio assistants. See David Davies, *El Greco* (London: National Gallery, 2003), 190. These include one in the Metropolitan Museum of Art, New York and one, attributed to El Greco, in the National Gallery, London.

[18] See provenance notes for *St Jerome* at the National Gallery of Art, Washington, accessible at www.nga.gov/fcgi-bin/tinfo_f?object=12204&detail=prov.

[19] Pacheco, *Arte de la pintura,* 36.

[20] See Pacheco, *Arte de la pintura,* 404 and 698.

an undeniable asceticism and spirituality in the attitude of the saint, also clearly delights in his own minute depiction of each muscle, bone and sinew in the tough, elderly male body. Indeed, El Greco dispenses with all the recognized accoutrements of Jerome in this composition: apart from the book from which is he reading, presumably the Bible, or on which he has based his meditation, and the stone in his right hand with which he will beat his breast, there is no cardinal's cloak, no crucifix, no skull, no lion, no writing implements, no hourglass. Since he did include most of these, with the exception of the apocryphal lion, in his previous *St Jerome in Penitence* (1595-1600) held at the National Gallery of Scotland, this narrowing of focus must be seen a deliberate strategy to intensify the depiction of spiritual experience, which would be consistent with the increasingly ascetic tenor of all his other late work.[21]

Luis de Morales, nearly forty years earlier, achieves a similar level of iconographic depuration in three of his four extant St Jeromes, in the context of a mid-sixteenth century spiritual milieu in Spain which had, faute de mieux, developed an ultra-conservative, anti-intellectual garrison mentality, as Alfonso Rodríguez G. de Ceballos explains:

> Puestas a término las experiencias religiosas innovadoras del erasmismo y del alumbradismo por los tribunales de la Inquisición; publicado en 1559 el *Indice de libros prohibidos* por don Fernando de Valdés, en que figuraron, inficionadas de herejía, obras de personas tan venerables como San Juan de Avila, San Francisco de Borja, fray Luis de Granada y Bartolomé de Carranza; intimado por Felipe II el edicto por el que prohibía a sus súbditos salir a estudiar en Universidades europeas, a excepción de tres o cuatro muy seguros, Bolonia, Roma, Nápoles y Coimbra, por temor al contagio herético, al español de entonces no le quedaba otro recurso que refugiarse en la más estricta ortodoxia, en lo ideológico, y en el más

---

[21] *St Jerome in Penitence* (1595-1600), National Gallery of Scotland. This shows a seated Jerome in the desert as an old bearded man with a full head of hair, stripped to the waist and gazing on a crucifix. The image includes a cardinal's cloak, partially draped around his lap, a cardinal's hat hanging on a rock behind him and an hourglass, quill and inkwell, a skull and two books laid out on a rock in front of him. He holds the crucifix in his left hand and a stone with which to beat his breast in his right. A tiny trickle of blood may be seen where the stone hit the flesh. He appears to use the same model for all his Jeromes. See also David Davies, "El Greco's Religious Art: The Illumination and Quickening of the Spirit," in *El Greco*, 45-71 (56): "El Greco's very latest works [...] glow with unearthly beauty [...] There is a new spiritual energy".

riguroso ascetismo, en lo moral, guardándose como del diablo de toda aventura intelectual y de todo incontrolado misticismo.[22]

Rodríguez de Ceballos quotes the advice of Diego Pérez de Valdivia in his *Aviso de gente recogida* that "Acaben de entender confesores, devotos y devotas que más vale un dracma de mortificación que quintales de arrobamiento, dígolo por los grandes peligros que traen".[23] As Mateo Gómez observes, Morales thus, by choice or accident, "supo como nadie recoger el mundo de espiritualidad íntima" demanded by his times and his clients.[24]

This world in Extremadura was more febrile and more heightened than in other parts of Spain, largely owing to the quality and character of three of the four bishops of Badajoz who served during Morales's adulthood and were his patrons. In other respects, a minor bishopric in a relatively small and not particularly wealthy city, Badajoz nonetheless saw a succession of three outstanding episcopal appointees between 1545 and 1572, convinced champions of Tridentine reform and also sympathetic to the new emphasis on lay spirituality and meditational practice encouraged by the Jesuits and, more problematically, the *Alumbrados*. Francisco de Navarra (1545-1556) was a noted disciple of the jurist and ascetic Martín de Azpilcueta and he attended the first sessions of the Council of Trent between 1545 and 1547; Cristóbal de Rojas y Sandoval (1557-1562) once chaplain to Charles V, attended the second convocation of the Council of Trent and in 1560 called a diocesan synod to enact the measures recommended by Trent, he was also a protector of the Jesuits, inviting them to preach and teach the *Ejercicios espirituales* in his diocese; Juan de Ribera (1562-69), later canonized, was also a champion of Jesuit spirituality, a close friend of Juan de Avila and a correspondent of Fray Luis de Granada.[25] All three churchmen encouraged their flock to practise the type of spiritual contemplation described in Ignacio de Loyola's *Ejercicios espirituales*, Fray Luis de Granada's *Libro de oración y meditación* and Juan de Avila's *Audi filia*.

During the same period, in Extremadura, there had been a resurgence in *Alumbradismo*, with conventicles in Badajoz itself, Fuente de Cantos, Llerena, Fuente del Maestre, Usagre, Almendralejo, Zafra and Frenegal de

---

[22] Alfonso Rodríguez G. de Ceballos, "El mundo espiritual del pintor Luis de Morales en en IV centenario de su muerte," *Goya: Revista de Arte* no. 196 (enero-febrero 1987): 194-203 (194).

[23] Rodríguez G. de Ceballos, "El mundo espiritual," 194.

[24] Mateo Gómez, "Flandes, Toledo y Portugal," 15.

[25] Rodríguez G. de Ceballos, "El mundo espiritual," 195-96.

la Sierra: "Sólo en esta pequeña población de Frenegal se contaban seiscientos devotos y beatas, clérigos y seglares, que se dedicaban a intensos ejercicios de devoción."[26] *Alumbradismo*, "a single native heretical movement", began in Guadalajara around 1512 and was led by the Franciscan Tertiary, Isabel de la Cruz, later joined by Pedro Ruiz de Alcaraz, an accountant to local nobility who was also a property owner, married with children.[27] Coming, as it did, in the same decade as Martin Luther's *Disputatio pro declaratione virtutis indulgentiarum* (95 Theses, 1517), this initial movement was based very much on profound study of the Scriptures, the establishment of a relationship with the first person of the Trinity not mediated by contemplation of statues or other images, or by the practice of physical penance, a belief in the primacy of faith over good works (solfidianism) and a refusal to accept the existence of Hell in a world created by a merciful God, though a Purgatory, not mitigable by the purchase of indulgences or other such bargains with God, was considered commensurate with a "Dios de la Misericordia".[28] Prayer was silent, unstructured, and directed mainly at God the Father through awareness of Scripture. This form of prayer activity grew up outside the formal hierarchies of the Church. In a spirit of egalitarianism, it involved religious and lay people, and women in particular were prominent within individual prayer groups or conventicles and treated, in all respects, as equals. The major figures in Guadalajara, Inés de la Cruz, Pedro Ruiz de Alcaraz and María Cazalla, were all of *converso* descent, as, of course, were many of the most important religious reformers and contemplatives in Spain in the sixteenth century, including Santa Teresa, San Juan de la Cruz and even the notorious inquisitor and confessor of Isabel la Católica, Tomás de Torquemada.[29] A meditational practice centred on the figure of God the Father rather than Christ, however innocently entered into, would always be open to the charge of *converso* or *judaizante* influence, since acceptance of the Trinity had been the chief objection in the disputations

---

[26] Rodríguez G. de Ceballos, "El mundo espiritual," 198; Alastair Hamilton, *Heresy and Mysticism in Sixteenth-century Spain: The Alumbrados* (Cambridge: James Clarke, 1992), 118.

[27] Hamilton, *Heresy*, v, 26.

[28] See Hamilton, *Heresy*, 2; Augusta E. Foley, "El alumbradismo y sus posibles orígenes," in *Actas del VIII Congreso de la Asociación Internacional de Hispanistas*, ed. A. David Kosoff, José Amor y Vázquez, Ruth H. Kossoff, Geoffrey W. Ribbans (Madrid: Istmo, 1986), vol. I, 527-32 (529), available at Centro Virtual Cervantes at http://cvc.cervantes.es/obref/aih/pdf/08/aih_08_1_055.pdf; Antonio Márquez, *Los alumbrados: orígenes y filosofía, 1525-1559* (Madrid: Taurus, 1972), 177-93.

[29] Hamilton, *Heresy*, 16-28.

undertaken by scholars of Christianity and Judaism in times when such debate was possible in Spain, the last of these, between scholars of Christianity and Judaism, taking place in Tortosa (1413-1414). When the inevitable edict was issued against the *Alumbrados* by the Inquisitor General and Archbishop of Seville, Alonso Manrique, in 1525, coincidence or not, very few of the indicted were, in fact, *cristianos viejos*. It became a matter of course for the virulently anti-semitic inquisitorial process which took place in Toledo to perceive Jewish-derived heresy amongst the *Alumbrados* at every opportunity.[30]

The most important legacy of the Toledo *Alumbrados*, as they became known, was their development of a method of contemplative practice, called *dejamiento*. While this may have been based on the Franciscan system of *recogimiento*, as Alcaraz was to claim under inquisitorial torture, it is to be distinguished from the Franciscan approach by its utter lack of a prescriptive practice and by its insistence that *dejamiento* was a passive abandonment of the soul to the love of God, whereas *recogimiento* involved a guided inner concentration on the life and person of Christ and structured prayer out loud, *oración de recogimiento*, this latter activity frowned upon by Isabel de la Cruz as unnecessary.[31] Perhaps the key distinction here is that between contemplation of the life of Christ using recognized prayer forms and direct, inner communication with God the Father.

When *Alumbrados* were denounced again, in Extremadura, by the Dominican extirpator of all types of *magia*, Fray Alonso de la Fuente, there had been much change. Fray Alonso was born in Fuente del Maestre, in 1533, and after training in Seville, he returned to his native province in 1570, as a preacher in the Dominican convent in Badajoz, to find the entire region steeped in *alumbradismo*, including his native town. He began a campaign against the *Alumbrados* which was to culminate in the edict of faith issued against them in July 1574 and the *auto da fé*, held in Llerena in June 1579, though trials of suspected *alumbrados* would be held for at least a decade.[32] As Hamilton and others point out, the *alumbradismo* of Extremadura was a much less sophisticated kind of contemplative practice than that of the Toledo *Alumbrados*. It was led, in the main, by people without sufficient theological training to understand the precepts of such as Juan de Avila or Fray Luis de Granada properly. Even reading through

---

[30] Hamilton, *Heresy*, 28.
[31] Hamilton, *Heresy*, 30ff; Foley, "El alumbradismo," 528-29; Pedro Santonja, "Las doctrinas de los alumbrados españoles y sus posibles fuentes medievales," *Dicenda: Cuadernos de Filología Hispánica* 18 (2000): 353-392 (360).
[32] Hamilton, *Heresy*, 118-21.

the lines of the anti-semitic and misogynistic rhetoric of the Inquisition and Fray Alonso's overt distrust of mysticism in all its forms, it is clear that boundaries had been crossed from piety into outright mountebankery and heresy, largely involving *beatas*, holy women, making public spectacle of their visions and trances. While the growth of *alumbrado* conventicles was no doubt due to the fomentation of a culture of personal devotional piety by archbishops Rojas y Sandoval and Ribera, and their protegés the Jesuits, they neither condoned nor envisaged the extremes of "mystical extravagance, imposture and licentiousness" into which, in some conventicles, the movement would descend.[33]

On the other hand, the reports of how prayer was conducted by the Extremeñan *Alumbrados* from the Llerena trial records from July 1575 (the process was undertaken over four years from the issuing of the Edict in 1574 to the culminating *auto da fé* in 1579) suggest that the focus at this stage was entirely Christological and closer to the practice of *recogimiento*, with allotted times, designated places and a scheme of prayer.[34] As distinct from the Toledo *Alumbrados*, these conventicles were led by "clerigos sacerdotes y algunos predicadores" who seemed to minister to a largely female congregation and live off the food and accommodation provided for them by these women:

> Enseñanles que se recojan a la mañana y de noche en oracion y contemplacion una ora u dos donde recen cinco *paternoster* y cinco avemarias cada uno dellos a una de las llagas de Jesucristo y contemplen en cada una dellas lo que padecio y en la que les diera mas gusto que alli paren.[35]

The fact that these priests or friars would then encourage these women or *beatas*, ordered by them not to marry nor enter religious orders but "que se corten los cabellos y se quiten las galas y chapines y vistan una saya parda y ciñan con cordon y traigan manto negro sin cintas y traigan tocas blancas mal puestas y que anden desaliñadas y sucias y hagan voto de castidad" to concentrate on the bodily manifestations of ecstasy, "lo que an sentido en ella [...] si an visto o oido alguna cosa" is reported in the Inquisition indictment of 1575 in a relatively objective manner and, in spite of the extreme bias of Fray Alonso de la Fuente who initiated the investigation, it must be taken more or less at face value.[36]

---

[33] Hamilton, *Heresy,* 120.
[34] Márquez, *Los alumbrados*, 290
[35] Santonja, "Las doctrinas de los alumbrados españoles," 388.
[36] Hamilton, *Heresy*, 117.

What is interesting here for the study of Morales's depictions of St Jerome is the description of how the *beatas* were encouraged to dress and contemplate the wounds of Christ. Of the four depictions of St Jerome by Morales, one is anomalous by virtue of the amount of detail it contains. It belongs to the altarpiece of San Martín in Plasencia, chastized by López Martín for its dependence on Flemish engravings. Jerome as a white-bearded elderly man is placed in the foreground, in profile, dressed in his cardinal's robes and hat, seated at a desk with an inkwell and crucifix on it, writing with a quill in one book with another open on a stand showing an illustration of the enthronement of Christ. A window on the viewer's left gives on to a landscape which shows a nearly-naked Jerome kneeling before the mouth of a grotto, with a lion, and scourging his breast with a stone. On the road in the far distance some houses can be seen with three loaded camels outside them. This extremely conventional depiction of St Jerome was, in all likelihood, executed at the behest of those who supervised the commission after the death of Gutierre Vargas Carvajal, bishop of Plasencia, who had begun the project. He died in 1559, before Morales was chosen as the painter for the altarpiece.[37]

The other three paintings show a very different Jerome, one who might well have followed the spirit, if not the letter, of *alumbrado* practice as described in the Llerena indictment of 1575. This Jerome is bald, nearly naked and deprived of most of the attributes included in the Plasencia image. Before 1560, there are many precedents for the naked, bald, unencumbered Jerome, three notable examples being Leonardo da Vinci's unfinished *St Jerome in the Desert* (1480, Vatican Museum), Albrecht Dürer's *St Jerome in the Wilderness* (1495, National Gallery, London) and Lucas Cranach the Elder's *St Jerome in Penitence* (1502, Kunsthistorischesmuseum, Vienna). Of these, the closest to Morales's iconography, both of the saint and his surroundings and accoutrements, is the Leonardo, in which an aged, bald, beardless, emaciated, nearly-naked full-length Jerome holds a stone in his right hand and looks up towards a sketched-in cross on his left. He is accompanied by a lion and there is a rudimentary cardinal's cloak on his right. Both Dürer and Cranach portray the old man with a long white beard and long hair around a bald crown, bare-chested though covered from the waist down by his tunic, and surrounded by several of the usual accoutrements. The altarpiece of Arroyo del Puerto (now Arroyo de la Luz) was, crucially, effected at more or less the same time as Morales was working on the Plasencia commission. Indeed, he may very well have worked on both sets together

---

[37] López Martín, "Las tablas de Luis de Morales," 57 and 60-61.

in Arroyo del Puerto.[38] However, this is a very different Jerome: he is shown in half-length view, before the mouth of a grotto, bearded, bald, grey-haired, with his torso naked apart from the remains of a shirt tied from his left shoulder to the right side of his waist. He has a large stone clutched in right hand, with which to beat his breast, and he grasps his white shirt with his left hand as if baring his breast to make way for the stone. On the left of the image there is a crucifix, with a lifelike figure of Christ, and the red cardinal's mantle of the saint behind it. This panel is located in the bottom right hand extremity of the predella.

The version of St Jerome which hangs in Badajoz cathedral and which was completed very late in Morales's career, in 1580, offers an even more stripped-down representation of Jerome. It shows him in extended head-and-shoulders, with a semi-naked torso and a narrow white sheet or shirt knotted over his left shoulder and around the right side of his waist. He is bald and bearded as in Arroyo de la Luz, but brown-haired, therefore younger and closer, in fact, to Pacheco's ideal of a young man in his thirties. His hands are clasped over a skull, depicted in profile, and the cross which stands in the crook of his right elbow is unusual in that it does not have a figure of Christ suspended from it. The top of the cross upright and the left side of the crossbar are both cropped at the upper left corner of the painting. The pupils of Jerome's eyes are turned up and inward, not looking directly at the cross, rather in the opposite direction. The cross disappears upwards to the viewer's left, his eyes disappear into his eye sockets upwards to the viewer's right.

Between the Arroyo de la Luz panel and the Badajoz cathedral painting, Morales executed his other St Jerome, another *St Jerome in the Wilderness*, in the 1570s. This picture is kept at the National Gallery of Ireland, in Dublin. It was regarded as being the painting mentioned as part of the Standish Collection, sold at Christie's in 1853, and it was acquired by the National Gallery of Ireland in 1872. It was restored in 1922, to secure the two pieces of panel from which the painting is made.[39] Very little otherwise is known about its history. Here Jerome is presented in head and shoulders format, three-quarter profile, facing towards the left, bald, extremely emaciated and with a very, very fine beard. He appears younger than the Arroyo de la Luz Jerome and probably older than the Badajoz incarnation. Like the Badajoz Jerome, he wears a bluish white garment, knotted with the knot sitting on his left shoulder and looped over his right shoulder. His hands are clasped over a skull which is presented

---

[38] López Martín, "Las tablas de Luis de Morales," 61.

[39] Rosemarie Mulcahy, *Spanish Paintings in the National Gallery of Ireland* (Dublin: The National Gallery of Ireland, 1988), 40.

also in three-quarter profile, and he balances a crucifix in his right hand with a highly life-like Christ nailed to it who is fleshier, more warm-toned and vital than the ascetic contemplative holding him aloft. Jerome's eyes are cast upwards, towards the top right, but the pupils have not quite disappeared into his eyelids as in the Badajoz painting. He is emphatically not looking at the crucifix, not looking at the very human figure of Christ, and Christ's gaze, if his eyes are open, does not intersect with any part of Jerome's body. There are tiny, translucent tears on Jerome's left cheek and the delicate, exquisite hands are those of an aesthete and a scholar, not a penitent working for his daily crust of bread. To the viewer's left and behind the crucifix is an arch of cut stone, an indication of the cave or cavern in which Jerome lived in the desert, the anachronistic and anomalous arch of cut stone presumably evocative of the institution of the Church. In the Badajoz painting, there is no background, and, as already stated, no figure on the cross. In the National Gallery painting, in a palette of cold bluish whites for the fabric and skull, and tones from pale beige to brown for the flesh and stone, Jerome's apparel is more solid than his flesh. He is vulnerable, almost as delicate and translucent as his tears, the abstraction of his eyes and the inclination of his head as it pulls away from the cross and up in the opposite direction emphasizing his soul's absence from his own corporeal being.

In the past, this very attitude has been dismissed as overly sentimental and mawkish, and redolent of the worst excesses of second-phase *alumbradismo*. For example, no less a critic than Federico Zeri opined, in 1957, that "Morales's *St Jerome* is an example of the uncontrolled visionary mysticism of the *Alumbrados*, which is innate in the Spanish soul, the image being so exaggerated that it inspires ridicule rather than reverence".[40] Yet, if this image were to be viewed more as a metaphor for Christological devotion, with the body of Jerome rapt in contemplation of the idea of the crucified Christ and the nature of his sufferings taken not as a mimetic representation of the physical act of contemplating a crucifix in a half-starved state but as an allegory of the soul, of unworldly, inner prayer, of quiet, self-contained *recogimiento* of the kind which Jerome himself must have practised in the desert, it would certainly absolve itself of Zeri's rather essentialist charge. Indeed, there is nothing overtly histrionic in this image, there is great economy of physical gesture, the palette is subdued, the iconography is spare and there is no attempt to

---

[40] Paraphrased in Mulcahy, *Spanish Paintings*, 40; Federico Zeri, *Pittura e Controriforma: "L'arte senza tempo" de Scipione da Gaeta* (Turin: Einaudi, 1957).

display direct communication between the life-like figure of Christ on the cross and the saint in prayer.

In other words, Jerome is surely used here, and in the Arroyo de la Luz predella panel and the Badajoz cathedral painting, as a means of instructing the devout in the correct manner of properly informed, respectful spiritual contemplation, a riposte, in fact, to the excesses of second-phase *alumbradismo*.

Jerome himself described the travails of his own foster-brother Bonosus, who went to live as a hermit on an island near Aquileia, in a letter to Rufinus:

> Alone upon the island—or rather not alone, for Christ is with him—he sees the glory of God, which even the apostles saw not save in the desert. He beholds, it is true, no embattled towns, but he has enrolled his name in the new city. Garments of sackcloth disfigure his limbs, yet so clad he will be the sooner caught up to meet Christ in the clouds. No watercourse pleasant to the view supplies his wants, but from the Lord's side he drinks the water of life. Place all this before your eyes, dear friend, and with all the faculties of your mind picture to yourself the scene. When you realize the effort of the fighter then you will be able to praise his victory.[41]

This perhaps gives a flavour of the contemplation of Jerome in the desert as represented by Morales. It is a depiction of the "effort of the fighter" which deliberately takes place out of sight of ordinary humanity, as the contemplative attempts, quietly and privately, to achieve the union with God which the Toledo *Alumbrados* practised through *dejamiento*, abandonment to the love of God, and Franciscan *recogimiento* attained through a more structured method of subordinating the self to the will of God. Nothing in Jerome or in Morales's informed representations of him should be mistaken for mawkish or extravagant display.

---

[41] Jerome, Letter III, To Rufinus the Monk, in *Jerome, Letters...*, at www.ccel.org/ccel/schaff/npnf206.v.III.html.

Luis de Morales, c. 1520-1586, *Saint Jerome in the Wilderness*, 1570s, Oil on European oak, 62 x 46.5cm, Photo copyright National Gallery of Ireland.

ENGAGED BUT NOT MARRIED?: DIEGO VELÁZQUEZ'S *LA TÚNICA DE JOSÉ* AND *LA FRAGUA DE VULCANO*

STEPHEN BOYD
(UNIVERSITY COLLEGE CORK)

The purpose of this essay is to outline some arguments, largely based on relevant textual sources, that might support the notion that two history paintings, *La túnica de José* and *La fragua de Vulcano*, which Velázquez produced in Rome during his first extended visit to Italy (from August 1629 to December 1630), effectively constitute a pair.[1]

La túnica represents the culminating moment in the Old Testament story of the relationship between Joseph, eleventh of the patriarch Jacob's twelve sons, and his jealous older brothers. The origins of their ill-will towards him are recounted thus in the Book of Genesis:

> Habitavit autem Jacob in terra Chanaan, in qua pater suus peregrinatus est. Et hae sunt generationes eius: Joseph cum sedecim esset annorum, pascebat gregem cum fratribus suis adhuc puer: et erat cum filiis Balae et Zelphae uxorum patris sui: accusavitque fratres suos apud patrem crimine pessimo. Israel autem diligebat Joseph super omnes filios suos, eo quod in senectute genuisset eum: fecitque ei tunicam polymitam. Videntes autem fratres eius quod a patre plus cunctis filiis amaretur, oderant eum, nec poterant ei quidquam pacifice loqui.[2]

For their practical assistance and advice in the course of preparing this essay, I am grateful to Julie Alden-Lowry (Bodleian Library, University of Oxford), John Barry (Department of Classics, University College Cork), and Professor Terence O'Reilly (Department of Hispanic Studies, University College Cork).

[1] Reproductions of these paintings may be viewed on-line at *The Web Gallery of Art*: http://www.wga.hu/art/v/velazque/02/0213vela.jpg (*La túnica de José*), and http://www.wga.hu/art/v/velazque/02/0211vela.jpg (*La fragua de Vulcano*).

[2] Genesis 37. 1-4. All biblical quotations are taken from *Biblia Sacra Iuxta Vulgatam Clementinam*, ed. Alberto Colunga, OP, and Lorenzo Turrado, 5th edn (Madrid: Biblioteca de Autores Cristianos, 1977).

[And Jacob dwelt in the land of Chanaan, wherein his father sojourned. And these are his generations: Joseph, when he was sixteen years old, was feeding the flock with his brethren, being but a boy: and he was with the sons of Bala and of Zelpha his father's wives: and he accused his brethren to his father of a most wicked crime. Now Israel loved Joseph above all his sons, because he had him in his old age: and he made him a coat of divers colours. And his brethren seeing that he was loved by his father, more than all his sons, hated him, and could not speak peaceably to him.][3]

Some of Joseph's older brothers are said to be hostile towards him because he had reported their bad behaviour to their father, Jacob. All were jealous of Jacob's special regard for him, and of the future greatness (including dominion over them) that he predicted for himself on the basis of his dreams.[4] Eventually, having considered and rejected the possibility of murdering him, they sold him to some merchants travelling down to Egypt and sent his garments, stained with the blood of a goat, back to Jacob in order to make him believe that his favourite son had been killed by a wild animal:

> Tulerunt autem tunicam eius, et in sanguine hoedi, quem occiderant, tinxerunt: mittentes qui ferrent ad patrem, et dicerent: Hanc invenimus: vide utrum tunica filii tui sit, an non. Quam cum agnovisset pater, ait: Tunica filii mei est: fera pessima comedit eum, bestia devoravit Joseph. Scissisque vestibus, indutus est cilicio, lugens filium suum multo tempore. Congregatis autem cunctis liberis eius ut lenirent dolorem patris, noluit consolationem accipere, sed ait: Descendam ad filium meum lugens in infernum. Et illo perseverante in fletu. (Genesis 37. 31-35)
> [And they took his coat, and dipped it in the blood of a kid, which they had killed: Sending some to carry it to their father, and to say: This we have found: see whether it be thy son's coat, or no. And the father acknowledging it, said: It is my son's coat, an evil wild beast hath eaten him, a beast hath devoured Joseph. And tearing his garments, he put on sackcloth, mourning for his son a long time. And all his children being gathered together to comfort their father in his sorrow, he would not receive comfort, but said: I will go down to my son into hell, mourning. And whilst he continued weeping [...]

---

[3] English translations are from *The Holy Bible translated from the Latin Vulgat: Diligently Compared with the Hebrew, Greek, and other Editions in divers Languages and First Published by the English College at Doway, anno 1609 newly revised and corrected according to the Clementine Edition of the Scriptures* [by Bishop Richard Challoner], 4 vols (Dublin?, 1750).

[4] See Genesis 37. 5-11.

Velázquez's painting represents the climactic moment of this first part of the story of Joseph, when his bloodstained tunic is presented to his father.

Because they demonstrated that he could now execute history paintings in the grand Italian manner, *La túnica de José* and *La fragua de Vulcano* are generally regarded by scholars as marking a watershed in Velázquez's technical and stylistic development. As Jonathan Brown has put it:

> The *Tunic of Joseph* systematically solves the problems of *Los Borrachos*. [...] Within a short period of time, he has mastered the canons and conventions of the grand manner of Roman history painting, as well as the subtleties of Venetian *colore*, without surrendering his individuality.[5]

The two paintings do not appear to have resulted from a commission, so it seems likely that it was Velázquez himself who chose their subject matter. A few years after his return to Madrid, in 1634, the paintings, along with others, were bought on behalf of the King, and shortly afterwards displayed together in a *guardarropa* of the Buen Retiro palace.[6] Around 1665, *La túnica* was removed to the Escorial where it still hangs.[7] *La fragua* had been transferred to the Palacio Real by 1772 and was acquired by the Museo del Prado in 1819.

On the extreme right of *La túnica*, we see Jacob seated on a dais covered with a richly-coloured, patterned carpet. His hands are raised in a gesture of horror and disbelief. Because of the angle at which his staff is shown lying on the ground, we are led to imagine that he has just cast it down in despair. The other five figures in the painting represent some of Joseph's brothers.[8] It is clear from their dress that they have just come in from looking after animals in the open fields. Velázquez has taken great care with the depiction of their expressions and gestures: the brother on the

---

[5] See Jonathan Brown, "Velázquez and Italy," in *The Cambridge Companion to Velázquez*, ed. Suzanne L. Stratton-Pruitt (Cambridge: Cambridge University Press, 2002), 30-47 (35).

[6] Fernando Marías has suggested that it may have been "el guardarropa próximo a la alcoba [de la reina Isabel de Borbón]". See his essay *"La túnica de José* de Velázquez: la historia al margen de lo humano," in *Velázquez* (Madrid: Fundación Amigos del Museo del Prado; Barcelona: Galaxia Gutenberg, Círculo de Lectores, 1999), 277-96 (280).

[7] It was taken to Paris by Napoleon in 1809 and returned to Spain in 1815. For a detailed account of the early life of the two paintings, see Marías, 277-80.

[8] In this respect, Velázquez departs from the scriptural account (Genesis 37. 32), according to which Joseph's brothers sent messengers to Jacob to inform him of his son's death. For a discussion of this discrepancy, and a proposed identification of the brothers in the painting, see Marías, 290-95.

far left turns away from the sight of Joseph's bloodstained garments in a dramatic gesture of revulsion; the two brothers in the centre, who are displaying the clothes to their father, strain forward nervously, the expression on the face of the brother dressed in black (in the centre) clearly showing his guilt. He watches his father's reaction sharply, hoping that he will be duped, anxious in case he is not. In the background, almost completely engulfed in shadow, stand two more brothers: one looks down at the floor and coughs (or bites his thumb) nervously; the other turns his head to face away from his father, and averts his eyes from Joseph's bloodstained shirt. Both appear to be overcome with shame as they listen to their brothers lying to their father about the death of his son. In the right foreground, just at the edge of the carpet, we see a small dog in profile. Seemingly sensing that something is amiss, and ready to defend Jacob from its threatening presence, he barks in the direction of the brothers holding Joseph's tunic, his forepaws digging into the carpet as he crouches in a half-defensive, half-attacking posture.

It could seem that Velázquez's intentions in producing this painting were exclusively painterly, that he wanted, as Jonathan Brown has said, to show that he could convincingly arrange figures in a space defined, in the Italian manner, by a perspective grid (formed here by the chessboard-patterned, tiled floor); that he could use rich, glowing colours and modulate them in accordance with the play of the light; that he was a master of anatomy, and that he could capture subtle gradations of a single emotion, guilt, on the faces of the figures. Indeed, these are the qualities singled out for praise in one of the earliest surviving appreciations of *La túnica de José*. It appears in the second edition (of 1668) of José de los Santos's *Descripción breve del Monasterio de San Lorenzo El Real del Escorial*.[9] De los Santos was a Hieronymite priest who, in 1656, had collaborated with Velázquez in the redecoration of the sacristy of the Escorial. In the passage dedicated to this painting, he quotes what he claims Velázquez himself had said about it to some onlookers, and writes enthusiastically about its pictorial qualities, in particular of the modelling of the figures "con tal arte y disposición, que puede ser ejemplo para la Notomía". He also proposes a moral interpretation of the painting, seeing in it a warning about the deadly effects of envy: "a la verdad, la fiera [que había devorado a José] fue la envidia de los hermanos, que no puede haber

---

[9] José de los Santos, *Descripción breve del Monasterio de San Lorenzo El Real del Escorial*, 2nd edn (Madrid: Juan García Infanzón, 1668). It was originally published in 1657.

mayor fiera".[10] We might feel inclined to view such an interpretation, especially coming from a member of a religious order, as owing more to a culturally-conditioned moralizing reflex, than to anything inherent in the painting itself. It might seem equally beside the point to look in any depth at its biblical source or at the relevant traditions of biblical exegesis in order to understand it. Yet, when we consider some of the details of the painting, and more especially, when we consider the whole work in relation to *La fragua de Vulcano*, it does seem, at least, difficult to interpret it in purely painterly or psychological terms.

As we have seen, *La túnica* and *La fragua* were produced in Rome at around the same time, and for up to thirty years they hung together in the Buen Retiro palace. Scholars have debated whether or not they were painted as companion pieces, and some landmarks in the development of that discussion will be reviewed shortly. For the moment, however, it will be useful to glance at some of the undeniable visual correspondences between the two works. What emerges, when one looks at them together, is a fairly consistent pattern of complementary likeness and difference with respect to each of their principal features:

I. Figures

In both paintings there are six figures, all of them male. In each case, one is an older man and the others young men: Jacob and his sons (*La túnica*); Vulcan and his assistants (*La fragua*). Semi-nude figures are prominent in both paintings, but especially so in *La fragua*. In both paintings, the figures are shown from a variety of angles: back, side, and front. In at least one case (the brother wearing the dark pink tunic in *La tunica*; the assistant second from the right in *La fragua*), Velázquez appears to have used the same live model. In each painting, Velázquez shows a clear interest in portraying subtle gradations of a single emotion on the faces of all but one of the figures: nervousness associated with duplicity in *La túnica*; astonishment in *La fragua*.

---

[10] De los Santos, as quoted in José Luis Colomer, "De Madrid a Roma, 1630: Velázquez y la pintura de historia," in *Fábulas de Velázquez. Mitología e historia sagrada en el Siglo de Oro*, ed. Javier Portús Pérez (Madrid: Museo del Prado, 2007), 133-59 (154).

II. Composition

In both works, one figure is relatively isolated, placed to one side and shown facing inwards towards the other figures, who (in most cases, and especially so in *La fragua*) are oriented towards him: in *La túnica*, Jacob, the victim of deception, is positioned on the extreme right; in *La fragua*, Apollo, the revealer of deception, is positioned on the extreme left. In each painting, and in each case towards the left, a large aperture in the background wall affords glimpses of a mountainous landscape with a blue overarching sky. In both paintings, the illusion of spatial depth is enhanced by the angled positioning of objects or implements on the floor: for example, the two staffs in *La túnica;* the hammers of various sizes and the stone plinth supporting the smaller anvil in *La fragua*.

III. Colour

The colour of the background walls in both paintings is a neutral grey-brown. In general, however, the colours in *La túnica* are richer and more varied.

IV. Lighting

In *La túnica* the main source of light comes from the right, from behind the seated figure of Jacob; in *La fragua*, the main source of light comes from the left, from the radiant aureole around the head of Apollo.

When one takes into account these visual correspondences together with the virtually equivalent circumstances of time and place in which they were executed, it is not difficult to see why many scholars should have concluded that the paintings were designed to form a pair. Before identifying some other features that would support this notion, it is convenient at this point to review some of the milestones in the debate about their relationship to each other, beginning with the work of scholars who have argued for the existence of a thematic link between them.

Writing in 1888, Carl Justi was the first to identify deception as their common theme: "Son *pendants*: el engaño descubierto y el consumado".[11] Commenting on Justi's remarks in 1947, and apparently unaware of De los Santos's text, Diego Angulo Íñiguez pointed to

---

[11] Carl Justi, *Velázquez y su siglo*, tr. Jesús Espino Nuño (Madrid: Istmo, 1999), 282.

la coincidencia de que el origen primero de la trama de ambas historias es la envidia, la de los hermanos de José ante el favor de Jacob por éste y la de Apolo ante el de Venus por Marte.[12]

It might seem surprising that Angulo should speak of Apollo's envy, rather than of Vulcan's jealousy, of Venus and Mars. It is interesting to note, however, that in his commentary on Ovid's *Metamorphoses*, published in 1589, Pedro Sánchez de Viana (albeit indirectly) also imputes this emotion to Apollo: "[el] Sol, a quien el adúltero [Marte] tenía gran miedo, por ser naturalmente descubridor de secretos, y tenerle por persona invidiosa de semejantes contentamientos".[13] More recently, in his entry for *La fragua* in the catalogue of the 2006 Velázquez exhibition at the National Gallery in London, Dawson Carr (cautiously) proposed that, despite some persuasive arguments advanced for thinking otherwise, it is more likely than not that there is a thematic link between the two paintings:

> Scholars debate whether this painting was conceived as a pendant to *Joseph's Coat*. The choice of a scene from classical mythology to balance one from the Old Testament can hardly be accidental, even if this was only to prove his abilities in both realms. However, as both show scenes of revelation, one calculated to deceive the other to unmask deception, it is tempting to see them as intending to provoke comparison. The differing sizes of the canvases and conflicting evidence concerning the original dimensions of both make a definitive conclusion difficult.[14]

As Carr signals here, the crucial, unresolved question of the original dimensions of the two paintings lies at the heart of the debate about whether or not they were intended as a pair. In 1986, Jonathan Brown argued:

> Much has been written about the underlying thematic content of these two works, on the assumption that they were intended as a complementary pair. This assumption rests in part on the apparently uniform dimensions and the

---

[12] Diego Angulo Íñiguez, *Velázquez: cómo compuso sus principales cuadros y otros escritos sobre el pintor* (Sevilla: Laboratorio de Arte, 1947; repr. Madrid: Istmo, 1999), 182.

[13] Pedro Sánchez de Viana, *Anotaciones sobre los quinze libros de las Transformaciones de Ovidio* (Valladolid: Diego Fernández de Córdoba, 1589), as quoted in Santiago Sebastián, "Lectura iconográfico-iconológica de *La fragua de Vulcano*," *Traza y Baza*: 8 (1983): 20-27 (23).

[14] Dawson Carr, "Apollo at the Forge of Vulcan, 1630," in *Velázquez*, ed. Dawson W. Carr (London: The National Gallery, 2006), no. 18, pp. 154-57 (157).

common use of lofty subjects [...] regarded by artists and theorists as the
true test of a painter's mastery of his art. [...] The *Forge of Vulcan* and
Joseph's Coat now measure 2.23 x 2.90 meters respectively. But the *Forge
of Vulcan* was originally around thirty-three centimetres narrower, while
Joseph's Coat was originally about fifty centimetres wider. In other words,
there was once a difference of over eighty centimetres between the width
of the two words, a difference which would have implied to viewers that
they were looking at two discrete history paintings by a single artist rather
than a pair of related works. For this reason it seems reasonable to regard
each painting as a separate, self-contained entity as far as subject is
concerned.[15]

Especially since then, as Salvador Salort Pons has put it, "esta teoría [que
ambos cuadros se concibieron como una pareja] cada vez pierde más
adeptos".[16]

More recently still, and more radically, Javier Portús Pérez has
expressed scepticism, not just about any supposed thematic relationship
between the two paintings, but even about the validity of extra-pictorial
interpretations of each individual work:

Son obras, sin embargo, en las que la narración no parece estar al servicio
de la transmisión de un contenido devocional, moral o cívico, sino que
tiene un fin en sí mismo; y en ellas hay un continuo alarde de las
capacidades del pintor. Las dos escenas que representan son relativamente
raras entre los artistas y parecen haber sido elegidas precisamente por las
posibilidades que ofrecen al pintor de investigar en campos muy concretos
y de demostrar sus capacidades.[17]

---

[15]Jonathan Brown, *Velázquez: Painter and Courtier* (New Haven and London:
Yale University Press, 1986), 72.

[16] Salvador Salort Pons, *Velázquez en Italia* (Madrid: Fundación de Apoyo a la
Historia del Arte Hispánico, 2002), 49. Marías's remark (about the supposed
pairing), "esta idea debiera caer por su propio peso" ("*La túnica de José*," 281) and
José Luis Colomer's quip that Brown's arguments about the differing original
dimensions of the paintings are "bastantes como para pensar que la pretendida
pareja natural no fue sino un matrimonio forzado" typify this trend; see Colomer,
"Roma 1630. *La túnica de José* y el estudio de las 'pasiones'," *Reales Sitios* 36:
141 (1999): 39-49 (46). It should be pointed out, however, that, since then,
Colomer appears to have shifted his position. In 2007 (perfectly illustrating Carr's
point), he wrote: "la significativa equivalencia original en dimensiones de estos
lienzos—avatares posteriores explican la diferencia actual de anchura entre uno y
otro—indica, como todo lo demás, que debieron de concebirse como pareja"; see
Colomer, "De Madrid a Roma," 152.

[17] Javier Portús Pérez, "Velázquez, pintor de historia. Competencia, superación y
conciencia creativa," in *Fábulas de Velázquez*, ed. Portús Pérez, 14-71 (23).

It may, indeed, be conceded, in passing, that not all Spanish mythological paintings of this period are imbued with moral, much less specifically Christian, meanings, and even when they are, these may not correspond directly to the interpretations that mythographers such as Pérez de Moya or Sánchez de Viana propose for the myth or myths in question.[18] It should, perhaps, be clarified here that some of the scholars who argue against, or suspend judgement on, the "pairing" theory, do acknowledge a range of affinities, even some thematic ones, between the two works. Marías, for example, allows that: "ambas obras [...] poseen incluso el denominador común de contar dos 'revelaciones', dos 'engaños', aunque de muy diversa categoría".[19] One may say, too, that Portús Pérez's observation about the relative rarity of the two scenes as subjects for paintings tends, entirely unintentionally in this case, to reinforce rather than to weaken the argument for there being an intellectual link between them.

Without entering into the debate about the original dimensions of the paintings, and, therefore (for the moment) about whether or not, or the degree to which, they were intended by Velázquez to be considered in relation to each other, this essay will now look at some of the evidence from the classical and biblical source texts as well as one detail from the tradition of biblical exegesis which might suggest that, at least in effect, they do form a pair.

In his London exhibition catalogue entry for *La túnica*, Carr proffered an original and revelatory observation about the cyclical nature of the Old Testament narratives of the lives of Jacob and Joseph: "Velázquez depicted the culminating moment when the guile of generations comes together. The Hebrew patriarch Jacob [...] had long before deceived his father and now his sons would dupe him".[20] He is referring, of course, to the way in which Jacob had passed himself off to his father, Isaac, as his older brother, Esau, in order to usurp the latter's birthright as eldest son, and he mentions how, later, Jacob himself would be deceived by his father-in-law, Laban, who had agreed to let him marry his younger and more beautiful daughter, Rachel, but, on what should have been their wedding night, sent his older and less beautiful daughter, Leah, to Jacob's

---

[18] On this point, see Oliver Noble Wood, "Mars Recontextualized: Readings of Velázquez's *Marte*," in *Rewriting Classical Mythology in the Hispanic Baroque*, ed. Isabel Torres (Woodbridge: Tamesis, 2007), 139-55 (142-43).

[19] Marías, "*La túnica de José*," 282. See also Manuela B. Mena Marqués, "*La tunica di Giuseppe*," in *Velàzquez a Roma, Velàzquez e Roma*, ed. A. Coliva (Roma: Galleria Borghese, 1999-2000), no. 1, pp. 72-73 (72).

[20] Carr, "Joseph's Bloody Coat brought to Jacob, 1629-30," 152.

bed.[21] The tradition of Christian biblical exegesis bears out the pertinence of Carr's observation. For example, with reference to Jacob's words: "Descendam ad filium meum lugens in infernum" (Genesis 37. 35), the influential fifteenth-century biblical commentator, Denis the Carthusian, cites St Augustine's belief that Jacob's sorrow at the supposed death of Joseph was intensified by the guilt he felt about his own wrongdoing in the past: "Tamen (secundum Augustinum) verba haec Jacob forsan fuerunt verba perturbati dolentisque animi, et propias culpas exaggerantes" ["However, according to Augustine these words of Jacob were perhaps the words of a disturbed and grieving mind, exaggerating his own guilt"].[22] Interestingly, and possibly significantly, the story of Vulcan, Venus and Mars, as told by Ovid in *Metamorphoses* IV, also involves a comparable cyclical pattern. In this case, it is not so much a case of the deceiver being deceived, as of an accuser, Apollo, being afflicted with the same amorous desires that had motivated the behaviour of those whom he had accused. In the *Metamorphoses*, the story is recounted by the nymph, Leuconoë, in order, as she explicitly says, to explain how Apollo, the great god of the Sun, became subject to the vagaries of love, and how Leucothoë, the mortal girl he loved, and eventually raped, was transformed by him into an incense-bearing tree:

> et orsa est
> dicere Leuconoe: vocem tenuere sorores.
> "hunc quoque, siderea qui temperat omnia luce,
> cepit amor Solem: Solis referemus amores.
> primus adulterium Veneris cum Marte putatur
> hic vidisse deus; videt hic deus omnia primus.
> indoluit facto Iunonigenaeque marito
> furta tori furtique locum monstravit [...]". (*Metamorphoses*, IV, 167-74)[23]

[Leuconoë began, while her sisters held their peace. "Even the Sun, who with his central light guides all the stars, has felt the power of love. The Sun's loves we will relate. This god was first, 'tis said, to see the shame of Mars and Venus; this god sees all things first. Shocked at the sight, he revealed her sin to the goddess's husband, Vulcan, Juno's son, and where it was committed."]

---

[21] See Genesis 27 and Genesis 29. 15-23, respectively.

[22] *Doctoris ecstatici D. Dionysii Cartusiani Opera omnia in unum corpus digesta*, cura et labore Monachorum Sacri Ordinis Cartusiensis, 42 vols in 44 (Monstrolii: Typis Cartusiae S. M. de Pratis, 1896-1913), I, 383 ("In Genesim et Exodum").

[23] All references to Ovid are from *Metamorphoses*, tr. Frank Justus Miller, Loeb Classical Library, 42, 3rd edn, 2 vols (London: Heinemann, 1977).

Leuconoë then goes on to explain how Venus took revenge on Apollo for his betrayal of her:

> exigit indicii memorem Cythereia poenam
> inque vices illum, tectos qui laesit amores,
> laedit amore pari. quid nunc, Hyperione nate,
> forma colorque tibi radiataque lumina prosunt?
> nempe, tuis omnes qui terras ignibus uris,
> ureris igne novo; quique omnia cernere debes,
> Leucothoen spectas et virgine figis in una,
> quos mundo debes, oculos. (IV, 190-97)

> [But the goddess of Cythera did not forget the one who had spied on her, and took fitting vengeance on him; and he that betrayed her stolen love was equally betrayed in love. What now avail, O son of Hyperion, thy beauty and brightness and radiant beams? For thou, who dost inflame all lands with thy fires, are thyself inflamed by a strange fire. Thou who shouldst behold all things, dost gaze on Leucothoë alone, and on one maiden dost thou fix those eyes which belong to the whole world.]

In fact, this parallel between Apollo and Jacob is complemented by another, similar, and possibly relevant one between Apollo and Joseph: just as Apollo aroused the hostility of Venus by betraying her love affair with Mars to her husband, Vulcan, so Joseph also provoked the hatred of some of his brothers by bringing back tales of their wrongdoing to his father.[24]

It is possible to point to one further coincidence of this kind. Vulcan (known to the Greeks as Hephaestus), famously, was lame: according to some classical accounts, this was because his father, Zeus, had thrown him down from Olympus for trying to rescue his mother, Hera, from his wrath.

---

[24] See Genesis 37. 2 (quoted on p. 203 above). According to the exegetical tradition synthesized in the biblical commentaries (published in 1614) of the Flemish Jesuit, Cornelius a Lapide, their "crimine pessimo" was of a sexual nature: "de peccato, vel Sodomico, ut vult Rupertus, vel bestialitas cum ovibus, quas pascebant, ut vult S. Thomas, Abulensis et Hugo de S. Victore, quod proinde quia pudendum, horrendum et infame, noluit hic Moses nominare" ["Here Moses did not wish to name the sin, either sodomitical, as Rupert has it, or bestiality with the sheep that they tended, as St Thomas, Abulensis and Hugh of St Victor say, because it was shameful, repulsive and vile"]. See Cornelius Cornelii a Lapide, *Commentaria in Scripturam Sacram*, ed. Augustine Crampton, 21 vols (Paris: Ludovicus Vivès, 1857-1863), I, *In Pentateuchum Moisis. Genesis et Exodus*, 337.

Vulcan broke his leg in the process, and it never healed properly.[25] In *La fragua*, one can see how Velázquez has hinted at his lameness by accentuating the twist in his torso and the misalignment of his shoulders to a degree beyond what would be required to depict his gesture of recoil purely naturalistically. Jacob was also lame. He was made so as a result of the famous episode of his struggle with an angel:

> Qui cum videret quod eum superare non posset, tetigit nervum femoris eius, et statim emarcuit [...] Ortusque est ei statim sol, postquam transgressus est Phanuel: ipse vero claudicabat pede. Quam ob causam non comedunt nervum filii Israel, qui emarcuit in femore Jacob, usque in praesentem diem: eo quod tetigerit nervum femoris eius, et obstupuerit. (Genesis 32. 25, 31-32)
> [And when he saw that he could not overcome him, he touched the sinew of his thigh, and forthwith it shrank. [...] And immediately the sun rose upon him, after he was past Phanuel; but he halted on his foot. Therefore the children of Israel, unto this day, eat not the sinew, that shrank in Jacob's thigh: because he touched the sinew of his thigh and it shrank.]

Fernando Marías has pointed out that in Gian Paolo Lomazzo's *Trattato dell'arte della pittura, scoltura et architettura* (published in Milan in 1590), which greatly influenced Velázquez's teacher, Pacheco's *Arte de la pintura* (published posthumously in 1649) and was therefore probably also familiar to his pupil, Joseph's coat is commended as a subject for painting on two occasions, with specific mention made of how Jacob's lameness resulted from his struggle with the angel.[26] In *La túnica*, there seems to be nothing about Velázquez's rendition of the figure of Jacob itself that would suggest that he is lame. However, while it is probable that the staff thrown at his feet primarily recalls his status as a patriarch, and, perhaps, the feebleness of his old age, it is also possible that it is intended to remind the viewer of his infirmity.[27]

Finally, another way in which the paintings may be seen to be linked is through the role that light plays in each of them. In *La túnica*, the light

---

[25] "According to Homer he was one of her children by Zeus. Him Zeus cast out of heaven, because he came to the rescue of Hera in her bonds. For when Hercules had taken Troy and was at sea, Hera sent a storm after him; so Zeus hung her from Olympus. Hephaestus fell on Lemnos and was lamed of his legs." See (Pseudo-) Apollodorus, *The Library*, tr. James G. Frazer, Loeb Classical Library, 121, 2 vols (London: Heinemann, 1921), I, 1.3.

[26] See Marías, "*La túnica de José*," 289-90, and especially 294, n. 38.

[27] Jacob's staff as symbol of his authority is given special mention in Genesis 32. 10.

shines with greatest intensity on the two brothers placed farthest to the left. It illuminates their bodies with a golden radiance, and picks out the rich colours (blue, salmon pink and mustard yellow) of their clothing and Joseph's tunic. It is here, too, of course, that the most intense contrasts of light and shade are to be found. The two brothers in the background are reduced, by comparison, almost to the status of shadowy silhouettes despite the fact that they are placed in front of a light-grey wall. The figure of Jacob is a little more brightly lit and more clearly defined than they are, but much less so than the figures of the brothers opposite him. One has to look closely, in fact, to see that the light which bathes these figures on the left so generously first enters the room in the form of an attenuated beam coming from the far right, from behind Jacob. It first manifests itself as it shines softly on the upper part of Jacob's left sleeve. Then, suddenly much more brilliant and concentrated, it appears as a narrow strip along the side of his upraised left hand. Dimmer and more diffuse once again, it passes over his face, and seems virtually to disappear until, halfway into its trajectory, it illuminates Joseph's bloodstained white shirt and the whole left forearm of the brother dressed in black. As it diffuses itself across the room from right to left, it reveals the features, and the guilt, of each of Jacob's sons with increasing clarity. It hardly needs pointing out that in the Bible, and in Christian art and literature, in general, the divine presence, and, especially, divine truth and justice are repeatedly evoked in terms of the imagery of light.[28] It is difficult, because of the subject matter, not to see light performing this symbolic function in this painting. This is especially so because of the way in which it is shown entering the room and, initially, shining most brightly on the back of Jacob's upraised hand. Jacob was, of course, a great Jewish patriarch, a man especially favoured by God, and in that sense, identified with him. If the light does symbolize divine truth, it also implies a divine judgement on the deception that it reveals. The brother on the far left of the painting turns his whole body away and shields his eyes from the sight of Joseph's garments in a dramatic gesture that, in the first instance, indicates either feigned horror or genuine shame. Because, however, he is also the figure on whom the light shines most fully, it may well be that Velázquez intended his gesture to be read, on another level, as an indication that it is the light of truth that

---

[28] In his *De los nombres de Cristo*, for example, writing about the first coming of Christ, Fray Luis de León says: "porque la obra de aquella venida fue desterrar del mundo la noche del error, y como dice San Juan [John 1. 5]: *Resplandece en las tinieblas la luz.* Y así Cristo por esta causa es llamado *Luz y Sol de justicia.*" See *Obras completas castellanas*, ed. Félix García, OSA, 4th edn, 2 vols (Madrid: Biblioteca de Autores Cristianos, 1957), I, 447.

he finds unbearable and from which he tries to shield himself.[29] In *La fragua*, the main source of light is the brilliant halo around the head of Apollo. As the classical, pagan god of the sun and of light in general, from whom nothing is hidden ("videt hic deus omnia primus" [IV, 172], as Ovid put it), it is appropriate that it is he who should reveal Venus's infidelity to her husband, Vulcan. In both paintings, then, although in different ways, light as the attribute of God, or a god, is associated with the unmasking of an act of deception.[30]

In light of the multiple correspondences of different kinds between *La túnica de José* and *La fragua de Vulcano* that have been outlined here (some for the first time, as far as this writer is aware), it seems yet more difficult not to concur with Dawson Carr's opinion that "the choice of a scene from classical mythology to balance one from the Old Testament can hardly be accidental", even if one believes that there is insufficient evidence to show that they were formally intended to constitute a pair.

---

[29] Even if, as Fernando Marías has suggested, this figure is to be identified with Reuben (who dissuaded his brothers from killing Joseph, but was complicit in their lie), the argument put forward here is not fundamentally invalidated. Marías, too, speaks of this figure as "a la postre avergonzado"; see Marías, "*La túnica de José*," 293 and 295.

[30] It lies beyond the scope of this essay to enter into the scholarly debate about whether or not, in accordance with a well established iconographical tradition, Velázquez intended the figure of Apollo in *La fragua* to be identified with Christ, and about how this might affect interpretation of the two paintings as a pair. On these questions, see Diego Angulo Íñiguez, "La fábula de Vulcano, Venus y Marte y *La fragua* de Velázquez," *Archivo Español de Arte* 33 (1960): 149-81 (179-80); Brown, *Velázquez: Painter and Courtier*, 74, and Colomer, "De Madrid a Roma, 1630," 153.

INDEX

The Impact of Nationalism on the Muslim World

The Impact of Nationalism on the Muslim World

Edited by
M. Ghayasuddin

The Open Press
Al-Hoda Publishers

British Library Cataloguing in Publication Data

The Impact of Nationalism on the Muslim
   World.
   1. Nationalism—Islamic countries
   I. Ghayasuddin, M.
   320.5´4´0917671   JC311
ISBN 0 905081 39 0 Hb
ISBN 0 905081 40 4 Pb

The Open Press Limited
6 Endsleigh Street
London WC1H 0DS
UK

in association with:

Al-Hoda Publishers
76–78 Charing Cross Road
London WC2H 0BB
UK

Typeset by Joshua Associates Limited, Oxford
Printed by Biddles Ltd, Guildford

Contents

Foreword

The Muslims, once leaders of a dominant civilization, today stand perplexed and polarized within themselves and dominated and exploited by foreign powers. *Mulukiyyah*, or hereditary monarchy, remained the dominant mode of political organization for the greater part of Muslim history. Alienated from the masses and becoming increasingly secular in outlook, the *malukiyyah* was always vulnerable. It was overrun by a rival and hostile power outside Islam when it could no longer defend the lands and societies of Islam. To make its gains permanent, the new power, western civilization, set about the task of dismantling the world of Islam. The political fragmentation of the *Ummah* was achieved by the imposition of the nation-State system. If, despite this, the disintegration has remained peripheral, it is because of the political culture of the Muslim masses, which has resisted the breakdown of their traditional societies.

The Islamic Revolution in Iran represents a turning-point in Muslim political history. The political culture of the Muslim masses, has reasserted itself in one part of the *Ummah*, breaking the strait-jacket of nationalism and the nation-State system. It is challenging and threatening the imposed status quo.

Nationalism is an alien concept and was unheard of in the world of Islam until a hundred years ago. It gained currency in the wake of colonialism. A new elite emerged in the Muslim world which became 'nationalist', 'westernized', 'secular' or even 'Islamic' under the influence of orientalism. Nationalism is the instrument of continued western control and domination over Muslim areas of the world. The new nation-States and their institutions function as an extension of colonial rule and in the interests of the colonial powers. The west has managed to keep the power of Islam divided and defused. The map of the Muslim world today is the map of nation-States in which 'nationality' and 'national interest' stand above Islam.

The six papers which comprise this book were presented at a world seminar on the Impact of Nationalism on the Ummah held in London from 31 July–3 August, 1985. The seminar was initiated by Dr Kalim

Siddiqui, Director of the Muslim Institute. His paper, the first, provides a framework to stimulate new lines of inquiry and action for Muslims. The second paper, by Murtaza Garia, explains how nationalism is viewed by the Qur'ān and Sunnah. This is followed by case-studies from the Middle East, Southeast Asia, South Asia and West Africa: Dr Mohamed Yehia gives a critique of the idea of Arab nationalism; Dr Hasan di Tiro discusses Dutch colonial Islamic policy and the birth of 'Indonesian nationalism'; Dr Dabla focuses on the experience of Kashmiri Muslims under oppression by the Brahmins (an elite cultivated by the British to succeed them in India); Malik N'Daiye deals with the French Islamic policy in West Africa.

This book should help to develop a better understanding of nationalism in the context of Islam and the Muslim political culture that has survived colonialism.

M. Ghayasuddin

The Muslim Institute
6 Endsleigh Street
London WC1H 0DS

17 June, 1986

About the Contributors

Dr Kalim Siddiqui is Director of The Muslim Institute, London.

Murtaza Garia is Principal Assistant Secretary, Ministry of Education, Arts and Culture, Mauritius.

Dr Mohamed Yehia teaches English Literature at the University of Cairo, Egypt.

Dr Tengku Hasan M. di Tiro is President of the National Liberation Front of Acheh Sumatra.

Dr Bashir Ahmed Dabla is Assistant Professor in Sociology at the Aligarh Muslim University, India.

Malik N'Daiye   is Director of Dawah, Jama'at Ibad ar-Rahman, Senegal.

Chapter I

Nation-States as Obstacles to the Total Transformation of the *Ummah*

Dr Kalim Siddiqui
Director, The Muslim Institute

Today we come face to face with perhaps the greatest evil that stalks the modern world—that of nationalism. This monster needs to be described and analysed in detail. Muslims throughout the world recognize the evil of nationalism in general terms, but there is little literature on the subject. In our universities nationalism is presented as a positive force that helped to accelerate the departure of the colonial powers. The fact of the matter is that nationalism either as a political doctrine or as a popular emotion was unknown to Muslims until about a hundred years ago. For 1,300 years before that, Muslims had established large States and empires and ruled over vast territories of the world without ever having to appeal to anything which even vaguely resembled modern nationalism. Nationalism is a force which leads to the disintegration of the human personality and society at all levels.[1] My views on the subject are well known; it is nearly 10 years since I wrote my paper, *Beyond the Muslim Nation-States*.[2]

I do not propose to undertake a detailed theoretical or philosophical examination of nationalism. My purpose is to take a pragmatic, empirical view of the state of the *Ummah* under the impact of nationalism. I am aware, of course, that nationalism is also the root of other common evils such as national socialism, national capitalism, national democracy and national culture.

Most of the world's major languages existed for hundreds of years before nationalism, and yet have come to be known as 'national' languages. The 'national' tag is now applied even to dress and food. We are, therefore, dealing with a disease that affects a wide variety of human behaviour. Nationalism has tried to capture the entire human personality at all levels—body, mind and soul. However, the poison of nationalism has been injected, and continues to be injected and spread, through one and only one source: the control and manipulation of political power.

The point that has to be clearly understood is that the State is the ultimate source of all good and evil in any society. For the followers of Muhammad, upon whom be peace, this point should not need to be stressed. It is almost impossible to be a Muslim without either living in an Islamic State or being engaged in a struggle to establish an Islamic State. If one or other of these conditions is not met, then perhaps the bulk of the Sunnah of Muhammad, upon whom be peace, will be ignored. The end product of the Sunnah of the Prophet was the Islamic State of Medina. The message of Islam was completed not only in the Qur'ān, but also in the State created through a relentless struggle against the established power of *kufr*. The Islamic State is an essential and integral part of Islam. Indeed, Islam is incomplete without the Islamic State. Islam is not merely a set of rituals for personal piety, Islam is the Creator's own plan, prescription and prognosis for all mankind. A Muslim can neither live the 'good life' on his own nor pursue 'personal *taqwa*' in isolation. The Islamic State is Allah's chosen framework and the one in which the moral, political, social, economic and cultural goals of Islam are pursued by the Muslim *Ummah*.

All this is common ground among Muslims. There is, however, a great deal of confusion about how the Islamic State is established. On the face of it, the answer to this question too should be simple and easily understood by all Muslims.

The method of Allah's Messenger, upon whom be peace, ought to be as clear as the Divine Message. Confusion has, however, crept in and this is largely, though not entirely, due to the political dominance of the west over Muslim societies. Once under alien political tutelage, Muslim societies began to throw up intellectuals, philosophers and political leaders who also accepted the intellectual and cultural overlordship of the west. It must be noted that the west was not content with acquiring undisputed control of and dominance over the political, social and cultural structures that already existed in Muslim societies. The west's colonial ambitions included the outright abolition and destruction of all institutions in traditional Muslim societies. The colonial powers created 'colonial States' in the image of their European States. These colonial States then proceeded to establish European-styled administrative, military, economic, social, cultural and educational institutions and structures. The people of the colonies were offered 'progress', opportunity and participation in the new order only if they learned European languages, acquired western education in European-styled universities, and generally accepted the European outlook and way of life. After this, if they also practised Islam strictly for personal piety, the Europeans did not mind.

The new Europeanized classes were also encouraged to look forward to a day when the European colonial States would be handed over to them as 'independent' States. But before the newly Europeanized colonials could be considered fit for political emancipation, they had to become nationalists. As nationalists they were encouraged to mix a little Islam with their otherwise secular politics. This was in any case necessary for communication with the 'backward' Muslim masses. Thus we came to acquire Muslim 'fathers of the nations' who are buried in expensive mausoleums in our capital cities. Some of them were also called 'kings'. The 'independence' they bequeathed to us was, and remains, little more than a continuation of the European colonial States. This brings me back to something I have said and written repeatedly during the last ten years. These colonial States, now called nation-States, are replete with national frontiers, national flags, national anthems, national days, national languages, national dresses, national cultures, national airlines, national histories and, above all, national interests. Every new 'nation' is defined in exclusivist terms. No two nation-States can have identical 'national interests'. The impact of this on the Muslim *Ummah* has been devastating. The political map of the *Ummah* today represents the globalization of the nation-State system.

It represents the defeat and dismemberment of the political power of Islam. More than that, it represents the continued political, economic, social and cultural dominance of the west over the lands and peoples of Islam. The loss of Palestine to Zionism was also made possible by the prior dismemberment of the *Ummah* into nation-States. A greater tragedy of this period is that there also emerged a number of 'national' Islamic parties. Nowhere in the world have such parties succeeded in attaining even modest goals within their chosen 'national' political systems. Nowhere in the world has an 'Islamic' political party succeeded in setting up anything that could even remotely be described as an Islamic State. In my view, the 'Islamic parties' were and remain a peculiar product of the colonial period. What we must all recognize is that the founders of these

'Islamic parties' were men of great learning, integrity and *taqwa*; some of the books written in this period have greatly enriched the literary heritage of Islam. But the learning, integrity and *taqwa* of these great figures of recent Muslim history cannot be used to defend the record and political role of the parties they founded.

The position that the Muslim Institute has taken for more than a decade is that no progress in rebuilding the House of Islam is possible within the framework of the post-colonial nation-States. The path of the *Ummah* and that of the Islamic movement within the *Ummah* is blocked by the nation-States. These nation-States are like huge boulders blown across our path by the ill-wind of recent history.

All nation-States that today occupy, enslave and exploit the lands, peoples and resources of the *Ummah* must of necessity be dismantled. It is the nation-States that give life and respectability to nationalism. Nationalism is not an idea that precedes its political manifestation. With some exceptions, the idea of nationalism has been artificially planted in order to support an externally imposed State. The idea of the State based on nationalism is so alien to the moral genius of our people that every single nation-State in the *Ummah* is unstable, weak and forever on the verge of collapse. All Muslim nation-States in the world today are maintained by a mixture of internal oppression and external support. It is only the regular injection of military and economic 'aid' from the leading imperialist powers that keeps these States going. None of these States has solved any of its own problems let alone those of its people. Since these States have neither roots in the history of Islam nor in the history of their peoples, they will not be difficult to dismantle.

While the dismantling of the existing nation-States is unlikely to present many problems, a great many conceptual and organizational problems have to be overcome. These relate to the nature and organization of the Islamic movement, to the political map of the *Ummah*, and to the political, economic and social transformation of the *Ummah* that we now seek to bring about. Let us realize that the extent, depth and nature of the change that we now seek is the most profound transformation of a world community that has ever been attempted. It is quite clear that one *Ummah* must mean one Islamic movement, leading to one global Islamic State under one Imam/ Khalifa. From where we stand today, the prospect of a single global Islamic State under a single leader seems so remote that most people would regard such a goal beyond the bounds of realism. Those of us who assert the general proposition that the unity of the *Ummah*, at all levels, is a set of achievable goals, must be more precise if we are not to be dismissed as naïve, illogical dreamers dealing in trite absurdities devoid of substance. Before we can expect to be taken seriously we must go further and insist that a rigorous system of thought based on observation and experimentation be put forward by the *ulama* and intellectuals of Islam. The Qur'ān and the Sunnah will yield greater and greater knowledge and insight as our capacity to use and absorb knowledge expands. It seems to me that Muslims, so far, have barely begun to use the total potential of the Qur'ān and the Sunnah in the shaping of a programme for the total transformation. It is probably true to say that the need for the total transformation of the *Ummah* has at no time been as obvious and as urgently felt as it is today. In the period of rapid expansion of the domains of Islam and the political and cultural dominance of Muslims, the need for such a transformation was not felt at all. The rapid physical and political expansion was itself seen as transformation. In this period, the leading scholars of Islam concentrated their attention on the writing of extensive commentaries on the Qur'ān. Their assumption appears to have been that such maladies as were found in the *Ummah* would be corrected through the better and deeper understanding of the Qur'ān. Clearly, the Qur'ān is a fathomless source of knowledge. Modern writers have pointed out that the laconic style of the Qur'ān includes profound nuances only now beginning to be understood and after man has developed the microscope, the telescope and other tools of observation and analysis in such fields as biology, astronomy, physics, chemistry and geology.[3] These new insights into the meaning of the Qur'ān will not be reflected in *tafsir* literature for some time to come. It will be some considerable time before our purely religious seminaries adjust to the scientific knowledge that enhances our understanding of the Qur'ān. The Qur'ān is of course unchanging. It has remained unchanged since its Revelation and will remain so until the end of time. But our understanding of the Qur'ān can deepen with our own understanding of the processes of history, our experiences and our ability to absorb and use new knowledge. The same is true of the Sunnah of the Prophet. The Sunnah is also a record of the total transformation of the Hejaz and its people over a period of twenty-three years. The Hejaz is a relatively small geographical area and its population, at the time of the Prophet, was also very small. The entire *Ummah* during this time lived within the territorial control of the State of Medina. Therefore, from the

Sunnah that transformed only the Hejaz we have to derive a programme for the transformation of an *Ummah* that is now global. An added complication is that the *Ummah* we want to transform is now divided into about fifty nation-States, each claiming to be 'sovereign' and 'independent' though each is, in one way or another, subservient to *kufr*.

We must not underestimate the power of the nation-States and their ruling elites to exploit the nationalist emotions of our people. Only a year ago, when I said that 'national' frontiers between Muslim countries make no sense and that they should become 'open' or 'soft' frontiers as successive nation-States are converted into Islamic States, the controlled media of the Pakistani regime immediately accused me of advocating the disappearance of Pakistan; the media of the Jama'at-e Islami, in Pakistan, accused me of 'anti-national' activities and of serving 'foreign interests'. So the boulders of nationalism and the nation-States are not lifeless, inanimate objects accidentally blown into the path of Islam; they represent the mobilized power of *nifaq* and also some well-meaning but misguided 'Islamic parties'. These obstacles in the path of Islam are all armed and supported by the power of global *kufr*. They have, also, already made it clear that they are going to fight Islam at every step and all the way. It so happens that Islam, too, orders us to fight these forces until our victory is achieved with the Help of Allah.[4] For us there is no such thing as internal conflict and external conflict. The forces inimical to Islam are so deeply rooted in the fabric of the *Ummah* that all conflicts will be simultaneously internal and external. There are no clearly defined geographical frontiers between Islam and its enemies. Those within Muslim societies who insist on accepting the political, social, cultural and economic supremacy of the west are not only our rulers, country-men and neighbours but often members of our own families. Thus, the era of conflict we have now entered into is one of grave consequences for all Muslims. No Muslim can opt out of the consequences of these conflicts. These conflicts will not leave anyone unaffected. It is not a matter of choice whether or not we want to engage in these conflicts; those opposed to Islam have already declared war on Islam. As we have seen, the greatest manifestation of this declaration of war against Islam, is the era of nationalism and of the nation-States. There can be no compromise, there can be no accommodation and there can be no peace in the world of Islam so long as any traces of nationalism remain in our societies. No programme for the transformation of the

Ummah is either realistic or even based on the Qur'ān and the Sunnah of Muhammad, upon whom be peace, if it does not set out to exorcise the ghost of nationalism and all its various political, social, cultural and economic manifestations.

As far as I know, the total transformation of the *Ummah* from its present condition to the ultimate condition that Islam desires has never been stated as a set of achievable goals. In the last 200 years, Muslim political thought has been, entirely, a reaction to the decline of Muslim political power and the emergence of the west as a global political power and civilization. The west's scientific, technological and economic achievements so dazzled Muslim thinkers that they accepted 'progress' as defined by the west as essential for the future of Muslim societies. Much energy was spent in trying to reconcile the essentials of this 'progress' with Islam. It was this search for reconciliation between Islam and western-style 'progress' that led to attempts to admit nationalism, capitalism, democracy and latterly socialism into Islam. Such attempts are still going on with programmes of 'Islamization' that, essentially, do not alter the chosen course of 'progress' through westernization. How deeply ingrained this idea of the compatibility of Islam with the west is, is demonstrated by the support 'Islamic parties' are giving to programmes of 'Islamization' in Muslim nation-States whose rulers are both secular and subservient to the west. There are also some 'Islamicists' naïve enough to believe that the United States is a friend of Islam and a natural ally against 'godless communism'.[5]

Let us first of all realize that we cannot even begin to think about the total transformation of the *Ummah* without first taking up the position that there is no compatibility whatsoever between Islam and the west. It is only when we have taken this step that we have created the necessary spiritual, material and historical situation in which the total transformation of the *Ummah* becomes a logical necessity. In today's historical situation, the declaration of the incompatibility of the civilization of Islam with the civilization of the west is the only step that can free us from the psychological stranglehold in which the west has held us for so long. This declaration of incompatibility forces us to prove the point that we are in fact incompatible; it forces us to define our civilizational goals in terms of Islam and Islam alone; it demands that we find alternatives to such global sacred cows as capitalism, socialism and democracy; it makes it necessary for us to find our own solutions to the problems of underdevelopment, poverty and wealth. The power of Islam in the world can be developed and mobilized only if the sources of our power are within the house of Islam. For instance, military power that depends on arms purchased either from or supplied by the west cannot be used for the glory of Islam. Standing armies of mercenary soldiers and officers will not and cannot fight for Islam. Lightly-armed *muttaqi* soldiers who go out to fight and die for Islam are more powerful than the heavily-armed professional soldiers who fear death. The mobilized will of the Muslim masses, under a *muttaqi* leadership, makes the Islamic State an invincible force. Compare this with the modern nation-States, in which the people are either divided by competing political parties led by sectional interests or where professional soldiers provide some of the most oppressive regimes of all history. In the nation-States that are the creation of the west, where ruling classes and 'Islamic parties' regard Islam as compatible with the west, the political systems are subservient to the west. The economies of these States are also integrated into the world capitalist system. The path of the *Ummah* is blocked not only by the boulders of nationalism but by the entire log-jam of western civilization. Nationalism is the very foundation of the west as we know it. It is, therefore, not possible to deal with national-ism in isolation. The road to the total transformation of the *Ummah* is a long one. We have not become so deviated from our original course in a short time and we are not going to get back to where we should have been by now overnight. When we talk about the total trans-formation of the *Ummah* we are talking about a process of history-making that will occupy us for a very considerable period of time. However, the immediate change of direction that is required must, at the very minimum, include the emergence of a global Islamic move-ment that rejects nationalism and the nation-States in their entirety and regards the west as totally incompatible with Islam.

The declaration of the incompatibility of the west with Islam brings us face to face with another question to which I have often referred in the past: the question of leadership. Once we have taken up the position of incompatibility between Islam and the west, we have also taken the position that those educated in the western tradition have no part to play in the leadership of the Islamic movement.

When I have said this in the past, many brothers have regarded it as too harsh and unrealistic. Where, they have asked, are the *ulama* who can lead the Islamic movement? This is a question that needs careful consideration.

Those who react in this way seem to think that I propose to exclude western-educated Muslims from the Islamic movement altogether. This is not so. I am convinced that all Muslims, whatever their background, whether educated or not, have to be part of the Islamic movement. This clearly includes those educated in western-styled schools, colleges and universities. But those educated in the western manner must realize that their education has equipped them to serve the political, social, economic, cultural, administrative and military systems that we must destroy. Western education teaches a man to be arrogant and selfish. In all Muslim societies today, we have ruling classes who have been educated and trained to dominate and exploit our countries in the style of the western colonialists. The western-educated ruling classes of today are the children, grandchildren or great-grandchildren of those who welcomed the western colonialists and co-operated with them. It is through them that our societies have been severely damaged by western colonialists. In every part of the world today there are governments and regimes controlled by this class of people. All such governments and regimes are doing everything possible to prevent the emergence of Islam in a political role. Throughout history, there is not a single instance of a western-educated Muslim elite that has served Islam in any meaningful way. There are of course hordes of western-educated scholars of Islam who have taken degrees in Islam just as others have taken degrees in medicine, law, economics, history and so on. Their major role, however, has been apologetic. These are the 'scholars' of Islam who have been trying to write books on 'Islamic economics', 'Islamic politics', 'Islamic liberalism', and so on. These are the compromisers who have been trying to prove that Islam is compatible with their secular ambitions and western preferences. The leadership ranks of the 'Islamic parties' are full of such 'Islamizers'. In Iran, these westernized individuals and groups were given a chance to serve in the highest offices of the Islamic State. And what did they do? They tried to capture supreme power. They, in fact, tried to re-establish Iran as a liberal and democratic nation-State with a few cosmetic 'Islamic' features. But now that the nationalists, liberals, communists and *munafiqin* have been unmasked and defeated, the vast majority of the westernized elite's youth performs glorious deeds in the service of the Islamic Revolution and the new Islamic State.

A particular feature of the western-educated elite is that its members cannot see any role for themselves except that of leadership.

The fact is that they were created to lead our people during the era of our subservience to an alien power and civilization. Their leadership role was itself subject to the overall control and dominance of the west. We cannot find a single instance of a Muslim country or society having escaped the dominance of the west under the leadership of those the west itself had prepared and chosen to lead us. What we do find is that in the post-colonial period all parts of the *Ummah* have become even more subservient to the west than they were in the heyday of direct colonialism. The so-called leaders of our 'independence' and 'fathers' of our 'nations' have been some of the most slavish people the *Ummah* has ever produced. They and their successors have done the bidding of the west more than the bidding of Allah, *subhanahu wa ta'ala*. In the struggle against *kufr* that lies ahead, these men and their supporters are likely to play the political role of *kufr* and *shirk* against Islam. They will be the chief instruments of the west's war against Islam and the Islamic movement. It is not an accident that all the nation-States dividing the *Ummah* today are lined up behind Saddam Husain. Nor is it an accident that both superpowers are also on the same side.

The incompatibility between Islam and the west that we have established and the total transformation of the *Ummah* that we seek to bring about force us to seek a leadership which is also compatible with our goals. Such a leadership can only emerge from the roots of Islam itself, and not from those sections of the *Ummah* that are contaminated by alien influences. If such people, let us call them *ulama*, do not already exist, then we will have to wait until they do. However, I do not accept that such *ulama* do not exist. What is true is that most of the known figures among the *ulama* are, in one way or another, tied to the coat-tails of the secular regimes. They and their institutions are dependent on official patronage, and are, therefore, in no position to participate in a struggle that sets out to defy and destroy the prevailing order. There are other eminent figures who simply do not understand the contemporary political situation of the *Ummah* in the world at large. They have become eminent through a lifetime of service dedicated to keeping the basic beliefs and rituals of Islam generally understood in the *Ummah*. This they have achieved by choosing not to challenge the political power of *kufr*. They worked within the narrow confines of the 'religious freedom' offered by *kafir* systems. In the post-colonial era, especially in the last thirty years, some of these *ulama* and their poverty-stricken institutions have received enormous financial patronage from the oil-rich Arab regimes. This has made them and their followers even more docile and subservient than they were in the days of direct European colonialism. Some of these *ulama*, especially in British India, opposed the leadership of the secularized, westernized Muslims but failed to offer an alternative to the dominance of *kufr*. The Muslim masses largely ignored them. The Muslim masses also ignored the 'Islamic' alternative offered by the 'Islamic parties'.

Today, the historical situation has been transformed. On the one hand, the Muslim masses in one country, led by their *ulama*, have swept aside the power of *kufr* and established an Islamic State; on the other, the post-colonial regimes in the nation-States have been unmasked and exposed as instruments of the political dominance of *kufr*. It is true that the subservient *ulama* and the 'Islamic parties' are still trying to defend the status quo, but it is also true that large numbers of both ordinary and very influential people in the *Ummah*, including many *ulama*, have become convinced that the only way forward is through a succession of Islamic Revolutions in all Muslim areas of the world. This newly invigorated opinion in the *Ummah* has yet to assert itself to challenge and defy the established political order. The irrelevance of the established 'religious' order of the subservient *ulama* and of the 'Islamic parties' has also become obvious to many people. Thus, the new global Islamic movement represents a new confidence in the *Ummah* that the west *can* be defeated, and a heightened sense of expectation and optimism for the future. The evidence of this spiritual and intellectual ferment in the *Ummah* is everywhere—in Muslim homes, families, communities, cities and countries throughout the world. This new mood cuts across all other known barriers of nationalism, ethnicity, territoriality and sectarianism. This is especially so between Muslims following the Shi'i and Sunni schools of thought. Despite the efforts now being made by the enemies of Islam to drive a wedge between Shi'i and Sunni Muslims the fact is that, in the last six years, under the influence of the Islamic Revolution, more Shi'i and Sunni Muslims have come closer together than at any other time.

Throughout the world new relationships have been forged between Shi'i and Sunni Muslims. I know of many *ulama*, of both schools of thought, who are meeting and working together in many parts of the world. Throughout the world there have emerged *ulama*, intellectuals, students and others whose names are not yet household names. We have to remember that the world's press and media are entirely controlled by the enemies of Islam. The Islamic movement's own media is, as yet, in its infancy. Indeed, everything about the new Islamic movement is in its infancy. An entirely new phase in the history of Islam has been inaugurated. The greatest assets of the new Islamic movement are the Islamic Revolution in Iran, the Islamic State that has been established in Iran, the leadership of the *ulama* of Iran and, above all, the leadership of Imam Khomeini. To follow in the footsteps of the Islamic Revolution in Iran, the *Ummah* outside Iran also needs to develop a leadership that is primarily, though perhaps not exclusively, derived from the ranks of the *ulama*. The emergence of leadership is itself a complex process which we should examine in detail on some other occasion. All that we need to note here is that if the new Islamic movement sets out to achieve the total transformation of the *Ummah*, then the quality of the leadership will be determined by the nature of the struggle that is undertaken.

There is no doubt whatsoever in my mind that the total transformation of the *Ummah* will require a total struggle at all levels and in all fields of human activity. Our struggle will be spiritual, philosophical, political, social, cultural, economic, scientific and military. Since we seek the total transformation of the global *Ummah*, the struggle will be conducted at all levels and at different levels in different parts of the world simultaneously. Such versatility in a global movement presents many problems. In some parts of the *Ummah*, as in Iran today, the struggle may have reached a relatively advanced stage. Indeed in Iran there is already an Islamic State in existence led by an Imam. In other parts of the *Ummah* the struggle has barely begun.

I have long held the view that once an Islamic State has been established it becomes by definition the leader of the *Ummah* and of the global Islamic movement. Every Muslim must give his allegiance to that State. In my view, this is not just a functional necessity it is a Divine ordinance. I have said before that Islam is incomplete without the Islamic State. Equally, the life of a Muslim is incomplete without allegiance to an Imam/Khalifa. I realize that Imam Khomeini has not offered himself for the general *ba'ya* of the *Ummah*. His reasons for not doing so are not difficult to understand. But this should not prevent us from regarding both the Islamic State of Iran and the Imam as leaders of the global Islamic movement. It is important to realize, however, that Iran, too, is still in the process of transformation. Perhaps, Iran is still in the early stages of transformation. At a seminar in London more than five years ago I argued that the first Islamic State to emerge after a lapse of more than 1,300 years would be a 'primitive model' of the ideal. Clearly there are stages involved in the total transformation of the *Ummah*. The early stages of transformation in an Islamic State, established as a result of a successful Islamic Revolution, are different from the early stages in other parts of the *Ummah* that are still some years away from an Islamic Revolution.

The instrument for the total transformation of the *Ummah* can be none other than the global Islamic movement. The method of the Islamic movement is the *Seerah* of the Prophet, upon whom be peace. After a prolonged struggle, the speed of transformation is accelerated to a point at which it is referred to as an 'Islamic Revolution'. The Islamic Revolution is the stage at which the Islamic movement converts either an area or country into an Islamic State. The Islamic State is then invaded by the external enemies of Islam whilst internal enemies try to subvert it. After a prolonged struggle, the Islamic State defeats its internal and external enemies and acquires control over its immediate environment. There then follows a prolonged period of transformation of the society at all levels until a truly *muttaqi* and just society comes into being. It is now possible to state these as distinct stages in the making of history and relate them to the *Seerah* of Muhammad, upon whom be peace.

The first stage is clearly the stage of prolonged struggle against very heavy odds. In the *Seerah* this is known as the 'Makkan period'. In this stage, which lasted for thirteen of the twenty-three year prophethood of Muhammad, there were a number of distinct phases. For most of this period, the Islamic movement is small and weak and there is no reason to believe that such a fledgling band of believers can overcome the established and dominant order. The power and arrogance of the established order and the relative weakness of the Islamic movement do not persuade the Islamic movement to tone down its beliefs, ideas, methods or goals. Indeed, during this period the Islamic movement boldly declares that the established order and its belief systems are evil and must be destroyed. At this point, the Islamic movement is only a scattered body of individual Muslims who are exposed to the worst kind of oppression and torture.

In the new 'Makkan period', in which the bulk of the *Ummah* lives today, the Islamic movement has to define its position clearly, crisply and unambiguously. Our basic declaration of faith—'there is no *ilah* except Allah'—must be related to the contemporary objects of worship that we have acquired in recent history. In the Prophet's time the declaration that 'there is no *ilah*' was understood by the Quraysh of Makkah as referring to the hundreds of idols they worshipped and kept in the Ka'aba. The Makkans also understood clearly that the declarations of Muhammad, upon whom be peace, were a direct challenge to the established system of authority and hierarchy in Makkah at the time. The new global Islamic movement of today has to make equally forthright and unambiguous declarations. For instance, we have to state categorically that the only two collective identities we recognize are those of the House of Islam and the house of *kufr*. The Muslims are one *Ummah* and the *kuffar* are one *millat*. There is no third *millat* in the world. The Muslim *Ummah* recognizes no nationality as a basis of law, statehood or sovereignty. There is no compatibility between the civilizations of Islam and *kufr*.

Once such a declaration has been made by the global Islamic movement, it also means that all the pillars of western civilization, such as social democracy, capitalism, socialism, liberalism, republicanism, marxism, anarchism, populism, multi-racialism, unionism, and so forth, are part and parcel of the *millat* of *kufr*. All these ideas, beliefs and philosophies, often dressed up as 'science' and 'progress', have been institutionalized. The highest of these institutions is the nation-State. All nation-States which exist today, including those with predominently Muslim populations, are, therefore, *ipso facto*, integral parts of the global domination that *kufr* has acquired.

No exception is possible. It must not be argued, indeed it cannot be argued, that because there is *shura* in Islam, modern democracy is 'Islamic'; that because private property is allowed by Islam, modern capitalism is 'Islamic'; that because Islam believes in equality, there is 'socialism in Islam', and so on. We have to wipe the slate clean before we can write on it; we have to demolish what exists before we can build on any site. This is the meaning of the declaration that 'there is no *ilah* except Allah'.

It was this clarity of mind and singleness of purpose that the Prophet, upon whom be peace, first induced among a handful of his followers in Makkah. Once this step had been taken, all else in the *Seerah*, the first full-scale Islamic movement, followed as day follows night. It was this single, bold, definitive, uncompromising step taken in Makkah that ultimately led to the total transformation of the Hejaz. It is this single step, when it is taken by the global Islamic movement today, that will inexorably lead to the total transformation of the *Ummah*, indeed to the total transformation of the world.

There is one more condition to be met. The global Islamic movement cannot take the first step without a leader. This is a condition that was never met and could not be met in the days of the local, regional and national 'Islamic parties' and partial Islamic movements. In our day, there has emerged a leader who has successfully achieved the transition, in one part of the *Ummah*, from the 'Makkan period' to the establishment of an Islamic State. This transition has been achieved under the *muttaqi* leadership of the *ulama* of Iran, one of whom is their *imam*. There is no other holder of political office in the world of Islam today, no other living soul, who can possibly qualify for the leadership of the global Islamic movement. It so happens that the declaration of incompatibility between Islam and *kufr* has been the cornerstone of the Islamic movement in Iran. The ruthless and uncompromising eradication of the influence, power, control and culture of *kufr* is the most outstanding feature of the Islamic Revolution in Iran.[6]

There is a difference between the 'Makkan period' in Makkah and the 'Makkan period' of today. In Makkah under the leadership of the Prophet, when the *Ummah* was only a handful of Muslims, the meaning and commitment of the declaration that 'there is no *ilah* except Allah' was clear to the established order. Today, when the *Ummah* represents a global community of Muslims, our faith and its declaration do not carry purpose, conviction, programme and precise meaning. It is only in Iran that the Islamic movement has defined and achieved the goals of the 'Makkan period'. Today, the figure of Imam Khomeini is identified with the modern 'Makkan period'. By adopting him as the leader of the global Islamic movement we give notice that the entire *Ummah* is now prepared to wage a relentless struggle against the Muslim nation-States and against the control and dominance of *kufr* over the House of Islam. In any case, the global Islamic movement cannot be led by anyone other than the leader and religious and political head of the first Islamic State to emerge in modern times.

Another point of vital importance is that in the original 'Makkan period' the Muslim *Ummah* was not only small but also united. There were no schools of thought in Islam. Those differences which, today, exist among Muslims are a peculiar product of the course Islamic history has taken. My view is that because our history has been divisive we are divided. Once the course of our history turns towards the pursuit and achievement of the goals of Islam that are common to Muslims, of all schools of thought, history itself will make these divisions a distant memory. The same sentiment was echoed by Imam Khomeini in a message to *hujjaj* in September, 1980. He said:

> To love one's fatherland and its people and to protect its frontiers are both quite unobjectionable, but nationalism, involving hostility to other Muslim nations, is something quite different. It is contrary to the Noble Qur'ān and the orders of the Most Noble Messenger. Nationalism, which results in the creation of enmity between Muslims and splits the ranks of the believers, is against Islam and the interests of the Muslims. It is a stratagem concocted by the foreigners who are disturbed by the spread of Islam. More saddening and dangerous than nationalism is the creation of dissension between Sunnis and Shi'is and diffusion of mischievous propaganda among brother Muslims. Praise and thanks be to Allah that no difference exists in our Revolution between these two groups. All are living side by side in friendship and brotherhood. The Sunnis, who are numerous in Iran and live all over the country, have their own *ulama* and *shaykhs*; they are our brothers and equal with us, and are opposed to the attempts to create dissension that certain criminals, agents of America and Zionism, are currently engaged in. Our Sunni brothers in the Muslim world must know that the agents of the satanic superpowers do not desire the welfare of Islam and the Muslims. The Muslims must dissociate themselves from them, and pay no heed to their divisive propaganda. I extend the hand of brotherhood to all committed Muslims in the world and ask them to regard the Shi'is as cherished brothers and thereby frustrate the sinister plans of foreigners.

A little later in the same message, Imam Khomeini sends out this rousing call to the *Ummah*:

> Muslims the world over who believe in the truth of Islam, arise and gather beneath the banner of *tauhid* and the teachings of Islam. Repel the treacherous superpowers from your countries and your abundant resources. Restore the glory of Islam, and abandon your selfish disputes and differences, for you possess everything. Rely on the culture of Islam, resist imitation of the

west, and stand on your own feet. Attack those intellectuals who are infatuated with the west and the east, and recover your true identity. Realize that intellectuals in the pay of foreigners have inflicted disaster upon their people and countries. As long as you remain disunited and fail to place your reliance in true Islam, you will continue to suffer what you have suffered already. We are now in an age when the masses act as the guides to the intellectuals and *are rescuing them* from abasement and humiliation. For today is the day that the masses of the people are on the move; they are the guides to those who previously sought to be the guides themselves. Know that your moral power will overcome all other powers. With a population of almost one billion and with infinite sources of wealth, you can defeat all the powers. Aid Allah's cause so that He may aid you. Great ocean of Muslims, arise and defeat the enemies of humanity. If you turn to Allah and follow the heavenly teachings, Allah, *subhanabu wa ta'ala* and His vast hosts will be with you.

The Imam is not afraid of identifying the enemies of Islam:

The most important and painful problem confronting the subjugated nations of the world, both Muslim and non-Muslim, is the problem of America. In order to swallow up the material resources of the countries it has succeeded in dominating, America, the most powerful country in the world, will spare no effort.

America is the number-one enemy of the deprived and oppressed people of the world. There is no crime America will not commit in order to maintain its political, economic, cultural and military domination of those parts of the world where it predominates. It exploits the oppressed people of the world by means of the large-scale propaganda campaigns that are co-ordinated for it by international Zionism. By means of its hidden and treacherous agents, it sucks the blood of the defenceless people as if it alone, together with its satellites, had the right to live in this world.

Iran has tried to sever all its relations with this Great Satan and it is for this reason that it now finds wars imposed upon it. America has urged Iraq to spill the blood of our young men, and it has compelled the countries that are subject to its influence to boycott us economically in the hope of defeating us.

Unfortunately, most Asian countries are also hostile to us. Let the Muslim nations be aware that Iran is a country effectively at war with America, and that our martyrs—the brave young men of our army and the Revolutionary Guards—are defending Iran and the Islam we hold dear against America. Thus, it is necessary to point out, the clashes now occurring in the west of our beloved country are caused by America; every day we are forced to confront various godless and treacherous groups there. This is a result of the Islamic content of our Revolution, which has been established on the basis of true independence. Were we to compromise with America and the other superpowers, we would not suffer these misfortunes. But our nation is no longer ready to submit to humiliation and abjection; it prefers a bloody death to a life of shame. We are ready to be killed and we have made a covenant with Allah to follow the path of our leader, the Lord of the Martyrs.

O Muslims who are now sitting next to the House of Allah, engaged in prayer: pray for those who are resisting America and the other superpowers, and understand that we are not fighting against Iraq. The people of Iraq support our Islamic Revolution; our quarrel is with America, and it is America whose hand can be seen emerging from the sleeve of the Iraqi government. Insha'Allah, our struggle will continue until we have achieved real independence, for, as I have said repeatedly, we are warriors, and for Muslims surrender has no meaning.[7]

When that message was issued on September 13, 1980, the Iraqi regime had not yet launched its full-scale invasion of Khuzistan; Imam Khomeini's references were to skirmishes on the border that had been going on for some weeks. Now the imposed war is nearly five years old. The most significant point about this war is that, for the first time since the defeat of Germany and Japan in 1945, both the United States and the Soviet Union are on the same side. The two super-powers, both belonging to the house of *kufr*, want to make the world believe that their goals are so diametrically opposed that they must continue to arm themselves with the deadliest weapons either to deter or defeat each other. However, their common hatred of Islam is such that they have openly united in the war against Islam. They know that the house of *kufr* must unite in order to confront and defeat the challenge of Islam to the western civilization. At the same time these superpowers and their allies and friends—Israel, India, Japan, South Africa and the regimes in the Muslim nation-States— have also realized that they must prevent the Muslim *Ummah* from becoming united against them. They know that once the *Ummah* is even partially mobilized in a global Islamic movement it will become invincible. They have already experienced the power of Islam in Iran. For Muslims the unity of the *Ummah* is an article of faith and a functional necessity for the 'Makkan period' of the Islamic movement. The differences among the various schools of thought in Islam are insignificant compared with the issues that divide capitalism and communism. If the house of *kufr* can ignore its differences in order to confront Islam, can the House of Islam not sink its differences to defeat that house of *kufr*? For Muslims the unity of the *Ummah* does not require anyone to abandon his particular position.

However, we should acknowledge that there are major obstructions to the expression of this unity in the *Ummah*. The political, economic, social and cultural obstructions to the expression of the unity of the *Ummah* are enormous. The greatest of these obstructions is nationalism and the nation-States. There are also other powerful forces at work to keep the *Ummah* divided, weak and subservient. The major objective of the Islamic movement is to mobilize the masses under *muttaqi* leaders in all parts of the world. This goal will be achieved at different times in different parts of the *Ummah*. As it is achieved, those areas will be liberated from nationalism and the dominance of the west. New Islamic States will be established in the newly liberated parts of the *Ummah* until, one day, the entire *Ummah* will consist of Islamic States united in a hierarchy of institutions under a single Imam/Khalifa. This is perhaps looking too far ahead. At the same time, perhaps it is important that we should look as far ahead as possible. Clearly the new leadership of the *Ummah*, as it takes shape, will have to engage in a prolonged process of *ijtihad* to resolve the many new issues that will undoubtedly arise.

In the new global Islamic movement that we now have, there is one part that has successfully completed the transition to an Islamic State and there are those parts that still find themselves at the earliest stages of what we have called the 'Makkan period'. Thus the entire spectrum of the *Seerah* of the Prophet, upon whom be peace, is simultaneously relevant to the entire modern Islamic movement. The *Seerah* is the blueprint for the Islamic movement in all stages. The *Seerah* literature that is found today is almost entirely devoted to the recording of events that took place 1,400 years ago in more or less the same order. There is as yet little or no attempt to derive from the *Seerah* a programme for the total transformation of the *Ummah* in today's conditions. This is because the *ulama* of today and their institutions have not been part of an Islamic movement committed to the transformation of the *Ummah*. The only commitment of the *ulama* has been to study the original texts, to lead the Muslim communities in prayer and to help them perform religious rituals. The new global Islamic movement will motivate a new generation of *ulama*. Only those *ulama* who are actively engaged in the struggle will be able to derive from the *Seerah* a programme for the total transformation of the *Ummah*. *Ijtihad* will, henceforth, be a continuous dynamic process prompted and guided by issues that will emerge in the course of the struggle. In the meantime, it is possible to create a functional and operational unity in the global Islamic movement by reference to the original 'Makkan period'. The emergence of such a functional and operational unity of the *Ummah* in a global Islamic movement raises issues that cannot be dealt with here.[8]

It has been said before, and needs to be said again, that the goal of the total transformation of the *Ummah* presupposes a total struggle. In the space of this paper it has not been possible for me to proceed to the detailed description of the total struggle and its various stages that lie ahead. I have dealt only with the outline of the first stage of the total struggle. There is, however, one aspect of it that requires a brief treatment.

It is this. An important part of the method of Muhammad, upon whom be peace, was to acquire control over the environment around him. It is well known, for instance, that the Prophet always sought out the visitors to Makkah who went there either as traders or as pilgrims. He invited these *outsiders* to Islam hoping to create followers of Islam outside Makkah. The Quraysh of Makkah took this threat so seriously that they tried to prevent visitors to Makkah from coming into contact with the Prophet. The Prophet also used the larger environment to seek protection for the early Muslims. This is the significance of the migration of Muslims to Abyssinia. They were given refuge by the Christian King there. The Makkan Quraysh sent a delegation to the King asking for the Muslims to be turned over to them. The King of Abyssinia, after hearing the Muslims' case, presented to him by Ja'far ibn Abi Talib, rejected the embassy of the Quraysh. Many Muslims lived in Abyssinia until the migration of the Prophet to

Medinah. Thus, in the earliest days of Islam, the Prophet secured a sanctuary for the Muslims outside Makkah. The Prophet also travelled among the tribes around Makkah. The best known of these travels is the Prophet's trip to Ta'if. It was this ceaseless struggle to acquire a foothold outside Makkah that led to the two pacts of al-Aqabah, which ultimately led to the Prophet's migration to Medinah and the setting up of the Islamic State there. Having brought the greater part of the environment of Makkah under his control, the Prophet embarked upon the conquest of Makkah.

For the 'Makkan period' of the new Islamic movement today the lessons are clear. The Islamic movement recognizes no frontiers in the *Ummah*. The struggle for the liberation of any one part of the *Ummah* can be carried out from any other part of the *Ummah*. Every part of the *Ummah* is a potential asset for all other parts. This means that every obstacle in the path of the Islamic movement in one part of the *Ummah* is also an obstacle for the entire Islamic movement. Every Muslim engaged in the struggle in any part of the world, no matter how remote or isolated, is engaged in a global struggle. Every group that is engaged in the struggle, no matter how small or remote, is also part of the global struggle between Islam and *kufr*.

We have to eradicate all traces of nationalism from the Islamic movement before we can challenge and defeat the power of national-ism established in territorial nation-States and a worldwide inter-national system dominated by the mobilized power and resources of the enemies of Islam. Ultimately, the shape of the *Ummah* will be determined by the shape taken by the Islamic movement today.

Notes

1. See my paper *Integration and Disintegration in the Politics of Islam and Kufr*, presented at the World Seminar on State and Politics in Islam in London in 1983. It is available in English, Arabic and Farsi.
2. This paper was presented at the World Conference on Muslim Education held in Makkah, April 1977. It was published by The Open Press, London, in 1980.
3. For example, see Maurice Bucaille's interesting book, *The Bible, the Qur'ān and Science*, Indianapolis: American Trust Publications, 1978.
4. Qur'ān al 2: 208; 3: 142; 8: 74; 9: 16; etc.
5. Ismail Faruqi in *Arabia*, London, June 1982, p. 36.
6. See my paper, 'Primary Goals and Achievements of the Islamic Revolution in Iran', presented at a world seminar in London in August 1984. The paper is included in Kalim Siddiqui (ed), *Issues in The Islamic Movement*, London. The Open Press, 1985.
7. Extract from Imam Khomenini's message taken from Hamid Algar, *Islam and Revolution: Writings and Declarations of Imam Khomeini*, Berkeley. Mizan Press, 1981, pp. 302–6.
8. At the Muslim Institute we have pursued the goal of a functional and operational unity of the Islamic movement for the last fourteen years. See, for instance, the *Draft Prospectus* of the Muslim Institute (1974), and my two short books, *Towards a New Destiny*, 1974 and *The Islamic Movement: A Systems Approach*, 1976 both published by The Open Press Ltd.

Chapter II

Nationalism in the Light of the Qur'ān and the Sunnah

Murtaza Garia

Nationalism in its modern form is a product of colonialism. It had, however, its origin in the self-defence mechanism built up in Europe, particularly in western Europe, to defend itself against the overbearing authority of the Roman Catholic Church, and the struggle was initially carried out by Protestant elements within the Christian community. It drew its strength from the emotional reaction which is always at work in situations of external and alien pressures upon local residents. The 'outside' enemy could always galvanize the masses into resistance and eventually into liberation movements. The concept of nationalism was, therefore, at its inception, a development in the drive of people to free themselves from alien domination and foreign exploitation.

Nationalism was in the course of time destined to outgrow its role as a unifying element in the struggle against foreign powers. In the era of colonization, which gained additional momentum from the Industrial Revolution of the eighteenth and nineteenth centuries, nationalism was used as an instrument of deliberate policy for subjugating peoples in different parts of the world. Whatever the reasons might have been for appropriating peoples' lands (economic, military, political or for settlement purposes), the colonization process always resulted in the division of the world into masters on the one hand and slaves on the other. The masters, who shared among themselves different portions of the divided world, were at the centre and the slaves at the periphery. The latter's role was essentially one of 'doing what the masters bid'. They could do little else, since they were cowed down by the masters' might which, perforce, had to be right.

The colonization process was able to make much headway because, apart from the unprecedented scientific and industrial progress which had been taking place in Europe, military supremacy, which, hitherto, had been in Muslim hands, had suffered a serious blow at the hands of Europe. In 1774, the Ottoman Empire was defeated by Russia, setting the stage for further conquests in terms of political, economic and cultural penetration. Soon, wide tracts of Muslim lands came under foreign domination. Among these were Morocco, Algiers, Egypt and Turkestan.

Military defeat was, none the less, only one aspect of the general overthrow of Muslims. The main factor contributing to their down-fall was their progressive relaxation and gradual abandonment of the teachings of the Qur'ān which had historically been the main-stay of Islamic civilization and had led Muslims to world leadership. However, moral laxity, the temptations of ease and luxury, internal strife and dissensions, hairsplitting arguments among the *ulama*, all soon worked their way into the social fabric of Islam and wrought untold havoc among Muslims, resulting in their decline.

The first signs of the eventual collapse of the Muslim *Ummah* can be traced back to the period immediately following the reign of the four Rightly-guided Caliphs, when there began to be a cleavage between the political and religious in the religio-political order of Islam. Prior to this period, there had not been undue attention paid to worldly considerations. These were, in decisive moments, alto-gether discarded in favour of Allah's will, even at the cost of one's life. Such unwavering determination and unswerving allegiance to the cause of Allah had been the rock on which the ships of worldly temptation had foundered. But afterwards the situation underwent considerable changes at the hands of those who sought the comforts of this life and who relegated salvation to a secondary position, being preoccupied all the time with the temporal exercise of authority and power. Even some of the *ulama* of the time were ready to pander to the whims and caprices of these leaders, seeking their favours. Gradually, the hold of religion weakened, the Muslim community lay exposed to foreign penetration and un-Islamic tendencies wormed their way into the mainstream of Muslim life, with all the attendant evil consequences. Western Europe was mainly instrumental in bringing about the plight in which Muslims find themselves to this day.

Europe had at the time embarked upon a crass materialist policy, following its own struggle with the Church and the latter's defeat because of its hostility to the forces of reason and science. The

Church had all along adhered to untenable dogma and the clergy had become intellectually bankrupt. Moreover, the phase of the inquisition had alienated enlightened sections of the people who had begun to frown upon the Church's role as the fountainhead of morality, truth and knowledge.[1] However, the period which followed the expulsion of the Church from the arena of public life saw the gradual descent of Europe into the pit of materialism. Having broken loose from the authority of the Church, the next and logical step was to outlaw the Supreme Being from having any say in human affairs, in the name of science and the scientific spirit.[2]

This materialistic temperament was not given its fullest expression until all links with the Church had been severed.[3]

Once such a policy was agreed, there was nothing to prevent Europe going on the rampage to serve its own interests. The weaknesses of the Muslims only made the Europeans task much easier, since there was no effective resistance. The Muslims were in large part, thus, responsible for their own downfall.

With its military superiority, Europe could go further with its plan of conquest, subjugation and exploitation of foreign peoples. Europe was, however, wise enough to realize that it would not be able to hold on for long on the basis of military supremacy alone. Knowing from bitter experience that a resurgent Islam could still sound the death-knell of its dominance, it began a de-Islamization process, in the Islamic world, through the separation of religion from the State. In this endeavour, it was joined by other powers with the same intention, that is Islam was the common enemy and it had to be made impotent.

In order to achieve their design more efficiently, they enlisted the support of the elites of the local Muslims and used them as their clients. While paying lip service to Islam, these local elites are today ruling Muslim countries but the truth is that they are still in the grip of their masters. Otherwise, how can we explain the complete disarray in the present Muslim world; with one Muslim cutting the throat of another; with famine threatening the lives of millions of Muslims throughout the world; with illiteracy stunting the growth of Muslim countries; with Muslims in a state of dependence on others for their needs and aspirations in virtually all walks of life; in brief with the Muslim *Ummah* at the lowest rung of the ladder of nations with the other nations looking down upon it with contempt?

Though foreign domination has taken many guises in its historical development, from military superiority to technological supremacy, going through political, economic, social and educational phases, the underlying idea that has always been at work is the 'divide and rule' principle. This principle is nowhere more evident than in the Islamic world. The principle found expression in many ways, but we shall deal with just one manifestation—nationalism—which has been a source of untold misery to the Muslim world and which, in its modern meaning, has no grounding at all in Islam, indeed is totally alien to its teachings.

The first form of human association has historically been the family, with blood relations and heredity as its foundation. These biological characteristics provided the primary basis for love, co-operation, mutual support and protection against outside threats, when necessary. Relationships fostered by these characteristics are not only natural but find favour with Allah, who says in the Qur'ān:

> And among His signs is this, that He Created for you mates from among yourselves, that ye may dwell in tranquility with them, and He has put love and mercy between your (hearts); verily in that are signs for those who reflect (30: 21).[4]

These biological characteristics cannot be altered, though members of the family may live far away from each other and may not nowadays exhibit the degree of homogoneity normally expected of a traditional family.

At the second level of social organization, there is the tribe, which has in the course of time been extended to mean the nation, with biology, geography and politics as its anchors. The biological base relates to physical characteristics, for example, the colour of the skin, shape of the eyes, nose and mouth *etc.* which are inseperable from the individual. These too, are, however, Divinely ordained and are not subject to the individual's choice. Besides, these do not invariably extend to all members of the tribe or nation, though they are frequently true of the family. Therefore, it is a false claim to define nationalism in terms of biological factors.

With regard to the geographical base, natural boundaries such as rivers and mountains have determined the territorial limits of nations. This too is a false claim, as being born in a particular place constitutes no basis for defining a person, let alone for evaluating him. Moreover, with increasing possibilities for movement from one place to another (there have been massive migrations throughout history), living in a particular territory does not provide a sound basis for defining a nation let alone using such a basis for the practice of a policy of ethnocentrism, a value which is accorded the highest priority under nationalism.

There remains the political base. This finds concrete expression in the determination of a people to be a nation, with full autonomy of will and action, apart from all others. In this case, the pursuit of the nation's goals and objectives constitutes the supreme good even if in the process it becomes necessary to suppress the legitimate rights of others to be a nation as well. In this way, the most oppressive injustices have been perpetrated against other peoples and the foulest means have been used to further the nation's aspirations, irrespective of the costs involved in terms of human lives and values. Today, the world is groaning under the weight of nationalism, which has been presented to the ruling classes of different nations beautifully gift-wrapped. Little do these ruling classes realize or, if they do, they do not care that, in accepting this gift, they are only playing into the hands of the enemy, becoming mere pawns through which their lands and people are exploited for their enemy's benefit and prosperity. On the other hand, the enemy has taken good care to perpetuate his hold by amply providing for the ruling local elites and by coming to their rescue at decisive moments. History abounds with such examples of external inter-ferences when the situation at the local level threatens the interests of the foreign powers. The local elites, it must be remembered, have had their training and education in countries which have taken good care that they return home as 'authentic' nationalists to operate by proxy for their masters. This long distance operation is especially tragic for Muslim countries, among which artificial barriers have been erected to prevent them from fusing into one single Islamic *Ummah*, as their religion commands them.[5]

Nationalism as a political weapon has, therefore, been used to make people self-centred and thus better able to continue the exploitation and pillage of the world's resources for the welfare of the few to the detriment of the many. The feelings engendered by nationalism and patriotism take root so deeply in the minds of people that they are ready to lay down their lives in defence of it. If only the people would look behind the curtain or lift the veil, nationalism would stand unmasked in its true hideous colours. For, the national interest which these elites claim to serve is in fact their own group interest.

The Islamic concept of State differs fundamentally from the secular one in that while the latter perceives itself as a centre to which the rest of the world is only a means for its own progress and welfare, the former is an administrative unit for the efficient translation of the Divine will into practice. While the nation-State is the be-all and end-all of social action and has no higher values and motives than its own desires and impulses, the Islamic State has a mission to fulfill: to carry the Divine message to the four corners of the world, in ever-widening concentric circles, so as to make the Law of the Creator reign supreme over other systems of Statecraft.

Islam neither denies the existence of nations nor is it inimical to the practice of nationhood as a basis for social identification and differentiation, for this is Allah's pattern of creation; but it does deny the nation's ultimacy in the determination and conduct of affairs. The Qur'ān says:

> O mankind! We created you from a single (pair) of male and a female and made you into nations and tribes that ye may know eachother. Verily the most honoured of you in the sight of God is (he who is) the most righteous of you (49: 13).

It is, therefore, clear that nationalism cuts at the very roots of humanity and ascribes partiality to Allah in His dealings with His creatures. It is also evident that the underlying ideas behind classifying humankind into tribes and nations are complementarity and co-operation, and that these do not provide yardsticks for establishing one's worth, for honour in the sight of Allah transcends membership of a particular tribe or nation, being based on righteousness (*taqwa*).

Nationalism, thus, violates the very essence of Qur'ānic teaching, which goes against ethnocentricity, promotes universalism, embraces all aspects of life, advocates a free society and inculcates a brotherly spirit among members of the Islamic faith.

Islam regards all mankind as one nation. The Qur'ān says:

> Mankind was one single nation, and God sent Messengers with glad tidings and warnings; and with them He sent the book with truth, to judge between people in matters wherein they

differed; but the People of the Book, after the clear signs came to them, did not differ among themselves except through selfish contumacy (2: 213).

This unity of mankind is only natural in that all men stand in equal relationship with Allah and His creatures and it would be invidious of Allah to discriminate among His creatures on the basis of criteria other than His own, which relate to universal values rather than to considerations of race, language, territory and the like. Otherwise, His justice and transcendence would be in serious jeopardy. Partiality and favouritism are human traits and cannot be ascribed to the ultimate source of being.[6]

The God of Islam is not a spent god who has outlived his usefulness and has now left the immediate and ultimate in life in the hands of the living, but is Ever-living and watching man in his discharge of the Divine trust placed upon him with a view to actualizing the Divine will on earth in default of which man will eventually have to render his account.

The Islamic State cannot become a vehicle of sin because there will always be, in the Muslim's consciousness, the idea of personal responsibility and final answerability for his actions. This is not to say that people will not commit sin. It is simply stating that sin will not permeate through the entire fabric of social life because the Divine commandment to Muslims to 'enjoin what is right and forbid what is wrong' and the Muslims' care to remain within the limits of *halal* and *haram*, if only at the individual level. This is, moreover not a theoretical vindication of the virtues of Islam but is empirically verifiable by comparative studies on the impact of different religions on the lives of their adherents.

The universal character of Islam is evident from the very first verse of the Qur'ān, which proclaims Allah as Lord of the worlds (1: 2). The Deity of Islam is not for the Muslim alone, nor is He limited in space and time. Nor does anybody, in relation to Him, have to shoulder more or less responsibility than others in carrying out His will. All are equal before Him in their creatureliness. All have equal claim on His love and mercy. All are subject to His laws of reward and punishment.

It has been said earlier that honour in the sight of Allah is based on righteousness. The Qur'ān says about righteousness:

It is not righteousness that ye turn your faces towards east or west; but it is righteousness—to believe in God and the Last Day and the Angels and the Book and the Messengers; to spend of your substance, out of Love for Him, for your kin, for orphans, for the needy, for the wayfarer, for those who ask, and for the ransom of slaves; to be steadfast in prayer, and practise regular charity; to fulfil the contracts which ye have made; and to be firm and patient, in pain (or suffering) and adversity, and throughout all periods of panic. Such are the people of truth, the God-fearing (2: 177).

This verse is at the same time a unique declaration of universal human duties, virtues, faith and practice and a negation of formalism, or externalities, in the determination of a person's worth.

Nor does Islam's universalism envisage an exclusively Muslim world community, or aim to bring the whole world under its sway by force; for it is proclaimed unequivocally: 'Let there be no compulsion in religion: truth stands out clear from error' (2: 256).

While exhorting its adherents to exert themselves for the establishment of the Divine order on earth, it makes it possible for such an order to be achieved through different channels and provides specific injunctions concerning the dealings of Muslims with other communities. These should be conducted on the basis of justice and love. The Qur'ān says:

O ye who believe! Stand out firmly for justice, as witnesses to God, even against yourselves, or your parents, or your kin, and whether it be (against) rich or poor: for God can best protect both. Follow not the lusts (of your hearts), lest ye swerve, and if ye distort (justice) or decline to do justice, verily God is well-acquainted with all that ye do (4: 135).

Lest feelings of hate lead Muslims to commit excesses, the Qur'ān commands:

O ye who believe! Stand out firmly for God, as witnesses to fair dealing, and let not the hatred of others to you make you swerve to wrong and depart from justice. Be just: that is next to piety: and fear God (5: 9).

While Judaism considers Christianity as an extension of itself and Christianity considers Islam as a non-religion, religion having been concluded with the coming of Jesus, on earth and his redemption of humanity through his atonement for our sins, Islam regards both Judaism and Christianity as it regards itself, i.e. as divinely revealed. It is an article of Islamic faith to believe in the revealed books and prophets. The Qur'ān says:

> The Apostle believeth in what hath been revealed to him from his Lord, as do the men of faith. Each one (of them) believeth in God, His angels, His books, and His Apostles. 'We make no distinction (they say) between one and the other of His apostles!' And they say 'We hear and we obey: (we seek) Thy forgiveness, Our Lord, and to Thee is the end of all journeys.' (2: 285).

The revealed book of Islam, the Qur'ān, is not a book for Muslims alone but is a reminder to all men that Allah's message to humanity has been the same throughout the ages. Speaking to the Prophet of Islam, upon whom be peace, about religion, the Qur'ān says:

> The same religion has He established for you as that which He enjoined on Noah—that which We have sent by inspiration to thee—and that which we enjoined on Abraham, Moses, and Jesus: namely, that ye should remain steadfast in religion, and make no divisions therein (42: 13);

again,

> Nothing is said to thee that was not said to the apostles before thee (41: 43);

and yet again,

> Verily this is no less than a message to (all) the worlds (with profit) to whosoever among you wills to go straight (81: 27–28).

Islam is, thus, against nationalism and particularism. It calls upon its followers to aspire to a world community under its banner, not on the basis of violence and compulsion but through free acceptance. The Muslim is entitled only to the freedom to call and convince others of the truth.[7]

When Muslims were leaders of the world, adherents of other religions prospered side by side as separate *ummahs*, bringing about the kingdom of God on earth, on the basis of common moral principles. The ideal of world community found its greatest affirmation in Islam, and its greatest embodiment in the Islamic State.[8] Such a State guarantees the freedom to differ not only to the different *ummahs* under its umbrella as collectivities but also to the individual members of each *ummah* as well, since the Qur'ān addresses men in general.

The last sermon of the Prophet of Islam, upon whom be peace, gave the final blow to all discriminations based on ethnic, racial and geographical considerations when he admonished his audience in the following terms:

> Listen to me well, O people; God created you all descendants of Adam, and Adam He created of earth. No Arab has a priority over a non-Arab, no white over a black and no non-Arab over an Arab, or a black over a white, except in righteousness.

This complete levelling of human beings does not preclude differentiation on the basis of knowledge, faith and righteousness and so forth. All of these, however, relate to achievement, either individual or collective, and have nothing to do with ascriptive norms and values.

The Qur'ān does not admit any dichotomy between politics and religion, faith and reason, spiritual and material, theory and practice, and so on. Further, it does not regard any area of human activity as falling outside its purview, whether it be economic, social, political, cultural or whatever. It regulates all aspects of life and prescribes a complete code for living which does not need to borrow from outside of itself for its continued existence and progress. The purpose of man's creation is accordingly the execution of the Divine will. The State as a political institution is, thus, the 'executive' agency for the achievement of Allah's design in accordance with His laws and the State may not operate independently of such laws. Since the ultimate legislator is Allah, it follows that all that men do, as His vice-gerents, has to accord with and be subject to His laws.

The spiritual and material are not separate in Islam but are given their due importance in the Qur'ān, which says:

> But seek, with the (wealth) which God has bestowed on thee, the home of the hereafter, nor forget thy portion in this world: but do thou good as God has been good to thee (28: 77).

The material goods at the command of men are means whereby men may attain felicity; they are neither to be deprecated nor disdained. The spiritual may not be pursued at the expense of the material nor the material at the expense of the spiritual.

The aim of Islam, it will be seen, is to invest the individual with an integrated and well-balanced personality, imbued with high moral principles and caring for the well-being of everyone around him while at the same time tending towards self-fulfilment. This is quite the opposite of the objective of nationalism which turns people into egocentric, ethnocentric self-seekers who will not be held back in the pursuit of their own interests, whatever the cost to others.

Islam's view of life as a whole finds expression in its teachings, which cover all aspects of life both at the individual level and at the collective level. Its coverage extends to all areas of human activity be it economic, social, political, educational etc.; all undertakings are to be carried out with a view to bettering the lot of mankind generally and in accordance with the Divine pattern. In everything that one does there is to be service to Allah on the one hand and to the love of humanity on the other; this love is also to be extended to other creatures of Allah. There should be no despoliation of nature but, on the contrary, judicious use of its bounties. All human interventions in space and time must have for their objective the realization of the Divine Will.

Islam accordingly sets out broad principles which should govern the life of man on earth. However, since this life is preparatory to a life in the Hereafter, the Qur'ān teaches that man, in his various dealings in the world, should always bear in mind their ultimate implications.

It has been shown that nationalism violates Qur'ānic teachings and, therefore, has no place in Islam. The practice of nationalism, however, has also proved to be a failure both on the domestic level of nation-States and at the international level. On the domestic front, nationalism conceals glaring contradictions within the nation-States themselves because the nation is everywhere a conglomeration of diverse groups striving for diverse ends, often conflicting with each other. Common race, language, territory have not prevented these various groups from fighting, and killing, each other. The 'interiorization' and 'internalization' of parochial values have moved progressively from the national to the regional and thence to the local and family levels. All these groups try to safeguard their own selfish interests.

At the international level, the feelings of nationalism have always been impervious to any attempt at universalism: witness the debates at the United Nations meetings where all issues of universal import are finally narrowed down to serving vested interests. Further, in all international agencies, the same concern prevails and any openness shown to others is inspired and motivated by egoistic considerations. There is not a single forum that is not used as lever for the furtherance of one's own cause, in utter disregard of others' rights.

The main reasons for the continued practice of nationalism among Muslim States seems to stem from a crisis of identity and a lack of effective leadership among the *Ummah* generally, and among the ruling elites in particular. The latter have become so impregnated with western values that it has become practically impossible for them to visualize the broader perspective of Islam. They suffer from all the stresses and strains of a split personality, with the result that their view about Islam is defective. Many genuinely believe that western and Islamic values may be reconciled. They are thus unable to provide the type of leadership which is necessary for the *Ummah* to reclaim its lost identity and function as an organic whole. Their judgement has become blurred.[9]

The love of God, above all other precepts, is the supra-national value which must be inculcated again in the minds of Muslims in order to achieve 'ummatic' dimension. The Qur'ān says:

Verily, this Brotherhood of yours is a single Brotherhood and I am your Lord: therefore serve Me (and no other) (21: 92).

Notes

1. Abul Hasan Ali Nadwi, *Islam and the World*, Academy of Islamic Research and Publications, Lucknow, 1973, pp. 127–129.
2. *Ibid.*, pp. 133–135.
3. Muhammad Asad, *Islam at the Crossroads*, Dar Al-Andalus, Gibraltar, 1982, pp. 38–39.
4. Abdullah Yousuf Ali, Translation and Commentary, *The Glorious Kur'an*, The Islamic Call Society, Tripoli, 1973.
5. Masih Muhajeri, *Islamic Revolution Future Path of the Nations*, Tehran, 1982, p. 17.
6. Ismail Raji Al Faruqi, *Tawhid: Its Implications for Thought and life*, International Institute of Islamic Thought (IIIT) Publication, Wycote, Pennsylvania, USA, 1982, p. 127.
7. Mahmud Awan, *Trialogue of the Abrahamic Faiths Book*, IIIT Publications, Wycote, Pennsylvania, 1982, pp. 82–83.
8. Ismail Raji Al Faruqi *ibid.*, p. 58.
9. Said Ramadan, *Islam and Nationalism*, Crescent Publication, Silver Spring, MD, n.d., p. 2.

Chapter III

A Criticism of the Idea of Arab Nationalism
Mohamed Yehia

Arab nationalist propaganda has been aired increasingly in recent months from many organs in Arab countries, particularly Egypt. It is evident to observers of the Islamic movement that the rejuvenation of the concept of 'Arab nationalism' is underway as part of the current building of defensive strategies in the Arab region against the danger of Islamic 'fundamentalism'. It is appropriate that an idea that originated from the minds of Christian Levantine writers in order to serve as a weapon of disintegration against the Uthmaniyyah State should now be resurrected to serve once more against Islam.

In its latest incarnation, Arab nationalism is put to a different use from its employment by either Nasser or the Baʿathists as a means of masking personal or party ambitions. It is presented as a secular political creed that draws upon certain western concepts, such as 'nationalism' itself, for its frame of reference. These concepts, modernity, progress, socialism, among others, represent both its slogans of attraction and the intellectual criteria by which it views Arab reality.

The leading feature of the renewed nationalist propaganda is the emphasis on 'Arab' as opposed to 'Islamic'. The aim of this change is to substitute the former for the latter as an inclusive and fundamental point of departure for analysis, description, and thought about political and social facts. The limited 'Arab horizon' is designed to replace and take precedence over the Islamic horizon in the thoughts and feelings of those at whom the nationalist propaganda is directed. The insistence on 'Arabness' as an alternative to 'Islamicness' gives the entire game away. It is clear that in recent presentations of the idea of Arab nationalism a confrontation with Islam is intended. Advocates of Arab nationalism do not hide the fact that they attack

Islam but their use of the concept as a weapon of attack—the anti-Islamic climate now prevailing in many Arab countries—is hindered by the fact that its presentations are riddled with logical contradictions. This is what I intend to expose.

The idea of Arab nationalism suffers from two main contradictions. The first is the exclusion of Islam as a defining and constitutive element of that nationalism. The second is the completely westernized content of an avowedly 'Arab' movement that supposedly wants to revive 'Arab' values and culture.

The First Contradiction

The Arab nationalist message seems simple and consistent. The Arabs from the Gulf to the Atlantic are one people united by the ties of blood, history, language and common interest. They ought to be united in one political entity which is socially and culturally modern. This programme can be achieved by the Arab nationalists in the face of opposition from various forces, of which the Islamic movement is the most prominent.

Now, the appeal to blood ties and the argument from ethnography and race has largely fallen into disrepute. Still, it is not quite clear how we can speak of a pure Arab race after the long process of mingling between the original Arabs of the Peninsula and such peoples as the Egyptians, Mesopotamians, Berbers and Negroes. The Arabic phrase 'ties of blood' comes in conveniently to cover for the weakness in the nationalist view on this matter by its double reference to both race and kinship. The latter is usually the meaning that is immediately suggested by normal usage and it saves the nationalists from becoming involved in an ethnographic debate they would lose.

The invocation of geography does not advance the nationalist argument far. The Gulf-Atlantic axis is a rather arbitrary projection which overlooks other areas to which the original Arabs ventured. The crucial fact in this regard is that it was Islam that created this 'grand Arab homeland', as it is called, and which impelled the original Arabs to conquer that area and much more beyond it so as to spread the teachings of Islam.

The Arab nationalists perform a sleight-of-hand when they arbitrarily carve out of the grand Islamic homeland (which was made possible by the spread of the Arabs' religion) a smaller area—the 'Arab homeland'—which is then separated from the larger body and either made to stand against it or to take priority of allegiance *vis-à-vis* the rest of it. If, for the sake of argument, we adopt the same secularist stance as the nationalists adhere to, we can say that Islam is an Arab cultural and social phenomenon which has been propagated by the Arabs throughout a large part of the known world. In this sense, the Muslims of the world can be said to have been 'arabized' by the mere fact of their embracing Islam.

The Arab nationalists play the trick of separating a section of the 'arabized'—the Muslims—which happen to possess one added feature of 'arabism'—the language—and place it as an independent entity and identity against the rest of the Muslims. They do not include in their nationalism some Arabic-speaking minorities and ignore the vital role that Arabic, with its script, plays in the languages and culture of other Muslims.

The Arab nationalists may be indicted of contradiction according to their own secular view of Islam as a social growth. For, if it is 'the religion of the Arabs' as well as main motive for issuing out of their limited homeland in Arabia, it should be the defining feature of Arab nationalism. It is Islam, and not those cultural factors transformed by it beyond recognition, such as language or history, that should be the yardstick of Arab nationalism. Yet the nationalists are out-and-out secularists who either exclude Islam altogether or assign to it a servile position within their own creed as a vaguely defined 'spiritual factor': a servility negated by Islam's own claims.

This same criticism applies to the nationalists' call and talk about joint interests—presumably economic—as a unifying factor of the Arabs. Their definition is ambiguous. Why should common interests, of whatever sort, not exist among the Muslims, as they have always done? Once again we meet with the same trick: the arbitrary extrapolation of a certain section, within the general Islamic context, and its establishment as an independent entity. The keyword here is 'arbitrary'. Nationalism is stripped of any rational claim and its bare ideological bias, which it tries to mask either with pleas of modernity or by appeal to similar specious terms, exposed.

The major contradiction in Arab nationalist thinking that I have tried to sketch above is seen most flagrantly in the adoption of certain cultural elements, e.g. language, common history and heritage, and traditions as defining features of that nationalism while continuing at the same time to ignore Islam out of a deep-seated secular outlook.

Before Islam, the Arabs lived in what may be called their prehistory. They were a tribal, warring collection of peoples with various dialects and with little or no cultural life, especially on the intellectual plane. Islam introduced such an unimaginable qualitative change into the life of the Arabs that it would hardly be an exaggeration to say that it 'created' the Arab identity.

The Quraysh dialect of the Arabic language was raised into the richest language in the world and one of the most widely used. Islam won for itself adherents that came from non-Arab cultures and was responsible for turning itself into a tool of thought and expression in many fields of science and scholarship. In this way, Arabic, spread far beyond its original home and speakers.

Similarly, Arab society was totally transformed in its structure, customs, aims, and outlooks. Islam has been the constitutive principle of Arab social and intellectual life for the last fourteen centuries and the attempt to posit an 'Arab nationalism' either without Islam or in confrontation with it is inconceivable. At the same time, an Arab nationalism that tries to take account of Islam will find itself in an impossible position; for the universal claims of Islam and its insistence on full allegiance to its tenets, as well as on its priority over other attachments, ensure that it rejects nationalism as a modern form of ancient tribalism and as the *hamiyyat al—jahiliyya* (fanatical clinging to pre-Islamic outlooks).

The Arabic language and culture have been made by and contained within Islam, and not the reverse. Islam has not been a passing and limited stage in an otherwise independent and developed tradition of Arab culture and society that had its own line of growth. The same applies to Arab history, which, along with the history of the many peoples that accepted Islam, is Islamic history. In fact, Islam is the common denominator that ties the life and history of a great mass of humanity together. As a universal moral code, Islam shaped every facet of the societies that embraced it, and linked them together in a vast entity which often found political expression in the *khilafat* system. A non-clerical creed, Islam does not have, for instance, a separate, isolated history as a Church.

Arab nationalists, however, take certain cultural, social, and historical facts or elements and cite them as factors of Arab nationalism. They, therefore, ignore the decisive role played by Islam in the shaping of these elements.

Islam is deliberately banished from the Arab nationalists' considerations. It is excluded according to the principles of secularism. The cultural, social and historical facts forged by Islam are taken away from it and made to stand as supports and features of Arab nationalism. Moreover, the same facts, which can in all validity and legitimacy be adduced to substantiate the idea of Islamic 'nationalism' and identity, are arbitrarily 'stolen' from the Islamic framework and forced to become constituents of a secular idea that sets aside one group of Muslims—the so-called Arabs—and puts them above and at odds with the rest of the Muslims, who still share with this separated group the same cultural, social and historical elements of unity. This serves to enhance that artificially defined, extrapolated view of an 'Arab' identity from within the Islamic matrix. In their much-vaunted slogans about the unity of culture, heritage, customs, feeling, outlooks and hopes, the Arab nationalists use fruits from the trees of Islam while disowning the tree. This position, paradoxically enough, is their only logical move. For to recognize the claims and priority of Islam would be to deny their own existence, their own attempt to break Muslim ranks, and to establish a higher authority than religion. The Arab nationalists have to deny Islam, even at the cost of devastating logical inconsistencies; accepting Islam demolishes their own *raison d'être*. Islam neither permits a higher nor another locus of allegiance of authority and guidance; it cannot tolerate a breach of unity among the believers or a limitation of its universal message and validity. By rejecting nationalism, therefore, it is in turn rejected by it.

The Second Contradiction

The phrase 'Arab nationalism' sets up a certain expectation which is violently contradicted by the content of the idea carrying that name. It is reasonable to expect that such an idea will seek its content from peculiarly Arab intellectual and cultural sources, whatever these may be. Yet, the plain fact is that apart from some superficial slogans about the glory of the Arabs, for instance, the entire content of this idea is of western origin; from the very source referred to in nationalist rhetoric as the 'imperialist west'.

It is not a question of borrowing certain ideas and terms. It is, rather, a matter of the wholesale adoption, assimilation and 'internalization' of attitudes, frames of reference, *etc.* Arab nationalism is, indeed, a western phenomenon not just in the familiar sense of being induced by European sources but in the sense that it is merely an extension of western concerns and modes of thinking. It should, however, be added that presentations of Arab nationalism rarely, if ever, reach the degree of sophistication that would seem to be suggested here. Arab nationalism remains a crude rehearsal of certain set formulas designed primarily for mass consumption.

The major western 'import' is the principle of secularism, which Arab nationalists go out of their way to emphasize as their defining factor. Secularism is not an Islamic idea and it has not always been present in conjunction with nationalist thought in Europe itself. One thinks, for instance, of the role played by Protestantism in west European nationalism and that played by Eastern Orthodoxy in Serbian and Bulgarian nationalism. The insistence of Arab nationalists on an indissoluble bond between secularism and nationalism highlights their premeditated intentions against Islam. Secularism has been cultivated deliberately by the Arab nationalists, although it does not spring naturally from any 'Arab' source.

Secularism is only the first of many western intellectual goods appropriated by the 'purist' Arab nationalists. The most outstanding of these is the idea of nationalism itself, not as the recognition of the existence of tribes, races and peoples, but as a call for the establishment of a secular political entity around a vaguely defined nation which, in the event, turns out as often as not to be those people governed by a central authority that sets out to legitimize and mask its hegemony by fostering the 'national' myth of a glorious past and a unique identity with a future-oriented mission.

Thus a phenomenon that was deeply embedded in local European conditions, and which often came to validate certain power interests, is imported by the Arab nationalists or, rather, deliberately exported by the west to the Muslim world after being removed from its distinctive historical matrix and is transformed into an abstract, prescriptive programme. According to this formula certain entities are to be created and certain existing power interests are to be encouraged to repeat the European experiments and developments. With regard to this last point, one thinks of the attribution, after the fact, of nationalist tendencies to some rulers in the Muslim world in the nineteenth century who sought independence from the Uthmaniyyah State. Mere power-seeking was responsible for such famous 'nationalist' examples as Muhammed Ali's rule in Egypt.

Arab nationalists usually forget that European nationalism dealt with individual entities or 'people' within the larger European framework. Applied to Arab conditions, this justifies the division of the so-called 'Arab world' into such constituent nationalisms as the Egyptian, Syrian, Iraqi, Sudanese, and so on. This logical, 'nationalist' move is, however, rejected by Arab nationalists, who choose, for no apparent reason, to halt the division of the Muslim world at the 'Arab' frontier rather than carry the application of the nationalist principle to the legitimate level of a single people.

The secret behind this arbitrary halting is that their real concern is not the nationalist principle as such but rather its employment as a tool to destroy the larger Islamic unity. It is a good tactic to hide the disintegrative aims of that tool by pretending that it is still a unity-seeking idea—that is among the 'Arab peoples'.

It is clear that the Arab nationalists, both old and new, have not even been faithful to the principle of nationalism which they borrowed from Europe to plant in an Islamic environment. Secularism and nationalism comprise the outer frame that determines the various other loans of the Arab nationalists from the west. Having rejected Islam and posed themselves as the champions of a certain cause, they found themselves obliged to fill the vacuum and make good their claims by a programme of action or a 'project'. Upon inspection, this project turns out, in its various presentations, to be no more than a weaker version of the dominant western ideologies, also removed from their social matrix and imposed as abstract rules of action on the totally different Arab environment.

The strange variable content of Arab nationalism has passed through the entire gamut of western ideologies, from liberal, fascist, socialist, quasi-marxist and social-democrat. It has a tendency to be coloured by the ideology of the particular western power that happens to be dominant in the Middle East at a certain time or that which patronizes the Arab nationalist factions.

The western ideologies which came into being in response to certain social, political, and cultural conditions in Europe were adopted by Arab nationalist propagandists and presented uncritically as a 'project' for the renaissance of the 'Arab nation' that, according to their theory, was passing through a different path of development and which had not yet attained a stage comparable to that of the European Renaissance. Yet, apart from superficial modifications to suit political conditions and guard against charges of westernization, the Arab nationalists kept the main body of the ideologies they imported intact.

Not only were the western ideologies appropriated in the manner outlined above but their peculiar terms and methods of examining facts were also adopted wholesale. This attitude is seen most clearly in that Arab nationalists see Islam, for instance, with European eyes. In fact, Islam and all other aspects of Arab reality are defined, examined, reinterpreted, and judged in terms of one western ideology or another. Favourite ideologies for this purpose have been the secular-liberal, a diluted form of Marxism referred to as Arab socialism, and a collection of socio-political ideas of American origin. Thus, Islam is usually seen by Arab nationalist writings either as a socio-economic projection from a certain 'base', a flowering of the enlightened emancipatory spirit of the Arab nation or as a 'human revolution' against the reactionary and exploitative forces of Quraysh.

Our purpose here is not to study what Arab nationalism has adopted from the west; it is rather to expose its major contradictions. With its present content and terms, 'Arab nationalism' is neither Arab nor nationalist. Rather, it is western and *inter*nationalist. It is simply a tool for propagating and universalizing western ideologies. The terms 'Arab' and 'nationalist' are convenient masks facilitating the acceptance of surreptitiously disguised western concepts among the Muslims.

Arab nationalism is not condemned here for failing to adopt the general heritage of the Arabs (the Muslims). Nevertheless, a continuation and renewal of Arab heritage in all fields of life is certainly the natural attitude to expect from those who base their ideas on Arabism and build a huge emotional aura around that term, making it the centre of their propaganda. Instead, they have abandoned the Arab heritage altogether and opted for a westernized content for their idea.

The Arab (Islamic) heritage offers a viable wealth of major premises, concepts and so forth for anyone who wishes to undertake a revival project for the 'Arab nation', even if he has reservations about what may be called the purely 'religious' part of that corpus. Islamic jurisprudence, social and moral values, principles of government, and practical experience in running a flourishing civilization for many centuries are valid and fruitful bases that can be developed, modified, and enriched even by a secularly-bound Arab nationalism to yield a genuinely Arab project for renaissance.

Yet the Arab (Islamic) heritage is completely neglected by Arab nationalists, except for occasional mentions in propaganda, in favour of the western doctrines they pose as renaissance guidelines. The only explanation that can be advanced for this attitude is the inherent anti-Islamic nature of the idea of Arab nationalism and its essential alienness to the Islamic heritage and beliefs of the Arabs. Arab nationalism cannot envisage an Arab renaissance from within the Arabs' creed simply because that creed happens to be Islam and because adherents of nationalism have defined themselves from the outset against that religion and for the west.

Consequent Contradictions

The two major contradictions in the idea of Arab nationalism render this doctrine vacuous and negate its claims both to being Arab and to being nationalist, revealing its nature as an ideological tool for the spread of western influence. These two contradictions have been reflected in many of the positions and arguments of Arab nationalism, graphically illustrating its inadequacy.

I now propose to deal with several of these consequent inconsistencies, beginning with an examination of three positions adopted by the Arab nationalists, and concluding with a refutation of three of their most frequently repeated arguments.

Three Arab Nationalist Positions

The Attitude Towards Independence

Arab nationalist writings place a high value on their 'independence'. This was their battle-cry against the Uthmaniyyah State and has also been raised against the occupying powers in Arab countries. They even raise it against advocates of Islam, whom they accuse of hankering after the days of the 'Ottoman yoke' and of scheming to dissolve the cherished Arab independence in a universal Islamic State.

Arab nationalist definitions of independence are negative in that they regard it as freedom from external domination and influence. Independence does not have a positive content in that doctrine and this is understandable in the light of its use as an instrument of attack upon the Islamic *khilafat*. It is independence from something but with no alternative. It is not impelled by a desire to install Islam, for instance, in its place of the departing foreign influence.

Moreover, Arab nationalists have always defined independence superficially. It was first defined in exclusively political terms as the evacuation of foreign armies, to be replaced by native-rule. Later, other elements were added, such as non-alignment; the highest ceiling that these definitions have reached of late, and only in response to the west's debates on the matter, has been to make some noises about economic independence. Independence in worldview, values, attitudes, and ideologies is seldom, if ever, broached in Arab nationalist circles. These circles, that have been created by western thought, even in their way of seeing things, cannot be expected to push their cherished slogans to their logical conclusion and to their only meaningful usage.

The cause of this muddle is in the 'first contradiction' discussed above. As doctrinaire secularists, the Arab nationalists have rejected Islam as the only possible content of and justification for the call for independence. They chose to fill their creed with a thoroughly western content, while they also had to maintain the 'independence' slogan both as a *raison d'être* and as an element of attraction. This left them in such a position that they were forced to use only the negative, superficial meaning of 'independence' and to avoid its deeper implications, which inevitably suggest that Islam is the only true source of independence for the Arabs.

Arab nationalist positions on this issue are reflected in the practice of those who ruled under the banner of this idea, for example, Nasser or the Ba'athists. Their jealously advocated slogans did not prevent them from losing their independence to certain western powers— including the Soviet Union. At the same time the 'nationalist' intellectuals who call themselves 'Arab' are slavishly dependent on the cultural goods of the west. Arab nationalism has failed miserably both in theory and in practice to live up to the slogan which it made its essence. The rejection of Islam and the adoption of secularism have been responsible for this.

The Position On Palestine

Arab nationalists have recently coined a phrase to the effect that Palestine is 'the central cause of the Arab people'. Their propaganda is intended to portray them as the sole defenders of the Palestinian cause. I do not wish to dwell here on the sad and disastrous record of that 'championship'. Their intellectual failure in this slogan is perhaps more instructive. The establishment of a Jewish State in Palestine is unanimously explained by Arab nationalists as an imperialist plot against the Arab nation designed to retard Arab unity and to fritter away Arab resources. This explanation fails to account for many aspects of the question.

Arab nationalists cannot explain why the attempts to establish Israel started whilst Palestine was still a part of the Uthmaniyyah State. Instead, it is Sultan Abdul-Hamid's rebuttal of these attempts that explains much of the encouragement given to the idea of Arab nationalism by anti-*khilafat*, foreign powers at the time. There was no 'Arab nation' at that time to justify the fiendish imperialist plot but there was, rather, an 'Islamic nation' to be torn to pieces by colonial and Zionist schemes, in which Arab nationalism itself featured prominently. More importantly, they cannot explain, let alone come to grips with, the religious nature of that Jewish nationalism which has been planted by their secular western mentors in Palestine. They have been taught by the west that nationalism is built on material and cultural ties that do not include religion. This principle was shattered to pieces before the uncomprehending eyes of the Arab nationalists as they confronted the Israeli case. For here material considerations, such as unity of race and original homeland, did not ostensibly exist and the Jewish religion is supposedly the constitutive element of the Israeli 'nationalism'.

The only response that the Arab nationalists could bring to this situation was to invent a famous dichotomy distinguishing the 'Jewish' from the 'Zionist'. Judaism, it was maintained, is a religion which the secular nationalists respect. Zionism, however, is an imperialist movement, within Judaism, which should be fought in Palestine as the enemy of the Arab people.

The massive support of Jews all over the world for Israel gave the lie to this argument and, in spite of the waning of the Zionist trend inside Israel as time wore on, the State itself grew stronger. The Zionists were not the only party to share in the building of Israel;

socialists, communists and religious parties have enthusiastically joined in this process. The charge of imperialism directed against Israel and its backers rang hollow with the Arabs who saw the Soviet Union and the world communists as well as European leftists, who are the forces of good according to nationalist propaganda, supporting the new State wholeheartedly.

Arab nationalists cannot explain why the imperialists chose to perpetuate their influence in the religion through a Jewish State in the religiously significant Palestine rather than through military bases, client rulers and elites. Nor can they explain why Israel was set up at a time when the imperialist powers were already entrenched in the Arab areas that really mattered to them—the Gulf and the Maghrib. Finally, they fail to account for the fact that Israel was, and is, willing to live with all forms of secular, nationalist regimes in the area but not with an Islamic regime.

The establishment of Israel can only be understood fully in the light of designs harboured by the west on the Muslims of the Middle East. The seizure of a land holy to the Muslims (Jerusalem, al-Khalil) is an affront to Islam, and the establishment of a Jewish entity described as 'nationalist' was to provide a westernizing instrument and an encouraging example for the secular nationalism being fostered around Palestine since the beginning of this century. Israel is a phase in the long struggle between Islam and Judaism; if it serves any imperialist purpose it is in the context of the west's attack on Islam, not because of an Arab nationalism that did not exist when Israel was first conceived and that itself shares the anti-Islamic nature of that Jewish State.

It is no wonder that the Arab nationalists, who themselves were part of the strategy of confronting Islam, should fail to explain the nature of Israel, although it is allegedly their chief enemy. Both Israel and Arab nationalism have been tools in the attempt to disintegrate Islam. But the two tools are so different that the theoretical bases of the first demolish those of the second and the second stands in bewilderment before the first. Ironically enough, it is Islam that is the cause of this paradox. Religion is allowed as a basis of Jewish nationalism, but is unnaturally excluded from Arab nationalism.

The nationalists' confusion in this connection is reflected in the scandalous failures with which they met their management of the conflict with Israel, although they have been in control of the strongest Arab countries. Having excluded the Islamic dimension of the conflict, they found themselves thrown back on appealing to the 'nationalist' sentiments of the Arab masses. But the only sentiments that came out into the open were the 'local' nationalist tendencies that were far from enthusiastic about abandoning their own homelands to defend that of the Palestinians. The real sentiments of solidarity that impelled the Arab masses to support the struggle for Palestine were Islamic. The Muslim Brotherhood, for instance, was the only group in Egypt to fight in Palestine against the Jews, and Islamic motives led the Egyptian people to sympathize with the *jihad.*

Arab nationalists refused to draw upon the huge material and moral resources of the Muslim world in their conflict with Israel. This would have entailed forfeiting their secular principles and brought about the very disaster their western backers fear: an Islamic unity and a new *khilafat.*

The Position Towards Islam

Various indications have already been given as to the nature of Arab nationalists writings towards Islam. Islam's claims to the exclusive allegiance of Muslims are rejected. All aspects of Islam that contradict the secular outlook, such as the Shari'ah, the concepts of *jihad* and the Islamic State, are interpreted away as mere historical growths that were attached to the body of Islam in 'ages of backwardness'. Calls for Islamic unity are condemned as dangerous deviations from the nationalist path. Islam itself is subjected to various 'interpretations' (*i.e.* distortions) to prove that it really approves of nationalism. In the process, Islam is turned into what the nationalists call *turath* (heritage). This *turath* they regard as a cumbersome corpus of writings, beliefs, attitudes, *etc.*, which has no place either in the 'modern world' or in the project of Arab nationalism unless it be 'sifted', 'purified' and 'reinterpreted'. From what point of view the *turath* will be sifted, by whom, for what purpose, under what conditions, and what will be left of it are questions that the nationalists prefer to ignore.

The attitude of Arab nationalism to Islam can be summed up by saying that an intellectual violence is exercised on all aspects of Islam to make it amenable to their secular views and to justify its exclusion from any place of prominence in Arabs' lives. This is all done in favour of nationalism, but once more the nationalists fall into contradiction. The natural course would have been for them, first, to either find Islam inadequate or empty of content and then to set about building a social and political creed to replace it. On the contrary, the strategy of Arab nationalism was to attack the fullness and validity of Islam and to deny and throw doubt on its programmes so that it could justify its own project and doctrine.

This attitude towards Islam reveals itself in yet another contradiction. Arab nationalists have shown intense concern in preventing the Arab entity they carved out of the body of Islam from reuniting with that body. All political movements that call for even lukewarm and formal co-operation between Muslim nation-States are scoffed at for being reactionary and hindering the crystallization of the desired Arab entity.

However, the nationalists do not have any reservations about either linking or even incorporating that precious Arab entity into other international entities and movements, not only in the political but in the cultural and economic spheres as well. The majority speak in the current revival of their thought about a unified front of all the 'progressive' forces of the world. Other Arab nationalists speak of close ties between the Arab entity and western Europe as a cultural and political body that balances the two 'superpowers'. Some of these speak more specifically about a 'Mediterranean' entity which fuses the Arabs and the southern Europeans into a primarily cultural-economic system. This last variety is flagrantly anti-Arab in its implications of merging the Arab identity into an essentially western culture.

On the political front, the Arab nationalists envisage merging their cherished entity into such world movements as the Non-Aligned, the 'Third World' and the 'South'. These movements are really western-defined and inspired, despite their high-sounding rhetoric about imperialism, a just economic order, and so forth. The point I am trying to make is that while the Arab nationalists have no difficulty in co-operating with or even merging into internationalist movements of any other kind, they stand completely against any form of Islamic action, even if it were mere window-dressing.

Once again, Arab nationalism presents us with a contradiction that can only be explained by its anti-Islamic stance.

Three Arguments of Arab Nationalism

Arab nationalism is not a well-argued or defined doctrine, as has already become clear. It's advocates usually have a limited repertoire of arguments that derive their only strength from being tirelessly repeated, uncritically circulated as self-evident truths. These arguments are weak and reveal the contradictions we have examined. I now propose to round off my criticism of Arab nationalism by discussing three such frequently advanced arguments.

The Argument Of 'National Unity'

The star argument of the Arab nationalists is that their doctrine will solve the problems of the non-Muslim minorities in Arab countries by abolishing the principle of religious rule (by the Muslim majority) and replacing it with nationalist rule, in which the higher authority will be secular and under which the minorities will regain their 'rights'.

There are no religious minorities in the 'Arab world' except the Copts in Egypt, who have been assimilated into the Muslim majority in all walks of life, and the Christians and some deviant sects in the Levant. The latter have been hostile to Islam for centuries and have cultivated, in modern times, close ties with the imperialist powers and Christendom. It was from among such groups that the concept of Arab nationalism emerged to serve as an instrument of attack upon the *khilafat* and to separate the Arab countries from the rule of Islam—thereby making them an easy prey for the European imperialists and their clients, the westernized elites.

In the light of the confinement of disaffected minorities to a narrow corner of the Arab world, the primacy given to this issue by Arab nationalism raises doubts about this movement. It has very wide claims and it declares its intention to replace Islam as the guiding 'project' of the Arabs. When the major justification given to these bold claims turns out to be the solution of a minority problem that only exists in the minds of some members of the minorities concerned, suspicion is naturally aroused.

Religious minorities in the Arab world did not suffer from persecution under Islam or the Uthmaniyyah State. They attained a secure and advanced status that made them ambitious for more, particularly with the penetration of European influences into the Ottoman-ruled Arab provinces. The Maronites in Lebanon used their links with France to agitate against the Uthmaniyyah State, calling for an independent Christian-dominated enclave in the Lebanon which was realized almost a century later. This agitation against Islam's tolerant rule was motivated, primarily by religious sentiments and was coupled with enthusiastic entry into alliances with such colonial powers as the French and the British in the nineteenth century. There was no talk, at first, about either an Arab dimension or 'nationalism' to this minority plotting an insurrection.

The 'Arab' dimension was suddenly introduced into the context to serve both as a cover for these moves towards minority secession and as a skillful tool to engage Arab Muslims in a struggle against Islam and its rule. For 'Arab' is a critical and sensitive term. It has been so indissolubly tied to Islam as almost to become synonymous with it. At the same time, it does not clearly indicate Islam and may be filled with non-Islamic, if not anti-Islamic, content—by reference to the pre-Islamic age, for instance. In this way, it can be used for deception and propaganda purposes with the first meaning displayed and the second either implied or intended. This is how it came to serve the conspiring minorities of the Levant by disguising their far from 'nationalist' ties to the west. It dragged with it the idea of nationalism, with its secular essence, as a further aid in disguise and in luring the unsuspecting Arabs from their allegiance to Islam.

This basically religious agitation against Islam and its rule is exposed fully in the insistence of Arab nationalism on the argument of 'national unity'. It explains why a movement that is supposedly secular and engrossed in a 'project' for the renaissance of the Arabs should pay such exaggerated attention to an imaginary problem that does not arise in Islam either theoretically or in practice; and that, if it arose, could easily find a solution within Islam's tolerant precepts. This argument only reveals that the main concern of the Arab nationalists is to continue the plan of the Levantine minorities, namely independence from Islam and ties with the west instead.

It is ironic that the Arab nationalists, who ask the Muslim majority to shed their allegiance to Islamic teachings on unity and to Islam's priority in and authority over their lives, come also with a call for more commitment from the non-Muslims to their own creeds. They completely ignore the fact that their alleged championship of the numerically small minorities comes at the expense of the overwhelming majority of Muslims whom they address. This is because their definition of minority rights is entirely negative. These rights will be secured only against Islam, when Islamic rule has been abolished and the Muslims have been secularized and westernized. In fact, these last few words point to the paradox involved in the Arab nationalist view. The rights of the minorities will be guaranteed and their problems solved only when the majority of Muslim Arabs have become like the Christians of Europe; that is, like the Christian minorities in the Arab world.

The nationalists who are so concerned about minority rights make no attempt either to find them within Islam or to work for them under its rule. They do not even care to define these rights and problems except in the negative sense described above. Thus Arab nationalism poses itself, primarily, as the solution to certain undefined problems of some small minorities at the expense of the Muslim majority. The proposed nationalist entity which has so far failed to solve the minority problems, witness the renewed sectarian tensions in some Arab countries, will also create other problems. It will clash with the strongly entrenched local nationalisms in many Arab countries, it will come into conflict with racial and linguistic minorities in these countries, and it will clash with universally-oriented movements such as Islam.

The grand scheme of Arab nationalism boils down to a suspicious obsession with a so-called minority problem, the solution to which will create a host of other problems, foremost among which is the obliteration of the identity of the Arab Muslim majority in practice. These problems have actually been created and Arab nationalism has, in that sphere, proved itself merely a tool for achieving the hegemony of religious and political minorities.

In Syria, it was the Christians and then the Alawites who used Arab nationalism as a cover to disguise their personal power-seeking, which ended in tragedy for the Muslim majority. In Iraq, it is the secularist-Christian minority that rules under the banner of Arab nationalism and leads the Muslim people of their country to attack the Muslims of Iran. In Lebanon, the Christians raised the same nationalist slogans, only to drop them and uncover their real designs and alliances with the enemies of Arabs and Muslims alike.

The Argument of 'Modernity'

There is a constellation of words that are always present in Arab nationalist propaganda and which are produced as arguments in favour of this idea. These words include 'modernity', 'progress', 'the age', 'reason', 'enlightenment', and similar phrases that supposedly support the Arab nationalist doctrine against its Islamic opponents, who are usually described by a counter vocabulary like 'reactionary', 'backward', barbaric, uncivilized, and so forth.

It is obvious that mere repetition of a group of terms does not, in itself, constitute an argument but that it has, rather, only a propaganda value. However, when these words are used in Arab nationalist writings they usually carry a westernized content of a leftist character. This is more evidence of the essentially dependent nature of a doctrine that brags about its 'Arabness' and 'independence'. Modernity, in nationalist usage, means establishing a society similar to that of the west and progress is measured with reference to that model. Enlightenment and reason mean thinking and behaving in the secular, materialist modes of Europe.

Islamic thought has come in recent years to analyze and criticize the arsenal of favourable terms circulated by the Arab nationalists and, indeed, by all sections of the secularist spectrum. It is usually pointed out that these terms are relative and abstract and must be placed in a certain frame of reference when used. However, it can easily be demonstrated that, even in the context of the western content of the Arab nationalists' terms, nationalism cannot be described either as modern or enlightened. Nationalism of the kind that prevailed in Europe since the Renaissance has been superseded by 'the modern age'. An 'enlightened' and 'progressive' socialism or marxism thinks in global terms and defines man in universal material terms that are basically socio-economic and neither racial nor cultural. A new 'nationalism' has been created in the Soviet Union that cuts across old nationalistic lines and unites and merges people on the basis of an internationalist creed.

The same can be said of the United States, where a new 'nationalism', perhaps it could better be called identity, is created through the famous 'melting-pot'. It is basically a cross-national entity built round a peculiar secularist ideology: 'the American dream'. There is also the example of Israel, which is supported by 'enlightened progressives' the world over. All these entities, and others in China and Australia for instance, build nations on the basis of certain ideologies that are essentially religion-surrogates. The building of nationalism on racial, ethnographic bases is not the mode of the 'age' in the leading powers of the world.

The enlightened and rational secular ideas or attitudes that the Arab nationalists display are usually hackneyed remnants of nineteenth century positivist-materialist thought which are now dead museum-pieces. It is certainly neither rational nor enlightened to present vague emotional echoes mixed with outmoded racial thoughts as the basis for Arab nationalism.

Arab nationalists usually argue that they are working in the spirit of the age to create a larger entity out of local nationalisms in the Middle East area, just as is now being attempted in Europe through various 'unions'. This, however, does not hide the fact that their call is essentially disintegrative and not unifying. To unite some local nationalisms, a task in which Arab nationalists have failed miserably, is surely a paltry thing compared to the serious schism which Arab nationalism has caused in the Muslim world, with the help of non-Arab chauvinism. In fact, Arab nationalism has a chronic tendency to degenerate into local nationalisms.

The Argument of 'Practicality'

With the weakness of their ideas being felt more and more, the Arab nationalists have developed this argument in the face of criticism from Islamic quarters. Islam is seen by them as an unfit alternative to nationalism. Its civilization failed many centuries ago and its political expression, the *khilafat*, is gone for ever after displaying its inherent defects. Moreover, Islam does not really have anything to offer beyond some general moral tenets. The social and political spheres are thus open before an Arab nationalism that offers a practical alternative.

It is tempting to quash this argument by appeal to the practical record of Arab nationalist forces that have ruled most Arab countries for differing periods throughout the last thirty years or more. They have ruled in dictatorial fashion, liquidating all other political tendencies and singling out the Islamic for particular harshness in order to prevent the evolving of a credible Islamic movement and, hence, a viable alternative to their rule. However, their failures in the social, economic and political fields have been resounding. All of the famous 'socialist experiments' introduced by the Arab nationalist regimes and elites have ended in ruin and their political and military efforts have been unable either to unify the Arabs or to confront Israel.

Arab nationalist regimes led by military, intellectual and sectarian elites of secularist and westernized preferences have practised dictatorship at its worst, strangling all sorts of liberties and human rights. They have enforced western ideas and values on Islamic societies, thereby causing chaos and deterioration. Their much-vaunted development schemes have mostly been ill-conceived and badly planned, as well as incompetently and corruptly managed.

In contrast, one can point to many practical successes of Islamic rule throughout history, though the comparison would be unjust to Islam because the Arab nationalists have such power in their hands as not even the most despotic Muslim ruler could have dreamt of. It may be more to the point to refer to the contemporary success of Islamic movements on many social and intellectual levels, even when they have been subjected to severe persecution and the distortion of their ideas and goals. The case of the Muslim Brotherhood in Egypt and that of the Islamic societies in recent years may be considered in this connection.

Arab nationalism is in a worse condition, in the estimation of viability, than that it thinks Islam is in. If we grant that both movements currently exhibit signs of failure and weakness, Islam has to its credit the fact that it has been forcefully excluded from the sphere of action in its own countries for more than a century by repeated colonialist and nationalist attacks. Islam is viable as a living creed which shapes the believers' values and view of life; it is not a travesty of certain nineteenth-century European ideas that have outlived their interest there. The argument from practicality is reduced, in fact, to the contention by Arab nationalists that since their elites are in possession of power and influence, their idea is more practicable than Islam, which has been excluded, by them, from the sphere of action.

They consider that the wider and deeper Islamic ideas, which go beyond race and view man in his entirety, are impracticable. They reject the comprehensive Islamic 'project', whose features they consistently distort by their secularist approaches, and present a limited, racially based, vaguely defined, and practically disproved idea as a viable alternative to it for no other reason than that they happen to be in or near power and that they resent an Islamic change.

Conclusion

This chapter has set itself the rather narrow task of criticizing what it described as logical inconsistencies bedevilling the current, and old, presentations of the concepts of Arab nationalism. It suggests that these contradictions, which affect the positions and arguments, can be explained by the fact that Arab nationalism has been envisaged from the beginning not as an intellectual creed or philosophy but rather as a political instrument to achieve certain ends; *i.e.* the arousal of some eastern Arab provinces against the Uthmaniyyah State. These ends have later developed to include the secularization and covert westernization of the Middle East Muslim Arabs, the pushing of non-Muslim or anti-Islamic elites into positions of influence and power, the legitimation of leadership ambitions, either by certain dictators or by Arab nationalist parties, and the establishing of an 'Arab' entity that is separate from the Islamic entity and made to stand against it after using some of the elements it created.

Arab nationalism was primarily conceived for an emotional, demagogic mode of propaganda and dissemination: hence the contradictions. The Arab crowds, it seems, could be sufficiently aroused by a jumble of slogans. Arab nationalism, that is, started life with a derogatory veiw of the Arab mentality.

When Arab nationalism began to feel the need for intellectual development, it could only magnify the contradictions inherent in itself in the way that I have traced. With its overwhelming western content Arab nationalism has, in fact, lost its independence and become a mere branch of some ideologies of the west but minus the intellectual sophistications. As I have earlier emphasized, it has practically ceased to be 'Arab' or 'nationalist' and has turned into a Trojan horse for internationalist forces encroaching upon the Muslim world. It combines with other secularized and westernized nationalisms fostered in various areas across the Muslim world to yield a pattern of attack upon the unity of that world and its identity.

The various brands of nationalism use the unification elements created by Islam to promote their own claims of independent and separate entities *vis-à-vis* Islam. They disintegrate the universal Islamic identity but they do not, as might be expected, end up in several entities. Rather, they are reunited again into another global system, that of western civilization in its widest sense. The nationalisms are claimed as smaller but more valid entities than the larger identity of Islam; but they soon reveal their essentially *dependent* westernized nature and merge into the universal western system in any or all of its political, economic, and cultural manifestations.

The crucial point in this development is the two contradictions that I isolated. The nationalisms represent intermediate stages in the confrontation between Islam and the west. They are seccessions from Islam which claim an independent identity but their essential content is inescapably western and secular. This content and the practice of the ruling nationalist elites leads inevitably to identification with, involvement in, and gradual incorporation into the universal western 'project'. The nationalist elites cannot revert to Islam even if they wanted to because they have destroyed its universal system.

Thus nationalism of any type can be seen, from the strategic point of view, as an intermediate phase between the disintegration of a total Islamic polity and identity and either the incorporation or assimilation of the resulting nationalistic identities into the global western polity. This is the logic that is inherent in the content of the idea of nationalism itself as it was, and still is, presented across the Muslim world: a secularist, westernized content. Nationalism can only lead to western *inter*nationalism; it is in essence a temporary, unstable phase of political development that has been forced on the Muslim countries, ultimately throwing them into the lap of the west. No amount of chauvinism and calls for a return to either 'original culture' or 'the roots' can save the nationalisms from that fate.

The mere idea, terms, mode of perception, and outlook of the nationalisms have been western-oriented and inspired from the start. When they abandoned universal Islamic claims to priority, allegiance, unity, and political and social expression, they had no alternative but to join the west, the other global system that confronts Islam. Nationalist illusions of independence and identity were only preparatory stages in this development. They are good rallying cries against Islam, while they hide the western content of the nationalist doctrine. When the nationalisms have performed the destructive part of their mission, the separation from the Islamic identity, and attempt to embark on some form of building their own 'identity', they find themselves drawn to the western vortex. All the secularized nationalisms of the Muslim world, from that of Atatürk to the Arab variety, can be explained by and studied according to this formula. All the grandiose attempts to solve desperate problems of the nationalisms—using such concepts as 'the South' or 'the Third World'—can only increase the malaise because they are of western origin and conception and because they are confined to partial views in the economic field which only help to remove tensions in the global polity dominated by the west.

Finally, note that the framework defined here can also serve to criticize the similarly artificial revival in some Arab countries recently of the doctrinaire secularist tendency which has been moribund in

Egypt, for example, for many years. Secularism uses the same arguments of Arab nationalism and suffers from the same contradictions and even more. It insists that Islam be evacuated from the sphere of social, economic, political, and cultural action and guidance only to replace it with western views and values, some of them of Judeao-Christian origins while the rest are atheistic.

Chapter IV

Indonesian Nationalism: A Western Invention to Contain Islam in the Dutch East Indies

Tengku Hasan M. di Tiro

Introduction

The problems of 'Indonesian nationalism' cannot be understood without knowing the geographic setting that governs it. The former Dutch colonial empire of the East Indies, whose territorial 'integrity' is still kept intact, *i.e.* un-decolonized, and has got away with only its name changed from the 'Dutch East Indies' to 'Indonesia', is not a natural geopolitical entity. The entire region has been brought under one single super-colonial administration by the bloody sword of Dutch colonialism that held sway over the vast region from the beginning of the sixteenth century to the present time, although since December 27, 1949, the supercolony has been administered by the Javanese on behalf of the Dutch and other western interests under the name of the pseudo-nation of 'Indonesia'. Henry Kissinger had aptly observed long ago that Indonesia was nothing but a 'geographic expression' until the Dutch found it more efficient to unite the islands of the Indies under a single administration.[1] This was indeed the genesis of the present-day 'Indonesian nation' and 'Indonesian nationalism', created solely to justify the unified administration of the huge colony as a preserve of western imperialism.

As a geographic expression, 'Indonesia' covers an area equal in length to the distance between Moscow and Lisbon, and in width equal to that between Rome and Oslo, with a population in excess of 160 million, composed of as many diverse nationalities, languages, and cultures as are found in continental Europe. As there is no sense in talking about the existence of one European nationalism today, so there is equally no sense in talking about the existence of an

'Indonesian nationalism', although western media and scholars have naïvely propagated this concept.

Islam and the Dutch East Indies

There is only one common denominator among the various peoples of the Dutch East Indies, namely Islam: the religion of 95 per cent of these peoples. However, the Dutch could hardly build anything on the basis of Islam which had been their number one enemy to begin with. Had they not in fact wrested control over these huge territories from half-a-dozen Muslim States that had existed before their arrival, such as Banten, Demak and Mataram on the island of Java; Bandjar on the island of Borneo (Kalimantan); Bone and Macassar on the island of Celebes (Sulawesi); Ternate' on the islands of the Moluccas; and finally Acheh on the island of Sumatra, against which the Dutch had to fight the biggest war in all their history? As the Dutch historian, Paul Van 't Veer commented:

> The Netherlands had never fought a war greater than the one against Acheh. In terms of the time of its duration, this war can be called the eighty years war. In terms of casualties—more than 100,000 dead—it was a military event that has no equal in the history of our land. For a century, Acheh War was the centre of our diplomatic, military, internal and international politics. . . . No place in the Dutch East Indies—Indonesia—can be compared with Acheh. A war that lasted that long, casualties that many, costing more than half a billion good 19th century Dutch gilders were the proofs of that. We did not know that in 1873 (when the Dutch first invaded Acheh). But we know that now. Let that stand, so the people in Holland, and even more so in Java, can have some ideas what kind of men the Achehnese are.[2]

But the Achehnese are simple Muslims. They are the living proof of the strength of Islam in the East Indies. General Van Swieten, who was the commander of the Dutch second invasion of Acheh in 1873–1874 (the commander of the first Dutch invasion, General Kohler, was executed by the Achehnese forces) and who was hailed, somewhat prematurely, as 'the conqueror of Acheh', finally came to the conclusion that 'there was no way to defeat the Achehese in war', and he recommended withdrawal and a negotiated peace.[3] The Dutch government rejected his proposal and so the war went on.

It was the continuous defeat of the Dutch that finally brought the orientalist and 'Islamicist' Christian Snouck Huurgronje to the forefront. He was considered a genius by his people and was described by Multatuli, a famous Dutch writer, as the second most important man in the history of Dutch colonialism in Indonesia during the nineteenth century. In orientalist circles he was regarded as one of the two foremost European authorities on Islam (the other one was Ignaz Goldziher of Hungary).

Huurgronje was asked to use his knowledge of Islam to find ways to defeat the Achehnese Muslims. His official instructions from the Dutch government read, in part, as follows: 'To study the conditions of the religious party in Acheh after the death of Tengku Tjhik di Tiro, and to find out their new disposition and to make recommendations.'[4] The Dutch had entertained high hopes that the martyrdom of the Achehnese leader, Al-Malik Tengku Tjhik Muhammad Saman, on January 25, 1891, would bring the Achehnese resistance to an end. That, however, did not happen; the resistance continued. This was why Huurgronje was dispatched to Acheh. Ultimately, he failed to achieve his objectives in Acheh because the Achehnese Muslims refused to co-operate with him; he could not influence them. However, despite his failure in Acheh, Huurgronje did emerge as the architect of the Dutch government's 'Islamic policy' in the Dutch East Indies, now Indonesia. His recommendations were accepted as official policy to the very end of the formal Dutch control of the East Indies, until the time of the illegal transfer of 'sovereignty' to their marionette, Javanese Indonesia, created in their own image, on December 27, 1949.

The Dutch 'Islamic Policy'

Christian Snouck Huurgronje formulated, in no uncertain terms, the objectives the Dutch colonialist regime must attain: namely, that Islam be destroyed as a politico-religious faith, albeit slowly and very subtly; Indonesia must be secularized and westernized, preparing the way for an eventual lasting union with the Netherlands that would be made possible on the grounds of a 'common' culture obtained through the success of his policy. This end, among others, was to be achieved by isolating the Muslims of the Dutch East Indies from any contact with the *Ummah* outside the Dutch East Indies. For this purpose, pilgrimage to Makkah and Hajj was to be very strictly controlled. Huurgronje was for using violent tactics, if necessary, to depoliticize Islam; for the Achehnese he even prescribed torture to destroy their 'over-confidence' and 'superiority complex' *vis-à-vis* the Dutch. In Huurgronje's own words, 'de Atjehers gevoelig te slaan en zo hun superioriteitswaan te ontenemen' (Achehnese must be hit in the most sensitive painful manner so that their superiority complex can be destroyed).[5] This was strange advice from a student of theology. But it was to no avail because it merely strengthened the Achehnese resolve to achieve martyrdom. Huurgronje had mistaken the proper Achehnese Muslims' attitude towards the invading infidels for a 'superiority complex'. In short, the Islam that was to be allowed in Indonesia, under Huurgronje's scheme of things, was in the form of rituals only. Meanwhile, the educational system for Muslim children was to be secularized. Finally, the overall supervision and leadership to implement these policies was to be entrusted to the Javanese aristrocracy, the group that Huurgronje trusted would be willing and able to secularize and westernize Indonesian Muslim society according to Dutch prescriptions.[6]

However, when Huurgronje permitted that a ritual Islam be allowed to continue, he had, in fact, conceded practically the whole thing, because Islamic rituals are in a different category from the rituals of other religions. Islamic rituals are in themselves the fount, the living, vibrant roots of the faith. This escaped Huurgronje's comprehension because he was not a Muslim. Islamic rituals are yearly, monthly, weekly, daily, nightly, even hourly 'rites of passage' that renew the Muslims' commitment to Islam anywhere, any time and under any situation.

In the event, Huurgronje's advice was fully adopted and enforced as the official 'Islamic policy' of the Dutch colonial government towards the *Ummah* in the Dutch East Indies until the outbreak of World War II, and again when the Dutch returned from 1945–1949. The Dutch wanted to keep every inch of their conquered territories united under a single administration in Jakarta for maximum profit, economy and ease of control, but they recognized the need to create a new common denominator to replace Islam among the peoples. This new common denominator was to be a secular, westernized culture in common with the Dutch culture to facilitate the eventual political union between

Indonesia and Holland. So the Dutch search for an alternative to Islam as a base for Indonesian 'unity' was a principled and most serious pursuit. The idea of secularization led naturally to the idea of an Indonesian 'nationalism'. But how can one inclusive 'nationalism' be created in a multi-national empire, covering an area as large as western and eastern Europe put together? If one European nationalism could not be created until now, with all the background unity of a European civilization, a European culture and an integrated system of communication, and a contiguous territory to boot, how could the creation of an 'Indonesian nationalism even be contemplated in a vast non-contiguous region, composed of myriads of archipelagoes, with one part separated by thousands of kilometres from others, without either a common language, culture, economy, or history? A unity under the banner of Islam would have been the most natural and desired by the overwhelming majority of the peoples of all nationalities, but that was against everything the Dutch stood for and wanted. A unity based solely on the force of the sword would have been fragile and illusory: that was admitted by all Dutchmen. So, a secular Indonesian 'nationalism', purged of any association with Islam, was accorded a consensus among Dutchmen of all persuasions, left, right, centre, liberal and conservatives alike, except for the most obtuse.

'Indonesian Nationalism'

Despite all the contradictions, however, an 'Indonesian nationalism' was promulgated and made a key part of Indonesia's State ideology, the *pancasila*. But for all intents and purposes, 'Indonesian nationalism' became, in fact, a cover-up for the nascent Javanese nationalism, that of the real new ruling class, whose aims, purposes and symbolisms were projected to represent 'Indonesian nationalism', that is the projection of a sectional, partial, local interest as the national, general interest. This fact can be easily observed. For example, all symbols of 'Indonesian nationalism' are expressed in Javanese language idioms: the State ideology is called *pancasila*, Javanese for 'five principles';[7] the Indonesian 'national' motto is *Bhinneka tunggal ika*, Javanese for 'unity in diversity'; the names of all Indonesian State decorations are in Javanese; the status of first-class national hero is reserved for Javanese and all positions of power and prestige in Indonesia are reserved for the Javanese. In addition the names of the State's administrative divisions and the titles of functionaries are expressed in Javanese: *desa* for a village and *lurah* for a village head; *kecamatan* for sub-district and *camat* for head of sub-district; *kabupaten* for district, and 'bupati' for its head, and so on *ad infinitum*. The supposed official language may not be Javanese yet, but this is only because nobody would understand Javanese in 95.4 per cent of Indonesia's territory; therefore Malay has to be used.[8]

The Javanese are in a favourable position to expropriate 'Indonesian nationalism' for themselves for a number of reasons: first, they are the favoured groups by the deliberate choice of the Dutch— did not Eduard D. Dekker, the Dutch novelist, write: 'Serving his Master is the *Religion* of the Javanese'? Second, although not the majority, they represent the largest single group among the inhabitants. Third, their homeland happened to be on the island of Java that was chosen by the Dutch to be the centre of the colonial administration because it was the first to be colonized and because of the 'reliability' of its population from the Dutch point of view, thus facilitating Javanese control over it. Finally, it was indeed to them that the Dutch had officially transferred their 'sovereignty' over all of Indonesia on December 27, 1949, to the exclusion of all other nationalities.

Even Acheh Sumatra was given to the Javanese instead of being returned to the Achehnese, the indigenous people of that country, who have more claim to the territory because the Dutch had taken it from them and not from the Javanese. Nor could this fact have been forgotten easily, because the Dutch had to fight the Achehnese for almost a century. Yet instead of returning the country to the people of Acheh Sumatra, the Dutch gave it to the Javanese. In doing so, the Dutch violated all the known rules of international law and decolonization procedures of the United Nations which prohibited any transfer of sovereignty over any colonial territory by a colonial power and stipulated that sovereignty over each colonial territory belongs to the indigenous people of that territory, who must be set free without any conditions and without further delay.[9] The real reason, however, went even further than the mere calculation of economic interests: if the Dutch had turned Acheh Sumatra over to the Achehnese it would have become the first Islamic State to re-emerge in Southeast Asia.

All these, however, did not alter the fact that Java represents only 7 per cent of Indonesia's territory. The other 93 per cent of Indonesia's territories are overseas from Java; some are two to three thousand kilometres away and inhabited by peoples of different nationalities, races, languages, and cultures totally alien to the Javanese, making the 93 per cent of Indonesia's territories in fact overseas colonies of Java, as it were. For, in the simplest terms, 'colonialism is rule over peoples of different race inhabiting lands separated by salt water from the imperial centre'.[10]

Thus, to make a sham 'nationalism' look real, a geographic expression has been called a 'country' and a 'nation'. Malay, a language of Sumatra, was commandeered to become 'Indonesian', although the Javanese do not speak (let alone write or understand) it. So today they have ruined it—they have made it the equivalent of Pidgin English to the English language. This so-called 'bahasa Indonesia', alias Javanese Malay, is a kind of 'Pidgin Malay' where the grammar of the classic Malay—a Muslim tongue—has been violated and its syntax disregarded. Further, it has been mixed up indiscriminately with unassimilated and unnecessary foreign words of assorted European languages, making it no longer intelligible to the Malay people themselves. Javanese Malay has become a grotesque language that is no longer fit for literature, poetry or serious discourse as far as the Malay peoples are concerned. The name of Indonesia itself is Greek to the peoples of the East Indies, a foreign nomenclature that bears no relation whatever to their history, language, culture and literature.

To complete the paraphernalia of the 'new' nation and the brand new 'nationalism', an upside-down Polish flag was adopted as the 'Indonesian flag'—a flag without history and without glory as far as the peoples are concerned. The plagiarized Yale Boola-Boola song was adopted as the 'Indonesian national anthem'. And to top it all, a two-sentence, thoughtless 'declaration of independence', devoid of any idea, much less a philosophy or a programme, was issued. Among civilized nations, a declaration of independence is a symbol, next to the flag, a statement of moral excellence and legitimacy, a brief for that nation's *raison d'être*. Indonesia's 'declaration of independence', however, was but a brief news bulletin.

The whole affair would be a farce if it were not for the river of blood that it has been spilled and which still continues to flow to this day. The farce inaugurated forty years of continuous bloodshed, of anarchy of the State. Forty years of officially condoned massacres, resistances and repressions that finally brought the military back to the helm— that is back to the stark reality of colonialism, and the exercise of its illegitimate and illegal power. The Dutch sword has merely been replaced by Javanese guns—to keep the 'unity' of the 'Indonesian nation' for no other purpose than western exploitation as the cheapest source of raw materials for the west's industries. Western journalists and scholars have found it agreeable to call this 'stability' and 'economic progress'.

Indonesian Nationalism and the Javanese Military State

The emergence of the Javanese colonialist State is patent proof of the death—in fact of the non-existence—of 'Indonesian nationalism'. Since the sixteenth century, Indonesia has always been (with the exception of Acheh Sumatra) a colonial empire and a colonial empire can only be ruled by force of arms. Colonialism and militarism are inseparable; one cannot exist without the other. The Dutch had created and preserved this colonial empire by force for 350 years, from 1599–1949, when they transferred it to the Javanese. Since then, the Javanese mercenaries have carried out the 'white man's burden' with catastrophic consequences for all colonized non-Javanese peoples of the East Indies, from Acheh Sumatra to West Papua and from the Moluccas to Timor. Since 1949, the time of the illegal transfer of sovereignty, hardly any island has not been used as a battlefield, and there is hardly any non-Javanese nationality whose blood had not been shed by Javanese troops. There have been revolts against Javanese colonialism on every island, just as there were revolts against Dutch colonialism before.

The Dutch East Indies were never decolonized, in contrast to all colonial territories in the rest of the world. The Dutch merely transferred their colonies to the Javanese, lock, stock and barrel, without returning even one inch of territory to the rightful people of that territory as prescribed by the Decolonization Law of the United Nations. The Dutch simply made the Javanese—for an agreed price—the heir of their colonial empire, disregarding the rights of the non-Javanese peoples to self-determination and independence. The Dutch and Javanese conspiracy against the International Law and Decolonization principles of the United Nations was justified by the fiction of 'Indonesian nationalism' and an 'Indonesian nation'. Yet the massive and desperate struggles for self-determination, waged by the Muslim majority and even by non-Muslim minority groups, were and have never been truthfully reported in the western media, which insisted on calling the freedom-fighters 'separatists', 'fanatics', or 'insurgents'. One book written by a western journalist is even called *Rebels Without a Cause*, as if there are peoples on earth eager to die for no cause. All this resistance against the Indonesian State proves that the peoples concerned knew that 'Indonesian nationalism' and 'nationhood' were merely a hoax to disenfranchise and colonize them.

The ink of the Dutch and Javanese signatures had barely dried on the Treaty transferring Dutch 'sovereignty' to the Javanese, when the Muslims in Pasundan (West Java) declared an Islamic State there, under the leadership of Imam Kartosuwirjo. In April, 1950, the people of the South Moluccas declared their independence from Javanese Indonesia, under the leadership of Dr. Soumokil. In 1952, the Muslims of the Celebes (Sulawesi), under the leadership of Abdul-Qahar Muzakkar, declared the establishment of an Islamic State there and severed all relations with the Javanese regime of Indonesia. The Muslims of Borneo (Kalimantan) followed suit under the leadership of Ibnu Hadjar. In 1953, the Muslims of Acheh (Sumatra) also announced the re-establishment of the Islamic State there and severed all relations with Javanese Indonesia. These armed resistances against the Javanese republic of Indonesia, in 93 per cent of the territory claimed by the Javanese republic, should have been enough evidence for all thinking men and women about the non-existence of the so-called 'Indonesian nationalism'.

Instead, the Western press chose to call these wars of liberation and self-determination of the non-Javanese peoples the 'growing pains' of the Indonesian republic. The Javanese colonialists called these freedom-fighters 'traitors' but on their own homelands they were called heroes of the peoples— *mujahideen*. Could this sort of thing have happened if there were a real Indonesian nationalism that really united these peoples? Clearly, there was no shared 'collective pride and humiliation, pleasure and regret' between the Javanese and the rest of the peoples of the East Indies. These are sentiments which, according to John Stuart Mill, are key indicators of the existence of a nationality. Apparently none existed in Indonesia. By 1965, all the leaders of Islamic liberation movements, such as Imam Kartosuwirjo of West Java, Abdul-Qahar Muzakkar of Sulawesi, and Ibnu Hadjar of Kalimantan, were martyred—murdered by the Javanese regime. Dr. Soumokil of the South Moluccas, who was a Christian, was also murdered by the Javanese Indonesian forces.

There is still more proof of the counterfeit nature of Indonesian nationalism: the atrocities committed by the Indonesian 'National' Army against fellow Indonesians. Mass murders and massacres have been the order of the day from the issuance of 'the bulletin', *i.e.* the declaration of independence, of Javanese Indonesia, in August 1945. To date, approximately 5 million people have met their death through the State's inflicted wounds all over the 'Indonesian' archipelago. 2 million were recorded in the six month period at the end of 1964 and the beginning of 1965 when the Javanese military seized power. Before and after that, over a much longer period of time, the victims were less carefully tabulated. There was, for example, the massacre of Pulot Tjot Djeumpa in Acheh in 1956, where the Indonesia National Army lined up 200 men, women and children as well as the elderly, and machine-gunned them to death. This was not a rare occurrence in Javanese Indonesia. Other such massacres took place in Kalimantan, Sulawesi, the Moluccas, West Papua and East Timor. Atrocities and tortures of the most bestial kinds are perpetrated daily by the Indonesian National Army against fellow 'Indonesians'. Any human being imbued with the most rudimentary sentiments of 'national' feeling would not be capable of behaving thus against his own kind. This indicates that a true Indonesian national consciousness does not exist. The sociologist Franz Oppenheimer probably put his finger on the problem when he stated that, 'we must not conclude the existence of a national consciousness from the existence of a nation, but on the contrary, the existence of a nation from the existence of a national consciousness.'[11]

Although the Indonesian army is called Tentera 'Nasional' Indonesia, most of its rank and file are Javanese gunmen who look down upon the non-Javanese peoples as foreign and so subject to the Javanese 'masters'. The army is also organized according to ethnic categories for more effective use in suppressing ethnic rebellions that have become the real reason for its existence. Thus, if the Moluccan people were rebelling, then the Javanese regime would send non-Moluccans, say Sundanese troops, to suppress them. If the Achehnese were rebelling, then the Moluccan troops would be sent to suppress it. And so on, following the old familiar practice of the Habsburg empire of sending Czech batallions to crush Slovak rebellions, or Hungarian regiments to suppress Croatian uprisings, to make sure that no emotional ties exist between the people to be crushed and the troops. In the short run, this policy will ensure the effectiveness of the repression; in the long run, it serves the policy of divide and rule, by enhancing antagonisms among the ethnic groups and thus guaranteeing the perpetuation of the authority of the central regime. During the Habsburg empire, this policy ensured the perpetual power of Vienna; in today's Indonesia it guarantees Jakarta's control of the outlying colonies, called 'provinces'. In such a situation, it is ludicrous to imply the existence of an 'Indonesian nationalism', just as it would have been naïve to imagine the existence of an Austro-Hungarian 'nationalism' under the Habsburgs.

Another proof of the non-existence of a true 'Indonesian nationalism' was provided by the experimentation with the party system before the emergence of the Javanese military colonial State. The last fairly, free elections held in Indonesia were in 1955 and 1957. The results of both these elections showed that the PNI (Partai Nasionalis Indonesia, i.e. the 'Nationalist' Party of Indonesia) got the bulk of its votes only in Central and East Java, the homeland of the Javanese ethnic group. The party got either few or no votes at all in non-Javanese territories, except from Javanese immigrants called 'transmigrants' there. By contrast, the Muslim party (Mashumi), although winning very few votes in Javanese ethnic territories, received most of the votes cast outside Java. The Muslim party was the only 'nationwide' party. Clearly these results demonstrate the widespread appeal of Islam to the population of Indonesia, irrespective of their national origins, in contrast to the limited, sectional, almost local appeal of 'Indonesian nationalism' to the Javanese ethnic areas, where secularism and nationalism have been propagated.[12]

Javanese Nationalism and Imperialism

Under the cloak of an impossible 'Indonesian nationalism' a Javanese nationalism has been given an opportunity to emerge triumphant. Although 'Indonesian nationalism' is itself a fake, it has become an effective mask for a real Javanese nationalism and its will to project its exclusive special and sectional interest as the 'national' one over the heads of the non-Javanese peoples and their homelands, while mediating with foreign powers for recognition of Javanese primacy and hegemony over this vast region (which constitutes approximately

80 per cent of the territory of Southeast Asia). This Javanese primacy and hegemony, however, can never be maintained without the tacit approval of neighbouring States. This is the strategic vulnerability inherited by Javanese Indonesia from the Dutch East Indies because even the Dutch colonial empire could never have existed for even a single day without British diplomatic and even (at times) military support and protection. This is so, primarily because Indonesia is not a natural geopolitical entity.

The Dutch East Indies existed by courtesy of the British when the British lost patience with the Dutch, as they did during the Napoleonic Wars. Stamford Raffles moved easily from Singapore to Java, and sent the Dutch packing. The fact that the British decided to give the East Indies back to the Dutch is yet another demonstration that the then Dutch East Indies, like the now Javanese Indonesia, existed only by courtesy of the neighbouring States singly, as was the case with the British then, or collectively, as is the case with ASEAN now. If another proof is needed, then here it is. During World War II, the Dutch empire of the East Indies, already called Indonesia, collapsed simply by the mere presence of the Japanese army in Singapore! Today, the existence of Javanese Indonesia depends on the courtesy of Singapore, Malaysia, Thailand, Vietnam, Brunei, the Philippines, Papua New Guinea, Australia, and, by extension, the United States and the Soviet Union. This is advisedly said, because even the superpowers cannot protect Javanese Indonesia from its tiniest neighbour. That is why Indonesia needs ASEAN as no one else does.

Javanese Indonesia is a State that cannot antagonize any State. It cannot confront any other State because any confrontation with anyone means the end of Javanese Indonesia as we know it today. Last time they were lucky to have ended the confrontation with Malaysia just in time. Otherwise there would be no Javanese Indonesia today. Consequently, Javanese Indonesia cannot have a foreign policy unless it be that of getting along with everybody.

Java, like Holland before it, has unreasonably tried to hold on to so vast a territory that it is absolutely impossible for it to do so let alone defend it. No country the size of either Holland or Java—especially Java without any industrial base and among the most backward of the backward countries—can defend an empire with coastlines in excess of 25,000 kilometres with a hostile population. The much-bragged-about Javanese defence plan for 'territorial war' (*Perang wilajah*) by waging a guerrilla war against any invader was just that: braggadocio! You cannot wage a guerrilla war when the local peoples are against you. This situation has obviously escaped the observation of the powers that are now so busy arming the Javanese Indonesian army, or else they are just interested in relieving the Javanese of his ill-gotten cash while they can and while he still has it.

James Soudon, the cautious Dutch Minister of Colonial Affairs, wrote the following words at the time of the mounting Dutch conflict with Acheh, reflecting his worries about the consequences of acquiring more territory: 'I see each further spreading of our authority in the East Indian Archipelago as a step further toward our over-throw, and the more so as we are already now grown far above our own strength'.[3] When a few years later, on March 26, 1873, the Dutch attacked Acheh and were roundly defeated at the Battle of Bandar Acheh, a member of the Dutch parliament in The Hague stated that, 'the repulse in Acheh and the enterprise taken altogether, will prove the last blow to the authority of Holland in the Eastern World'.[14] This was no exaggeration, as history has subsequently shown.

'Great empires die of indigestion', Napoleon observed. That had been the fate of the Roman Empire and of the Dutch East Indies. It is also the inevitable fate of Javanese Indonesia, although it survives for the time being by the courtesy of its neighbouring States. Javanese Indonesia, which is held up in the west as a paragon of 'stability', is in reality the sick man of Southeast Asia.

Notes

1. Henry Kissinger, *Nuclear Weapons and Foreign Policy*, 1957, Harper, Ox. p. 256.
2. Paul Van 't Veer, *De Atjeh-Oorlog*, 1969, p. 76.
3. J. Van Swieten, *De Waarheid over onze vestiging in Atjeh*, 1879.
4. Paul Van 't Veer, *De Atjeh-Oorlog*, p. 187. Cf. C. Snouck Huurgronje, *De Atjeher*, 1906.
5. C. Snouck Huurgronje, *De Atjeher*, 1906.
6. C. Snouck Huurgronje, *Verspreide Geschriften*, Vol. IV, pp. 111–248, Bonn & Leipzig 1927, *passim*, *Ambtelijke Adviezen*, 1889–1936, The Hague, Nijhoff, 1965, *passim*, *Nederland en de Islam*, Leiden, E. J. Brill, 1915, *passim*.
7. These principles are: belief in God (including animistic gods), Indonesian nationalism, democracy, humanitarianism and social justice. *Cf.* Tengku Hasan di Tiro, *Democracy for Indonesia*, New York, 1958, pp. 79–82; also *Crescent International*: 'Javamen opt for paganism', Mar. 16–31, 1984; 'The Menace of Pancasila', Feb. 16–28, 1985; 'Islam outlawed in Indonesia in favour of pagan Pancasila', July 1–15, 1985; 'Islam abolished in Indonesia', July 16–31, 1985.
8. The island of Java represents only 7 per cent of Indonesia's territory but Javanese is spoken in two thirds of it because West Java is populated by Sundanese who speak their own language. Thus, Javanese is actually spoken only in 4.6 per cent of Indonesia territory.
9. United Nations' General Assembly Resolution 1514–XV, *Declaration on the Granting of Independence to Colonial Countries & Peoples*, December 14, 1960.
10. Rupert Emerson, 'Colonialism: Political Aspects', *Encyclopaedia of Social Sciences*.
11. 'Wir Mussen nicht aus der Nation da Nationalbewusstsein, sondern umgekehrt aus dem Nationalbewusstsein die Nation ableiten', Franz Oppenheimer, *System der Soziologie*, Vol. I, p. 6.
12. *Cf.* Tengku Hasan M. di Tiro, *Masa Depan Politik Dunia Melaju*, New York, 1965; Atjeh, 1984; *Demokrasi Untuk Indonesia*, New York and Atjeh, 1958.
13. Paul Van 't Veer, *De Atjeh-Oorlog*, p. 15.
14. *The New York Times*, May 6, 1873.

Chapter V

Nationalism and Kashmiri Muslims
Bashir Ahmed Dabla

Introduction

The emergence of nationalism in eighteenth century Europe, as one of the dominant ideologies, provided the doctrinal basis for the historic transformation—from empires to nation-States—to a new political order of our time. As other parts of the world came under European subservience the currents of nationalism swept through the colonized world. It became the creed of the new secular world order. It became a rallying force, in the hands of the newly emerging elites, for their struggle against alien rulers.

Hayes has described nationalism as a, 'modern emotional fusion and exaggeration' of two phenomena—nationality and patriotism.[1] It is used, generally, as a, 'consciousness, on the part of individuals or groups, of membership in a nation, or of a desire to forward strength, liberty, or prosperity of a nation.'[2] It is associated with the following characteristics of the nation: the idea of a common government; a defined territory; distinguishing features, such as language and descent; common interests; and a certain degree of common feeling or will.[3] Nationality seems to be a condition attributed to either a person or group of persons, 'who speak the same language, have common historical traditions and regard themselves as a distinct cultural society'.[4] Thus, nationalism is a political creed that underlies the cohesion of modern societies and legitimizes their claim to authority. It centres on the, 'supreme loyalty of the overwhelming majority of the people upon the nation-state either existing or desired'.[5] In brief, nationalism has three important features. First, it is a concept which demands the loyalty of the individual and the group, primarily, to the nation-State. Second, it represents a desire of a people to be united as a sovereign nation. Third, it is a phenomenon which exists in the form of either a state of mind or a general will.[6] In short, nationalism represents an ideology in the secular sense of the term and it affects the whole way of life. The indoctrination of the nationalist ideology, necessarily, means the replacement of other ideologies, particularly those of a religious nature.[7]

The swift growth of nationalism in the east can be related to the conditions of the colonial rule of the European powers. All the nationalist movements in the Muslim world were primarily irreligious and devoid of the basic contents of Islam.[8] They triggered a debate in the Muslim world about the religiosity of nationalism. Arguments have been made for and against the 'Islamicity' of nationalism. Our opinion is that nationalism, essentially, represents a parallel ideology to that of Islam. The reasons for this assumption are four. First, while nationalism concentrates upon a particular group of people having certain characteristics, Islam has a supranational character and is addressed to all individuals and groups without any differentiation. Second, the adoption of nationalism as an ideology means the preference for the secular borrowing from the west which, in all probability, accelerates the process of secularization. Third, nationalism initiates and intensifies the cultural plurality and social antagonism between various units and sub-units of the Muslim world. Fourth, nationalism, in all cases, dilutes the impact of Islam as the dominant ideology of the people as well as of the state.

Nationalism in Kashmir[9, 10]

Nationalism swept the Muslims in Kashmir as a result of the impact of colonialism. In fact, the history of modern Kashmir can be considered as the history of the emergence and assertion of Kashmiri nationalism, referred to as *Koshuriat* in Kashmir. It gave rise to a mass movement, in 1931, which represented the first organized effort of the Kashmiri Muslims against alien (*nuebrim*) domination, exploitation and feudal rule. This movement initiated the process of general emancipation, in the secular sense, of Muslims in Kashmir. Before 1947, when Kashmir came under the control of two countries, India and Pakistan, *Koshuriat* remained a dominant ideological creed and became a rallying force in the struggle against the feudal rule of the Maharaja. After 1947, it became the State ideology propagated and perpetuated by the National Conference party under the leadership of Shaikh Muhammad Abdullah.

There is hardly any study which has analysed the Kashmiri Muslims' problems from an Islamic perspective. Our endeavour in this paper is two-fold. First we intend to evolve an Islamic/Muslim critique of *Koshuriat* and its impact; and second, to develop an objective assessment of all the developments in Kashmir in the past decades. Our effort will be to concentrate upon the reality of *Koshuriat*, how it emerged, how it determined subsequent developments, how it affected the Kashmiri Muslim intelligentsia and the Kashmiri Muslim masses, and, lastly, how it benefited the intelligentsia and betrayed the masses.

Though the 1931 mass movement in Kashmir initiated around the Muslim grievances against feudal rule, it gradually became secular. The Muslim Conference, which represented the interests of the Muslims in Kashmir, changed into a National Conference in 1939, advocating secularism as its policy and programme.[11] The secular character of *Koshuriat* was mainly a result of the strong influence of the Kashmiri Pandits,[12] leaders of the Congress party, especially M. K. Gandhi, Jawaharlal Nehru and Maulana Azad, and the Hindu Communists. The 'Naya Kashmir' (New Kashmir) document, which was adopted by the National Conference, unanimously, in 1944, was a programme for the future socialist reconstruction of modern Kashmir. This document has been called a 'socialist manifesto' in its content and essence and a 'communist manifesto' in its actual construction.[13]

The Muslim perspective of *Koshuriat*, which prevailed in the early 1930s, could not withstand the changes. First, the traditional Muslim leadership in Kashmir functioned within the framework of a feudalized Islam' whose interests coincided with the maintenance of the feudal system. This leadership often lent its support to the feudal rulers, even non-Muslims, in order to safeguard its interests. Since it did not come out openly against the alien rule, its legitimacy was lost among people whose leadership was taken over by young revolutionary Muslims. Second, the young Muslim leadership, which had undergone a western education, was deeply influenced by the ideals of nationalism, secularism and socialism. The adoption of the irreligious path by this leadership may be explained in terms of its lack of historical sense and anticipation of future catastrophes, its distorted understanding of Islam and the grand promises and pressure tactics of the Kashmiri Pandits, Communists and Congress leaders. Third, the

Islamic perspective of *Koshuriat* could be neither conceived nor developed mainly because of the absence of any organized Islamic movement in Kashmir in the 1930s.[14] The *rishi* (*Sufi*) influence on Islam in Kashmir had made it more of a folk religion than an ideology for change. This kind of Islam could not provide an alternative to the secular-socialist *Koshuriat* in its formative stage.

The Impact of Koshuriat

Political Impact

The adoption of *Koshuriat* necessitated certain political changes in its formative stage. That is why the conversion of the Muslim Conference into a National Conference and the adoption of 'Naya Kashmir' (New Kashmir) as the national programme was carried out successfully in 1939 and 1944 respectively. The logical outcome of these two attempts was Kashmir's accession to the Union of India in 1947. These attempts represent the basic betrayal of the Kashmiri Muslims. The argument is supported by three points. First, the Pandit-Congress-Communist leaders gave rise to these ideas and implemented them through the ruling Muslim elites even though the Muslim masses of Kashmir were neither consulted nor made aware of the reality of these attempts. Second, these attempts put a significant restraint on the Muslim-Islamic character of Kashmir. The chances for the emergence of Islam as a revolutionary ideology, a state religion and a social movement were subverted. Third, the accession isolated the Muslims of Kashmir from the rest of the Muslim *Ummah*. It married them with a country which had neither a history, geography, culture, language nor religion in common with Kashmir. It put them in a land where they had no identity and no respect. The argument of the Kashmiri nationalist stalwart that the accession would lead to the prosperity of Kashmiri Muslims proved baseless because their fellows outside India attained relatively better standards. At this stage, one historical fact must be emphasized: that while all factors—religious, historical, geographical, economic, political, social and cultural—had gone against the accession, it was materialized mainly on the basis of the ideological synonymity, their common faith in secularism, between the Kashmiri and Indian nationalist leaders.[15]

The Response of India

After the temporary accession, the Kashmiri nationalists began implementing their ideals for land reform, the abolition of usury and the availability of free education. But such hurdles were created by their opponents that the very essence of these reforms was negated. In this way, the reality of secularism came to the fore. The Indian leaders' commitments to equality for Muslims under secularism proved baseless. The Kashmiri Pandits, the Dogras and other Hindu communalists in Kashmir, Jammu and Delhi made a tirade against the Muslim Kashmiri nationalists, especially Shaikh Abdullah, as the change had affected the Hindus. Their sole objective was to reverse the trend of change which had benefited the poor Muslim peasants and workers of Kashmir. The outrage of these forces led to the utilization of brute state power against the Muslim Kashmiri nationalists, resulting in their arrest in 1953. Two developments followed. On the one hand, Shaikh Abdullah adopted an anti-Indian posture, but it did not contribute to the Islamic-Muslim perspective of *Koshuriat*.[16] On the other, India began the rigorous Indianization process of Kashmir. A well-planned policy was initiated by the Indian government *vis-à-vis* Kashmir which had two important facets. First, a series of unrepresentative and corrupt governments were imposed upon the people of Kashmir. This was done consciously so that the puppet regimes followed every order from Delhi and eroded the 'special status' of Kashmir, guaranteed under Article 370 of the Indian Constitution. Second, the Muslims in Kashmir were always divided so as to make their voice ineffective.

Historic Surrender and Aftermath

Though the people of Kashmir suffered, they chose the Shaikh's side, primarily, because he represented their aspiration for the right to self-determination. The 1950s and 1960s saw the struggle of the Kashmiri Muslims for their independence.[17] The struggle enabled them to remain aloof from the national mainstream of India. However, the Kashmiri Muslims had to face humiliation at the hands of their nationalist leaders in the early 1970s after the fall of Dhaka to the Indian forces. Shaikh Abdullah abandoned his struggle for the freedom of Kashmir which he had led from 1953–1974. He was re-installed as chief minister of Jammu and Kashmir in 1975. He was kept on tenterhooks and finally removed in 1977.[18] The Shaikh realized that, despite promises, the policy of the Indian government had not changed but he could do little except resent his betrayal by India. At one stage, he challenged Mrs Indira Gandhi, Prime Minister of India, for her policies towards Kashmir.[19] But the fact is that the Shaikh had enmeshed himself completely. He could not revolt but simply complain that the north Indian communalists were bent upon changing the demographic composition of Kashmir so that the Muslims would be turned into a minority. The Shaikh's death, in 1982, intensified the Indian hold on Kashmir. The agents of Delhi in Kashmir, who would never come out during the Shaikh's lifetime, began roaring in the streets of Srinagar. When Farooq Abdullah, Shaikh Abdullah's son, challenged them on the basis of mass support, his elected government was toppled in 1984.[20] Thus the way was paved for the permanent policy of installing puppet rulers and adopting the tactics of divide-and-rule in Kashmir.

Economic Impact

The political decisions taken under the influence of *Koshuriat* had serious economic implications for Kashmir. A relatively self-sufficient and independent economy was made a dependent economy in the course of post-accession. Economic growth was halted by the closure of the Jhelum Valley road, the only natural gateway to the valley of Kashmir, so denying easy road contact with national and international markets for Kashmiri domestic products. Instead, a dangerous road from Jammu to Srinagar was opened which meant only delay, loss and discouragement. Until this time, the famous Kashmiri fruits could reach national and international markets through the Jhelum Valley road in one or two days; through the Srinagar-Jammu road it took more than a week.[21] A conscious policy was adopted by the central government *vis-à-vis* Kashmir to make the latter economically dependent in order to pave the way for political integration. This policy was implemented efficiently and significant success was achieved. The degree of dependence of the present Kashmiri economy is so great that if the Jammu-Srinagar road closes for some days, the city of Srinagar faces riots because of the shortage of essential commodities, all, of which come from outside. It crudely reflects the common saying in Sriniagar that, 'Kashmir imports everything from India except the water of *Chashma Shahi* (the Shahi spring)'.

Economic Costs

Since all political regimes in Kashmir were sponsored by Delhi, they never concerned themselves with long-term planning. As a result, the Kashmiri Muslims could not control any organized sector of the economy. Though the Muslims have a monopoly over the world-famous traditional arts and crafts, they are nevertheless under-developed. Their organization is primitive, technology obsolete and profits meagre, especially for the workers. The average worker receives between 300 and 400 Indian rupees for working 10–12 hours a day and six days a week. The profitable and productive sectors, such as industry, trade and commerce, the professions and employment, have always been dominated by non-Muslims. Hindus (who constitute about 30 per cent of the population) hold 95 per cent and 55 per cent of jobs in central and state governments respectively.[22] The Hindu-dominated Jammu province is economically developed and this is reflected by the number of industrial units—1019—in 1971, when compared with 833 in the Muslim-dominated Kashmir.[23] Moreover, the Muslim rulers in Kashmir have often succumbed to the pressure of Jammu Dogras under orders from Delhi. That is why Jammu was able to snatch more funds from the state government. Even during the era of Shaikh Abdullah's rule, from 1975–1982, the Jammu province received a larger share of the allocated funds (in Indian rupees) than its entitlement while the Kashmir province received less than its due share, which can be seen in the following statistics:

	Kashmir (in lakhs)		Jammu (in lakhs)	
	Entitled Share	Allocated Share	Entitled Share	Allocated Share
1975–76	2,025.17	1,753.88	1,725.77	1,812.59
1976–77	2,648.30	2,388.47	2,256.78	2,271.06
1977–78	3,776.05	3,584.22	3,217.80	3,102.83
1978–79	4,820.68	4,012.99	4,107.99	4,431.84[24]

(one lakh = 100,000)

Thus the economy for Muslims, in Kashmir, remained static. If it changed, it benefited the Hindus more than the Muslims.

Social Impact

First, the adoption of *Koshuriat* and the subsequent political developments, especially the accession of Kashmir to India, took Kashmiri Muslims out of the Muslim social unit and put them into the broader Hindu social milieu. The sociological implications of this change were far reaching. On the one hand, the Kashmiri Muslims were cut off from the Muslim *Ummah*, though they constituted the majority in their homeland. On the other, they were taken into a cultural milieu which had no similarity with their own culture, traditions, norms and modes of behaviour.

Second, the Kashmiri Muslims faced the problem of cultural aggression. Since they had turned themselves into a minority, they were bound to be influenced culturally by their interaction with the Indians. Moreover, a well-planned policy of cultural assimilation was followed by the Indian Government through publications, newspapers, magazines, radio, television and film *etc.* The net result was the strong impact of Hindu culture upon the Kashmiri Muslims. This influence has also been referred to as the Hinduization of Muslims.

Third, the ideological indoctrination of Indian nationalism was made the supreme objective. In addition to other efforts, education was utilized fully for this cause through its central organization and in school syllabuses. Its effects were deeply felt. Muslim children in Kashmir learn about India but know hardly anything about Islam and Kashmir. As a result, a new generation of Muslim youngsters is growing up whose commitment to Islam, Muslims and Kashmir is questionable.

Fourth, Muslim social customs and the demographic composition of Kashmir experienced significant changes. Hindu-Muslim and Kashmiri-Indian marriages were encouraged. The demographic change lessened the dominant position of Kashmiri Muslims, whose proportion in the state has gone down from 68 per cent in 1961 to 65 per cent in 1971 and 63 per cent in 1981.[25] One of the major factors for this is the migration of Punjabi Hindus to Jammu. Moreover, the family-planning programmes have affected the growth rate of Kashmir, which declined to 26.42 per 1,000 in comparison to the Indian national growth rate of 30.57 per 1,000 during the decade 1971–1981.[26]

Fifth, systematic attempts were carried out to develop a generation with a completely secular outlook.

The Causation

Simple Questions

Several questions arise from the above analysis. How did all this happen? What factors were involved? Why could the traditional Muslim leadership not assert itself? Why did the young Muslim leadership adopt socialism and secularism? Why were the objectives of *Koshuriat* not fulfilled by the Muslim Kashmiri nationalist leadership? Why could Islam not be made the political ideology of the people of Kashmir who are known for their religious devotion?

Muslim Elites and Masses

As is clear from the above course of events in Kashmir, *Koshuriat* followed its natural path of development. Everything developed as it would for a secular-socialist ideology. In fact, *Koshuriat* in its infancy emerged from the aspirations of the Kashmiri Muslims for their emancipation after a long period of oppression, torture and exploitation. But it was soon diluted and distorted. It was secularized and socialized by the Hindu-Pandit-Communist intelligentsia and the feudal Muslim elite. The Muslim masses were hardly aware of these minute ideological details. In reality, they were not made sufficiently aware of what they were fighting for. Their ignorance permitted the ideological manipulation of the Muslim leadership. In this way, the Kashmiri Muslim leadership, which represented the first generation of local leadership after a long gap, could neither represent nor materialize the real aspirations of the Kashmiri Muslims.

Failure of the Religious Leadership

The traditional leadership in Kashmir had changed into an interest group: it was more concerned with safeguarding its own interests than with those of Islam. It was not antagonistic towards the alien rule. It neither provoked people nor led the revolt against the feudal rulers, though there were sufficient grounds for that. When the young Muslims with their modern education arrived in Kashmir, they realized people's aspirations and revolted against the alien domination. The Muslim masses supported them wholeheartedly and they assumed the leadership. In this way, the legitimacy and authority of leadership shifted from religious to non-religious people in Kashmir and Shaikh Muhammad Abdullah emerged as the most powerful leader of the masses. As their understanding of the history of Islam, Muslims and Kashmir was meagre they were easily swayed by the alien ideologies. Socialism and secularism were dominant ideologies in those days in Asia, especially after the October revolution in Russia in 1917, the young Muslim leaders were attracted to these ideologies, which they considered revolutionary.

Young Nationalist's Failure

The young nationalist leaders were committed to certain basic changes according to the 'Naya Kashmir' programme. So, they had high hopes and expectations from the Indian leadership. The Indian leaders, however, had developed their own preferences and priorities. When the Muslim Kashmiri nationalists served their interests, they were applauded. When, however, they hurt their feudal interests, they were condemned, criticized and finally jailed, not once but repeatedly. When the Kashmiri nationalists demanded the restoration of basic human rights for Kashmiris, they were labelled 'anti-national'. When they raised their voice against the sufferings of Muslims in Kashmir, they were called 'communal'.

Islam and Islamic Movements

Islam has been the dominant religion in Kashmir. But it was not made the political ideology of the people at the crucial time of their history. This was mainly due to three factors. First, Islam in Kashmir developed a folk (*rishi*) character with roots in pre-Islamic traditions which place more emphasis on ritual. This kind of Islam could not provide the revolutionary ideology necessary at the initiation of the struggle against alien non-Muslim rulers. Second, the role of the traditional religious leadership was not completely Islamic; in some cases it was un-Islamic. It was often used against the Muslim interests in Kashmir. It was interested in the status quo because its status, authority, power and interests lay in the maintenance of the feudalized religious institutions. Third, modern Islamic movements had not emerged on the scene at the time of the initiation of the Kashmiri Muslims' struggle for freedom in the 1930s. They emerged in the following decades but remained primarily fringe or peripheral movements in Muslim society. Their role as mass movements was almost non-existent.

The *Jamaʿat-e Islami* movement alone attempted to provide an Islamic dimension to *Koshuriat*. It strongly emphasized the Islamic identity of the Kashmiri Muslims, their relationship with the Muslims of the world, the liberation of Kashmir and the establishment of the Islamic State. It provided a strong critique of the Kashmiri nationalist leadership but it lacked the leadership and necessary intellectual tools for a revolutionary Islamic movement. While it preached the independence of Kashmir, it participated actively in Indian electoral politics. Finally, it started a political battle against the Kashmiri nationalists without mobilizing and preparing the masses, which led to its disastrous defeat.

Conclusion

The above analysis shows that the ideology of *Koshuriat* hurt the basic interests of the Kashmiri Muslims. In reality, it negated all that the Muslims stood for. Their political subjugation, economic exploitation, social segregation, cultural domination and educational backwardness continued in different forms. Though their commitment to Islam has not been challenged, the dominant alien impact is certainly draining them of their Islamic nature. Thus, it can logically be inferred that any ideology lacking roots in Islam can neither prove beneficial nor serve the fundamental interests of Muslims in any country.

Notes

1. C. J. H. Hayes, *Essays on Nationalism* (New York, Macmillan, 1926), pp. 5–29.
2. Royal Institute of International Affairs, *Nationalism—A Report by a Study Group of Members of RIIA* (London, Oxford, 1939), p. xvii.
3. *Ibid*.
4. R. S. Chavan, *Nationalism in Asia* (New Delhi, Sterling, 1973), p. 4.
5. Hans Kohn, 'Nationalism', *International Encyclopedia of the Social Sciences*, edited by David L. Sills, Vol. 11 (USA, Macmillan, 1968), p. 63.
6. J. Kennedy, *Asian Nationalism in the 20th Century* (London, Macmillan, 1968), p. 3.
7. See Carlton J. H. Hayes, *Nationalism: A Religion* (New York, Macmillan, 1960).
8. This does not necessarily mean that these movements were anti-Islamic in character. However, the movements de-emphasized Islam as an ideology and as the unifying force of Muslims.
9. Kashmir represents the territorial unit of Jammu and Kashmir State, comprising the regions of Kashmir, Jammu and Ladakh. At the time of partition of the Indian subcontinent in 1947, Kashmir could not accede to Pakistan, as was the wish of the Kashmiri Muslims, mainly due to the role of the Hindu Maharaja. Subsequently, one-quarter of Kashmir territory came under Pakistani control (it was liberated by the Muslim rebels and given the name of 'Azad Kashmir'), two-thirds under India's control and some areas were grabbed by China. The total area of the Jammu and Kashmir state in 1981 was 80,900 sq. miles (Pakistani Kashmir 4,144 sq. miles and Indian Kashmir 16,773 sq. miles and the areas of Ladakh, Astore, Baltistan and Gilgit 63,554 sq. miles), See Mohammad Yusuf Saraf, *Kashmiri's Fight For Freedom* (Lahore, Ferozsons, 1977), Vol. I, p. 1. The total population of Kashmiri's, inside and outside Kashmir, is 8 million (6 million in Indian Kashmir, 2 million in Pakistani Kashmir, and 1 million in different parts of the world, see *The Voice of Kashmir* (London) estimates in the early 1980s). While the Kashmir valley has a 94 per cent Muslim majority, Jammu and Ladakh provinces have Hindu and Budhist majorities respectively. The Muslims constitute 95 per cent in Pakistani Kashmir and 63 per cent in Indian Kashmir. The Kashmir valley is the most beautiful part of the

state. While the scenic beauty of the valley has compelled outsiders to call it 'a paradise on earth' and 'Switzerland of Asia', not many people have concentrated upon the cruelties and brutalities perpetrated upon the inhabitants of this earthly paradise of land by its alien rulers in the last four centuries.

10. Muhamad Ishaq Khan, *Perspectives on Kashmir: Historical Dimension* (Srinagar, Gulshan Publishers, 1983), pp. 20–21.
11. Ghulam Hassan Khan, *History of Freedom Movement in Kashmir* (Delhi, Life and Light Publishers, 1981), pp. 322, 325–6.
12. Kashmiri Hindus are generally known as Kashmiri Pandits outside Kashmir. Their proportion in the population of Jammu and Kashmir state in 1981 was 2.7 per cent. Their literacy rate is 100 per cent and they are highly westernized. They have dominated the major sectors of the economy for many centuries. They represent a highly conscious and extremely conservative community in the Indian subcontinent.
13. M. A. Fazili, *Socialist Ideas and Movements in Kashmir, 1919–1947* (New Delhi, Euraka Publishers, 1980), p. 106.
14. The modern Islamic movements like that of *Jama'at-e Islami* emerged on the Kashmir political scene after the 1960s.
15. Even the Pandit nationalist leader, Prem Nath Bazaz, was not in favour of Kashmir's accession to India. See his book *Inside Kashmir* Srinagar, Kash. Publications, 1941.
16. See Shaikh Abdullah's statements and letters at that time.
17. See Mohammad Farooq Rehmani, *Azadi Ki Talash* (In Search of Freedom) Srinagar, 1981, and Saraf, *op. cit.*
18. For the Congress policy towards Shaikh Abdullah after 1975 see Mohammad Kasheer, '1983 Assembly Elections: Sociological Dimensions', *The Muslim*, Friday Special (Islamabad), October, 1983, p. 1.
19. Quoted in A. B. Ganei, *Kashmir National Conference and Politics, 1975–1980* Srinagar, Gulshan Publishers, 1984, p. 129.
20. For how the Congress party at the Centre masterminded toppling of the elected government of Dr. Farooq Abdullah in 1983, see J&K National Conference, *Toppling Game in Jammu and Kashmir* (Jammu, JKNC, 1984) and Farooq Abdullah, *My Dismissal* (New Delhi, Vikas, 1985).
21. The accession of Kashmir to India put a halt to the growth of the Kashmir economy. See Abdullah Lone, *Economic Consequences of Kashmir's Present Political Situation* Srinagar, 1968.
22. Bashir Ahmad, 'The Unfortunate Muslims of Kashmir', *Radiance* (New Delhi), 8 April, 1979, p. 9.
23. *Ibid.*
24. Jammu and Kashmir Government Statistics.
25. Census of India, *Jammu and Kashmir* (Provisional).
26. Census of India, *General Statistics*, 1981.

Chapter VI

Nationalism as an Instrument of Cultural Imperialism—A Case Study of French West Africa*

Malik N'Daiye

Introduction

The need for commercial expansion as a result of the industrial revolutions in England, France and Germany gave rise to increased competition over newly acquired territories as a source of raw materials. A multitude of new companies was formed to develop Africa commercially.

European competition over the control of Africa culminated in the Berlin Conference of 1884–85; the agreement reached resulted in the division of the Continent into English, French, German, Belgian and Portuguese spheres of influence. The stage was now set for these countries to colonize their respective spheres of influence.

In order to give way to a subservient political order, the colonies underwent a total transformation; new institutions replaced the old. Secularism became the new driving force for progress and development, and nationalism the new 'cementing' element in the modern societies. This was achieved through the introduction of a myriad of new ideas developed in Western Europe.

A new elite was created through education and patronage to perform the role of intermediaries. When power was transferred to this new elite to run the newly emerging nation-States that came into existence at the departure of the colonial powers, subservience became a permanent condition.

Africa had been prepared for colonization by three centuries of the slave trade, which had removed millions of young African men and women from their homes to become slaves in America. This coupled

---

* This is an abridged and edited version of the Arabic original. Translation into English by H. Shaheen Azmi.

with the long period of oppression made Africa an easy target for European occupation.

West Africa had known Islam since the ninth century CE. In the course of history, Muslims in Africa produced great centres of learning and commerce and created great empires. When the French occupied this area, during the nineteenth century, the Arabic language functioned as the official language of discourse between monarchs and governors. It was also the language of scholarship and all legal and diplomatic proceedings. The use of Arabic was not only restricted to Muslim kings but extended even to pagan rulers.

Initially, the French colonial administration accepted Arabic as the language of communication. Official proclamations and announcements of the period were routinely written in Arabic in the official newspaper of the day, the *Moniteur du Senegal.* During the period of French military conquest, mainly before 1900, Muslim opposition led by *Ulama* such as Mamadu Lamine, al-Hajj Umar and Samory was ruthlessly crushed. Once this period was over, pragmatism took over as the French policy towards Islam.[1]

French Islamic Policy

The problems associated with administering large territories with only a small number of European personnel, necessitated the creation of a class of intermediaries. The Muslims who supported the French took up this role. They had the crucial advantage not only of being literate but of having experience in the art of ruling.[2]

In 1879, the Director of Political Affairs for Senegal encouraged his best interpreters to learn Arabic, which was also used by commercial houses in their transactions in the hinterland.[3] During this period the French even allowed the application of Islamic Law to be continued simply becaue it was easily available in book form and was familiar not only to the Muslim population, but also the non-Muslim.[4]

These measures were based on the twin assumptions of pragmatism and the widely held view that, 'Islam represented a necessary stage of cultural evolution between pure barbarism and the understanding of higher French civilization'. Quellien was voicing the administration's view when he said: 'Muslim propaganda is a step towards civilization in West Africa, and it is universally recognized that the Muslim peoples of these regions are superior to those who had remained fetishist, in social organization, intellectual culture, commerce, industry, well-being, the struggle for life and education'.[5] O'Brien has called it 'assimilation policy in retreat'; the difficulties of direct assimilation having been considered insuperable, Islam was found useful as an intermediate stage in the development from 'fetishness' to French status.[6]

The impact of men like Auguste Comte (1798–1857) on the development of human thought and civilization had a considerable effect on the thinking of French and British colonial officials. Comte considered the history of Europe as synonymous with the history of the human race and believed that all civilizations would necessarily develop along the same lines as western civilization. He maintained, in his 'Law of the Three Stages of Intellectual Development', that human thought gradually evolves, passing from the lowest stage, the theological stage, to an intermediate stage, the metaphysical stage, to the most advanced stage, the scientific or positivist stage.[7]

The thinking of Comte, coupled with the Darwinian theory of evolution, provided the moral justification for colonization; Europe was not only right to exploit the mineral resources of Africa, but also had a civilizational mission. In the early stages of colonial administration, therefore, Islam was 'encouraged', as Governor Faidherbe, who laid the foundations of French Islamic policy in West Africa, believed that Islam could be used both as a vehicle for the diffusion of a higher degree of civilization among Africans and as an instrument for the unification of French-occupied West Africa.[8]

This necessitated the creation of 'a controlled, a malleable, a pliable Islam that they could twist and bend to their purposes'.[9] To achieve this, Muslims were, on occasion, given special privileges, donations were made towards the construction of mosques, and passages were paid to Makkah. But where there was any hint of opposition Muslims were either harrassed, imprisoned or deported. This patronage helped in creating a breed of pliable *ulama*, or religious elite.

The secular Muslim elite was created through education, starting with *medersas* or Franco-Arabic colleges. These '*Medersas*' taught French language and culture in combination with Arabic and Islamic sciences 'to create an Islamic elite both loyal to the regime and equipped with the requisite skills to serve the administration'.[10] An analysis of the curriculum reveals that in each week twice as much time was spent on French studies as on Arabic.[11]

However, during the early period the French administration was more concerned with using leaders of Sufi orders either as informal or even as formal agents of administration than with the secular Muslim elite. Apart from Faidherbe, other administrators who contributed greatly in developing a coherent policy included Robert Arnaud, Xavier Coppolani, Emile Combes and La Chatelier. Many of them had previous experience in dealing with Muslims in Algeria, where France had successfully constructed a sort of 'official Islam' with 'administrative mosques', the faithful covered by a census, civil service *cadis*, pilgrimage by authorization and a new model code, the bastard product of Muslim law and French jurisprudence.[12]

Combes proposed a similar policy for West Africa as well as other colonies:

> In the first place it would appear useful to study the possibility of placing the spiritual and temporal heads of the religious brother-hoods under our direction ... They could help to attract the sympathy of our Muslim natives if, instead of keeping them at a distance, out of a sort of traditional distrust, we could give them the title of *Imam* of their various *zawiyas*, and make them submit for our approbation the diplomas they give their *moqaddim*. Once these dispositions had been taken, the choice of the *chioukh* themselves would be ratified by our administration. We would place the *Chioukh-El-Islam*, supreme heads of the Muslim religion, who would be intermediaries with an interest in aiding our work of surveillance and moral reform.[13]

Robert Arnaud suggested procedures which might be used to win over the leaders of the brotherhoods:

> The first method constitutes a sort of decapitation of the brotherhood: it means winning over the leaders with material advantages which are easy to find when one has the administra-tive resources of the country at one's disposal ... A second procedure is to encourage the internal dissensions which the ambitions of certain persons excites within the brotherhood ... the principle of *divide et imperas* is here more applicable than ever.[14]

In 1906, Arnaud was entrusted with a mission by Governor-General Roume to travel throughout West Africa to prepare a report on the situation of Islam. This was followed by a series of studies by Paul Marty on Islam in the various French territories of West Africa. The object of such studies was, in large part, to provide assessments of individual Muslim notables, particularly with regard to their attitudes towards the French authority. These studies were also pre-occupied with the 'threat of pan-Islamism'. As concern for the protection of the Uthmaniyyah Khilafat grew among the Muslims of West Africa 'localization' of Islam became a major concern of French administrators. Anything that encouraged concern for the wider *Ummah* was discouraged. In 1908, Arabic newspapers from abroad were banned. In 1910, some local Arabic newspapers were seized; the instruction from the Governor-General was to exclude 'all pan-Islamic' propaganda in West Africa. This included everything in Arabic except the Qur'ān and 'strictly religious' books.[15]

Froelich has summarized the policy adopted towards the leaders of the brotherhoods: 'We have favoured the heads of the brotherhoods and organized the travels of the great *marabout* while asking them, in exchange, to pacify spirits; we have treated them with the greatest honours; we have, at their demand, constructed schools, *medersas* and even mosques'.[16] Once success had been achieved in this area, French policy took a new turn.

The appointment of William Ponty as Governor-General (1908–1915) introduced a new twist to French Islamic policy. Ponty favoured what he termed a *politique des races*, under which traditional chiefs were given greater powers than they had so far possessed. The aim of such a policy was to preserve ethnic particularism by ensuring that each ethnic group had a chief appointed from among its own people. The *politique des races* encouraged ethnic separatism and was intended to prevent the spread of Islam to non-Muslims. The use of Arabic for official purposes was now to be avoided.[17]

Ponty's successor, Governor-General Clozel, gave further encouragement to the *politique des races*. He believed in a greater degree of respect for 'fetishism' and for the use of traditional (*i.e.* pagan) rather than Muslim law in courts. According to him, the *ulama* were to be watched carefully and allowed to travel only with an administrative permit. Mosques and Muslim schools were to be built only by administrative authorization which was rarely given.[18]

Clozel's policy was primarily designed to 'build barriers' in order to prevent the further diffusion of Islam by making use of traditional pre-Islamic beliefs. It was realized that Christian missionaries could offer no effective opposition to Islam.[19] Their activities were regulated, but the motive was not religious, as religion was merely the tool of the policy.[20] This failure of the Church made secular education imperative; if the Muslims could not be converted to Christianity they must be secularized.

British colonial policy towards Islam in West Africa was no different. It was grounded in similar notions of social, cultural and intellectual development and guided by similar political considerations.[21]

French opposition to Islam manifested itself in four ways. First, in the persecution of resisting Islamic leaders. Second, in the persecution of teachers of traditional Islamic sciences. Third, in the separation of the Muslims in West Africa from co-religionists in other parts of the Muslim world. Finally, in the distortion and 'paganization' of Islam.

In its attempts to contain Islam the colonial administration actively persecuted those religious leaders who had not pledged allegience to French colonial rule. Slanderous fabrications were officially spread to discredit them. Some were detained, others exiled from their homelands and some even executed. French persecution was particularly intensive from 1905–1912, when a chain of imprisonments spread across French West Africa, from Senegal to Niger and from Mauritania to Guinea.

Robert Arnaud, whose advice on Islamic matters was extremely influential in the period before the First World War, justified these actions: 'Even if we don't admit ourselves the right to meddle into the religious affairs of a people, we are compelled to concern ourselves with individuals who desire to lead it [West Africa] in the direction of Islamic revolution'.[22]

The teachers of traditional Islamic science also came under strict surveillance. Arnaud said:

> It is not enough that we require a Qur'ānic *medersa* (school) to be licensed, it is also incumbent that we closely observe those responsible for it. The *medersa's* teachings and its effectiveness must be a subject of concern, at all times, for the officials of the various departments. They should know what might result from teaching on application to public and private life. They must be aware of what influence visiting Shaikhs, roaming Shaikhs and returning pilgrims must have. . . .[23]

As stated above, after occupying West Africa, the colonialists concentrated on separating the Muslims of West Africa from the rest of the Islamic world. Visits from foreign Muslims were restricted; observers were appointed to supervise those visits that were sanctioned. Those who wished to perform the Pilgrimage were required to obtain licences and procedures were made highly complicated. On this point Arnaud writes: 'As far as the colonial authorities are aware, those Senegalese who have travelled to Makkah in the last five years do not exceed in number eleven pilgrims or a handful'.[24]

In order to create disharmony among the Muslims, Islam was distorted by the infusion of local characteristics. Arnaud wrote: 'We have before us an honourable task in promoting in West Africa the development and persistance of an "African Islam"—in its fullest sense. We should administer its formation in accordance with the particular ideology of every group'.[25]

Likewise, the colonial administration sought to entice minds in West Africa into re-envisioning Islam through the notions of black consciousness, on the pattern of Black Christianity in southern Africa. Towards this end Arnaud wrote: 'In southern Africa Christians (whose numbers are many) are proceeding to found a completely black church—named "Habashiya". It befits us to move towards the founding of a "Habashiya Islam" in this region of West Africa'.[26]

French Education and its Goals

The French education system in West Africa reflected their policy of assimilation. An official document of 1909 relating to French Guinea states that one of the main aims of French education should be to 'make of the school an instrument for the diffusion of our civilization'. The other two aims were to train local auxiliaries, clerks, telephonists and so on, and to train skilled artisans. The curriculum in these schools was entirely French; Arabic and Islamic studies were excluded.[27]

As graduates from these schools started to come off the production line, the French insisted that all African employees of the administration must be qualified from French schools and be fluent in French. This created a demand for French education and gradually attracted young men away from the Islamic system of education. To further this aim, financial inducements were provided for parents to send their children to French schools. Teachers in Qur'ānic schools were offered financial bonuses if they included the French language in their curricula.

The Governor-General of French West Africa decreed on 15 July 1903, and 12 June 1912, the following:

— The requirement of licensing for all new Qur'ānic schools.
— The power to close Qur'ānic schools for public safety or for reason of unsanitary conditions.
— The prohibition of the religious instruction of children between the ages of six and sixteen during public school hours.
— An annual grant of 300 Francs to every Qur'ānic school that agreed to teach the French language for at least two hours every day.

Such measures were intended to extend a degree of control over Islamic education. But the offer failed to lure any teacher. No one agreed to alter his curriculum or requested a licence to open a Qur'ānic school. However, having lost their place of eminence as centres of learning and scholarship which they had occupied prior to the coming of the French to the area, they were soon reduced to insignificance.

Christian Evangelism: its Growth and its Goals

The first arrival of a monk to Senegal was in 1779. He took up residence in Saint Louis, the occupied portion of Senegal at that time. In 1840, three Senegalese were elevated to the position of priesthood for the first time. Monasteries were established in 1819 in Saint Louis, thus preparing the way for the arrival of a wave of missionaries in 1845. In the earlier years, with the support of the authorities, Christianity rapidly spread. In 1857, a large school for monks was opened. In 1863, Rome sent an Episcopal representative to Seneghambia.

The problem of Islam, however, soon confronted the bishops. It became clear to them that the conversion of the pagan regions was significantly easier than that of the Muslim regions. Senegal was considered a Muslim region. Missionary groups responsible for Senegal decided that it was more advantageous to send the best of their missionaries to regions more likely to accept Christianity such as Cameroon, the Congo and Gabon. Senegal, considered impenetrable, was left to the colonial administration to deal with. Despite this there were some 5 per cent Christian converts at the time of independence in 1960. Power was transferred to this minority as it could be relied upon more to uphold colonial norms and values. (Leopold Sedar Senghor was president of Senegal for twenty years, 1960–79.)

Christian missionaries were an integral part of colonialism. Missionaries in a particular colony were largely nationals of the colonizing State. Nationals of another European state were required to register with the colonial administration, especially if they were aligned with conflicting sects within Christianity (for example, Catholics as opposed to Protestants).

The Missionary Approach

Education

All levels of education, from nursery to university, were employed as a means to spread the gospel. The first school in Saint Louis was opened in 1821. At that time schools were under the control of the Christian Society for Brotherhood. It was soon realized, however, that Muslim parents had an aversion to missionary schools. As a result, the first secular school in Senegal opened in 1860. In 1906, this school, then known as the School for the Sons of Chiefs, was renamed a *medersa*, or Franco-Arabic College. Similar *medersas* were established at Timbaktu, at Djenne and at Boutilimit in Mauritania.

Medicine and Relief

A conference of missionaries held in Senegal, in 1924, declared that 'medicine is one of the best means to proselytize to Christianity'. Concern for health in Africa first came from missionary societies in 1840. The goal at that time was to protect European missionaries from African diseases. The first medical mission was sent to West Africa in 1892 by a missionary church. Another medical mission dispatched to the coast soon followed, and remained there from 1895–1907.

In recent times, aid coming from western countries through either relief agencies or international Christian missions is distributed to the poor and bereaved through local church socities. This aid, especially if in the form of medicines, helps reinforce the wealth of local churches, and assists them in their missionary task. The drought in areas of Africa has provided missionaries with an opportunity to extend their influence. The fact that no Islamic organization exists to provide any aid whatsoever, either at the local or the international level, has created a vacuum for the missionaries to fill.

The Challenges to Islamic Society

The undermining of three fundamental pillars of Islamic society, Islamic doctrine (*'Aqidah*), Islamic Law (*Shari'ah*) and Islamic brotherhood (*Ukhuwwah*), has been the goal of all western education.

Islamic doctrine (*'Aqidah*) was made a target of attack because of its important role in guarding Muslim societies from the assimilating effects of subservience to western thought. The Islamic Law (*Shari'ah*) shields Muslim societies from the circulation of vice and immorality amongst its individuals and communities. Because of its role in arming Muslim society against exploitation, it was targetted for elimination. The Islamic brotherhood (*Ukhuwwah*) was targetted, because it acted as a strong bond between the individuals and communities of a single nation as well as between Muslim nations throughout the world.

Instruments of French Policy Implementation

Secular Education

Secular education was envisioned as the main instrument leading to the distortion and disintegration of the grip of Islamic doctrine on Muslim society.

The Law

A secular legal system, with legislative bodies, was imposed over the long established Islamic legal system, where legal decisions (*fatawa*) of the religious scholars (*ulama*) played the legislative role.

Nationalism

Nationalism was imposed over the traditional perspective of Islamic brotherhood. This was intended to cause the disintegration of Muslim unity through the construction of internal and external barriers between Muslims.

Neo-colonialism

Colonialism prepared for the colonists' departure by appointing nationalists and secularists to succeed them. Positions of authority were restricted to them, in the hope that they might be able to prise Muslims away from Islam and instead attach them to western ways.

They claimed and boasted that they were the harbingers of freedom and independence. They were, on the contrary, no more than the henchmen of the departed colonialists. They would, hypocritically, claim to be the protectors of the people, while at the same time perform as their hangmen. Marching hand in hand with their foreign sponsors, they deceived and misled many.

In each departed colony, colonialism left behind a time-bomb that would explode at a propitious time in the future. As the civilian nationalist elite failed to deliver the goods, these time-bombs began to explode. These bombs were in the form of the military of the new States. Soon the military elite began to take charge of the civilization goals of their former colonial masters with much greater vigour and oppression.

The period of colonialism is not over yet.

Notes

1. D. Cruise O'Brien, 'Towards an Islamic Policy in French West Africa', *Journal of African History*, Vol. VIII, 1967, pp. 303–16.
2. A. Gouilly, *L'Islam en Afrique Occidentale*, Paris, Larose, 1952, p. 257.
3. Report of Directeur des Affaires Politiques, Senegal, 8 July 1879, *Archives Nationales*, Section Outer-Mer (A.N.S.O.M.), Senegal VIII, 23 *bis*.
4. P. Marty, *Etudes sur l'Islam au Senegal*, II, Paris, Leroux, 1917, pp. 287–8.
5. A. Quellien, *La Politique Musulmane dans l'Afrique Occidentale Française*, Paris, Larose, 1910, p. 100.
6. D. Cruise O'Brien, *ibid.*, p. 305.
7. P. B. Clarke, *West Africa and Islam*, Edward Arnold, London, 1982, p. 189.
8. J. D. Hargreaves (ed.), *France and West Africa*, London, 1969, p. 148.
9. P. B. Clarke, *ibid.*, p. 190.
10. P. B. Clarke, *ibid.*, p. 191.
11. D. Cruise O'Brien, *ibid.*, p. 312.
12. A. Le Chatelier, 'Politique Musalmane', *Revue du Monde Musalman*, Vol. XII, September 1910, p. 80.
13. President of the Council (Combes) to Minister for the Colonies, 1 August, 1902, *A.N.S.O.M.*, Missions 115F.
14. R. Arnaud, *Précis des Politique Musalmane, 1, Pays Maures de la Rive Droit du Senegal*, Algiers, Jourdan, 1906, pp. 119–23.
15. D. Cruise O'Brien, *ibid.*, p. 310.
16. J. C. Froelich, *Essai sur les causes et methodes de l'Islamization de l'Afrique de l'Ouest du XIe siècle au XXe siècle*, mimeographed paper, International African Institute, Fifth Internal African Seminar, Zaria, 1963, p. 7.
17. D. Cruise O'Brien, *ibid.*, p. 314.
18. J. Brevie, *Islamisme Contre 'Naturisme' au Soudan Francais*, Paris, Leroux, 1923, pp. 257–62. Brevie was an adviser to Clozel and was later himself Governor-General.
19. D. Cruise O'Brien, *ibid.*, p.315.
20. D. Cruise O'Brien, *ibid.*, p. 308.
21. P. B. Clarke, *ibid*, p. 191.
22. R. Arnaud, *L'Islam et la Politique Musulmane Française en Afrique Occidentale*, Paris 1912, p. 126.
23. *Ibid.*, p. 129.
24. *Ibid.*, p. 129.
25. *Ibid.*, p. 122.

26. R. Arnaud, *op. cit.*, p. 133.
27. Mervyn Hiskett, *The Development of Islam in West Africa*, Longmans, London, 1984, p. 293.

Index